50p

GW00672359

DIANE CILENTO

My Nine Lives

DIANE CILENTO

My Nine Lives

VIKING

an imprint of

PENGUIN BOOKS

MICHAEL JOSEPH

Published by the Penguin Group
Penguin Books Ltd, 80 Strand, London WC2R 0RL, England
Penguin Group (USA) Inc., 375 Hudson Street, New York, New York 10014, USA
Penguin Group (Canada), 90 Eglinton Avenue East, Suite 700, Toronto, Ontario, Canada M4P 2Y3
(a division of Pearson Penguin Canada Inc.)
Penguin Ireland, 25 St Stephen's Green, Dublin 2, Ireland (a division of Penguin Books Ltd)
Penguin Group (Australia), 250 Camberwell Road,
Camberwell, Victoria 3124, Australia (a division of Pearson Australia Group Pty Ltd)
Penguin Books India Pvt Ltd, 11 Community Centre,
Panchsheel Park, New Delhi – 110 017, India
Penguin Group (NZ), cnr Airborne and Rosedale Roads, Albany,
Auckland 1310, New Zealand (a division of Pearson New Zealand Ltd)
Penguin Books (South Africa) (Pty) Ltd, 24 Sturdee Avenue,
Rosebank, Johannesburg 2196, South Africa

Penguin Books Ltd, Registered Offices: 80 Strand, London WC2R 0RL, England

www.penguin.com

First published by Penguin Group (Australia), a division of Pearson Australia Group Pty Ltd, 2006
First published in Great Britain by Michael Joseph, 2006

1

Text copyright © Diane Cilento, 2006

The moral right of the author has been asserted

Cover and text design by Debra Billson and Karen Trump © Penguin Group (Australia)
Front cover photograph by Waugh © popperfoto.com. All rights reserved
Back cover photograph by Image © Corbis/Australia Picture Library
Author photograph (back flap) by Mike Lawn/Rex Features/Austral International

Typeset in 11.5/17 pt Legacy Serif Book by Post Pre-press Group, Brisbane, Queensland
Printed in Great Britain by Clays Ltd, St Ives plc

A CIP catalogue record for this book is available from the British Library

ISBN-13: 978-0-718-14925-3
ISBN-10: 0-718-14925-4

ACKNOWLEDGEMENTS

Having just finished reading the marathon madness of my life at one sitting, (more or less), it struck me forcibly that I could never have managed to live it, let alone get it down on paper, without the assistance, support and patience of so many people. I shall endeavour to mention some of them. It would be impossible to name them all unless I undertook another tome, and, believe me, I have no plans to do that.

It would be churlish not to begin with my teachers, Yat Malmgren, J.G. Bennett, Hasan Shushud, Bante and Bulent Rauf. Without these remarkable men in my life, I would never have been able to complete this book. Then my brother-in-law, Geoffrey Maslen, wrote me a letter when I had all but given up and thrown the half-written manuscript in the too-hard basket. Without that letter, it would have remained there mouldering. My sister Margaret, Geoffrey's wife, has been a constant ear on the end of the phone listening to all my woes and urging me on.

I want to thank Linda van Noonen for her editing and pulling lots of bits together, and her husband David, for walking me with his dogs every morning. Delini Wijeyesekera, Derani Zealand and her three sons, Dusty Stahle, Carol Davidson, Janet Austin, the two Lynnes, Jade and Heath for keeping me fit, and Gaye Osborne for keeping a cool head in London.

I am indebted to WWOOFers of all nationalities, German, French, Danish, Japanese, Swedish and English, who have passed through Karnak and worked to keep the jungle from closing in on us. To David and Gillian Helfgott, Jane Rutter and her son Bertie, Jacqui Carrol and John Nobbs of Frank Theatre, Carol Lloyd, Tania Heben, Linda Jackson, Victor Spinetti, Margo Gordon, Susie Hines, Bryan Wiseman and Matthew McCarthy for volunteering their invaluble services to the theatre. I thank my daughter for her culinary skills, Nigel Pegrum for his musical ones, and Dean Holland for making the lasers shine. I am eternally grateful to all of you.

Finally, I would like to thank all the students who have passed through Karnak, for their work in the garden, participation in study, meditation, cooking and creative projects. Come back when you wish to renew our journey together.

To Giovanna, Jason and Dashiell,
so they know

CHAPTER ONE

*T*he Spit, Mooloolaba. We have to lug everything up the beach, sometimes in the moonlight, to reach the house – food, saucepans, bedding, tackle, boxes of fruit, swimming togs, oars and hurricane lamps. There is the smell of kerosene, salt air and seaweed. The moon makes a broad silver pathway across the water to my feet, as though it has followed me there and is shining directly on me. The waves glint and quiver before they crash down and slither up the sand, dumping a spurt of foam up my legs.

Arrival. The house is a weather-beaten old Queenslander with a lopsided verandah. Its walls are stained dark brown with creosote to stop the incursions of white ants. Some rooms have red satin curtains put there by the previous occupant, an opera singer. In the front bedroom is a big, sagging brass bed where the younger kids sleep, three or four together. We climb in, not bothering to wipe the sand off our feet. The spider-leg leaves of the she-oaks sizzle on the dunny roof outside. 'Sweet dreams,' calls my mother. A chorus of tired voices reply, as always, 'Passionfruit.' I fall into slumber like a ripe mango tumbling off a tree. Tomorrow, the beach.

The beach is my dreamtime. It is the launching pad where my inner life takes off. The beach is the place where, for the first time, I know for sure that I am not just my body, that I am a free spirit who can *be* anyone and *do* anything. I am certain that even now the shadow of a small female in faded Speedos, with long, tangled blond hair and a peeling nose, still haunts that beach looking for shells or bits of coral, popping dried bluebottles with her heel, talking to herself and singing, oblivious to the rest of the world. She is as much a part of the scenery as the pelicans that languidly cruise the battered shore or the oily strands of seaweed that wash up on the sand.

Every morning, before the sun is up, I run the length of the Spit on the Moolooloo River side, through the mangroves and down the path to Clark's shop to pick up the milk, which I carry home in a wide-lipped steel jug so it won't spill. By the age of six I am an adept, handling the whole operation with ease, but one morning, as I dawdle back, I hear a strange noise, a sinister sound like a slavering beast sucking on the entrails of a recent kill. I stop short and wait. The sound, coming from the mangroves above my head, is getting louder every second. I crouch down as a shadow falls over me. A hairy face looms in to examine me. It has chomping jaws, loose lips and dingy yellow teeth that are masticating mangrove leaves. It peers down at me through large, dozy, protuberant eyes fringed by thick lashes. I cannot move, so terrified am I of the beast. Its smell overpowers me as it spurts a spray of putrid stuff out of its mouth that lands on my arm. It is the shock of green spittle that galvanises me into action. Dropping the milk, scraping at my slimy arm, my legs working like pistons, I do not feel the mangrove shoots perforating the soles of my feet until later. I run and run and never stop until I am up the back stairs, through the kitchen and into the womb-like centre of the big sandy bed, where I remain all day.

My close encounter with a camel left me with a wary eye out for large, ruminant, cushion-footed quadrupeds. I could never be persuaded to go for the milk again. I was told that it was quite common to encounter a camel on the Spit, that a travelling circus always wintered in

Mooloolaba and they let their animals wander there because they knew no-one lived there . . . just us. That kept me clinging to the waterline for months. I was alert and ready to dive into the sea at the glimpse of any animal, even just a big dog.

When he was studying medicine, my big brother Raffles was a lifesaver with the Mooloolaba Surf Life Saving Club, whose members, mostly university students, were all volunteers. They travelled up the coast at weekends in the back of an old truck and patrolled the surfing beach between the flags, one of them sitting up on the lookout with a loudhailer to call out to bodysurfers who swam outside the lines or got into rips. I became the official mascot and youngest honorary member of the Mooloolaba Surf Life Saving Club, and was allowed to daub yellow sulphur solution on people who had been stung by bluebottles or jellyfish.

Raff was my idol, my hero, when I was little. He was very beautiful, with sun-bleached wavy hair, curling golden lashes and smooth brown skin. To me, he seemed immensely strong and muscular as he swung me about, took me for rides on the crossbar of his bike and carried me on his back way out past the largest breaking waves to bodysurf where only the bravest ventured. We would shoot the big boomers together, a small blond shrimp attached like a limpet to the back of the large brown youth as he waited and then accelerated to catch the perfect Pacific breaker. We would linger, suspended for an instant on the crest of the wave, contemplating the chasm below. Then there was the adrenaline rush of dread and delight as the roar of rushing water broke over us, shooting us forward and downwards at what felt like the speed of light. I loved the last bit, when the wave lost its fury and carried us gently along. Raff knew how to waggle his whole body like a fish to attain more distance; sometimes we'd get nearly all the way to the beach.

The first time I experienced pure naked terror was when Raff left me out in the middle of the ocean. All the other surfers had caught the massive wave as well. It was too good to be missed. I was not hanging on to my brother's back tightly enough, or perhaps he had too much sun oil on, but he slipped away from under me and I was alone in the gargantuan sea, aware of the dark shark shadows moving beneath me, too light to catch any of the new waves that built up. I knew very well that if I started swimming towards the shore I would be dumped and churned senseless by the ferocious middle surf. I would be carried out half a mile underwater, never to be seen again. I tried to become invisible and tread water so softly that only seabirds would be aware of my presence from miles up in the sky.

I waited for what seemed like years before Raff came back. My heart was pounding like a captured bird's and I was taking enormous gulps of air along with seawater through chattering teeth, which covered my tears of relief. I knew that I must pretend I hadn't been frightened at all. My brother noticed that I was more closely riveted to his shoulders and he kept flicking me off.

My next elder brother, Carl, and his friends once built a raft out of pandanus wood. They strapped the scabby logs together with beach vines, put me on it and launched it off some rocks at Alexander Heads to test whether it would float. That pandanus wood is porous became obvious after about three minutes, and I held on while the logs began breaking apart. I was in imminent danger of being smashed as I drifted towards the rocks.

'See? You owe me your Swiss knife. I told you it wouldn't float,' one of the boys screamed at another.

'Jump, you silly dill!' shouted my brother as the boys wandered off, disinterested now that the raft was proven to be unseaworthy.

But I could not jump. I had to hold on in the hope that I could somehow escape being picked up by a wave and dashed against the jagged rocks. I waited until there was a lull between waves and then pushed myself as hard as I could out into the open sea, away from the breaking waves, diving as deep as I could and swimming furiously underwater. Two hours later I lay in the shallows, too exhausted to drag myself

4

ashore. My brother and his friends had disappeared. I saw Carl at the skating rink later that afternoon.

'What happened to you?' he asked.

'Oh, I was just trying to fool you that I'd drowned,' I said.

'Well, don't do it again,' he said sternly.

It is easy to learn the basics of how to be a Stoic when you are at the lower end of the pecking order in a large family. There were six children, three boys and three girls, and I was the youngest daughter. The youngest of my three brothers, David, was my mother's pet and I was my father's. We each had different methods of not becoming disempowered within the Cilento clan. Amongst a competitive bunch like our family, you had to learn quickly to give as good as you got.

I had my revenge on Carl for the raft business. Further up the Moolooloo River there lived a lady with an army of bleating goats and an idiot son called Clyde who spent his days banging with a stick on an old piece of galvanised iron in the yard. She giggled a lot and used to squirt me in the face with the milk squeezed from the long udder of her favourite Nubian nanny-goat, Jessica. She'd make goat's cheese by mixing the milk with lemon juice, tying it in a piece of cotton and hanging it up to drain on the barbed-wire fence at the back of her house. Goat droppings, little dark lozenges of perfect size and proportion, covered the ground around her house. I collected some of the hardened dry ones, wrapped them in silver paper with a twist at each end like Fantales, put them in a chocolate box and gave them to Carl for his birthday. He had already swallowed two before he realised it wasn't toffee.

My eldest sister, Margaret, had bright red hair and fair skin, so she burnt. It is a curse to have to cover up every time you venture out of doors into the sunlight. Marg was always distinguishable as the blob on the landscape, shrouded in towels, sketching under an expansive mushroom hat. When my parents were not in residence at Mooloolaba (which was frequently), it was Margaret or my godmother, Cappy, who looked after us. Cappy's real name was Maia Bomford. A British spinster who became a nanny, she invested all her emotions in whatever young person she was nurse to at the time.

Cappy had deep scars on her body made by the claws of a goanna. I never tired of hearing the story of how she got them. It happened when she was transporting a beautiful baby girl in her charge from Brisbane out west to the family cattle station, travelling in a truck with cattle dogs and cowboys employed by the child's parents. At a rest stop in a treeless spot, the dogs rousted out a huge goanna, which ran up Cappy's back while she was holding the infant. 'I stood there, Diane, holding that baby and I knew I couldn't let go. The thing's head was up over my shoulder and its tail was hanging down on the ground.'

'So what did you *do*?'

'I called out to the men, handed the baby to one of them and then got down on my knees. The dogs were all going mad, barking and trying to kill it, and I put my head on the ground but it kept digging its claws into my neck. See here? It was lashing out at the dogs . . . worst moment of my life. I thought I was going to die.'

'Did they shoot it?'

'No, they were too frightened the bullets would hit me. One of the dogs got hold of the thing's tail and pulled so hard that its claws ripped even deeper into my skin. It seemed like an hour before it ran off me . . . and all the dogs after it. I was bleeding so bad they took me to the hospital and the baby was crying . . . but I still held her.'

'I thought you gave her to one of the men.'

'Yes, but he gave her back to me.'

'Why?'

Cappy did not answer.

'Why do you think it thought you were a tree, Cappy?'

'Perhaps it was the size of my ankles.'

How could you not love a heroine like that? Every time she told the story, I would want to see her scars again and stroke them for good luck.

My sister Margaret had another ongoing story devised to scare the life out of me. It was about the wicked Witch Wheeza, who whistled through the cracks of the house on windy nights. Her time was spent chasing children, and if she caught you she'd turn you into a yellow-bellied black snake so that the only way to escape from her was to burrow under the earth. At night she hid in the dark, waiting until you went to bed, when she would whisper nasty things in your ear. Like most kids, I became terrified of the dark. Even the thought of venturing outside on a windy night when Witch Wheeza might be about was enough to turn me into a gibbering wreck.

I was shuddering by the stove one evening when my father noticed my fear and asked me to come for a walk with him. I told him I had a sore foot. He insisted he would carry me. I sat on his shoulders until we reached the sea, where the water glowed a luminous grey way out over the Pacific Ocean. As we walked along the beach with the she-oaks swaying and rustling behind us, I knew Witch Wheeza was hiding there, watching and waiting. I clung to my father's leg, and he stopped and took hold of me. Then he spoke in the special voice that he reserved for me.

'You don't have to be frightened. I will always be with you in your heart. I will be right in here.' He rubbed my chest and then laughed. 'Don't forget that it is me in there with you. We are the most frightening things out here. If you remember that, you will never be frightened again. Whatever is out here in the darkness is likely very frightened of *us*. Come on, D, stand up and walk straight . . . that's the way . . . and no-one can ever hurt us.'

After breakfast I was free to do what I wanted all day, as children were in those days. The danger of skin cancer was a thing of the future and, although my nose peeled so many times that I had to wear a piece of sticking plaster over it, I cannot remember keeping a hat on for more than a few minutes. I never came back to the house for lunch but stayed on the beach, either around the surfing area or at the back of the Spit, playing around in an old rowing boat. The boatshed was manned by one of Mooloolaba's special eccentrics, a certain Mr Bell, who had a shiny, domed head covered by a knotted handkerchief, sandy side-whiskers, trousers rolled up to the knee and twelve toes. The sixth little toe curled up over the top of each foot like a little snail. I spent a lot of time in Mr Bell's company. His toes enchanted me.

We stopped going to Mooloolaba so often when our house fell into the sand one day. There was a back-up shack at Caloundra, some miles down the coast, which had push-up galvanised-iron shutters. My dad filled it with every Penguin book ever printed – green for detective, blue for travel, orange for fiction and I can't remember the subject of the yellow ones. There were creepy damp holes filled with reptiles all along Moffat Headland. They had been dug as air-raid shelters but kids crept down into them to play spooky games or to use them as loos if they weren't filled with pools of water.

Back in Brisbane we lived in the house at Annerley, a roomy wooden Queenslander with verandahs. It was built-in underneath, painted green and white and topped by faded red tiles. I walked to Yeronga State School every morning with my school port containing my neatly wrapped peanut-butter sandwich, which I always threw away. I played through the lunch break and had no time to eat. Initially, I was sent to the Catholic school on Ipswich Road but, after a day or two there, I came home and asked my father where Hell was.

'Why do you want to know?' he puzzled.

'Because that's where I'm going,' I answered confidently.

'Who told you that?'

'My teacher.'

I was transferred to the State school shortly after that.

My dad read to us every morning. In some ways, it was the best time of the day. My brother David and I were allowed to get into bed with our parents, but only after the 'greenies' had flown through, parrots that then flew in flocks of hundreds, shrieking and swooping through the sky. They were the wake-up call, the alarm clock of the skies and, when they had gone, I would crawl in beside my dad and David next to Mum. Dad would take his glasses from the bedside table, stretch them round his ears and ask, 'Now, what will it be today?'

His selection of books was an extraordinary one for young children, though not for an academic catching up on his reading. Machiavelli, Dante and Cavalcanti were mixed in with Rudyard Kipling and Robert Louis Stevenson. Ezra Pound's translations of Petrarch's love poems were baffling, as were Chaucer's *Canterbury Tales*, but my father did also read us *Gulliver's Travels*, Banjo Paterson's poems, Henry Lawson's short stories and Kipling's *Just So Stories* as some acknowledgement that we were children. I didn't care what he read as long as I could listen to his voice and watch his facial expressions. He could imitate any accent and become a different person in an instant. I don't know if it was then that I learned to love the theatre but those morning readings became the stuff of my imagination. Even if I didn't understand most of it, my dad did and one day I would too.

My unconscious leaning towards theatricality came out in dressing up. I received an authentic sailor's suit for Christmas one year when I was about five, with a little round cap that had 'HMAS' written on it. I would not take it off, even to go to bed, unless it was forcibly removed. I insisted that everybody called me Jack. I was no-one but Jack the Sailor.

There was a big dressing-up bag in the linen closet that had filled over the years with fancy-dress creations my parents had worn at balls on various boat trips abroad. The one I liked the best was a bat costume with spreading wings and an evil little mask that fitted over the face. It had fangs and a small protruding red tongue and I was certain that, once I put it on, no-one would ever guess who I was. This was the period when I was a nocturnal being and wholly identified with my cat Phenos. Together, we roamed the gardens and backyards of Annerley, yowling. I learned to speak Cat from Phenos. I would climb out onto the balcony that was attached to the sleep-out where I slept, spread my wings in my bat outfit and leap off, *believing* I could fly. Sometimes I really did, and other times I came a cropper . . . but nothing that a few moments of lying on the ground miaowing did not remedy.

Once, my friends Betty, Joyce and Lyndall and I collected heaps of mushrooms in a paddock after school. We cooked them in a stolen frying pan over a fire behind the golden bamboo clump and took them up to my dad's study with several forks. We sat in a circle on the floor with my dad, each of us eating one mushroom at a time until they were finished. There seems no reason to recall this small incident except that it was an unforgettable afternoon. Although they may look the same, the mushrooms that grew in fields then are a different species from the mounds of farmed things found in supermarkets today.

On our way home from school through Yeronga Park we'd pass some tennis courts, behind which was a shed where all the line-markers and garden tools were kept. It was here that a small man dressed in grey, with a grey cap worn low over his eyes, used to lurk. We called him the Grey Ghost, or just GG. We thought that he had some sort of stomach growth, because whenever we went past he would expose an angry-looking red stump on his lower abdomen. We supposed that he was a jockey who had injured himself in a horserace.

I was nearly nine at the time. It is hard to believe but, in those days, none of us schoolgirls knew what it was. Of course, we had all seen our little brothers naked but this was not a small, pale protuberance used for peeing; this was a massive carbuncle. We knew instinctively that there was something frightening about this grey figure with the outstanding feature, so we started coming home another way, by the road. After a while we forgot about him altogether until one day, in an old spare allotment in Villa Street, we were playing Chinese Gardeners –

a curious game in which each player collects various coloured leaves, grasses or flowers, arranges them in neat patterns on a piece of tin and then barters to get the best variety into their Chinese garden. The bartering is done in pretend Chinese. Suddenly, we heard '*Ding dung doodley oodley oo*,' as the Grey Ghost stepped between us, jingling money in his pocket.

Our Chinese gardens flew in the air and we scattered in all directions as GG drew back his grey coat to reveal a monstrous scarlet post. 'Ever seen one of these before, eh, girls?' he asked.

We ran, our bulging eyes looking backwards at the object uncovered before us, which he seemed to be waving at us. I raced all the way home to my mother's surgery under the house, where her secretary, Mrs Ekhart, held court. I was puffed out and inarticulate but, from what I managed to splutter, she got the message that there was a disturbance with a man in Villa Street. She interrupted my mother, who was with a patient, and there was a short conversation behind closed doors. My mother then appeared and fixed me with a piercing gaze, her stethoscope swaying around her neck. 'Now, D, what happened?' she asked. 'Is there something wrong with this man?'

'He's got this thing sticking out of him and . . . it's all red. It's a tumour . . . I think.'

'Where?'

I indicated. There was a long pause.

'Where is this man?'

'He's down in the spare allotment in Villa Street.'

'Ah,' said my mother. She was tight-lipped as she disappeared back into her office with Mrs Ekhart. I heard a hurried conversation and a telephone call before Mrs Ekhart came out of the office. She was wearing a sewn-up owl's face. Beckoning me towards her with her finger, she opened the drawer of her desk in which she kept little toys and other pacifiers for children who were being given the needle. 'Would you like a lolly, dear?' she asked. I took a purple one and turned to go but

Mrs Ekhart placed a restraining hand on my arm. 'You'd better wait, dear. I think your mother wants to talk to you.'

There was something in her manner that suggested trouble and I tried to read the signs for what I might have done wrong. I sat down and sucked on the lolly. At last, my mother said goodbye to her patient and ushered me into the examination room. I always hated the smell in there – a mixture of ether and disinfectant. Ever since I'd jumped on a hidden hayfork in the pottery barn and my mother had probed the wound with some sort of cold metal object, I had steered clear of the surgery.

'Did this man try to touch you or any of the other girls?' my mother queried.

'Not really. He wanted to buy some of our Chinese gardens but everyone knows they're not real. We thought he had a growth. It looked pretty bad.'

'No, D, what you saw was not a growth. It was a penis, a male member.'

It was an awkward interview. I had no idea what she was talking about when she quoted from a book about 'exposing the male member' and 'excitation causing tumescence'. She showed me some pictures of what looked like GG's growth, talked about babies and asked me if I knew how they were born.

'Of course I do,' I told her. 'They come out through the belly button. Doctors undo it when the baby's ready and then it comes out. That's why it's called a belly *button*.'

'No, D, it's not exactly like that.'

Thus it was that I was initiated into the mystery of women's business. I was frankly incredulous when my mother explained the actual process of birth, using diagrams. I looked at her tummy covered by its starched white doctor's wraparound and, for the life of me, I couldn't imagine myself in there, let alone coming out. 'Well, anyway,' I said, 'I'm never going to get married or have any of that stuff happen to me, so it

12

doesn't really matter, does it?' With that, I flew out the door before she could tell me more. I really hoped I would never grow up.

My father's stories of the Cilento ancestry were extremely colourful and perhaps apocryphal. He had charted our family back to Normandy, to the rise and demise of Roger, King of the Two Sicilies, also known as Roger the Cruel. As I understand it, Roger was one of the younger sons of a Norman noble who had no hope of inheriting. Like many ambitious but disinherited younger sons, Roger decided to try his luck in Naples, acting as a supplier for the Crusades. This was a very lucrative venture and ruthless Roger became so powerful that he took over the reins of government and proved to be a tyrant. He was overthrown, or perhaps assassinated, his family fleeing into the hinterland. My father said that Roger had very blond hair, which is why the Cilentos were still fair-haired.

They seem to have been a rebellious lot because my father's grandfather, Rafael Salvatore Cilento, who came from Seiano in the province of Cilento near Naples, was a follower of Garibaldi when that revolutionary led an unsuccessful insurgency in the 1860s. Rafael Salvatore was sentenced to death by King Ferdinand of Naples but was smuggled out of Italy. He arrived in England with two manservants and high hopes. They did not last long. His money ran out, the manservants went back to Italy and he signed on to the English trading vessel *Telegraph* bound for Australia. When the ship landed in Port Adelaide in 1865, it was immediately quarantined because of suspected typhoid aboard but Rafael Salvatore jumped ship. Branded an absconder, he lay low until the vessel had sailed. Rafael Salvatore remained in South Australia, where he married and raised seven children, one of whom, Raphael Ambrose, was my grandfather.

My mother's paternal family, the McGlews, were refugees from the massacre of Glencoe, arriving in Australia through Fremantle in the 1830s. They were pioneers and some of their descendants still live in Western Australia. McGlew & Co was a well-known trading company selling horses (Walers) and primary produce to South-East Asian countries in return for spices, silks and rice. My grandfather, Charles Frederick McGlew, left the family business to the managers in each port when he went off to serve in World War I.

My grandmother's grandfather, Captain James Henry Walker, was the master of a barque, the *Thomas King*, which came to grief on the shoals of the Great Barrier Reef off Cape York in the 1840s. Leaving the passengers and some of the crew behind, he set out to walk south to the nearest civilisation. Only he and his boatswain survived the journey. His companions were massacred and he lost half his body weight in the months he marched. My father wrote a book about his adventure called *Captain Walker's Marathon*, which he dedicated to my mother and had privately printed. The irony is that the passengers and crew left behind were rescued a few days after Captain Walker and his men set out.

Captain Walker's son Henry built the Bank of New South Wales in Cooktown as the gold rush began on the Palmer River. He sired thirteen children but, unfortunately, died soon after taking up residence in the grand house that's still standing in the main street of the town. His wife succumbed to Hodgkin's disease shortly afterwards and the children returned to Sydney, where they were farmed out to various relatives. My grandmother, Alice Walker, married Charles Frederick McGlew and my mother, Phyllis, was their only child.

My father, Raphael, had sparkling green eyes behind rimless glasses, flared nostrils and an expressive mouth. He was very attractive to women, although he would spend hours in deep conversation with his male cronies. His hair grew straight upwards on his head and, when I was little, I thought the hairs looked like thin saplings on the edge of a miniature forest.

Every night after dinner, my father would smoke a cigar. I loved to watch the ritual he went through. First, he would remove the gold paper ring and give it to me. Then, he would use a little silver knife that he kept in his waistcoat pocket to prepare the end. I would put the ring on and wear it until it fell off. Freud would have had a field day. I was a daddy's girl.

My mum had dark, bright, very vigilant eyes and long hair that she used to brush downwards from the nape of her neck over her eyes every morning. She would then coil it around her head. Small boned, she had an extraordinarily sweet smile and the remarkably flexible hands of a born healer. She had what is sometimes called 'the common touch'.

I never met either of my grandfathers but both our grandmothers lived with us at the house at Annerley. Gran, my dad's mother, lived upstairs while Nanny, my maternal grandmother, lived in a granny flat downstairs, next to the surgery. They both played the piano but their tastes in music were spectacularly different. If Gran launched into a Chopin Prelude upstairs, it would not be long before a dirge from the hymnal would override the tinkling sounds from above. The grand-mothers rarely met, as Nanny preferred to eat her meals in solitude, away from the turbulent population upstairs. Gran wore a heavy iron calliper on her leg (the consequence of a horse-riding accident, she told me, although I later learned she had tripped over a garden hose), which ensured that she seldom ventured downstairs. When she did, she carried a stick made of light bamboo that had three monkeys – See No Evil, Hear No Evil and Speak No Evil – carved on it.

If Gran was in bed, she would catch you around the neck with the crook of her stick and draw you down to sit close to her. As Gran's room was not large, she kept most of her belongings either under the bed or hanging on hooks around the walls. She was vain and kept a netting bag that held every hair that fell from her head and a blue Bristol glass bottle that was the repository of all her tears. I was her sole audi-ence when she recited the litany of her beauties. Her complexion was alabaster white with blue veins clearly marked, 'just like the cheese,' she would say, laughing. Her eyes were forget-me-not blue and she had long ear lobes like the Buddha, 'but so do elephants,' Gran noted. She had the skin of a young girl and the tapering fingers of a lady of leisure.

All these attributes she repeated to me daily, sometimes as a ventriloquist with the voice of Simon, her 'pet' fox fur, which hung on the back of the door. When she dressed, she wore a big feathery hat and Simon around her neck, just poking his head over her shoulder. She had style, my Gran. Even in the torrid Brisbane summer, she held her head high and wore her fox furs with aplomb.

Nanny was a diminutive woman who reminded me of a hairy-nosed wombat. When she was grumpy she had the face of a burrowing animal thrust into the daylight against its will, but when serene she had the torpor of a dozing koala. Nanny was deeply distrustful of me because I had given her whooping cough when I was two, and she warned my mother continuously that I would come to no good. Extremely religious, she was convinced I had the devil in me.

There were differing reasons why we never met our grandfathers. Nanny's husband, Charles Frederic McGlew, was gassed in France in the First World War. An ambulance bearer and conscientious objector, he never returned to Australia, living out the rest of his days in southern Italy. I thought he might have gone to the war to get away from Nanny. Gran's husband, Raphael Ambrose Cilento, still lived in South Australia and my dad once brought me some walnuts from him. 'These are a present from your grandfather,' he said. 'He has a walnut plantation in the hills behind Adelaide. One day you may meet him but he can't come up here. Your grandmother would have a fit. He has lived with an Italian woman since she left him.'

The match between my parents, a McGlew and a Cilento, was frowned upon from the moment of its inception at the University of Adelaide, where my mother was the first female to graduate in Medicine. She had entered university to study art, but anatomy and the workings of the human body had drawn her away from the easel. Phyllis McGlew became the only female student amongst the eighteen males of her year. An only child, whose doting dad gave her a new red Saxon sports car (Australian-made) for her twenty-first birthday, she zoomed around campus, by all accounts, with many admirers 'clustered like flies on the running boards'.

Young Raphael Cilento was not the choice of husband her parents would have made. From an Italian family, he had worked as a smelter's labourer, he still soled his own shoes and, on Friday nights, he boxed the preliminary bout at the Adelaide Stadium. He wrote about himself at this time:

> It is said that adversity moulds character . . . but, in my case, five years of penury have warped my viewpoint. Pride and poverty combined to make me a solitary, wrapped in a protective cloak of disregard for any opinion except my own.

He may have been a 'solitary' but he had a great ability to make accurate anatomical drawings and this gave him an entrée into the inner circle. He illustrated faculty papers and lecture boards, often sitting opposite Phyllis McGlew, drawing little people upside down running towards her to amuse her. She did not encourage him, as she was engaged to someone else at the time, but somehow he must have charmed his way into her heart because, by the time they graduated, Raphael Cilento and Phyllis McGlew were engaged to be married.

My dad enlisted in the Army and was posted to New Guinea with the Occupational Force, which took over from the Germans. My mother went to the Great Ormond Street Hospital for post-graduate work and made a tour of the WWI trenches with her mother. When my parents finally tied the knot after Dad's tour of duty in New Guinea, they became physicians to the Sultanate of Perak in Malaysia and set sail for the port of Teluk Anson, where my mother was gazetted as 'lady medical officer'. My father decided to channel his energy into specialising in tropical diseases.

The young doctors made their first home in a thatched bunga-
low on stilts in the grounds of the native hospital, far away from the
European section of the town. It was here that my father delivered
his firstborn son in the middle of a flood. After the birth of Raphael
Charles Frederick (known as Raffles), a sturdy blond boy with broad,
high cheekbones, a round forehead and green eyes, my father presented
my mother with a set of scalpels to impress upon her that he did not
wish her to discontinue her medical work because she had become a
mother.

My father's treatment of yaws with organic arsenic proved outstand-
ingly successful. He introduced quinine for malaria and de-wormed half
the population. In no time, he was speaking their language, becoming known as Lyda Mas – Golden Tongue. He would sit cross-legged
under the house in the evenings, discussing metaphysics and medicine
with tribal elders (*pengulus*) and devouring durian in season with all the
other devotees. He was more at home in Asia than he ever had been in
Adelaide.

Before he left Malaya, my dad conducted a tour, walking through
all the villages dressed in a sarong and turban as the Sultan's man, pro-
liferating ideas about mosquito control. The die was cast: he was to
be an administrator and a diplomat as well as an innovator in tropical medicine. He was knighted for his services to medicine in 1935.
My father's stance on native health attracted bureaucratic attention
in Canberra and he was repatriated to Australia to become director of
the Brisbane-based Tropical Hygiene division of the Commonwealth
Department of Health. Thus it was that the rest of us children, after
Raffles and Margaret (Ruth, Carl, David and I), were born in that big
country town called Brisbane.

I walked to Yeronga State School every day through the park, and
every year on Anzac Day we made wreaths to hang on trees that marked
the driveway to the school. Each child was allotted a tree under which
was a little plaque bearing the name of the dead Anzac who was their

special soldier. I can still smell the fresh scent of chrysanthemums in the early morning as we fashioned the circles and big 'A's embellished with flowers. It was a game, a competition and a sacred duty all in one. Then the park was suddenly closed off by barbed wire. The Americans had arrived and set up camp there.

Long queues of women formed outside my mother's surgery every evening after work, hundreds of girls who were pregnant or suffering from venereal diseases. During the day, the house was jammed with people – friends of my brother who made illegal liquor in a make-shift laboratory under the house, visiting children from the country, Americans invited by my sisters, nurses taking classes from my mother, patients, grandmothers and women who sewed, washed and ironed. I used to sit in a tree and talk to my bantams, my obsession at the time.

When my father went overseas, I decided to live in a tree. I chose a spreading poinciana. A few boards placed strategically between two boughs formed the floor of my cubby-house, and a fruit crate served as a makeshift roof. My mother had had some new orange cushions made up for the sitting room, so I purloined them for my tree house and, waving my torch around like a beacon, settled down for the night. Soon the wind began to blow and I had to hang on to stop myself from falling. The rain came down in buckets and, in no time at all, the cushions became sodden heaps, oozing orange dye.

It is difficult climbing down a tree in the dark. The bark gets slippery and you miss vital footholds. I was half-expecting to find lanterns lighting up the driveway, voices shouting my name, the clamour of an anxious family suddenly relieved to see their prodigal daughter again, but I should have known that, in our family, no-one had even noticed that I was gone. The only consequence of the event was my mother's bafflement as to the whereabouts of her precious new orange cushions. Had she looked up, she would have noticed a poinciana tree shedding lumps of grey stuffing and strips of discoloured material from its upper branches.

What I truly loved more than anything in the world was to dance. I attended ballet classes every afternoon at the home of Frances Davis, a tireless and loving teacher. Her mother played the piano while five or six of us young ballerinas lined up to do our *entrechats*, *grands jetés* and *pirouettes*. After class, we went around the garden to her mulberry tree. If it was in fruit, there was no better treat than to sit up in its branches munching mulberries until our tongues turned black.

At Gran's insistence, I was taught the violin by Theodora Benson, a dark-haired melancholic with chipped teeth and moles all over her face. She was hopelessly in love with Yehudi Menuhin and had painted at least fifty portraits of him from photos. These crude daubings hung on the walls of her classroom and my clearest memory of her classes was the face of Yehudi sneering from every wall at my feeble attempts at Fritz Kreisler exercises.

Meetings at the Alliance Française were held in French by Monsieur Denat. Antoine Denat was one of those dedicated beings who opened the world of Colette, Jean Cocteau, Coco Chanel, Jean-Louis Barrault, Jean-Paul Sartre, Simone de Beauvoir, Verlaine and Rimbaud to children who exhibited Francophile tendencies. To me, the French seemed to live in a rarefied world of brilliance and style that made everybody pale by comparison. I saw my first French films at the Alliance Française, and they were unforgettable – *L'Éternel retour*, the *Fanny*, *Marius* and *Caesar* trilogy, *La Belle et La Bête* and *Le Facteur*. I picked up the language quickly by ear but not the grammar, which is wicked, and used to go around speaking with a French accent, pretending I had been in the Resistance as a child messenger.

In hindsight, I am sure these manifestations were a direct result of the fact that my father had left Australia and gone to Europe. As soon as the Second World War was over, because of his unquestionable adroitness in administration and ability to handle medical disasters, he was made a Lieutenant General, head of the United Nations Relief and Rehabilitation Administration (UNRRA) in the British zone of Germany.

Given the task of clearing up Belsen-Bergen, he recruited ninety-six of the most optimistic graduates of London University. The results were immediate. Within a week the death rate had halved, and within a fortnight it had halved again.

However, in Australia, without my father's presence in the house, my mother and I clashed like cymbals and the dynamics of the family skewed. My brother Raff became the arbiter and pseudo-patriarch, dispensing punishments, taking sides unfairly and driving a wedge between my mother and the rest of the children. I am sure it was not all his fault and I know I was unmanageable.

On one occasion, I irritated my mother so much that she picked up a hairbrush and was about to strike me with it when our border collie, Mac, bit her hard on the leg as she drew her arm back. I laughed shamelessly and ran away, which only enraged her more. It was soon after this incident that my mother and Raff decided that I should get some counselling. Unluckily, my brother sent me to a friend of his who had just graduated from medical school and had never had a patient, let alone a recalcitrant twelve-year-old with attitude. I had known this friend of Raff's all my life and had always considered him a boring Mr Pecksniff who put too much grease in his hair. It was no contest. He gave up after two appointments. 'Incorrigible' was the adjective he used in his report.

The upshot was that I was sent as a boarder to the Glennie Memorial School for Girls in Toowoomba, far away from family conflagrations. It was hoped that I would acquire manners and some of the genteel attributes of womanhood. I would return home docile and prepared for marriage to some dreary professional chap who would keep me in funds and out of trouble for the rest of my life. As I had no interest in medicine, the only profession considered worthwhile by the Cilento clan, I could not be deemed a serious person.

Glennie was a large institution built around the turn of the last century to educate the daughters of well-heeled cattle-station owners from Outback Queensland. It was constructed along the lines of most colonial hospitals and schools from Calcutta to Karachi: a quadrangle in the centre, with classrooms, kitchen and common rooms clustered around at ground level. Dormitories, lecture rooms and ablutions blocks took up the other levels and the Mistresses occupied a wing overlooking the front drive. The dormitories were divided into Houses – (Horrible) Hale, (Terrible) Tufnell, (Dirty) Donaldson and (Wonderful) Webber. Obviously, I was a Wonderful Webberite and slept on the third floor of a dormitory.

There were roughly two hundred boarders and the same number of daygirls. No males were ever seen on the premises, except the Reverend Tinpants (I never knew his real name as no-one ever called him anything else within my hearing), who conducted Chapel every evening. The lesson was read by Miss Dowson, Head Mistress of Glennie, who would finish by extolling the virtues of abstinence and piety.

Miss Dowson wore a pageboy wig, dyed black, that moved all of a piece. She had the myopic gaze of an introvert and the rich brown Raj accent of one born and brought up in Poona. She wore a tweed suit under black university robes in the daytime and floral Indian silk batwing blouses with a calf-length skirt of 1920s vintage in the evenings.

Food at Glennie was shepherd's pie or stew and sinker, a dessert made from quantities of flour, water and small black currants, which was so called because it hit the pit of your stomach like lead. After dinner, we would retire to the large sitting room to listen to Miss Dowson reading Ngaio Marsh detective stories while the goodie-goodies sat on the floor simpering as they sewed their trousseaus or knitted. It was ghastly.

Most of the girls had never been to school before but rather had done correspondence courses from their dusty cattle stations near Winton, Longreach and Goondiwindi. Some had been boarders since the age of five and knew nothing but an institutionalised lifestyle. They were given to 'crushes' on fellow students, twittering and squawking like flocks of budgies.

Nobody spoke to new girls, though the established inmates came up and stared fixedly at your nametag, mouthing out the letters and making comments about your origin, especially if the name was C-I-L-E-N-T-O. You had to wear the nametag on the front and back of your uniform for a week to allow everybody to get used to you.

From what memories I can dredge up of those first few uncomfortable days, the talk was all about who had the most money and what boys from Toowoomba Grammar were sexy. The daughters of the squattocracy were only concerned with snaffling themselves rich husbands. I knew before the first week was out that I was in the wrong place and went to tell Miss Dowson that I wished to leave.

I remember the interview well. It took place in a small annexe overlooking the quad while Miss Dowson arranged a profusion of larkspurs and delphiniums in vases. She wore gloves and had a little pair of secateurs attached to her waist. Miss Dowson knew immediately why I was there. The scene was one that must have been played out a hundred times, with variations, but she chose to ignore my presence and continued snipping and shifting the blooms, stepping back to contemplate the effect. When she sensed that I was about to leave, she gave herself a little nod of approval and turned to face me with an expression of concerned inquiry.

Miss Dowson listened to my argument, head averted and eyes darting back every second to regard her handiwork. When I had finished, she gave me a wan smile and patted my shoulder with her long gloved fingers. 'My dear child, you will settle down within a day or two, make scores of friends and just *love* it here. It's all a matter of *adjustment* and getting into the swing of things. You're such a sweet gel.' She cupped my face in her gloved hand, stared sympathetically into my eyes and then her gaze reverted to the larkspurs. This was her way of marking the end of the interview.

'Adjustment' consisted of being accepted into a clique and being given a nickname. I became Chilly-bum. 'Getting into the swing of things' meant joining the swimming, tennis and hockey teams and doing outrageous things after Lights Out (such as climbing down the fire escape to have midnight feasts in the empty swimming pool or raiding other dormitories for fights with pillows loaded with books). Any sexual shenanigans went on under covers after Lights Out, when crushes on prefects, Mistresses or film stars were discussed with bated breath. It is no wonder that the atmosphere was one of suppressed sexual hysteria, with all the passionate outbursts, Chinese whispers, loathings, lovings and lurkings that accompany it. And the GOSSIP! Something overheard from the next shower cubicle would be around the school in a matter of minutes, grossly distorted and sometimes very funny.

The teachers all had nicknames too. Miss Lake, a PE instructress with huge knobbly calves, was known as Puddle; Miss Gower, who taught Elocution, was called Lizard because she flicked out her tongue when she over-enunciated her words; and Olive Green, our mathematics teacher, was dubbed the Hag, for obvious reasons.

It wasn't long before I was seriously plotting to get out of Glennie for good. I took to sneaking out during the afternoon tea break and running to the telephone booth two streets away. It started as an attempt to call home and plead with my mother to come to rescue me, but when I couldn't get through, I rang the school's number and asked to speak to Miss Dowson, stating that it was Lady Cilento speaking. She came to the phone immediately.

'Good afternoon, Miss Dowson,' I heard myself say in my best deep, maternal voice. 'I'm ringing to find out how little D is getting on and to tell you that I shall be in Toowoomba at the weekend lecturing. I wonder if you could put her on the bus to town on Saturday morning as I won't be able to collect her myself?'

'Of course, Lady Cilento,' effused Miss Dowson. 'She's such a sweet gel – a little high-spirited and headstrong perhaps, but she's settling down nicely now, getting into the swing of things, making scores of friends. It's all a matter of *adjustment*, you know.'

After a few pleasantries we concluded the conversation and I fell back in the booth, almost fainting at my own temerity. It had been so easy! I'd just 'jumped' into my mother!

When I was called to Miss Dowson's study later that afternoon, I was careful to wear a face of concern, as though she was going to tell me that there had been a death in the family. She held back the revelation that I was to be permitted to go to downtown Toowoomba on Saturday to meet my mother, prefacing the news with a long dissertation on how she had informed my mother of my misdeeds and naughtiness. She pointed out that her decision to allow me out was due only to her respect for my mother, and that I should show my gratitude for her kindness by swearing to behave properly in the future.

After I got over my astonishment that I had actually got away with it and had had my day of freedom in the un-marvellous fleshpots of downtown Toowoomba, I looked back over the experience and two things stood out. I realised that, if I *believed* myself to *be* my mother and made that little leap in my head, I *was* my mother! Her words and voice came out of my mouth as long as I didn't *think* about it, allowed it to flow without hesitation and *knew* she was me! What I had stumbled upon in that telephone booth was the secret of 'acting' – and the mystery behind every successful confidence trickster, spy, practical joker and defrauder in the business. You have to know beyond any shred of doubt that you *are* who you say you are. It's as simple, and as difficult, as that.

What I also learned from that day was that I would never pull the same trick again without taking friends along with me. In reality, I had a miserable time after the initial exhilaration of getting away with it faded. I went to the movies but a raincoated man sat next to me and I was horrified to feel a clammy hand climb up my leg in the dark. I had to move twice before I escaped him, finally finding a seat between two large matrons with lots of parcels and bags. For the rest of the day, I wandered around looking in shops with no money to buy anything and ended up at the bus terminal early, eating tepid fish and chips out of newspaper while waiting for the bus to take me back to my prison.

On the weekend of the Toowoomba Show, the Ecca (Exhibition), I took four girls with me but didn't tell them that my mother wasn't coming. The girls, whom I shall call Pip, Bazza (short for Beverley), Hookey (who had one eye) and Kristina, were friends. They were older than I was and fun, and I had seen that they had lots of money hidden away. It was against the rules to keep money at Glennie but nearly everybody had a few notes secreted in photo frames, stashed in the bottom of sewing baskets or buried deep in boxes of dusting powder. Glennie money often smelt of lily of the valley or tea rose and had a fine coating of talc. I told them to bring as much of it as they could, as we would be going on all the rides at the fun fair attached to the Ecca. I urged them to bring some real clothes to change into instead of the bulky serge tunics, grey stockings and red, gold and purple ties that marked us out as Glennie 'gels'.

It was pouring with rain as we boarded the bus. I have always loved the smell of new rain on hot tarmac. We booked into the big hotel and changed into 'frocks', and the rest of the day is a blur of madness and fun. We watched the bulls and horses being paraded at the Ecca showground, went on every single ride, including the Big Dipper, shied at coconuts, and Hookey won a monkey on a stick. We joined up with some Toowoomba Grammar boys and went to a freak show where a two-headed pig and other animal deformities were on display, suspended in huge glass bottles of formalin. We saw Hermie the Hermaphrodite, half-man and half-woman, dressed in a tuxedo and with half a moustache on one side and wearing a slinky evening dress and ankle-strap high heels on the other. We flirted and smoked cigarettes in an alley while the rain made channels that ran over our smart shoes. We drank thick shakes, ate chunky potato scallops and went to the double bill at the cinema. This time, the hands up the legs were warm and fumbling and we squirmed away from the funny boy smell. Everyone forgot the time.

26

By some miracle, the last bus was late and we managed to catch it back to Glennie. As we changed into our uniforms in the back of the bus, Kristina exclaimed, 'Oh, my God! What happened to your mother?' I explained how I'd rung up 'Dowie' Dowson, impersonating my mum, and did imitations of Miss Dowson and 'my mother' discussing me. We giggled all the way back to school, swearing that we would never tell anyone about our excellent escapade.

Thursday morning was Assembly Day at Glennie. The Head Mistress, in her mortar and black robes, took the podium for her weekly summing-up and inspirational lecture on how Glennie girls should think and behave. On this particular Thursday morning, about five months later, we noticed that a sort of pall hung over the whole room during the reading of the lesson and the hymn singing. Miss Dowson cleared her throat and gave us all a baleful glare before she spoke in her mellifluous voice: 'Gels, it has come to my attention that five of you behaved in public in a deplorable manner when you were granted the privilege of representing the school at the Toowoomba Exhibition some months ago. I want those gels who know they are responsible for their part in this deplorable episode to stand up.'

Everybody looked around at each other, not knowing exactly what she was talking about, but when I saw the mortified face of Bazza as she slowly got to her feet, the saliva left my mouth. I knew in one blinding instant that she was talking about *us*! Bazza had recorded the whole incident in her diary and they had read it.

Miss Dowson continued, 'Yes, Beverley, you may well look ashamed. Stand up Kristina, Sonia [Hookey's real name] and you, Pip. I do not blame you for the instigation of the plot to take the school down. You were innocent dupes but, once you *knew* the stratagem, you should have returned to the school and reported the matter immediately.'

By this time I'd got to my feet and Miss Dowson turned her attention to me. 'This gel,' she said, pointing her long finger at me, 'is the epitome of deceit, the exemplar of disruption. She planned the whole affair, making me believe that *she was her mother!*'

Someone laughed out loud and there were some muffled sniggers from around the Assembly Hall. Miss Dowson must have realised how odd her last statement sounded. '. . . *on the telephone,*' she added. 'I will say no more about this grievous occurrence, except to gate all of you for the remainder of the term. No outings, all silent meals. But you, Diane Cilento, you will resign from your House. You are the first gel ever to be put into Blank House. Any further disruption to the peaceful running of this school will *not* be tolerated and I put you on notice that I shall speak to your mother . . .'

Here Miss Dowson paused mid-sentence. She must have been reminded of how often she had spoken to *me* as my mother and that I knew perfectly well what she had said to 'my mother' about me. 'Your mother shall *really* be informed about this, mark my words,' she concluded ominously. 'Assembly dismissed!'

The story of our adventure flew around the school, gaining momentum with every telling. By the end of the day, it had us spending the night with Toowoomba Grammar boys at the hotel, getting roaring drunk, dancing down the corridors naked, taking my mother's car for a joy-ride and evading the police by jumping into a creek.

I liked Blank House. There were no prefects to hassle you and you didn't have to feel guilty about receiving black marks or letting the house down. It was great and I stopped getting into so much trouble. How could I? I was Head Prefect and Secretary. In fact, I was everything. I was the CEO of Blank House. I put up a notice on the main board to the effect that, as the inaugural member of Blank House, I would welcome anyone who wished to resign from their present House and join me beyond the pale. Then I entered myself into the Swimming Events as the representative of Blank House. Several girls put their names down on the list, expressing their desire to join Blank House, and I think I interviewed one or two of them. By the end of that week I was told to pack my bags, as my brother was coming up from Brisbane to collect me.

Life at the Annerley house had changed, and I felt my father's absence even more keenly. My mother was mortified by my untimely departure from Glennie but she did not interrogate me about what I had done. Perhaps she had heard some version from Miss Dowson and felt somehow implicated because I had been imitating *her*. However, she was compelled to search for a suitable school for me. In the end, I expect the only one that would take me was Somerville House, where both my sisters had been schooled. I was to be a daygirl and travel every day from Annerley to Vulture Street by tram.

One of the addictive joys of riding the tramcars in those days was to jump off before they stopped, an art form practised by many. The trick is to stand on the lower step as the tram begins to slow down and to ascertain the exact moment and speed to step off. You take a few little nimble steps and then slow down to a cool saunter. This way, you don't have to wait for the long grinding halt and jostling by the crowds trying to get off at the same time. I considered myself one of the best exponents of the art of tram jumping. I liked showing off to the Churchie boys (Church of England Boys Grammar School), and could match any of them for distance before the stop and quickness in slowing down.

As a student of Somerville House, you were never to appear in the street without gloves, stockings and hat. On the tram, we were meant to travel in the Ladies' Compartment up front. If that was full, we could sit in the middle section for mixed sexes at a pinch but were forbidden to enter the Men's Compartment or travel at the back of the tram, where larrikins and drunks tended to congregate. Leaping off trams before they stopped was such a remote probability for a girl from Somerville

House that it hadn't even been included in the formal list of things you weren't supposed to do.

Coming home was the best fun of the day. I would divest myself of my Somerville House hat and gloves and stuff them into my school bag. Then I would join the Churchie boys out the back of the tram. We had a game going, taking turns jumping off at every stop and getting back on again just as the conductor rang the bell.

Inevitably, one afternoon I was unlucky enough to jump off the tram too soon and sprawl headlong along the road, grazing my stockinged knees and ending up in front of Miss George, Deputy Head of Somerville House. She had alighted from the Ladies' Compartment and walked back to see what was going on. With her eagle eye, she had enumerated my many misdemeanours before I had risen to my feet – NO HAT and NO GLOVES – while all the Churchie boys stood around laughing and dusting me down in a familiar way. I knew I was a goner as soon as I looked into her little, steely grey eyes. My mother was asked that I be withdrawn from Somerville House by the end of the term.

In the meantime, on the other side of the world, my father had moved to New York City. His work at Belsen with UNRRA having finished, he led the first UN delegation when the World Health Organization came into being. He was allocated an apartment in Peter Cooper Village, a new complex built to house the UN delegates and staff, situated on First Avenue and 20th Street. Soon afterwards, my sister Margaret won a Wattle League scholarship for painters and joined him there.

After my Somerville House debacle, my mother began pressuring me as to what I intended to do with my life, other than be a delinquent. I told her what I really wanted was to dance professionally. She was filled with misgivings. 'But, D, you can't just be a dancer,' she exhorted me. 'It's so precarious. It's over so soon. You *must* have another string to your bow.' This left me puzzled, as I thought she meant my violin bow, which had at least fifty strings attached to it at all times.

30

Around this time, my mother's weekly articles in Brisbane's *Courier-Mail* began to focus on wayward teenage girls, with advice on how to curb their unruly spirits. She advocated parental control, especially from the parent who holds most sway over the child, and cited the absence of one parent as a possible cause of the waywardness. I took her at her word and pleaded that there could be no better 'parental control' for me than in New York with my dad. She was unconvinced by my entreaties at first, but when my sister relayed strong messages to her about my father's growing attachment to his secretary, Ursula, there was a rapid reappraisal.

With eight other passengers, my mother, my brother David and I set sail for Boston on the *Pioneer Star*, an old iron Liberty ship carrying a cargo of onions and lobster tails. We traversed the Pacific across its widest part, stopping at Pitcairn Island, Tonga, the Friendly Islands and the Panama Canal. Once through the canal, we headed for Trinidad, then San Dominique and on to Boston.

After what seemed like an endless voyage, suddenly we were docking and there was my dad looking so familiar and yet so foreign, wearing his continental beret, and my sister, her red hair blazing in the autumn sunlight. They were gazing up, their eyes lit in anticipation. I watched them for a long time before they saw me, savouring the lines of their faces. They were beloved strangers and I was unnerved at being related to such exotic beings.

CHAPTER TWO

*I*t was a chasmic leap from the repression of Glennie and Somerville House to the jumpin' jivin' corridors of PS 83, Washington Irving High School, on Third Avenue and 17th Street, New York City. At first I couldn't understand anything anyone was saying and the large classes of thirty-five or forty students, mostly African-Americans, unsettled me. What's more, I could not tell the students from the staff because no-one wore a uniform.

For the first three weeks in New York City, I was intimidated by everything – the noise, smells, giant high-rises, buses belching black smoke and the COLD. Never having been out of a sub-tropical climate, and with blood as thin as vin rosé, my fingers froze and the rims of my ears crackled with ice. It was agony and I could not fathom the folly of building one of the largest cities in the world in such an inhospitable climate. No wonder the people were so cranky. They snapped at you if you were slow getting the hang of their money and elbowed you out of the way on the bus. People mumbled to themselves in the streets or occasionally shrieked for no reason at all but nobody took any notice. Weirdos, drunks, derelicts and poor old bag ladies plodded about the city, dodging yellow taxis hurtling down the avenues, and everybody shouted.

I quickly learned to wear several layers of clothes – gloves, balaclava, anything to keep out the bitter cold and soothe the inflammation of my mucous membranes. I took to walking around Manhattan, initially to economise on bus fares and keep out of the way of the savage hordes, and I began to appreciate the cryptic New York humour, the frenetic energy and the human torrent that swept up Fifth Avenue to the Plaza and spilled into Central Park. It was a new, unexpected theatre of reality I had entered and now I was part of it. I watched the great red sphere of sun sink between the skyscrapers on the West Side and the East River glittering in the morning light. I stood under the elevated railway as it rumbled down Third Avenue, its giddy girders casting criss-crossed shadows on the cobbled streets below. In my mound of shapeless garments, I felt invisible and invulnerable as I wandered the city in a daze of delighted shocks, devouring every impression. I couldn't get enough. I was fifteen, and I was hooked on the streets of New York.

Soon, it wasn't just the streets. I discovered the Metropolitan Museum, the Hayden Planetarium and the Museum of Modern Art. Instead of going to school, I would take my twenty-three cents and go down into the basement of MOMA where classic films, undreamed of in Brisbane, were screened every day – D. W. Griffith's *Birth of a Nation*, all of Erich von Stroheim's films, including *Greed* and *Foolish Wives*, John Ford's *Grapes of Wrath* and so many other wonders. I saw Greta Garbo, Sarah Bernhardt, Eleonora Duse and Anna Pavlova. I was like a drunk in a brewery. I would emerge bedazzled, transfixed and infused with a strange new inspiration, walking all the way from 57th Street to Peter Cooper Village without noticing the distance.

I had stopped attending classes at PS 83 after another of my disastrous clashes with an authority figure at school. At the insistence of my mother, who was still going on about the 'second string to my bow', I had enrolled in the Secretarial Studies course. Although I could hardly understand what anyone was saying, I felt anonymous and secure amongst the forty other students. We were learning how to lay out a formal letter when I heard the teacher's strident voice.

'Miss KILL-EN-TOE!' she called, stabbing her finger into the list of students' names while sweeping her other hand around the room. I had no idea that she meant me. 'Miss KILL-EN-TOE!' she repeated.

I raised my hand fearfully. She held up a piece of A4 paper.

'What do I have when I have this?'

I looked at her stupidly. What did she mean? Was it a trick question? After an excruciating pause, while she showed her impatience, I answered, 'Well, if you *have* it, you've *got* it.'

There was another pause. This time, she emphasised every word as if I was deaf.

'I said, Miss KILL-EN-TOE, what do I *have* when I HAVE this?'

She shook the paper in my face. The vehemence she put into the words commanded the attention of the rest of the class. I began to shake and stutter.

'Well . . . it . . . it . . . it seems to me, Miss, that if you HAVE it . . . you've got it!'

The whole classroom began to pick up the refrain. Someone started the chant, 'If ya HAVE it, ya GODDIT! Yeah, baby, if ya HAVE it, ya GODDIT!'

In the midst of the bedlam, I suddenly got it. What she meant was, 'What do I have when I HALVE this?' Americans pronounce 'halve' the same as 'have'. I tried to shout out the explanation but the noise was now thunderous, with kids standing on their seats, chanting and whooping. The teacher had left the room. She returned accompanied by a senior member of the staff, the Principal, I presume. I was singled out as the instigator of the riot and sent out of the class. It was this ridiculous incident that set me off on my New York Odyssey.

At home, a palpable tension filled the apartment. My mother was suddenly free from the surgery, Mothercraft meetings and delivering multitudes of babies, and she didn't know what had hit her. After twenty years as an indefatigable doctor and mother, she was demoted to housewife. She waffled about for a few weeks, not knowing what to do except shop and cook too much food. Yet, as the weeks went by, her mood became progressively more subdued as both of us watched my father in the mirror as he whispered into the telephone in the evenings after dinner. He did not realise that he was fully revealed in the large looking glass opposite him and that, even though we could not hear the words, it was impossible to misunderstand his murmurings – what my grandmother would have called 'sweet nothings'.

My brother David never noticed anything because he was either making model airplanes in his room or trying to get topsides of the different educational system. He had been sent to the McBurney School in Manhattan but it wasn't long before he was begging Mum to let him take a sickie, pleading headaches, tummy pains, sore ears . . . anything rather than go back to the bear pit of daily bullying that was McBurney.

My sister Margaret did not live with us. She had studio space at No. 4 MacDougall Street. I loved visiting her down in Greenwich Village, where the streets crawled with eccentrics of all ages, sexes and colours, and passionate discussions, music and arguments filled the air. They didn't care if they made a spectacle of themselves or shouted obscenities.

I took two jobs to pay for ballet lessons at the Michael Fokine School of Dance at Carnegie Hall. I babysat on the sixteenth floor of one of the other buildings in Peter Cooper Village, except that my 'baby' was actually a large girl of nineteen years who was a victim of cerebral palsy and confined to a wheelchair. Her parents, from the Deep South, were thrilled to have found someone to play with their daughter. They hardly ever took her anywhere or communicated with her but she was actually very intelligent. She had a telescope set up by the window and, after the parents had left, she would show me where to point it and we would perv on the inhabitants in the opposite building, just like Jimmy Stewart in Hitchcock's *Rear Window*. We were sure we'd see a horrendous murder one day. Sometimes we would laugh and laugh for no reason. I liked her a lot and thought I had a good deal at five dollars an hour, though I was a bit worried that one day she might fall out of her wheelchair laughing. She must have weighed fourteen stone.

My other job was in a factory in Brooklyn, where figurines of horses, merry-go-rounds and fairytale characters were fashioned for the display windows of Saks and Macy's on Fifth Avenue. My job was to apply glue, sprinkle on coloured sparkle and glitter, pat it into place and wipe away the excess. It wasn't difficult but by the end of the day my jeans were so caked with glue and glitter that I couldn't bend my legs. I had to stretch them out on the seat of the subway or else stand up all the way back to 23rd Street in Manhattan.

For the first time in my life, I knew what it was to work in a sweat shop all day with no breaks, except to get a chilli dog from the Mexican guy on the corner. Nothing ever tasted so good nor had I ever felt so tired. Once I went to sleep on the subway coming home, missed my change and ended up at 23rd Street on Long Island. I have never loved my mother so much as when I finally staggered through the door around midnight. She gently pulled the filthy, stiffened garments from my collapsed body, bathed me tenderly and carried me to my bed, where she tucked me in like an infant.

Ballet lessons at the Michael Fokine School were conducted in a big dusty room with *barres* on one side and mirrors on the other. To my horror, instead of the six to eight students I had expected, there were at least fifty squeezed in to do their *pliés* and they were all ancient, or so they seemed to my fifteen-year-old eyes. The teacher stood on a little raised dais and shouted out each new exercise while the usual Chopin pieces were thumped out on the piano. Anton Dolin, the celebrated British dancer and choreographer, once took a class. The man who stood in front of us constantly shifting mucus around his sinuses and running his fingers through a sparse crop of dyed red hair bore no resemblance to the magnificent creature I had seen sweeping his partner effortlessly into the air in *Swan Lake* in Brisbane. The vision of myself as a prima ballerina was growing fainter every time I went to class.

The elevator at Carnegie Hall was large and slow, with a squeaky grille that had to be dragged across and latched securely before it would move. People went up and down to classes all day long cursing it – singers, trumpeters, violinists, flautists, drummers and young actors studying at the American Academy of Dramatic Arts, which occupied the entire top floor. I used to ride up and down with them just to listen to their chatter. They fascinated me greatly. They were so lively and excited, not at all like the dancers, who tended to be a morose lot, fretting about their turnouts and their elevation.

Amongst the young actors was one especially beautiful brunette with the classic features of a goddess I'd seen on a Greek vase at the Metropolitan Museum. She was always laughing and talking. I watched her covertly as she threw her head back, her hair swishing back and forth. From what I could gather, she was about to finish her course and leave the comparative safety of drama school for the gaping maw of the Great White Way – Broadway. One day in the elevator going up, she touched my cheek and said, 'You're such a pretty girl. What's your name? Are you thinking of starting at AADA when you're old enough?'

I could feel my ears pulsing with pleasure and embarrassment as I answered, 'No, I'm going to be a dancer. My name's Diane . . . Diane Cilento.'

'Cilento?' she repeated, pronouncing it 'Ch' in the Italian way. 'You must be an Italian with a name like that. But you're so fair. You must be a fair Venetian. I'm Italian too. You couldn't get more Italian than me. My name's Italiano, Anna Maria Italiano, but I'll probably have to change it if I'm gonna make it in the big time.' She laughed and swung her hair around again. 'But *you* won't have to,' she continued. 'They love dancers with foreign names . . . dancers and movie monsters. Did you know that Boris Karloff's real name is Jim Pratt?'

We arrived at the top floor and she swung the creaking door open. 'Why don't you come and have a look around? Come on,' she urged. 'No-one's going to bite you.'

And so I was ushered into a new world that opened up in front of me – a world I stepped into as easily as I had stepped out of that lift. I knew immediately that I had found what I *really* wanted to do.

Anna Maria Italiano *did* change her name – to Anne Bancroft – and she *did* make it in the big time and was sensible enough to marry a man who made her laugh and with whom she was not in competition. He changed *his* name too, from Melvin Kaminsky to Mel Brooks.

Some days later I ventured up to the top floor again, this time with a mission – to meet the Principal of the American Academy of Dramatic Arts. He was a small, fine-boned man whose wizened face lit up when he smiled, revealing perfectly even false teeth that moved ever so slightly when he spoke.

'My name is Mr Gellinger but they call me "the Old Guy",' he said as he handed me an audition form. 'They've all been through here. I've seen them all and they all know me. I'm a living legend. I'm the Old Guy of Broadway. Come back when you've learned the "Gallop apace" speech from *Romeo and Juliet*. You're about the same age as she was. Hope you'll have a better outcome than she had. Shakespeare was tough on broads.' He cackled at his own joke.

I had no idea what he was talking about, but the mention of Shakespeare was disconcerting. At Glennie we had waded through *Julius Caesar* but the only Shakespearean acting I'd ever seen had been a horrendous production of *Macbeth* murdered by my brother Carl's class at Churchie. I dreaded having to try to make sense of, let alone act out, the daunting words that crowded the soliloquies.

I took the subway home, wedged in at rush hour, reading the words over and over, trying to understand what Juliet was getting at.

Gallop apace, you fiery-footed steeds,
Towards Phoebus' lodging: such a wagoner
As Phaethon would whip you to the west,
And bring in cloudy night immediately . . .

Who was Phaethon? Where was Phoebus' lodging? What a weird girl Juliet must have been to talk like that. Suddenly, I remembered the lesson of the telephone booth when I had jumped into my mother – but I knew nothing about Juliet, so how could I jump into *her*?

That night at dinner I asked my dad who Phaethon was. 'Phaethon was the son of Helios, god of the sun,' he explained, 'who drove his golden chariot across the heavens every day. Phaethon was a spoilt boy who induced his father to grant him any favour he desired. What he desired was to drive his father's chariot across the heavens, but when he did he couldn't control the immortal horses and so wreaked havoc by scorching the earth. Seeing the danger, Zeus threw a thunderbolt. End of Phaethon, end of story.'

'Why don't you tell us another mythological story?' said my mother.

My father put down his knife and fork and tapped the bridge of his nose, a sure sign that he was launching into loquacious mode. Basically, I suspect he was relieved to talk about an impersonal subject that would fill the deadly pauses brought on by a wife who knows that her husband is philandering and a husband made wordless because he knows that she knows he's cheating.

'What about the story of Narcissus?' suggested my mum in a quiet voice.

My father regarded her through narrowed eyelids. Narcissus was the man who fell in love with his own image. It was a tricky situation to be trapped between one's parents at this sensitive moment in their lives. There could be a conflagration at any moment, and we were all alert to the shifts in mood that preceded a passionate outburst.

Just then the telephone shrilled. I leapt up to answer it before anyone else could get it. We all knew that Ursula, Dad's secretary/mistress, always called just as we were getting up from the table after dinner. Speaking concisely in her Sloane Street accent, she requested to speak to Dad. Mimicking her toffee-nosed voice, I asked who was speaking.

'His secretary, Ursula,' she replied tersely.

'Oh, sorry, Ursula. I didn't recognise your voice. We're in the middle of a very important family conference this evening, Ursula, and my dad is not taking any calls.' I spoke urgently and quietly, as though not wanting to interrupt what was going on at my end, and then added cheerily, '*Byyyeeeeeee!*'

I explained to Dad that Ursula had said it was nothing of any consequence and that she would be in the office the next day. I didn't dare ask any more questions about 'Phoebus' lodging' or Phaethon, as my dad was wearing his don't-come-near-me face.

The next day, I went to the New York City Library and researched *Romeo and Juliet*. I learned that the whole speech is about Juliet's impatience to make love with Romeo. There were still some bits that I didn't understand because I'd never experienced them, but I hoped to one day. 'Lovers can see to do their amorous rites by their own beauties.' I loved reciting the 'Gallop apace' speech as soon as I had memorised the words. I can still recite the whole speech today.

I began hyperventilating in the elevator as soon as the old grille clicked shut and we began our upward journey towards the top floor where the audition for AADA was to take place. At every floor I was tempted to leap out and run down the stairs back to the anonymity of 57th Street. By the time I reached the room where my future was to be decided I was breathing like a dog on a hot afternoon, although it was the middle of winter. I stood in front of the examiners, scarcely able to repeat my own name, and when they asked me what piece I was offering, nothing came out of my mouth, just rasping breath. It was the Old Guy who took pity on me. Holding out a glass of water, he told me to sit down.

'No, no . . . can't do it sitting down,' I choked out. 'It wouldn't work like that!'

Finally, they told me to go outside and deep breathe until I was calm. They said I could come back and that they would pretend they had never seen me before. They waited fifteen minutes before I had gathered the strength to make a proper entrance and get on with it. In the end, they were as relieved as I was when I reached the final words of my speech: 'And every tongue that speaks but Romeo's name speaks heavenly eloquence!' It was over, and they were smiling encouragingly.

My audition was successful and, although I was so very young, it was agreed by the adjudicators and the Old Guy that I should start immediately – with my parents' consent. That was the predicament. How was I to explain to my parents that I had not attended high school for an entire term, that I had no intention of ever going back, but that I wanted five hundred dollars to study acting?

Before I could broach the subject, my mother received a letter from PS 83, Washington Irving High School, reporting my truancy. She was tight-lipped and exceedingly disappointed in me. This was the third time she'd had to bear the brunt of my defection from school. I could see in her eyes that she was despairing of my future, and foresaw a life of either covering up for my blunders or literally paying for my mistakes.

'I'm going to have to tell your father about this,' she announced. 'What are we to do with you? If you have no education, you will never get a proper job. You will always be a burden. What have you got to say for yourself? What have you been doing every day instead of going to school? I'm *very* upset.' I could see tears welling up in her eyes.

'Listen, Mum, don't be worried about me. I *know* what I want to do now . . . I do . . . I really know. I'm going to *act*.'

'That is an idiotic idea! It's the most precarious profession in the world. Only about one in five hundred, male or female, make a living at it. You can't just hare off and say you're going to act. At least, you ought to have another string to your bow.'

I knew it was useless to say anything more to her, so I waited until my father got home and then told him. His reaction was altogether different from my mother's. He listened carefully. I started by telling him I had been selected by audition as a student at AADA. As for my truancy, after hearing my story of, 'If ya HAVE it, ya GODDIT!' at PS 83, he laughed and looked at my mother. 'Well, what do you think, Phyl, let her put her ability as a mimic to good use? If you're going to act, you'd better be good at it. There's nothing less forgivable than bad acting.'

I knew what my mother thought. She thought I'd got away with it again.

When the spring semester came to an end, summer hit New York City like a sledgehammer. We sweltered, and, like migratory birds, every member of the family took off for other parts of the planet. My father went back to the Middle East, where he had been assisting Count Folke Bernadotte in the mediation process between Israel and Palestine. Margaret went to Cassis, in the south of France, where she joined an artist colony. My brother David went back to Australia for good, having had enough of McBurney School, and my mother began researching vitamins, the newest phenomenon in medicine, in New Mexico, where she had relations.

I was sent as an apprentice to the Barter Theatre of Virginia. I was not paid a salary but got food and board at the Barter Inn in exchange for understudying most of the female roles, playing children's roles, doing props and working as an assistant to the stage manager. I shared a room at the Barter Inn with two other apprentices, Barbara van Ornam and Dorothy Brentlinger.

The cherubic Barbara, who was four years older than me, wore contact lenses and her dark hair was combed in loose sausage curls over her forehead to cover a deep indentation, the legacy of a forceps birth. She had modelled herself on Doris Day. I don't know what Dorothy Brentlinger was doing as a theatre apprentice. She was a large, voluptuous blonde, sluggish in her movements, who loved nothing so much as sleeping. Dorothy suffered horribly from period pains and had to lie in bed for a whole week every month with a warming pad on her stomach, moaning 'Shit, shit, shit, shit,' like a mantra. The first night I was there,

Dorothy told me that she despised live theatre and only wanted to get into movies.

Although I had grown several inches since I left Australia, I was still small and was always called upon to play children of both sexes. I had learned to use make-up at AADA and was at last beginning to develop breasts (which I had to bind in order to play boys). I had never felt the pangs of teenage love for anyone except the first mate of the *Pioneer Star*, Mr Chittenden, who had hair that grew like moss and who smoked a pipe. At the Barter Theatre, the stage manager took a fancy to me and pursued me with dogged persistence until Bob Porterfield, the theatre proprietor, told him that I was 'jail-bait'. I think that was why he fancied me but I had learned long ago the art of getting out of the way of persistent men with groping hands. At the beginning of the season, there was much drinking and testing by the guys to see which girls they could sleep with and who would just be pals. Dorothy Brentlinger quickly became the girlfriend of one of the directors and started taking all his notes, sitting very close to him in rehearsals. She moved in with him after a few weeks, and Barbara and I slept much better without her moaning.

The lighting director I shall never forget. His name was Alvin Aucherland and I was appointed his assistant. He had a special trick for new apprentices, saying, 'Now just hold this for a minute while I test it. Is that okay? Yes? Is *that* okay?' Then he would give you an electric shock. I heard he did it every year to his assistant, but after the first time I took care to wear rubber gloves whenever I had to work with him.

Later in the season, the Barter Theatre went on a tour of one-night stands to many small towns. We travelled in our own bus through Iowa, Ohio, Georgia, Alabama, Kentucky, North Carolina, South Carolina and as far up as Wisconsin, playing theatres, colleges and halls. We even set up the show in an empty swimming pool at one stop. We took two plays, *You Can't Take It with You*, by Kaufman and Hart, and Molière's *The Imaginary Invalid*.

Each new venue was a challenge. We'd arrive, look over the stage with the other tecs, climb into overalls, unload the truck, assemble the lighting grid in front of the acting area, heave a dozen 'Leucos' up a ladder, attach them to the grid, focus them, cover the grid with black velvet, grab a banana, shower, set up the props, do the show, change back into overalls and then repeat the whole exercise in reverse. For this I was paid thirty-five dollars a week, my first theatrical earnings. I lived on chocolate milk, Hershey Bars, French doughnuts and bananas. I saved what I imagined was a fortune. I played a child in the Molière and was a walk-on and understudy to all the female parts in *You Can't Take It with You*. The acting bit of the day was a doddle compared to the other work.

It was my mother's hope that by the end of the tour I would have had all the theatrical nonsense purged from my system and be ready to go back to school. However, my experience at the Barter Theatre only served to strengthen my resolve. I was determined to continue to learn the skill of acting.

I travelled back to New York by train ready to begin the winter term at AADA, but in my absence the situation at home had changed once again. My father was now permanently in the Middle East and, since Count Bernadotte had been assassinated, his workload had doubled. He had taken Ursula with him as one of his two secretaries and my mother was very despondent. In her heart, she believed that her marriage was over. She had decided to give up the apartment in Peter Cooper Village and return to Australia by way of the UK to renew old friendships and follow up on her research into vitamins and nutrition, which was to become the backbone of her fame in later years. Mum argued that as my sister Margaret had given up her place in MacDougall Street, there was no place for me to stay in New York and continue my studies at AADA. She had already booked our passages on the *QE2*.

It was a dismal day when the great liner docked in Portsmouth. The Channel was the colour of weak tea and I was not impressed. The first thing I read in England was on a toilet wall:

Ain't no need to stand on the seat
Portsmouth crabs can jump six feet.

It was the 1950s, and the British shops were so dreary compared to Bloomingdale's or Macy's, the food so insipid and the people so dispirited and dowdy that I was amazed. What was all that 'but it's better back in Britain' stuff we'd been hearing from whingeing Poms all our lives? I was desperate to join my sister in Paris within a few days.

Jane Austen was correct in her assertion that what concerns a mother above all things is to see her daughter married to a suitably well-heeled bloke, ready to produce the grandchildren who will become the source of endless hours of conversation and concern in the future. I wondered why my mother had insisted that we should go to Bristol before heading to London. We went to the home of her old flame, the fiancé she had jilted for my dad. His name was Sir Harold Boyce, and since their university days together in Adelaide he had taken up residence in the UK, made a fortune in constructing railway carriages and become the first Australian Lord Mayor of London. Sir Harold had a son called Richard and my mother was blatantly matchmaking from the moment we arrived.

It was a vain hope. Richard was pimply and pompous, about as attractive to me as root-canal surgery, and my two days in Bristol were a sort of torture. I could not wait to get to London to explore the possibilities of getting into RADA (the Royal Academy of Dramatic Art). I had letters of recommendation from the Old Guy, Mr Gellinger, to Sir Kenneth Barnes, his counterpart at RADA.

As a veteran of summer stock and a couple of terms at AADA, I did not hyperventilate when I went for my audition at RADA, but my offerings of Juliet's 'Gallop apace' speech and then Hilda Wangel from Ibsen's *The Master Builder* were greeted with stony-faced silence by the panel of adjudicators ranged before me. A turbaned woman with a magnificently articulated voice asked me how I had achieved such an interesting 'hybrid' accent.

I wasn't sure what 'hybrid' meant but she went on to inform the rest of the panel that the sounds I was making were of a Cockney and New Orleans origin. When I told them that I was an Australian who had worked in America, they all nodded their heads knowingly and murmured words to each other that I couldn't catch. After a few more questions, I was dismissed. They informed me that I would know their decision in two weeks' time. I felt dejected after the interview, and did not hold out much hope of success, but whatever my fate I was determined to weather any adversities and forget about RADA if they turned me down. In the meantime, I managed to persuade my mother to let me join my sister Margaret in Paris.

Paris in the fifties was a city in full flight. It was humming with excitement. Margaret took me to Les Deux Magots in the Boulevard Saint Germain, where I sat all day over one cup of coffee, waiting breathlessly to get a glimpse of my heroes: Juliette Gréco, Edith Piaf, the two Simones – Signoret and de Beauvoir – Jean-Paul Sartre and Jean Cocteau. My sister was sketching three musicians who arrived to play in the street – a gangling blond guitarist, a small, dark, gay accordionist and a sad-eyed girl who played the flute. When they finished playing, the accordionist shuffled around with a bowl. Two people put money into it. Then they came over to our table to see what my sister had produced and she bought them a drink. I was disappointed to find that they were not French but Danish.

The two men were talkative but the girl stared over my shoulder with cloudy eyes as she sipped her vin rouge. Only once did she catch my eye and twitch her lips in a shy smile. She touched my blouse. 'Pretty,' she whispered.

'Why don't we exchange them? I like yours too.'

She smiled then and suddenly snatched my hand and pulled me to my feet.

'We come back!' she shouted to the others and scampered along the pavement, dragging me with her.

We ran, weaving through the pedestrians along the wide boulevard and into a back street, up four flights of stairs and into a dingy room that smelt of dirty clothes. She sat me down on the bed. 'I am Ebba. What is your name?' I could see a bunch of dead violets on the window ledge behind her head.

'Diane.'

'Diane,' she repeated. 'Will you help me?'

'How?' I asked. 'I'm sorry, I don't have any money.'

'No,' she said. 'You will *take* the money.'

I was confused. 'Take it from where?'

'When we play,' she said. 'I will show you.'

She undid the buttons of my blouse, her fingers fluttering like little moths, and eased it off my shoulders. Then she unlatched the frogging on the front of her blouse and, in an instant, we were both naked to the waist. Her breasts were twice the size of mine and I'd never seen brown nipples before.

'You are a child,' she said, taking my hand and placing it over one of her breasts.

I could feel the blood rush to my head and she must have seen doubt come into my eyes.

'Come,' she said and withdrew her hand. 'I will make you look right.'

I let her outline my eyes with kohl and cut my fringe into a ragged line. I looked at myself in the mirror and saw someone new, a fugitive girl. When we returned to the café, my sister did not recognise me at first.

'What have you been doing?' she asked anxiously. 'Mum will have a fit if she sees you like that.'

Ebba had explained to me that I was to play deaf and dumb, standing with them while they played. When they finished, I was to walk around with the bowl and just stand there until the patrons put some money in it. It was quite a successful ruse but Margaret did not approve, so I only did it for two days. I thought it was a terrific acting lesson. The only way to do it is to *believe* you are deaf and dumb, and not react to anything. It is a difficult feat, especially if you are on the lookout for celebrities.

A young American wearing thick bifocals followed us around both days. He knew I was faking it, though he put lots of money in my bowl. On the second day, he brought a friend and they sat in front of me discussing whether I was a virgin or not. I think my eyes must have flickered because he said to his friend, 'I win! You owe me lunch at La Tour d'Argent!' I did not wait to take the money after that set but went back to my sister's table and sulked. When he had gone, I said goodbye to the Danes, who gave me some money and warm hugs.

Even though Paris was so entrancing that I could happily have stayed for months, my sister and I boarded the train for the south of France, en route to a farmhouse on a property called Clos St Michel, situated halfway between the railway station near Cassis-sur-Mer and the sea.

Cassis was a small fishing village at that time, made famous because Winston Churchill had stayed at the hotel, Les Roches Blanches, and painted seascapes from there. Margaret Olley, Fred Jessup and Wolfgang Cardamatis knew Margaret from the National Art School, East Sydney Technical College, but other artists, mostly Australians, came and went all the time I was there. In the tradition of the Impressionists, the colony occupied the original stone farmhouse at the vineyard where the grapes were fermented. The house wine flowed day and night.

I slept in the main room next to the fire, over which all the food was cooked. I didn't bother to work out who was in love with whom, as they swapped around quite often, but I was aware of people padding around half the night, whispering or talking loudly, occasionally squealing or stifling laughter. Our food was simple – large aromatic stews full with vegetables and wild thyme, crunchy baguettes with home-pressed olive oil and garlic, farm-made goat's cheese and tomatoes from the vine outside.

The owners of Clos St Michel, Monsieur and Madame Magnan, appeared to Australian eyes as a comic couple. Monsieur Magnan, a grumpy old Frenchman, wore an ancient floppy tennis hat and sand-shoes. For a shortish man, his feet were enormous, size seventeen at least, and he walked with his toes pointed outwards like a perform-ing seal. Madame had fair, dry skin like parchment and wispy grey hair pulled back in a bun but her eyes burnt like black embers, half-hidden behind pale rounded lids. I kept out of her way until she caught me feeding the half-starved dog that was tied up to guard the chateau.

She beckoned me to follow her. I thought she was going to have me thrown out but she led me to a big new barrel, a *tonneau*, which had been put in place in the cellar of the farmhouse to hold the next vintage of Clos St Michel vin blanc. She indicated that I should climb inside through a hole in the top. '*Ma fille est trop grosse,*' she said by way of explanation. A bucket full of brandy was lowered in, along with a sponge, and I was to douse the inside walls of the barrel with cognac so that it soaked into the wood. I could see one of Madame's burning black eyes watching me through a hole in the side of the barrel. I came out only when she shouted 'Okay, *ça suffit,*' by which time I was unable to stand up straight.

I'd hardly had time to savour the splendours of Provence before I received an acceptance letter from RADA, confirming that I was included in the course that was to begin in a week's time. I dashed back to Lon-don, swearing that I would return to Cassis at Easter, after the first term. My mother had found a place for me to stay within walking distance of RADA in Gower Street, the YWCA opposite the British Museum, where I took up residence immediately. The culinary contrast between the canteen cabbage lying dormant for days in the stainless-steel bain-marie and the steaming caldron full of succulent French onions in Cassis was painful, but I wasn't in England for the food.

The first person I met at RADA was the American with bifocals who had followed me around in Paris. He was in my class. I hoped he wouldn't tell everyone about our previous meeting but, of course, he did. His name was Theodore J. Flicker. He was from New York and his father had made a fortune printing Bibles. There was another Australian in our class, Michael Blakemore, who has since become one of the most outstanding theatre directors in the world. Michael had already spent three years as Robert Morley's secretary and was worldly and nicely cynical. A student called Timothy Forbes-Adam had been invalided out of the army after being shot in the foot by friendly fire in Normandy. He was older than all of us and upper class. Gay Veitch, a Scottish lass from Hawick in the Borders, became my friend on the first day when the voice teacher singled us out as having the worst accents in the class. Some of the girls were at RADA not to become actresses but as a sort of finishing school and there was an American, Jack Salamanca, who intended to write. Also in our class were two Iranian students, one of whom was the best-looking man I have ever seen. His name was Manouchari Anwar.

The first term flew past. I had to learn to breathe again, to use *all* my lung capacity, not just the upper part, to sound my final consonants, to fence and to mime. It was full-on and the teachers were extremely professional. My only appearance on stage that first term was a walk-on part in the final show for graduating students and I was only in it because I spoke Italian. Joan Collins was leaving that term and the play was called *See Naples and Die*. I was a fruit vendor, shouting as I crossed the stage in a marketplace scene, pushing a barrow of oranges. I hammed it up disgracefully.

'*Arance! Son buone, mie arance! Vedi Napoli e Mori!* See Naples and Mori!'

Afterwards, I received a letter from a theatrical agent, James Fraser of Fraser & Dunlop, but I forgot all about it in the rush to get back to Cassis by Easter. I was excited because my dad was breaking his journey in Marseilles to visit us at Cassis. Madame Magnan had invited him to lunch on Easter Sunday.

For the Magnans it was a special occasion because they were opening some rooms in the chateau that had been closed since the Germans had commandeered the house for the duration of the war. I found out that the little boy laid out in a coffin whose photo I had seen was their youngest son, who had been run over by a German truck at the end of the war. They had closed the rooms after his death. For them, that Easter was to mark the end of their grieving. The whole household and the artist's colony took part in the preparations for their classic Easter feast.

Plump ripe tomatoes were selected, hollowed out and drained. Real mayonnaise was prepared with egg yolks, olive oil, lemon, garlic and salt. This was folded in with fish and herbs and the tomatoes were stuffed with the mixture. The final touch was the cross of anchovies on top to denote Easter. Roast kid with wild thyme and hundreds of garlic heads, which were squeezed to make a gravy, was next. Hand-churned vanilla-bean ice-cream for dessert and cherries soaked in eau de vie for afters. I have never forgotten the care that was taken to make everything perfect.

My dad gave the Magnans the gift of a carved inlaid box made from cedar of Lebanon. Later in the afternoon, my dad and I walked to the foot of La Couronne de Charlemagne. The sun was hitting the white rocks that jutted out like a stone tiara on the forehead of the mountain and we sat down with our backs to it, watching the play of light and shadow.

'I think your mother's given up on me,' said my dad.

I just kept looking at the mountain, noting the curlicues of pink clouds rising into the sky.

'I've been travelling for so long. I'm tired, Diane. This job is like trying to move that mountain with a shovel.' He was quiet for a while. 'Yes,' he sighed. 'I think your mother's had enough.'

He said nothing more about Mum. I thought he was going to confide in me about his affair with Ursula, but instead he talked about Charlemagne and his son Pippin, the hero Roland and the ways of chivalry. As we wandered back in the dying light of the evening with the scent of pine in our nostrils, he said out of the blue, 'You will be an extraordinary woman, Diane.' Walking along the pathway back to the chateau, he put his elbow under my chin and gave me three small backward hugs. 'But I don't have to tell you that, do I?' His car was waiting in the driveway and, after he had said goodbye to everyone, he disappeared into the night.

During the next two terms at RADA, we were introduced to many classical playwrights, including George Bernard Shaw, Christopher Marlowe and Ben Johnson. We began to rehearse scenes with a professional director. At the end of each term, plays were produced on the small stage attended by the Principal, Sir Kenneth Barnes. Performances were often interrupted by conversations about Sir Kenneth's dog, Marsha. A loud stage whisper would cut through some sensitive scene:

Sir Kenneth to Sargeant, the doorman: Did she *do* it?
Sargeant: Yes, Sir Kennuf.
Sir Kenneth: *Both* of them?
Sargeant: I'm not sure if it was both of them, Sir Kennuf.
Sir Kenneth (vehemently): Then take her out *again* and make *sure* this time!

Then there was a crisis. My mother had gone back to Australia, certain that the marriage was over. My father was in the process of organising the United Nations High Commission for Refugees (UNHCR). He had addressed the second conference of the World Health Organization, which he had also set up, and then dashed off to Greece to report on the state of the 900 000 refugees there. He was pressured from every side but his greatest concern was for the refugees. He put together a conference of the Arab states called the Beirut Seminar, which was a huge practical success, putting in place training programmes and addressing the problems of shelter and food shortages. For this, he was made Commander of the National Order of the Cedar of Lebanon. He sent me a photo of himself receiving the award, having scrawled underneath: 'Here is a photo that suggests I am being publicly strangled'. A second conference was called in Cairo, again to be organised by my dad but, this time, his immediate superior, Henri Laugier, refused permission. He gave no reason and there was a monumental row.

It was at this moment, fatefully, that my father received a letter from my mother saying that she thought it was no use going on with the marriage and that she was on her way back to Brisbane. The real probability of losing his wife tipped the scales and my father resigned from the UN. He arrived in London and booked our passage home before I actually had a word to say and, in the end, I said nothing. He was so obviously distraught. We embarked on the P&O liner *Strathaird* and headed back to Brisbane.

CHAPTER THREE

*T*he boat docked and, like a junkie in search of a hit, I rushed to the beach at Mooloolaba. My old white surf ski with the green mermaids stencilled on the side was still standing under the surf-lifesaving club. All day I stayed in the water. I was dumped but I didn't care. I revelled in the sun and the squeaky white sand, the lazy curlers breaking and re-forming. This was my home, where I belonged. For me, there was no more seductive place on earth. Why had I ever gone away?

That night I lay in bed in agony, covered in chamomile lotion. I had forgotten about the sun. I peeled all over for weeks. I had been away for more than two years, and in that time I had not finished school. I had not finished RADA. Except for my back, I was half-baked and had no idea what I was going to do with myself.

It took a week for the culture shock to kick in. Everyone in Brisbane seemed to have taken shots of novocaine, and everything that I had yearned for now maddened me. I took a job modelling sports clothes at a shop called Players, walking around in tennis outfits, bathing costumes or jodhpurs, smiling at customers. It was deadly dull and difficult, as I was bad-tempered most of the time.

I learned to drive on the back roads around Mooloolaba but my stomach churned when I thought of RADA. I could feel the tentacles of apathy closing around my heart and I knew I had to go back and finish my course. I wrote to Sir Kenneth Barnes, asking whether I could take up the scholarship that had been offered to me, and was overjoyed when I received an affirmative reply. I waved Sir Kenneth's letter in my parents' faces but they were unimpressed. Shocks were required before they would take me seriously.

I covered my body with green make-up and seaweed, extended my mouth, spiked up my hair and lay in wait for my parents on the beach behind a vine-covered dune. They were deep in conversation when I leapt up and delivered Puck's speech to the First Fairy from *Midsummer Night's Dream*. As I delivered my final lines – 'I go . . . I go . . . swifter than arrow from Tartar's bow' – I front-flipped, landing at their feet, and then flew into the sea, staying under the water for as long as I could. I cannot say they weren't impressed. My passion was evident and I was not to be denied. At last my return to London became a reality.

I saved every penny, gave dancing lessons and did radio broadcasts. My mother came around and donated, as did other relations. In quite a short time I had enough loot to book a passage on the same old *Strathaird* that had brought me home, but this journey was steerage, below the waterline in a stuffy little cabin with four other women.

London was bathed in sunshine when I arrived. I had led my parents to believe that my scholarship provided a living allowance but that was not true and I had to find some way to support myself. Olivelli's was a restaurant in Store Street, a turning off Gower Street. Frequented by old vaudevillians and comedians, it had rooms to let upstairs. Luckily for me, their off-licence wine shop opened at 5.30 p.m., the same time as my classes at RADA finished. I would dash from Gower Street to Store Street, ready for the first customers at 5.35 p.m.

Old Pappa Olivelli paid me £4 10s a week plus one meal a day. He kept a bottle of sweet Cinzano under the counter and spent his evenings wandering in and out of the shop. Mamma Olivelli knew perfectly well what he was up to. She would bustle into the shop after him while he cursed under his breath, '*Porca miseria! Porca puppazza!*'

I would eat as much pasta and cheese as I could manage, stuff my pockets with bread for the next morning and cycle back to my digs exhausted. My room was a poky cupboard with a gas ring that only worked when fed money. Never having used one before, I tried to cook an unopened tin of baked beans on it. It blew up, coating the walls in a fine layer of orange sludge that refused to budge.

One evening, Pappa Olivelli came into the shop fondling the hand of a strangely familiar man whose few remaining hairs were dyed a pale orange. He was dressed in a crushed-velvet evening gown.

'Ere ee iss!' announced Pappa Olivelli. 'You see dis man? Ee maka me laugh more den enyone! Issa geniuss!' He grabbed a bottle of Chianti Ruffino. 'Thissa for you. Chianti Ruffino! Best in da whole world . . . because *you* da *best*!'

The man turned his long, mournful face towards me. I knew that face from somewhere . . . but from where?

'Dis is Stan Laurel! Da Great Stan Laurel an' Ardee!'

And then there was Derek, a fellow student from the new class at RADA, who was from South Africa and wore a big russet teddy bear coat. He came to Olivelli's every night to eat a four-course meal and do business. He would sit at a table up the back, quietly masticating while anyone who wanted to borrow money would wait in line for an interview. Once the IOU was signed he would reach into the depths of his coat, pull out a huge wad of notes and peel off the amount requested. 'One week,' he would say, 'and it's ten per cent. It goes up the second week.'

Derek conducted poker games in a hotel suite somewhere near Marble Arch and modelled himself on Van Johnson. Inevitably, I became heavily in debt to him – fifty pounds. I was meant to pay him back by the end of the week but I knew I couldn't. It was then that the dancers amongst the female students at RADA were called into the Principal's office to meet the casting director for the major American movie *Moulin Rouge*, which was being shot at Pinewood Studios. José Ferrer was playing the part of Toulouse-Lautrec (on his knees), Zsa Zsa Gabor was playing Jane Avril and John Huston was directing. We were to be the young trollops who nightly danced the Can-Can at the Moulin Rouge. We were all ecstatic when we heard that we were to be paid real money. Lessons in shrieking and throwing our legs in the air for the classic Can-Can followed. They dressed us up in full skirts and frilly knickers, although I'd read that the real attraction of the Can-Can, with its high kicks, was that the dancers never wore knickers at all.

The art director reproduced the famous Lautrec posters and there were doubles who wandered around the set, drinking cups of tea, puffing on fags and being very un-French and cosy. With her *jolie-laide* face, Jill Bennett was perfect for the role of Sarah, the girl behind the bar, and Katherine Kath as La Goulue was a dead ringer for the original (whose real name was Louise Weber). José Ferrer had a horrible time adjusting to the little boots he had to attach to his knees to transform himself into Toulouse. Zsa Zsa Gabor loathed us. She couldn't abide a bevy of nubile girls giggling and flirting on the set. She would sweep past us, her lips curled in a sneer of disapproval, as she took her place for a scene, calling 'Darrlink, darrlink,' to John Huston in a loud guttural accent while waving her fan in front of her face to rid the air of our execrable emanations. We did imitations of her in the dressing room and cheeked her at every opportunity. When *Moulin Rouge* was finished, I was able to pay Derek back.

By the end of the term at RADA, I had appeared as a drowned girl in a BBC drama directed by Lance Sieveking (playing dead does not require acting – just learning not to breathe, a handy thing to know), as a princess in *The Princess and the Swineherd* at the Mercury Theatre in Notting Hill Gate and a young witch in a film called *Halloween*, shot by a brilliant young cameraman named Nick Roeg.

At Christmas, I got a job at Bertram Mills' Circus at Olympia. I wore the traditional fishnet stockings, incredibly high heels, a bum-revealing little green flared skirt, a pillbox hat and gloves that were shocking pink and sequinned. In this outfit, I rode an elephant called Maggie in the

Grand Parade. Performing elephants are all females, as the male of the species becomes unwieldy when a secretion called musth flows from its temporal glands, between the eyes and ears, causing elevated testosterone levels, aggressive sexual behaviour and violent frenzies. Female elephants have been known to fall in love with their *mahouts* (keepers) when sexually deprived, making gentle noises in their throats whenever their love objects are near. My particular elephant used to shuffle onto my feet if I stood too close to her. I was never unafraid of her jealous temperament.

There were three shows a day, presided over by the well-loved clown Coco. Coco wore a wig with a bald top and fringe of hair that he could make stand on end whenever he wished. It was magic to see two thousand men, women and children explode with delight as he plodded across the arena in his elongated boots. All he had to do was stop, turn askance, make his hair stand on end, turn his toes up, open his cavernous black mouth into a round 'O' and the audience was his.

I loved the camaraderie of the changing rooms at the circus. The circus people were cosmopolitan, speaking many languages; they walked around completely naked except for their boots, reading the *Circus Times* and chain smoking. There was a strict pecking order amongst their ranks. The magnificent Lipizzaner white stallion equestrian acts were at the top of the heap, followed by high-wire and trapeze artists. Specialised animal trainers were superior to human cannonballs, tumblers, dwarves and knockabout clowns. The 'Clean Clown' was higher in the ratings than other clowns, and midgets were in a special category of their own. Transients like me were not ignored, just tolerated.

A lady contortionist called Frau Delilah Schreiber, who sat in the canteen knitting endless scarves and whistling through her teeth, fascinated me. She did an ingenious act with two men in top hat and tails. It began with the two swaying drunks in evening dress coming home from a party with their balloons and rattles. They spot a box under a lamppost and wobble over to examine it. One of them tips the lid, out flies an arm and they run away in fright. They sidle back up to the box and gradually unpack the body of a grotesque doll, which is so pliable that it does not seem to be human. They contort it into obscene shapes and use it in suggestive ways. Finally, having exhausted all physical possibilities, they fold it back up into its box, close the lid and sit on it. The most impressive moment came at the end of the act when the men flipped the lid up and out came the mask-less Frau Delilah Schreiber, wearing a sexy leotard and looking like a million dollars. One of the men draped her in a red silk cape while the other presented her with a massive bunch of lilies.

When I asked Frau Schreiber how she removed the doll suit inside the box, she cackled and crowed: 'Secrets . . . secrets, darlink. I von't tell you how old but I am over sixty. Public vants to look at young meat, darlink . . . young meat.'

The clowns are the most interesting group of performers in a circus. They expose the joke of life and show us the pitiful vulnerability of the human condition. You can feel the whole audience lift when the clowns come on. I was witness to an event during my time at Olympia that illustrates the greatness of clowns.

There was an act that was called 'the Jaws of Death'. A number of dwarf clowns came on, shouting, turning cartwheels, doing flips and hanging onto the hands of a very tall, dome-headed clown, who was suddenly lifted into the air. Up and up he went on a rope that pulled him up to a cage set high in the roof of the Big Top. The 'jaws' were two steel gates that formed the floor of the cage. The clown then climbed onto a Harley-Davidson motorcycle that was lying on the cage floor, revved it up and began to ride around inside the cage. The faster he went, the further up the sides of the cage the bike climbed, until he was riding sideways, horizontal to the ground. Meanwhile, as he gathered speed, the rider stripped off his clown's outfit, underneath which he was wearing black leather. With a roll of kettle drums, the gates opened as he continued to ride around the cage, a gaping hole beneath him and only air separating his body from the ground sixty feet below. In a death-defying finish, he stretched out his arms and leaned backwards on the bike. The crowds cheered, the band played and, when the drums stopped, the Jaws of Death closed and the leather-clad figure took his bows.

On Boxing Day, a big noisy crowd gathered for the evening show, still reeling from the excesses of Christmas Day. Everything went exactly as it had at the afternoon performance except that somehow, as the motorcycle rider ripped off his clown costume, his trousers became caught in the back wheel. As the kettledrums rolled and the Jaws of Death opened, the back wheel jammed and the machine stalled. Slowly, the front wheel turned towards the gaping hole below. The rider, gripping the handlebars, did not attempt to leap to safety but sat bolt upright, staring in front of him as his machine slid down and teetered on the rim of the cage. For what seemed like forever, the Harley-Davidson balanced precariously before it fell to the ground with a sickening crunch. The rider was still clutching the handlebars and the wire wheels were still turning as the troupe of little clowns rushed on whooping, just as they had at the commencement of the act. They surrounded the fallen man, holding his head and shoulders up, whispering comfort into his ears and keeping his last moments hidden from the audience, who began to applaud, thinking it was all part of the act. The crowd rose to their feet and went on applauding while the clowns carried the long, lifeless black body off, like ants transporting a dying dragonfly back to their nest.

Later, I heard two men discussing the act as they left after the show.

'How do you think he did it, falling from that height and still hanging onto the bike?' asked one.

'He was on wires,' said the other. 'Didn't you see them? I saw them straightaway. They must be bloody mad to smash up a Harley-Davidson every show, eh?'

When I wasn't astride Maggie in the Grand Parade, I showed people to their boxes and sold souvenir programmes and circus jigsaw puzzles during the interval. To supplement my paltry earnings, I learned to gee for the concessionaires. The scam was simple. I would go to the archery stand and try to hit the bullseye. Even if I missed, I would win a big fluffy teddy bear or a massive box of chocolates. A barker would start talking it up as soon as I hit anything at all.

'Come along, Maid Marian, let's see what you can do! One more go and you'll be onto the big one! Just one more score and you've got yourself a lovely teddy! A nice big teddy to snuggle up to in bed at night!'

A crowd would gather to watch and, amid cheers and side bets, I would win! I would hug my teddy, as crowds of punters lined up to have a crack themselves. Later, I would take Teddy back and pick up my ten shillings. I reckon I won the same bear about ten times.

It was around this time that I swore an oath that I would never again live in a tiny room with nowhere to walk to outside the door except a hallway and stairs. I felt so desperate to see the sea one weekend that I persuaded two girls from my new class to hire bikes and ride with me to Brighton. We ended up stranded in an empty, freezing hostel, warding off the attentions of a lecherous caretaker.

When we eventually came to the beach, cold, exhausted and hungry as wolves, it was almost invisible, swathed in fog and drizzle. The miserable waves sucked up the pebbles and dragged them back into the grey maw of the English Channel. It was so far removed from the iridescent blue water and shimmering sands of Mooloolaba that I found tears falling from my eyes, without being conscious of crying.

All the friends from my earlier terms at RADA had left, except for Timothy Forbes-Adam. He had a walk-on part in a West End play called *Quadrille*, written for the Lunts (Alfred Lunt and Lynne Fontaine) by

Noel Coward. It was probably Timothy who saved me from starvation after my time at the circus finished. He bought me meals, lent me money and, at Easter, took me to Yorkshire to meet his family.

The estate was in the East Riding of Yorkshire, and Timothy's father and mother had given over the original family mansion to a girls' school. So many impoverished upper-class landowners were unable to meet death duties or pay the enormous costs involved in the upkeep of such a building. Timothy's parents were like characters out of an Evelyn Waugh novel. His mother, who was almost deaf, spoke in a piercing, querulous voice. She had three sons, the eldest of whom was Timothy. Mrs Forbes-Adam was the daughter of Lord Wenlock, whose family name appears amongst the signatories of the Magna Carta at Runnymede in 1215. This information was imparted within the first five minutes of my setting foot in their house.

'I was in labour with you for forty-eight hours, and when you came out you had a head like a turnip,' she informed Timothy, who cringed visibly.

'Are you sure it wasn't a pumpkin? Or a squash?' he asked weakly.

'No, darling, it had a little pointy bit on top exactly like a turnip.' She put her hand up and tweaked the top of his head as though the point was still there.

Her husband's larynx had been blown out in the First World War but he learned to speak using the belch method. The sounds he made became very muffled while he was eating, so he used a small microphone at the dinner table. Mrs Forbes-Adam had a hearing aid attached to a little box and during one evening meal it began to emit a high-pitched whine.

'What's he saying, dear? Oh dratted thing!' Whack! Whack! She hit it with great force, which only made it louder.

'What does she want to know?' Timothy's dad belched into his microphone. The whine of the hearing aid set all the dogs howling in unison and we abandoned dinner without eating a bite.

Timothy had relinquished his inheritance in favour of his brother Des, who had three small daughters. On Easter Sunday, these little girls along with ten or twelve other children from like families were invited to afternoon tea for an Easter egg hunt in the garden. I have never seen such a collection of spruced-up designer children paraded by their proud young mums and even prouder nannies. The girls wore little organdie frocks with ribbons to match, jewelled hairclips, satin bows and sable collars while the boys sported seersucker pantaloons and handmade shoes. Just one of their outfits would have kept me fed and clothed for several months.

I had expected that the nannies would form a gossipy group and let their charges run riot in search of the chocolate eggs. I was looking forward to seeing the pristine little darlings besmirched with chocolate and grass stains. However, while the mothers, grandmothers and guests drank tea and ate cucumber sandwiches at a safe distance, it was the nannies who fossicked about. Peeking through the daffodils, they called, 'Oh do come along, Felicity. Come and see what's hiding in here. Oh, it's so exciting! Isn't it fun! No, don't you open it, Stephen. You'll get muck all over your new shirt. Let nanny do it. There's a good boy.'

I was horrified. No wonder the English grew up to be so peculiar and inhibited. They never had a chance to do anything but be clean and docile. I looked around but no-one else seemed to think there was anything at all strange about the scene. On the contrary, the parents expected the nannies to behave as they did.

Back in London, the spring term, my last at RADA, was commencing. The winter of my discontent was over. The malaise brought about by hunger, bone-chilling winds, sullen skies and irascible landladies gave way to clear, blue, crisp spring mornings. Starry pink and white blossoms appeared on trees, people stopped huddling about with their shoulders around their ears and sticky buds turned into pussy willows. It lifted my spirits. Even my rumbling belly felt less of an affront and more of a blessing. At least there would be no worries about getting fat.

I was rehearsing Strindberg's *Miss Julie* at RADA, but I couldn't forego the chance of assisting backstage at the Arts Theatre, where a young mime artist named Marcel Marceau was performing. I was unprepared for the impact that my initial viewing of Marceau would have on me. He was so mesmerising that the audience hardly moved when he was on stage. He would begin slowly, walking up stairs, becoming trapped in a small room, the walls of which became real when he touched them, and would engage in a tug of war. I was determined to learn from his show, *The Seven Ages of Man*, and he gave the RADA volunteers lessons in his method, which was to practise in front of a mirror working through sections of the body. It was an exceptional experience just to watch the process in action. Marcel Marceau sparked a resurgence of interest in mime throughout the world that has never diminished.

I met another man who was physically the antithesis of Marceau, though they were both tall men. Tony Richardson was a gangling North Countryman so out of contact with his own body that he sometimes appeared spastic. He spoke in great gasps, expelling breath in bursts to emphasise words. His favourite word was 'marvellous!' He was a true enthusiast who surrounded himself with talented people. When we met he was about to direct two plays at the Contemporary Arts Institute – *The Changeling*, a revenge tragedy, and *The Apollo of Bellac*, a two-hander by Jean Giraudoux. He asked me to be in both and I said yes, because I said yes to everything in those days.

I went to his apartment overlooking Hammersmith Bridge and it was truly 'marvellous'. It took up the whole top floor of actor George Devine's house, where George lived with his wife Motley, the designer. George and Tony were in the process of acquiring the bombed-out old Royal Court Theatre in Sloane Square where G.B. Shaw's plays had been performed. They were planning nothing less than the overturning of the Establishment theatre. Under their guidance, the new Royal Court would produce radical new British playwrights like John Osborne and Arnold Wesker, mount controversial works by Jean Genet, Samuel

Beckett, Tennessee Williams, Giraudoux and Pirandello, and break the fossilised West End mould. They would send theatre-goers reeling into the streets, their minds humming with brave new ideas and images.

We'd all sit around the big kitchen table at George's house drinking plonk while George and Tony would hold forth about the diabolical state of the theatre, the stranglehold Binkie Beaumont of Tennents Management had on it, how real meaty plays were overlooked in favour of rubbish and how certain actors were always in favour while others were overlooked. George would clamp his pipe between his teeth and his steely twang would silence every other voice.

'Horrible fucking revivals! Ghastly drawing-room comedies! That's all Tennents ever dish up! What's that little ditty you made up, Johnnie, the one about Binkie B? Go on, sing it! It's great!'

Then John Osborne, the actor who was writing *Look Back in Anger* at the time, would sing:

A stands for Arsehole,
Poo Poo,
B stands for Buggery.
If you wanna get a job
You godda sell your knob
To dirty old Binkie B.

We called George Devine 'God'. Tony Richardson was Jesus and John Osborne was John the Baptist. They were rousing times.

The production of *The Changeling* was a joyous affair. It had wickedness, madhouse scenes (always an excuse for over-acting) and a finale piled high with dead bodies. I had to learn to sneeze convincingly for this play. My sneezing scene as Diaphanta brought the house down. For the first time, I knew the heady rush of making an audience come with me all the way and cheer at the end of our ride. Stand-up comics must dream of this audience participation when they go over their routines in bed at night. There is an indefinable moment when an audience decides to love you and wishes the affair would never end.

George, Tony and John were pivotal in nurturing the growth of a generation whose ideas led to Britain becoming the most exciting place on earth in the sixties. Battles over censorship with the Lord Chamberlain's Office (theatre censor until 1968) were rife. John Osborne always wrote plenty of offensive words into his plays (fuck, shit, cunt, etc.), which he used as trade-offs for things he *really* didn't want to lose. John's failure to compromise on the most important scene in his play *A Patriot for Me*, by making the cuts required for the work to be licensed for public performance, forced the Royal Court to become a theatre for 'club' audiences for the duration of the production. John's first play, *Look Back in Anger*, was saved from oblivion when critic Kenneth Tynan extolled it in a review as the most original work of the decade from an English playwright.

I was hurrying down Wardour Street one morning when a violent storm hit the city. Having no coat or umbrella, I took cover in the shallow entrance of an unimposing building. As I backed up to shelter from the deluge, my eye fell on a brass plaque affixed to the front door. It read Fraser & Dunlop. The name sounded familiar but I could not place it and then suddenly I remembered . . . the theatrical agent! It was James Fraser of Fraser & Dunlop who had written to me after my appearance as the Italian orange vendor in *See Naples and Die*. With no hesitation at all, I pushed open the door and climbed the rickety stairs to their office on the first floor. A tall, thin, camp man, with a Scottish brogue and a cleverly concealed comb-over, answered my knock.

'Hu-lllooo. How arrre ye?' he greeted me. '*Sooooo*, Miss Cilento, ye've condescended to pay us a visit, have ye? I expect you'll be just about finished at Gower Street by now, won't you?'

'Umm . . . er . . . yes, well, I was going to write to you but then I had to go back to Australia and I . . .'

'There's no use apologising. We don't expect actors to reply to anything. You're all thoughtless babies. We know that. I take it you are here to seek representation?'

I said I'd come to find out what it meant to be represented by a theatrical agent. It meant 10 per cent of all salaries, hand-holding, encouragement, advising on parts, mediating between the actor and the management, pep talks and flattery, he told me. That was a lot of work to undertake for such a small remuneration, considering what I earned, I pointed out. He said that we would see about that. Jimmy opened the door and called through to the other office across the landing. 'Oooh, Peter, can you step in here a minute?' His partner, Peter Dunlop, a pear-shaped man in a cardigan with a handlebar moustache and kind eyes, shook my hand and looked me over. Jimmy introduced me as if I was already his client.

'Would you like to come down to Lyons Corner House and have a bite of lunch?' Jimmy asked.

I said yes, as anyone who offered me food at this time assumed the status of deliverer, and we set out together under a large umbrella. When we arrived at the café, a stately woman wearing a huge cartwheel black hat beckoned to us but Jimmy Fraser did not go to her table at once. Instead, he ordered for himself and me and then requested two whole servings of shepherd's pie for the lady in the big hat, pointing at the table where she sat. My first thought was that she was a distinguished character actress from the provinces, but when we approached the table I looked at her round, ruddy, unmade-up face and knew she was not a theatrical person.

'You're late,' she said grumpily in an accent thicker than Jimmy's. 'Here, give me that.' She took the dripping umbrella out of his hands and shook it vigorously. 'Look at you. Every day, you've got less hair. You used to be such a bonnie wee angel with lovely downy skin and blond hair. What a pity it all changed!'

67

'This is my mother,' said Jimmy by way of introduction.

Almost immediately after my meeting with Jimmy Fraser, I landed the part of Louka in G. B. Shaw's *Arms and the Man* at the Arts Theatre. A sure-fire crowd-pleaser, the piece was set to music soon after Shaw wrote it and titled *The Chocolate Soldier*. Our production starred the actor/director Alec Clunes. I've always believed that the part of Louka, the saucy gypsy girl, is a much better role than that of the insipid leading lady. My understudy was a young actress called Susan Hampshire.

Opening night saw me revert to old problems that dated back to my Barter Theatre days. I threw up before the curtain and spent a few horrible moments in the wings before my entrance wondering whether I would be able to control the nervous giggles threatening to overcome me. But I held my nerve and felt the love tide wash over me before I left the stage.

Much to my amazement, the *Daily Express* and several other papers devoted more than half their reviews to my performance. The next night, Stuart Latham, director of the Manchester Library Theatre, came backstage to offer me a season playing Juliet in *Romeo and Juliet*, the leading role in *Eurydice* by Jean Anouilh and chorus work in *Murder in the Cathedral*. I accepted without hesitation.

I'd felt destined to play Juliet ever since that first audition at AADA. In rehearsals, I was like a greyhound out of the traps, gabbling the lines I knew so well from auditions, floundering about in the scenes I had not learned. Stuart Latham took me aside after a week and told me to calm down, not to try so hard, to think about getting inside Juliet's skin, understand the Italian temperament . . . blah, blah, blah. No more shilly-shallying. I was to know all my lines so well that they would be literally engraved into my brain.

On the weekends, along with armies of ramblers and backpackers, I used to take the bus into the Cheshire countryside where I would declaim the Potion Scene into the empty landscape and puzzle for hours over the text. Basically, I didn't understand what it was all about. When Juliet says, 'Learn me how to lose a winning match played for a pair of stainless maidenhoods,' was she talking about a maidenhead, meaning hymen? What was so special about virginity that it became the focus of so many plays written in the Middle Ages? I remembered the old New York joke about the Statue of Liberty – she is supposed to turn a leaf in her book every time a virgin passes on her way to Staten Island.

What I could not grasp in my exploration of Juliet was her overwhelming passion for one man and the desire to make love with him forever. Juliet could not bear to live if Romeo was dead. I spent much time contemplating what it would be like to plunge a knife into myself. Whom did I know who felt a passion so strong that death was preferable to life? The answer was no-one.

When Timothy Forbes-Adam turned up from Yorkshire, we went out on the moors and he listened to my lines. We talked about love and death and he told me he loved me. I was curious and desirous at the same time – not so much for him but for what Juliet *felt*. I wanted to experience sex and love together to understand the passion and impatience that made Romeo and Juliet the most celebrated lovers of all time. I allowed myself to be seduced out there on the Cheshire moors. It was not very satisfactory because I was too small and he was too anxious. I knew it wasn't real but something new had happened and we came back on the bus wrapped in each other's arms.

The play was an instant success when it opened. There were queues all the way around the Central Manchester Library, and we played to packed houses for every show. I wore glorious costumes made of gauzy pastel materials that floated out and moved with me. They had been Jean Simmons' dresses when she played Ophelia in the film *Hamlet* with Laurence Olivier. For my death scene, Wardrobe had sewn a little pocket under my left breast to slip the knife into so it would stand upright when I stabbed myself. One night, I slipped the knife into the wrong place and stabbed myself for real, right down to the rib. I felt no pain but bled copiously on my beautiful costume. In the last scene, when the Capulet and Montague families come to claim their dead children,

I felt a heavy weight fall across my body. Seeing the real blood, the actress playing my mother had fainted right on top of me.

When the season ended, the Mayor of Manchester with his Council hosted a reception for the actors. I can hear him now: 'You've made brass!' he proclaimed in his flat Manchester accent, 'and that's important because no other acting company has ever made brass here before!' Long before the speeches were over, the actors had descended like locusts on the tables of food and devoured nearly everything before the dignitaries even got to their feet.

Unbeknownst to me, a casting director had come to see *Romeo and Juliet* and he was convinced that I would be perfect for the lead in a new film called *The Angel Who Pawned Her Harp*. Nothing in my life so far had prepared me to play an angel. Dispatched to Beaconsfield Studios to test, I was dressed in a floating white costume and photographed with a harp. I thought I looked ludicrous but the director liked it, so I was whisked away to stay at the Saracen's Head in Gerrard's Cross, close to the studios. Jimmy Fraser signed the contract because I was still underage.

Set in an East End pub and at the dog track, where endearing Cockney characters hang out, it was one of those little English 'luvvy' flicks about an angel who descends to earth and pawns her harp to get money to bet on the dogs in order to help a boy. The formula was perfected with *The Lavender Hill Mob*, in which a sweet, innocent old lady survives nefarious plots and ends up the winner. Exchange the angel for the old lady, expunge the darkness of the murders in *The Lavender Hill Mob*, and you have it – except that our film wasn't written and directed by a genius.

My memory of the actual shoot is sketchy, though I do remember the strong impression of ceasing to be a human being and becoming a sort of doll that hairdressers, make-up artists and dressers could primp and poke at. They followed me around with powder puffs, combs and hairspray wherever I went, and I was relieved when each day finished and I was driven back to the Saracen's Head to rest until the 5.30 call the next morning.

My narrow room overlooked a square where a picture-postcard church stood surrounded by yew trees. The dining room was empty most nights and there was nothing to do but sit upstairs looking out the window, just as I had done when I was a child. One night, instead of the desultory groups of locals hanging about, the whole square was alive with people. Enormous arc lights known as 'brutes' were being dragged into place to light up the church and graveyard. A crowd was gathering to watch what was happening, which was what is generally happening on film locations – nothing. Then a buzz went around, which I could hear from my perch on the windowsill above them. SOMEONE was coming! The crowd pressed forward as a long black limo inched its way along the street and came to a halt. A female with a scarf covering her head emerged and, flanked by hairdressing and make-up minions, entered a caravan. The crowd settled back to await the next exciting piece of action.

The director walked up and down the path to the church looking through a viewfinder, followed by the cameraman and continuity girl. I could tell it was going to be a long night. After a while, I could stand it no longer. I slipped out of my room without bothering to put on a coat on that balmy night and joined the rubbernecks. I quickly found out that it was an American film being shot at Pinewood Studios and that the scarfed woman was Gene Tierney of *Laura* fame. She was having coffee in her caravan and had ordered a shandy and cigarettes from the pub. My informant was a lady who worked at the local chemist, who knew everything about everybody.

They fired up the brutes and the whole square was lit in a ghastly white light that made faces glow unnaturally. While the crowd was mildly interested in the director and the camera crew moving about like shadows in the graveyard, it was the door of the caravan from which the star might appear at any moment that held their attention. There was a man standing next to me who was the only one not fixated on the door. He was staring at *me*.

71

I moved away and embedded myself in the crowd but he moved with me. After four evasions, I decided to go back to the hotel. As soon as he saw me walking purposefully towards the Saracen's Head, he closed in and I got a good look at him. He was not tall, nor was he young. His hair was receding and he had large, dark Italian eyes. He was dressed in expensive clothes and under the lights his skin had the yellowish tinge of someone who takes Atabrine for malaria. He was definitely not English.

'You're very lovely,' he said. 'Who are you? Can I take you for a drink? Or maybe you're too young . . .'

Oh God, I thought, not another one, and kept on walking.

'No, wait, I want to talk to you!'

But I was gone.

Up in my room again, I surveyed the scene below. At last, they were ready to shoot. I heard the director's voice shout, 'And . . . ACTION!' A female figure darted out from behind a yew tree and ran the length of the pathway, looking back in terror. There were two cameras on the scene, one shooting from above and the other positioned so that the woman was running towards it into close-up. 'CUT!' cried the director. Then the assistant director's voice sliced through the night. 'Will you be QUIET this time please, people? PLACES, please. We're going again.'

I was so engrossed in the scene that I didn't hear the tap on the door. When I did eventually turn around, the door had opened and the man who had pursued me in the crowd was standing there smiling. 'Hello. So this is where you are,' he said.

I was dumbfounded. I could not believe that I had forgotten to lock the door. What an idiot! Now this nutter had come in, bold as brass. I caught my breath and told him with as much authority as I could muster that he must leave, that I had to get up very early the next morning and was about to go to bed.

'That's exactly what I had in mind,' he said, taking off his overcoat. 'I had a feeling I'd meet someone like you tonight. I generally avoid these locations like the plague.'

Having backed up to the bed, I picked up the telephone on the night table and dialled reception. The desk was slow to answer. I had seen the night attendant outside watching the filming. 'This is Miss Cilento, Room 217. Please send some security men to my room straightaway,' I demanded urgently. 'There is a man here who is trespassing!'

'There's no-one on the end of that phone,' the man said as he took the receiver from my hand. 'Nice try.'

He sat me down on the bed and I began to feel really frightened.

'No . . . no . . . no, don't be frightened. I just want to make love to you. I'm a very good lover,' he murmured, running his hands through my hair and down my shoulders. 'Don't worry. It will be wonderful for you.'

He had pinned me to the side of the bed by now and I was starting to panic.

'You'll thank me afterwards.' He was rubbing me down hard now as though I were a horse. 'They all do. You don't know who I am, do you?'

I began to struggle for real now and it turned out to be a long tussle, with him making little comments all the time. 'What a little spitfire! Oh good, you have a lot of spirit! Such silky blonde hair!'

At last, managing a mighty kick to his groin, I squirmed out from underneath him and dashed for the door. I ran all the way down the stairs and into the street, mingling with the densest part of the crowd. It wasn't until some hours later, after the first assistant had shouted 'IT'S A WRAP,' that I returned to the hotel, went straight to the front desk and had them change my room.

The next day at the studios, I received an enormous basket of red roses with a card that read: 'I love your spirit – Aly Khan'.

'Ooooooh . . . Look everybody! Our angel's got flowers from Gene Tierney's boyfriend!' crowed my waspish little make-up man, reading over my shoulder.

On my return from shooting *The Angel Who Pawned Her Harp*, once again I had to find somewhere to live, somewhere central and near the park. I found a place right next to Harrods on the adjacent corner of Hans Road, above a Barclay's Bank. Hardly had I settled in and met the ancient concierge, a miserable woman named Madame Berault who shuffled around in scuffed slippers all day, when Jimmy Fraser phoned in a lather of excitement.

'Dennis van Thal has asked whether we can come to 146 Piccadilly to meet the Big Man.'

'What does that mean? Who's the Big Man? Tell him to postpone. I'm too busy.'

'Sir Alexander Korda, head of British Lion Films. He never asks to see anyone unless he's got a plan, so we'll just show a little patience, won't we.' Jimmy was always like that with me – a camp mixture of castigator and confidante. 'I fixed the meeting for Tuesday, so you've got time to get yourself something to wear and not turn up looking like a scruff.'

'But I start rehearsals on Monday for *The Big Knife*,' I pleaded.

'Och, dear, say you've got a dentist's appointment . . . anything. Korda doesn't like changing dates.'

I have no idea what I finally wore but I know I changed my clothes at least six times before I had to admit that I had nothing left to try on. I was very nervous. Now 146 Piccadilly no longer exists. Where it once stood, 250 000 cars a day cross from Hyde Park Corner into the park. I believe Queen Elizabeth II was born there before her father ascended to the throne. At the time of my appointment with Sir Alexander Korda, it was the official headquarters of British Lion Films and very grand offices they were.

We waited in the monolithic outer office until Dennis van Thal, the legendary producer and casting agent, led us through to the back of the building overlooking Hyde Park. Before we reached the door, it opened to reveal, silhouetted against the light, a tallish stooped man whose head thrust forward and slightly to one side. He stood back to facilitate our entrance and we took our places in chairs set strategically lower than his desk. He moved to take his seat behind it, still a mysterious figure against the light.

'This is the young lady you wished to meet, Sir Alex ... Diane Cilento ... and her agent, James Fraser of Fraser & Dunlop.'

'Ah,' he said, 'but Cilento is an Italian name. Dennis tells me you're Australian.' Without waiting for a reply, he went on, '*La lingua Toscana nella bocca Australiana.* Ha, ha, ha! You see? I speak *la lingua Toscana* like an Italian waiter.'

There was no answer to that, so I kept quiet.

Jimmy was fidgeting around in his chair, anxious to speak, but Korda continued unperturbed, 'You have been playing an angel, I hear ... ha, ha, ha ... a very difficult role to undertake in this day and age. Not many role models for the part, eh?' He spoke in a pedantic manner, highlighting his faint Middle European accent. 'I have seen a rough cut of this film. In fact, we are going to re-edit it. I think you make a delicious angel.' He twinkled at me from behind his desk.

I had the impression that, although he was playing Uncle Holly, he could become a fiendish tyrant if crossed. I still could think of nothing to say, so I just sat tight. Jimmy Fraser was gathering himself to utter something again when Korda cut him off as words began to tumble out of his mouth.

'I invite you to think about the possibility of signing with British Lion if we can negotiate a satisfactory contract but, for today, I just wanted to meet the little angel and see that you were not about to take wing ... ha, ha, ha ... What will you be doing next?'

Jimmy seized his chance. 'Och, well, she's just gone into rehearsals with Sam Wanamaker for a play in the West End. It's opening ...'

'Why don't you let her speak for herself, Mr Fraser?' Korda interrupted. 'She's surely got a tongue to answer with.'

'It's a play called *The Big Knife* by Clifford Odets,' I croaked, wondering why my voice sounded so peculiar.

'You will receive first-night tickets, Sir Alex. I'll send them to Dennis,' interjected Jimmy sycophantically.

I felt very uncomfortable and couldn't wait for the interview to be over, even if I was being offered the glittering prize. Sensing my discomfort, Sir Alex was on his feet almost immediately, intimating the termination of the interview.

'Never fear, Mr Fraser, Dennis will be in touch with you. In the meantime, I shall say *arrivederci*, my dear. I expect we shall be meeting again very soon.'

I was off down the passage before I realised the others were still standing near the doorway talking. I checked myself, not knowing whether to go back or not. After some minutes, the silhouetted figure of Sir Alex beckoned me.

'Dennis tells me that you are frightened of me,' he said, gently taking my hand.

I mumbled something. I don't know what.

'Well, my dear, I shall make a prophecy here and now. In ten years time, I will be frightened of *you* . . . ha, ha, ha.'

When we eventually stumbled out of 146 Piccadilly, I was disoriented. I thought the interview had been a disaster.

'Not at all! Not at all!' Jimmy Fraser shrieked when we were back at his office. He was stirring his coffee so forcefully it spilled all over his desk. 'He *loooved* you. He absolutely *looooved* you. Couldn't you tell?'

'No, I never said a word. He probably thought I was mentally deficient.'

'Och, you don't understand anything yet. That's the way people like him *want* people like you to be.'

I had no time to worry about what Sir Alexander Korda thought of me, so completely pre-occupied was I with rehearsals and costume fittings for *The Big Knife*, going on tour and opening in London. Sam Wanamaker was a dynamic actor and director from Chicago who, fearing that the House Committee on Un-American Activities might blacklist him during the McCarthy era, had relocated to the UK.

I was playing a vulnerable young Hollywood starlet who is eliminated for being in the wrong place at the wrong time. I had one long scene with Sam in which I was supposed to be drunk. On tour in Brighton, I decided to imbibe an entire bottle of wine at lunch before the matinee to see how it felt to be really tipsy for the scene. I went on and played the scene absolutely brilliantly, I thought, but the moment he left the stage, Sam came to my dressing room so furious that he was shaking.

'Don't you ever *ever* do that again, do you hear? You were flying out there! Your timing was shot to pieces. You were all over the place. Now, sober up and never do that again!'

I was chastened. I was also beginning to feel sick and spent a few ugly hours throwing up before the evening show. It was a salutary experience. I have never drunk more than a couple of sips of champagne before a show since that day.

Harold Hobson, critic for *The Sunday Times*, reviewed the play twice. His first review was a sour little piece accusing the playwright, Clifford Odets, of making his hero unacceptable because he calls his best friend 'darling' and makes noises like an owl. Sam replied to the nit-picking critic, pointing out that Hamlet calls Horatio 'Core of my heart' and behaves eccentrically throughout the play. Harold Hobson saw the play again and subsequently wrote a rave notice – but the damage was done. We dropped below the break figure and Sam was outraged to discover that one of the box-office women was being paid to tell potential customers that there were no seats available. All hell broke loose, and we were transferred to another venue, the Saville Theatre, where we had a visit from one of my all-time heroes.

During my salad days in New York, my habit of wagging school to watch classic movies in the basement of the Museum of Modern Art enabled me to discover the marvellous films of Erich von Stroheim,

Hollywood's top director long before censorship. I was an aficionado of *Greed*, *Foolish Wives* and *Queen Kelly*. Imagine my excitement, then, when this icon appeared in a box for an evening performance. I peeked through the curtain and there he was, ramrod straight, monocle in place, accompanied by an elegant French woman at least a head taller than he was and dripping with jewels.

After the show, we all lined up on the stage to meet the great man and his svelte mistress. He did not disappoint us. Though not a tall man, his presence was electric and his duelling scars shone dully in the onstage working-lights. His manner was exactly as it was in *Sunset Boulevard* when he played Gloria Swanson's ex-film-director butler. When it was my turn to shake his hand and ask a question, von Stroheim was so courtly that I became tongue-tied. He covered my embarrassment by lavishing compliments on my performance.

'Is Hollywood really as bad as Clifford Odets has painted it in this play?' I finally managed to ask him.

He pondered this question for some time with his head lowered before raising his rather reptilian eyes to mine and saying with deliberation, 'My dear young lady, it isss VERSSE!'

That year, 1956, I received the Variety Club Award for Best Newcomer of the Year. My progress was being reported in the Australian press and my dad wrote that my mother was quite astonished. I was quite astonished myself.

In the meantime, Jimmy Fraser was lining up work for me. At the same time as I was doing the play with Sam Wanamaker, I was acting in a film called *The Passing Stranger*, starring Lee Patterson and the lugubrious Duncan Lamont. On the way to an impossibly early call after an evening performance in the theatre, I grabbed a tube of cream on my way out the door. I remember lying back in the limo smearing the cream over my face, feeling a burning sensation and smelling pepper-mint. I'd covered my features with toothpaste and had nothing with which to wipe it off.

The killer early-morning film calls were averted for two whole days on weekends, a time of blessed relief, even though there were two shows on Saturday. I would lie luxuriating in my bed all morning, sleep being a respite from the relentless cycle of travelling to the theatre, make-up, warm-up, playing the show, removing the make-up, showering, eating and going home.

One sunny Saturday morning that summer, I felt constrained to drag myself out of bed and walk in the park. I was on my way back to Hans Road when I was approached by one of the most beautiful young men I have ever seen. His skin glowed the same colour as his eyes, a warm tobacco brown, and he was wearing a Mediterranean-blue shirt that was open at the neck. He asked me in Italian where he could find a swimming pool.

'Scusi, signorina, ma Lei sa dov'è una piscina?'

He was very formal, very correct. I told him there was one called the Oasis in the West End and that he could catch a bus to get there. I wondered why he had addressed me in Italian, as I didn't think I looked European. I walked on. He followed. I let myself in the side door with-out looking back. I climbed the stairs and could not help peeking out the window. There he was on the pavement gazing up. He was sensa-tional, Michelangelo's *David* come to life. As if he knew I was watching him, he smiled and turned away, raising his hand in salutation.

I went to dress for a lunch date with the producer and the direc-tor of my new project. At the smart West End restaurant, I listened in a sort of daze to their ideas about the forthcoming film, *Passage Home*, my first after signing with British Lion. I was to play a young governess sent home from South America, the only woman on a broken-down freighter with a crew of no-hopers and ratbags. The captain was to be played by Peter Finch, a compatriot, and Anthony Steele had the role of the first mate. Suddenly, I saw a figure standing outside the plate-glass window, staring in. It was the unmistakable outline of the beautiful boy who had asked me directions to the swimming pool. I watched him scanning the faces of those inside until he found me and his head stopped moving. After a few moments, he disappeared from view. I tried to concentrate on what my future colleagues were saying but they were talking into a void. I could not take my eyes off the place where the boy had stood.

Outside in the slanting sunshine, I looked around for him but the streets were empty. It was 3.45 p.m. and the matinee would begin at five. I could already hear the alarm bell sounding faintly in my ears and realised I would have no time to go home before the show. I hailed a cab, leaned back and watched the sunlit streets sail by. I wondered if the boy was stalking me.

Once back in the familiarity of my dressing room, I went through the ritual preparation that precedes any performance – make-up, costumes, voice exercises to speak the words trippingly off the tongue, a quick stretch to loosen the limbs and onto the stage to play my designated role. When I'd completed the two shows, my marathon week would be over. I would forget everything – the play, the other actors and the boy. I would seek only the deep comfort of my bed, nuzzling into cool sheets and slipping into blissful unconsciousness for at least ten hours.

It was not to be. As soon as I had run the gauntlet of autograph hunters outside the Stage Door, I saw him. I was stopped in my tracks by the burnished perfection of him as he stood under the streetlight leaning against a silver Sports Vespa.

'Ciao,' he said. 'I just watched you two times. Can I carry you home?'

I moved nearer to him like a somnambulist. A taxi slowed down and one of the actors from the show leaned out the window and shouted, 'Hey, D, want to share a ride home?'

I wavered on the pavement for a second or two and then turned towards the beautiful boy. 'Thanks,' I called back, 'but I'm okay.'

I sat side-saddle with my right arm encircling his slim waist as we skimmed across the glistening streets of London. I was dizzy with pleasure, as if I'd been re-united with a twin I never knew. Maybe now I'd know how Juliet felt, I thought.

He did not stay that night but, by 10 a.m., he was back again, ready to collect me on his borrowed Vespa. We went to the swimming pool, where he talked nonstop in a barrage of Italian, French and mangled English. He came from Rome, but was never going back. A law student who dropped out, he wanted to be a racing driver. He loved his mamma but hated his father. He had a sister, Ludovica, and an adopted brother, Roberto Vaiano, who was a cripple. We swam and lay in the sun. I could not stop looking at him, with his brown fingers and curling upper lip. He stroked my hair and called me Dianetta. His name was Andrea Volpe.

In hindsight, I can see that everything had been set up to fuel my attraction to inferno heat – my father's mythologising of our Italian ancestry, Andrea's astounding beauty, the romantic way he'd approached me in the street, my just having played the besotted Juliet. Much to Madame Berault's chagrin, Andrea moved into Hans Street within days of our meeting. We were inseparable every second I was not engaged at the theatre or on the film set.

Andrea was nocturnal and idiosyncratic, leaping up in the small hours of the morning to munch on bread and dark chocolate – but only crunchy baguettes and dark Lindt chocolate he bought at a patisserie. At other times, he would practise ski turns at midnight, bending and rising on one knee and twisting his body into grotesque shapes. Most of all, he loved speed and wanted to be a racing driver like Stirling Moss or Juan Fangio. His only English friend was a mechanic called Bob, who was wordless until the topic of conversation turned to crank shafts or gearboxes. We soared around London on our new green Vespa, my hair streaming and skirt flying, oblivious to danger, laughing as we threaded our way through traffic jams. There were no crash helmets or protective gear in those days.

While all this was going on, Jimmy Fraser and Dennis van Thal were putting the finishing touches to my seven-year contract with British Lion Films. I was to receive a rising weekly salary and be at their disposal for as many films as they wanted. I had no script approval but I could do plays on the stage as long as they would enhance my career.

Jimmy and I were summoned to dine at 146 Piccadilly. The large dining room was on the first floor and we were the only guests. The walls were adorned with works by Vincent van Gogh and another painter who also signed himself Vincent. Korda explained that these paintings were by his brother, Vincent Korda, artistic director and production designer of such great films as *Jungle Book*, *Thief of Bagdad* and *The Longest Day*.

After Sir Alexander had sat down at the head of the massive table with us on either side of him, he rang a bell and a sensible-looking housekeeper wheeled in a vast, domed silver platter on a trolley. She slid back the lid to reveal an entire baron of beef. Korda never did things by halves. While we ate, he kept us amused with lively tales of actors and directors he had signed with British Lion since its inauguration. He told us how he had changed his wife's name from Mary O'Brien to Merle Oberon and how her new name had made her a star. We learned that Diana Dors' real name was Dora Fluck and that when she went to open a fete in her native Swindon, the young vicar introduced her as, 'Our very own Dora Clunt.'

All this I knew must be leading up to the question of what I should change my name to. Jimmy Fraser said he thought both names should start with the same letter like Marilyn Monroe or Brigitte Bardot. I did not say anything. I was thinking about my dad.

'Perhaps you should ask your father first,' suggested Korda, as though he had read my mind.

'I don't feel uncomfortable with my name the way it is,' I said. 'And, it's true . . . I don't think my father would be pleased if I changed it.'

There was an awkward silence, broken by Sir Alex clapping his hands together to close the subject. 'In any case, the contract will be made out in the name of Cilento . . . but I'm disappointed I couldn't re-baptise you.'

My sister Margaret, who arrived back from Australia some weeks after the contract was signed, tells me that she distinctly remembers her first view of Andrea. It was when we came to Tilbury Docks to pick her up. She insists we drove a red Aston Martin right onto the wharf while all heads turned at the spectacle of the new young starlet in a spunky topless sports car being chauffeured by her groovy continental boyfriend – the ultimate cliché on wheels. I have no recollection of this incident. What I *do* remember is that we finally fled the muttering and hissing of Madame Berault and found a flat in Roland Gardens large enough for us all. By the time I finished the play, there were two whole weeks for a holiday, my first since I was at RADA.

The three of us took the train from Paris all the way to the Spanish border town of Port Bou, in Catalonia, where we were delayed for a day or two by Andrea's passport problems. Our destination was La Escala, a village built on the site of Roman ruins. Spain had not yet become the destination for the British masses, with egg and chips on every corner, and we had a splendid time exploring not just La Escala but Girona, Barcelona and Figueras.

My sister painted and sketched all the while, pictures I still have. One lovely, simple portrait of Andrea sits on my wall today to assure me that I was not just blinded by passion. He is a very beautiful creature.

Andrea took it for granted that I would marry him as soon as we returned to London, and because I could not imagine a time in the future without him, I took it for granted too. We took a flying trip to Rome before we were married, and Andrea showed me all the secret places of his city, places he had been going to since he was a child. Rome is a magical city at all times, but whirling around it at death-defying speeds on the back of a motor scooter, grabbing small cups of espresso and *frullati* at intervals to keep up the pace, gave me a regard for the Eternal City that has never diminished. We did not stay with his family because Andrea had officially left home forever but it was inevitable that we should meet them . . . and meet them we did with all the convolutions and brouhaha with which Italians like to conduct their lives.

It happened while we were driving around in a borrowed car savouring the glory of a Roman sunset, when the whole city pulses in a warm terracotta light. Traffic had slowed as workers choked the streets on their way home when, suddenly, Andrea pulled the wheel of the car sideways, as though to turn off to the left but our way was barred. We sat red-faced at right angles to the rest of the traffic while at least twenty road-raged drivers sounded their derision with hoots, claxons and explicit hand gestures.

'What's up,' I asked.

'It's my mother,' said Andrea, scrunching down in his seat.

'Where?' I was looking at all the occupants of all the neighbouring cars for any likely candidates.

'Don't look,' he yelled, huddling even lower in his seat. 'She's in the green BMW on the right.'

I turned and looked at a very elegant lady sitting bolt upright next to a red-faced man with thick white hair combed straight back from his forehead. They were both staring ahead and not speaking.

'Is that your father?'

'No,' he said. 'That's Guillermo Persichetti. He's an architect, the uncle of Clara Petacci.'

'Who?'

'You know, Mussolini's lover. She was killed with him.'

'I never heard of her.'

The traffic moved and Andrea extricated us with a flick of the wheel. Now we were behind his mother's car.

'Oh, *merde!* She's seen me. We'll have to go to the trattoria where they go every evening.'

'I don't think she saw you. If she did, she didn't blink an eyelid.'

'That's how I know she saw me.'

Andrea followed the BMW and then turned off. We drove around for a bit before turning into parkland near the river. The green car was parked under a tree. On the way, Andrea had explained to me that Persichetti was his mother's lover, and that he had a German wife and six children. They met late in the afternoon, not every afternoon, he stipulated, and later went on to an out-of-the-way trattoria in the Villa Glori, where they drank Campari and soda and ordered prosciutto. They never ate the prosciutto from the trattoria, as it was rather rank and inferior. Persichetti always brought some of the good stuff with him.

We could see the couple through the trees from the car. The Contessa Elza Volpe de Smaele and Guillermo Persichetti were sitting at a table under a rickety umbrella. They were talking to a waiter who was carrying a plate. The table was surrounded by cats. It made an interesting tableau – an incredibly smart matron with short, glossy, salt-and-pepper hair brushed sideways, wearing a beautifully cut grey suit and extremely high heels, about to distribute a plate of *prosciutto crudo* to an army of mangy, miaowing cats. At her side, the gentleman, in an equally expensive suit, was flicking his handkerchief at the more impetuous pussies to keep them from leaping onto the table. Instinctively, I knew that this was the wrong moment to be introduced to my future mother-in-law.

I did not get out of the car. Andrea looked at me quizzically and then re-started the car. 'No?' he asked.

'No,' I said. 'Tomorrow for lunch maybe?'

'Okay,' he replied and we drove off.

The next day, I chose my wardrobe with great care instead of throwing on any old thing as I usually did. I took great pains with my make-up and sauntered about in front of the mirror trying to assess what sort of first impression I might make. Then I took it all off and started again. My second attempt was reaching for the ingénue but I knew that bare legs and sandals weren't going to do it, so I went back to the first outfit.

I felt very nervous, as though I was going to audition for a part that might be wrong for me. The Volpe apartment took up an entire floor of a modern block in Rome's elegant Parioli quarter. We were let in by a manservant wearing a striped livery jacket and white gloves and shown into a vast sitting room. The furnishings were in tasteful olive and biscuit with touches of crimson. Tall vases of tuberoses were everywhere. Their heavy perfume was overpowering but wonderful. I could hear someone talking loudly in another room.

I was examining the photos on the grand piano when there was a flurry behind me as Andrea's mother flew into the room and flung herself upon her son with a cry only a distraught mother could make.

'Oh, my darling, where have you been? You wicked boy, going off like that and not telling me where you were . . .'

Andrea extricated himself from her embrace and indicated my presence near the piano. 'Mama,' he said, moving towards me. 'This is my *fidanzata*.'

Elza turned to me and drew in her breath. She became very still as she studied me minutely, a half-formed smile trembling about her lips. I could not tell if she was about to laugh or explode with anger and disbelief. Instead, she approached me slowly, extending her left hand. I put out my right hand and took her moist, pampered fingers in mine. I could feel my heart beginning to pound. She peered into my eyes. 'Yes, yes, yes,' she said. 'You are the reason this boy has forgotten his family and forsaken us. You cannot know how worried we've been. We haven't heard from him for months.'

She tempered her words with a sort of roguish gurgle, taking the edge off them so I wouldn't be offended. Her voice was deep and well modulated and she did not roll her r's like an Italian. She uvulated them like a French speaker.

She led me back to the piano. 'Did you see this photo of Andrea as a baby? He was so gorgeous. By this age, he was completely bald. For two years, he was completely bald.' She smiled lovingly at her son, ruffling his now abundant head of hair. 'It didn't start out like that, *caro*. When you were born, you had a mass of black ringlets like a Zulu. It fell out after two weeks. I wonder where that came from.'

Andrea had no intention of letting his mother indulge in an orgy of baby stories. He opened a door leading to a long passageway and shouted, 'Ludovica, where are you? I can hear you. Come and say hello!'

I had forgotten that, in Europe, the big meal is in the middle of the day. We sat around the large oval table in the Art Deco dining room in silence as two servants wearing white cotton gloves served the soup. There was an apprehensive mood at the table and I could think of nothing to say. Giovanni, Andrea's father, did not arrive until well after the soup had been served and, when he sat down, the dynamics of the table changed. It did not take long to realise that the entire family was engaged in a deadly power struggle – a struggle to capture Babbo's attention and approval.

Ludovica, the daughter, two years younger than Andrea, flirted outrageously with her father, vying with Mooma, a girl of the same age, who also lived at the apartment. Mooma was a soft, pouty adolescent with wings of dark hair parted in the middle. I later discovered that she was also a daughter of Giovanni Volpe. Her mother had died soon after the war when Mooma was a toddler.

Then there was Roberto Vaiano, a contemporary of Andrea, who silently wolfed down prodigious amounts of risotto Milanese while his eyes slid from Elza to Giovanni and back again. He was crippled. His body had never recovered from being crushed under a building during a bomb raid, in which both his parents were killed. Elza, who had been

87

a great friend of his mother, had adopted him. His clothes were covered with oil paint and he gave off a strong smell of turpentine and anger.

Andrea and his mother kept up a desultory conversation about the scandals of Roman society. Giovanni chose to ignore them both completely. In fact, it became obvious that husband and wife never actually looked at each other. They stared over each other's shoulders or up at the ceiling but never for the briefest moment did they establish eye contact. (In Laban terms, this is called Unacknowledged and it is probably the kindest way to describe their relationship.)

The best way to describe Giovanni himself was to say he was a 'Shrug', a large red-bearded Shrug on legs. Every reaction was a gesture of dissatisfaction. His shoulders lifted and his mouth turned down in a grimace, no words being necessary to define his disenchantment with the world. I could see and feel Andrea's acute discomfort in his fruitless endeavours to evince some response other than a shrug from his father. All his carefully worded questions and subtle flattery were to no avail. There was just no way in.

It was inevitable that mother and son bonded like the elements of iron in the freezing fire of Giovanni's indifference. Even at that one luncheon sitting I could see why Andrea had hotfooted it out of that household. The more effusive and loving his mother was towards him, the more wintry his father became. At least I could now fit the faces to the people Andrea talked about and had some inkling of the complication of his family life. I did not envy him.

As for myself, during all the years I knew Giovanni Volpe, he never once addressed me by the familiar form of *tu*, only ever using the formal *Lei*. For my part, I never thought of him as anything but 'the Shrug'. My grandmother would have said that he had been sleeping in the moonlight wearing that ugly grimace when the wind changed and he stayed like that forever.

The moment we returned to London, I was thrust into the filming of *Passage Home*, with Peter Finch and Anthony Steele. One thing is glaringly obvious when one starts the shoot of a film with two male stars of equal status playing the leads: a strange *mano a mano* begins. The two actors circle each other like dogs, appraising each other's strengths and weaknesses minutely, plotting how to get the edge, watching how the director treats the other guy and determining how they can enhance their roles to take the acting honours. It is an interesting game to observe from the sidelines, as long as one isn't suckered into taking sides. Sometimes it can result in pulling extraordinary performances out of mediocre actors or it can lead to punch-ups and chaos. It depends on the director. Female stars are less overt in their combatant style. They make ardent friendships but often play the bitch behind backs.

The battle between Peter Finch and Anthony Steele was a mismatch from the start. Peter was a fine classic actor with all the advantages of stage experience. He'd played a superlative Mercutio at the Old Vic and a villainous Iago with Orson Welles, and was acknowledged as a contender to take over Laurence Olivier's role as best actor in Britain. The problem for Peter when we were filming *Passage Home* was that he had stepped into another of Olivier's roles. He was engaged in a scandalous and public affair with Olivier's wife, Vivien Leigh. This evened up the scores with Anthony somewhat because Peter would drive straight from the set in Pinewood Studios to Stratford-on-Avon, where Vivien was playing. He would remain there until morning and then drive back to the set completely knackered. I know this because we shared a car. Paddy, our Irish driver, was nearly as whacked out as Peter was. Occasionally, Peter would keel over with fatigue after lunch, his eyes falling backwards in his head during a take. It could be very disconcerting to act with him.

I believe Vivien was a very demanding mistress and I could detect a distinct lightness of heart in Peter on days when he did not have to go to Stratford. He taught me the 'Sandfly dance' one evening in the bar at Pinewood, which he said he'd learned from some Aborigines in Cape York. It was an energetic stomp, punctuated with short snorting breaths and one waving arm. We always performed the Sandfly dance when Peter didn't have to go to Stratford.

Peter discovered early on that Anthony was a one-pot screamer, becoming legless after only a single drink. Peter's ploy was to buy himself and Anthony a line of vodka and tonics at lunchtime and challenge him to a contest to see who could drink them fastest and remain sober. Afternoon scenes with Anthony after these bouts often resulted in fifty-six takes. Eventually the director chopped Anthony's scenes into short bites so he could get through them. Of course, Peter was unaffected by liquor, his head being as hard as granite.

Anthony was not an actor in any sense of the word. He was an ex-army hunk who used to roll his sleeves up to his armpits so that his bulging biceps would be even more prominent. He was cleft-chinned and had a loose lock of dark hair curling over his forehead. When he spoke, it was more clenched lower jaw than stiff upper lip and it made everything he said sound intimate and urgent. Several years after *Passage Home*, he married Anita Ekberg, the Swedish Bombshell of *La Dolce Vita* fame.

When he wasn't almost comatose from tiredness, I always felt relieved to be acting with Peter. He was so assured and very protective towards me. I had identified him with my brother Raffles when I was little: they both had a voracious appetite for life, which hid a covert vulnerability that instantly made women their slaves.

The centrepiece of the film was a terrific storm that swamps the ship. The production team pulled out all the stops to make it realistic, even though it was shot on a sound stage. The whole deck was on giant rockers, which tipped to an alarming angle while hundreds of tonnes of water were released to simulate colossal waves. The same water was sucked up from the floor and used again. No prizes for guessing who was rolling about from one side of the deck to the other with each new wave, finally being saved by the Steeley arms of Anthony. Sean Connery told me that when he saw the film while he was on tour in the provinces with *South Pacific*, each time I rolled across the deck, the whole audience would fill in the sound effects: '*Whhoooooooah* . . . Here she comes again!'

After a week of being a good trouper doing my own stunts, I emerged with my hips a mass of bruises and my fingers water-wizened, vowing to kill the members of the crew who threw their old cigarette butts and other rubbish into the overused water wave. The management gave me a bunch of flowers taller than I was but it didn't make up for the monumental cold I caught or the sinking feeling of being stuck in these awful British Lion films where the female roles were as insipid as stale cornflakes.

Andrea and I were married at the Kensington Register Office that spring. I wore a brown velvet suit and carried freesias. Andrea was splendid in a white suit with a blue shirt. I'm afraid I could not stop giggling during the ceremony because when Andrea had to repeat the words 'lawful wedded wife', his English deserted him altogether and he said 'awful veddy life' every time. Soon everyone, my sister and the registrar included, were overcome with merriment. It probably did not augur well for the future of the marriage.

The wedding breakfast was at Skindles on the River Thames and Jimmy Fraser announced that Sir Alexander Korda had offered Andrea a job in his foreign department as a reader of French and Italian scripts, under the watchful eye of the Baroness Budberg. There was a long, weepy telephone call to my parents in Australia but I don't think Andrea mentioned our marriage to his parents. The next day, we left for Bermuda – not for a honeymoon, as might have been supposed, but to join Kenneth More, Sally Anne Howes, Cecil Parker, Jack Watling, Gerald Harper and a whole cast of castaway actors on location to film *The Admirable Crichton*, an adaptation of J. M. Barrie's comic play of the same name.

The Admirable Crichton must have been rather radical in its day, dealing as it does with the reversal of the master–servant roles. It is set on a deserted tropical island where an upper-class family has been shipwrecked with their servants. The servants take over as the practical leaders and save the puny aristos from certain death. The Head Butler, Crichton, becomes 'Guv', a benevolent despot, until they are saved, but once back in civilisation the status quo is re-established, the class system remains sacrosanct, and Crichton re-emerges as the Admirable Butler once again. Barrie wrote the play as a comedy, contrasting the toffs' inability to do *anything* with the cheerfulness and bravery of the servants, who actually do *everything*. He was well aware that the Victorians were more fearful of nature – insects, reptiles and wild animals – than anybody else in history. It was a blatant crowd-pleaser.

I played Tweeney, the between-stairs Cockney maid who worships the Guv (Kenny More) and ends up getting her man. It was a gift of a part and I grabbed it with both hands. The director, Lewis Gilbert, was a Londoner born and bred and basically loathed being forced to shoot out of doors in what he regarded as a hostile environment. He never let his bare feet touch the earth, sand or sea, wearing socks to protect his feet and walking around in a perpetual haze of insect repellent. Coming from Queensland, where monster mosquitoes can carry you off in the night, I found Bermuda very tame. Tourism had taken over from sugarcane and its only real claim to fame at that time was the British naval base and the fact that Noel Coward had made the island his home. These two features were closely connected, I suspect.

It seemed that the whole cast, except me, had worked with Noel, whom they called the Master. We were invited to his sumptuous villa overlooking the harbour, where he had undoubtedly coined the phrase 'Hello, sailor' while greeting young ensigns from his verandah. Noel, who described himself as having the face of an ageing Chinese actress, had the quickest wit I have ever encountered and kept up a barrage of one-liners that had us all weeping with laughter. We stood worshipfully around the concert piano while he tinkled his way through a medley of his best-known songs – 'Mad Dogs and Englishmen' and 'Don't Put Your Daughter on the Stage, Mrs Worthington'. Those were the days when I hungered for success and I was immensely impressed by the neatly bound set of a dozen or more books that adorned the piano: *The Collected Works of Noel Coward*.

Noel and I had an instant rapport and found pleasure in each other's company at the odd times and places we met for the rest of his life. I also became bosom buddies with Sally Ann Howes, who was funny and had a lovely singing voice (something that had been left out of my fairy godmother's gift basket when I was born).

Back under the grey skies of the British Isles, I threw myself with added zest into starring in TV dramas, a play and another British Lion film. Sir Alex was getting his money's worth out of me. I played a Hungarian chanteuse who sings in a lion's cage at the circus in a movie called *The Woman for Joe*. It starred George Baker, me and an Algerian midget named Jimmy Karoubi.

The Circus Rosaire was a genuine outfit, employed to set up their tents and caravans at Pinewood Studios so that we captured the real atmosphere of the Big Top. George Baker was cast as the manager of the circus. The great French actress Françoise Rosay, Man Mountain Dean, a well-known wrestler, and many other unlikely actors and freaks made up the rest of the cast. There was a ring with sawdust, spectacular young trapeze artists, lots of lions and a lion tamer who looked so ethereal that you thought any passing breeze would have bent his long tubular body in half. Unfortunately, he was mauled by his own lions and died soon after the film was completed.

The day they chose to shoot the lion scenes, several hundred extras were called to comprise the audience. They sat in one block, shifting to a different part of the auditorium to provide the background wherever the camera was placed. A sheet of glass was set up in the lion's cage to separate me from the animals; shooting only at right angles to the glass made it invisible to the camera's lens. After the lions entered the ring and did a few tricks, I was supposed to order them to sit on their up-ended tubs while I serenaded them. It was simple and effective on paper – except that the day they chose to put theory into practice, they failed to factor in one important variable.

There was an air of expectancy as I took my place in the cage. I rehearsed miming to the playback of my song both in English and in Hungarian and, at the given signal, the door flew open and into the cage sprang six great rangy beasts. It was a heart-stopping moment, even with the glass barrier between us. I was quaking as they snarled and bared their fearsome yellow teeth while they prowled around the confines of the cage, bumping and rattling the glass in their perambulations.

Even before the wispy lion-tamer entered the ring, it was apparent that something odd was happening. One of the lionesses lay down on her back and started to roll around in a suggestive manner in front of a huge male. It wasn't long before the courtship blossomed into something more serious and the crowd of extras shrieked with delight. They stamped and whistled as we witnessed two fully grown African lions fornicating with an intensity and rapidity that was a marvel to behold. In close-up from where I stood, practically by their sides, it was truly awe-inspiring.

The director motioned me to stay where I was, thinking that once they had done it they would be tired and get on with their act. How wrong he was. These lions were indefatigable. They mated all morning, with only very short recovery periods. They mated until even the rent-a-crowd grew bored. In Olympics terms, if these British Lions had been mating for England, they would have won gold. They mated until the director was tearing his hair out, calculating the cost of holding all the extras in place, plus crews, four cameras, danger money for the tamer, extra meals . . . a whole day's shooting down the tubes. He shouted to the poor tamer to stop them but we all knew it was a vain hope.

Not only did the mating couple continue but there were other lions in the ring who wanted to get into the act as well. Skirmishes broke out and the noise was deafening, with my playback bleating away in the background. I did not know whether to laugh or scream or just settle down and watch the most intimate live-show entertainment since the Roman Colosseum. I still think they missed the chance of a classic scene on film – me singing my turgid Hungarian song with the British lions going at it behind me. Think of that as a trailer for the movie!

Jimmy Karoubi stood three feet nine inches tall. He told me he had three brothers back in Algeria who were all over six feet but that he had never grown after being blown up in a mine accident when he was seven years old. Perhaps this was true, or perhaps a genetic fault was responsible for his size, but despite the vertical challenge, Jimmy Karoubi allowed nothing to quench his desire for the right to be treated like any other young male contender. He had a blue caste mark tattooed in the middle of his forehead. His limbs and head were perfectly in proportion and he was very vain about his looks.

The producers of the film had found Jimmy working in Paris as MC in a gay cabaret club, where he introduced the transvestite floor-show with, 'Messieurs et Mesdames . . . et les AUTRES!' Reportedly, he had once been part of the boxer Sugar Ray Robinson's entourage. He had never acted before. We all got to know Jimmy well during the shoot. He was talkative, full of naughty stories, and could curl up in an armchair and snooze at any time of the day or night. Andrea called him Bebe and he took to coming back to Roland Gardens after work and staying the night with us.

I shall never forget taking him to Portobello Road Market one Saturday morning. Because he smoked cigarettes and was growing a little moustache, children were drawn to him like a magnet. Here was what they took to be another child dressed in a midget suit, nonchalantly sucking on a cigarette and sporting a real moustache. They hooted and ran after him, trying to touch him and make him play with them.

He was a very reluctant Pied Piper, his face becoming suffused with blood. I realised with a sort of shock that he was infuriated, so I took his hand and ran with him. He was having a real panic attack but his small tormentors still pursued us, squealing excitedly. At last, he could stand it no longer. He turned on them, screaming invective in Arabic and French. It was not a joke. He was foaming at the mouth by the time I got him back to the car. Jimmy may have been a midget but the fury inside him was monumental.

My last meeting with Jimmy was several years after the film was finished. By this time, I was living in Caroline House on the Bayswater Road and I had a baby daughter, Giovanna. Much water had passed under the bridge. I was sitting with the baby's nanny and my sister Margaret when the telephone rang. The sun was just dipping below the roofs. A voice on the other end said, 'Hello. I don't think we've ever met but you may have heard of me as Fabian of the Yard, Scotland Yard. I believe you are a friend of Jimmy Karoubi?'

When I affirmed that I was, he asked how long it had been since I'd seen him. I told him I had not seen Jimmy for months but that he often telephoned to ask how things were and to tell me his news.

'Well, if he telephones you or gets in touch, I would like you to call me immediately. I'm afraid Mr Karoubi is wanted in connection with a series of murders. It is urgent that you know this.'

I was dumbfounded. 'Are you sure you mean Jimmy Karoubi, the small man, the midget who was in a film with me?'

'Please take down this number. Don't take any chances. He is wanted in connection with the murders of children. Call me at once. He may be dangerous.' He repeated the number again.

'I can't believe this. Are you sure there is no mistake?'

'There is a warrant out for his arrest. The murders took place in France some time ago, not here.' Then he added grimly, 'There's no mistake.'

I replaced the receiver and related to my sister what the man had said. I was not sure whether it was a practical joke. If it was, the man on the phone must be a consummate actor. Hardly had I got the story out when the doorbell rang. When I opened it, there stood Jimmy grinning, not looking at all worried. 'Hey,' he said, 'give us a French kiss and I'll tell you what you had for lunch.' It was one of his standard openers.

He came in and we all sat and stared at each other while my baby daughter gurgled and crawled to his feet. He did not take any notice of her, but asked if he could have some tea. The atmosphere was electric. No-one moved and no-one said anything. The sun was gone now and the temperature in the room had changed. Jimmy was aware in a flash that we all knew and, without another word, he was out the door and gone. I did not ring the number I had been given but afterwards I heard that Jimmy was arrested somewhere near Marble Arch later that evening.

I once received a letter from Jimmy while he was in prison on the Île Saint-Louis in Paris. It was short, telling me nothing but asking whether I had seen a copy of *The Stage* because his name was on a list of actors who had unclaimed money at the newspaper office. I wrote back but never heard another word.

CHAPTER FOUR

*A*uditions, especially for big shows with American directors, were always very fraught affairs. You had to turn up at the designated theatre in the morning with minimal knowledge of the play and make a conjecture about what sort of girl they were looking for. Then you were called onto the stage in groups of three or four at a time to be scrutinised by shadowy figures sitting in darkened seats of the auditorium. Whispered discussions took place as you continued to wait until, finally, a voice would ring out, 'Girl number two from the right, you can stay. All the others are excused.' There would be a rush for the wings and the three who had been dismissed would dash into a corner to rearrange their hair and change their blouses and make-up. Some girls even brought wigs. It always paid to have several changes of costume for an audition. I have seen girls dismissed twice and still get the part in the end. It's all a matter of getting past that first hurdle – the instant impression.

La guerre de Troie n'aura pas lieu ('the Trojan War will not take place') by Jean Giraudoux had been translated by Christopher Fry, whose success, *The Lady's Not for Burning*, had run on the West End for years. Under its English title, *Tiger at the Gates*, a prestigious production of Giraudoux's play starring Sir Michael Redgrave as Hector was to be mounted in London prior to opening on Broadway. Harold Clurman, the illustrious American director who had initiated the Group Theatre, was to direct the large cast assembled in London. The producer was Robert Joseph, son of Lazarus P. Joseph, the Controller of New York City. Everyone was agog with anticipation and eager to get a look at the script.

Andrea took me to the first auditions on our Vespa. We had headed off early that morning for an appointment at the headquarters of the Bank of New South Wales in Berkeley Square, armed with plans and figures for our first business enterprise. It was to be a Vespa hire company in partnership with Andrea's friend Bob, the mechanic, who would service the machines. Andrea was very excited and so was I.

We were ushered into the inner sanctum where I presented the idea enthusiastically, as Andrea's English was still less than understandable. We were both ill prepared for the mirth with which our proposal was greeted. I have learned over the years that when the older generation of Australian men address you as 'girlie', you're in trouble. They do not consider young females accompanied by good-looking Italian males who speak little English to be serious.

It was understandable then that, after such a putdown, I arrived at the audition in a rather flustered and angry state. I had no time to compose myself, being called onto the stage as soon as I walked through the door, and hadn't even removed my coat. I found that I was the only person on the stage, except for a faceless man standing with his back to the working-light that illuminated the stage. Without any greeting, he handed me a script as an American voice called out, 'Are you from Fraser & Dunlop?'

'Yes,' I called back.

'What's your name, honey?'

I spoke my name into the empty theatre.

'What? Who? Can you repeat that?'

I repeated my name twice and, each time I said it, it sounded more hollow and unreal echoing in the void.

'Can you spell that? Di-Anne, first name . . . Di-Anne who?'

Suddenly, I'd had enough. I threw the script on the floor and screamed some ugly words into the darkness. For the first time in my life, but not the last I'm ashamed to say, I threw a wobbly. I stormed off the stage and out of the theatre, catching up with Andrea just as he was about to speed off down Shaftesbury Avenue. I knew Jimmy Fraser would be furious with me but I didn't care.

We spent the day exploring the countryside outside London and into Wiltshire. Like most Italians, Andrea was endlessly amused by old pubs, English country life, hunting with hounds and stately homes. When we arrived back at Roland Gardens we were greeted by Rosa, the Sicilian girl who did the cleaning and cooking, who was in an agitated state. Jimmy Fraser had been to the flat, she told us, and had waited for half an hour. I was to call him as soon as I stepped through the door. While Rosa wrung her hands, saying how angry Mr Fraser was with me, we got back on the scooter and went to the movies on Fulham Road.

The consequence of this rebellion was that I landed the plum role of Helen of Troy the next day. I've often wondered whether throwing a wobbly and walking out is not the best way to secure anything. If they think they can't get you, they want you. You must truly not care about an outcome, acausality being the secret of the universe.

Apart from Michael Redgrave as Hector and Basil Sydney as Ulysses, the large cast included Robert Shaw (playing the small part of a sailor), Norman Rossington, Leueen McGrath (wife of George S. Kaufman) as Cassandra, Barbara Jefford, Catherine Lacey, John Laurie (of *Dad's Army* fame), Wyndham Goldie, Leo Cicceri and Peter Kerr. The set and costume designer was the legendary Australian Loudon Sainthill, a true genius. Lennox Berkeley composed the original score.

At the first rehearsal, which took place on stage at the old St James Theatre, one of the most beautiful West End playhouses ever torn down, we studied a model of the set. Someone remarked that it looked like an obstacle course fit only for goats. There were a great many different levels, battlements, ramps and buttresses, as well as some enormous

Gates of War that opened at the end of the play, signifying the commencement of the Trojan War.

Harold Clurman, the director, was a plump, bouncing dynamo with a wet cigar stuck perpetually in his mouth. He talked very fast and nearly all the time. I remember his first words as we all sat around in an elliptic circle on the stage while he paced up and down: 'I'm gonna throw a whole lot of information up in the air and you're gonna catch what you can as it comes down. We're gonna read the play over and over until you can recite the script backwards and the wonderful rhetorical language Christopher Fry has written is as familiar to you as *Three Blind Mice*.'

With that, we began our reading of the play and, true to his word, we were still sitting in a circle reading it two weeks later. Halfway through the third week, most of the cast were getting decidedly toey and John Laurie was heard to remark when he knew he was within earshot of the director, 'This is going to be the best-rehearsed *radio* play ever to be sat through on any stage!'

When we finally got to our feet to block the play, it was with great relief. The information Harold threw up in the air about my part was that I represented Nature. I had no idea how representing Nature could affect the way I was to play the part of Helen. There is always a terrible time in the preparation of a play when the actor is struggling with the words, lost to the meaning of the role and fearful that he is getting it wrong, making an idiot of himself. As the opening night creeps nearer every day, the feeling of despair and terror deepens. This is the time when actors have anxiety dreams and wake up howling in the night. I was no exception.

My mother turned up while we were in dress rehearsals in Manchester, using the opportunity of a post-graduate course in natural childbirth to meet Andrea and Jimmy Fraser. She was so pleased with me for not being a delinquent that she took me to see some films on women having babies 'naturally'. I suppose she was trying to encourage me to have one myself, as my mother's sole conception of marriage was just that . . . conception, babies and making a good many of them. In one of her many articles on motherhood, she wrote that she believed women got much more pleasure from breastfeeding a baby than from sexual penetration by their husbands. Needless to say, the films, which were very graphic, put me off procreation entirely.

For my role as Helen, Loudon Sainthill created the most beautiful dress I have ever worn – a champagne-coloured silk jersey, moulded around the breasts and hips and open to the waist in the front, but only visibly so when I walked. I had known Loudon Sainthill, a contemporary of my sister, since I was a child. He was a tanned and handsome man who never produced work that was less than sensational. I wore a fringe of sculpted Greek curls on my forehead, a golden ornament to hold my hair up in the back and wonderful golden sandals up to my knee, which were a delight to move in. They had to be because, once on that obstacle course of a set, we had to know exactly how many steps were required to get from one rostrum to the next. Our first dress rehearsals were occupied with just walking around the set, trying to get the hang of the levels and ramps.

Opening night was just as ghastly as we had all expected but held its most disastrous moment until the end of Act I, when the goddess Iris is meant to fly in, land centre stage, deliver a pithy, poetic summing up of what has occurred and present a tantalising glimpse of what is to come in Act II. Then, as we all stand transfixed by her speech, she flies off and the curtain falls. This role was performed by Olive Gregg, an actress with a dreamy voice and big operatic presence. Due to time constraints, we had never actually rehearsed the flying part, so her arrival was a first for the entire cast lined up on stage to witness the event.

A fanfare of trumpets sounded, but nothing happened. We all stood there, not knowing what to do. Then, quite suddenly, from the wings stage left and high up, an apparition came hurtling through the air on a lowering trajectory, knocking actors and scenery out of the way as it flew. Instead of the goddess Iris, upright and in control of herself, we saw an up-ended Olive, bottom in the air, underwear showing and arms waving, madly trying to right her balance while screaming as she swung in both directions. Actors were dashing about getting out of the way of the flailing arms and legs of Olive. The audience was applauding, Michael Redgrave was livid and all of us downstage were falling on the floor with laughter as she flew back and forth, gathering speed with each swing. No-one could stop her. The human pendulum seemed destined to swing for as long as the momentum carried her.

Of course, it was no laughing matter. Michael shrieked at the stage manager to take the curtain down and, when this was done, the sobbing Olive was wrestled out of the air and unravelled from her Kirby's flying harness. She was taken to hospital badly shaken and suffering from bruises to both her body and pride. Poor Olive, it was said, only ever performed on radio after this debacle. Harold Clurman deleted the role completely, so we had no more flying scenes.

As we toured through Great Britain to Edinburgh, Glasgow, Newcastle, Oxford, Bristol and Liverpool, I was experimenting with the part of Helen of Troy, trying to find the key to unlock such a complex but maddeningly transparent person. Every time I went on stage, I grappled with her intricacies and obviousness but I was never satisfied. Somehow, she was eluding me. When we opened in London, the reviews were very good but not raves. I was anxious. I felt I was not filling the role with the stuff of mythology – the stature that made Helen of Troy remembered down the ages as 'the face that launched a thousand ships'. Then, out of the blue, I received a letter. It was a long and respectful letter from someone named Yat Malmgren, who offered to teach me free of charge. He listed his history, from his childhood in Sweden and a gold medal at the Concours de la Dance in Brussels in 1939 to more recent work with Kurt Joos and an encounter with Rudolf Laban, originator of the theory of movement and author of *Effort*, a time and motion study.

At first I was sceptical, but when I talked to my friend, actor Harold

Lang, an original, dedicated cynic whom I had known and admired ever since I came to London, he was filled with genuine enthusiasm. I agreed to meet Yat on the stage of the Apollo Theatre, where we were playing, the next morning at 10 a.m. It was a meeting that changed my concept of acting in the theatre forever.

I agreed to lessons and would arrive at the theatre every morning. At first, Yat would let me do nothing but walk around the stage, becoming aware of the extraordinary power of *presence* within the space of a theatre, learning the difference between the dynamics of Weight, the thought penetration of Space, the kinetics of Time and the emotion of Flow. He was a mesmerising teacher, able to reignite my excitement in watching and analysing every gesture to uncover the secret of why people moved in such a way, why their bodies had begun to adopt certain expressions and positions, inexpressible in words but instantly recognisable in emotional content. Every morning, on my way to the theatre, I would sit at the front of the bus on the upper deck, enthralled by characters in the street below, scrutinising their every move, every gesture, and storing them in my memory.

When at last we came to grips with the role of Helen and what I was doing in movement in performance, I was already confident enough to experiment with the actual technique of what I was learning. I discovered how to be sustained in Time and how to use Space, how to glide and float instead of flicking and dabbing. The proof of the pudding was that, with every performance, I could feel audience reaction to my new assurance and timing. It worked! It was a miraculous and apparently effortless spell that one could cast. I began to get huge laughs that frightened the life out of me at first. Then, receiving a hand on exit assured me of the approval of the spectators.

For Michael Redgrave, it was not so easy to accept my newfound assurance. He wrote me a letter in which he asked me not to put the lower half of my body against his and to take less time with my lines. I was nonplussed, as I knew that what I was implementing was adding lustre to the play and I was sure there was no tactility – or no more than had been originally rehearsed. I asked my cunning old mum what I should do. She read the letter, thought for a while and then said, 'Go and put the letter on the noticeboard near the stage door.' I did so, and it was gone the next day. Nothing more was ever said on the subject. Working with a great actor is comparable to playing tennis with Andre Agassi when you've only had a racket in your hands for a few months: either you raise your game very quickly or you retire, never to play again.

I never stopped striving for Helen and she is a pretty slippery customer. I began to attend all Yat's classes in the old studios at the top of Shaftesbury Avenue – action classes, floor classes and classes in theory. It was a revelation, a tough, demanding workout in body, mind and feelings that left one exhausted but exhilarated. It was a joy to study with Yat.

At that time, Rudolf Laban was alive and living in Seven Oaks but I was never able to go there on the weekends because of the two shows on Saturday and my much-anticipated lie-in on Sunday mornings. However, I was required to produce essays about Laban's Inner Attitudes and how they align themselves to characters in plays. I remember writing out a whole treatise on *Mother Courage* by Bertolt Brecht. In Laban terms, the character of Mother Courage is mostly in the Inner Attitude of Stable. She is Strong in Weight (Dynamics) and Flexible in Space (Thought). It follows that she is practical and, in movement, most likely to use Slashing or Wringing gestures. This may sound rather dry and intellectual, but when it is incorporated with the doing, it is electrifying, and the most practical way to cut the crap out of acting. Of course, no-one would argue that the intuitive element comes first for an actor, but the process of working through a part using the Laban theory, with Yat's guiding eye, made every performance a fascinating experience.

I loved the terminology of Inner Attitudes – Stable, Mobile, Near, Remote, Awake and Adream. We all go through life in one or two (or sometimes even three) of these states without realising that our most

105

intractable problems stem from tunnel vision caused by becoming fixed into one of these Inner Attitudes to the exclusion of the others. None of them is better or worse than the other; they just *are* and it is through these Inner Attitudes that we image the world around us.

It was quite startling for me to learn that Rudolf Laban had won the Military Cross during World War II for his work saving millions of man-hours in factories. He toured various workplaces, devising and putting into practice movements by which workers used the minimum of space and the least effort to complete whatever task. His work, known as the Time and Motion Study, embraced manufacturers of bombs and theatre actors alike. In times of war, no-one is looking for nuances, just Quick and Direct – the more like a machine the better. What a blessing that machines have now been invented to reproduce man's movement and perform most of the repetitive tedious tasks once allotted to poor factory workers.

Tiger at the Gates played a limited season of six months in London before it was transported lock, stock and almost all barrels to Broadway to open the 1956 season. The barrels that remained in London were Robert Shaw and Norman Rossington, who would be replaced by American actors. Andrea was to continue working with Baroness Budberg in the scripts department of British Lion, both of us being convinced that the play would be an enormous flop, lasting only a few days on the Great White Way. I would not be gone for long and we would be in touch every day, thinking about each other every hour, parted only by distance, not in spirit.

Thus, I found myself back in the special madness that is New York City, staying at the Algonquin, rehearsing night and day. On the day before the day before we opened, there had been a particularly gruelling full dress rehearsal, stopping and starting to get the lights perfect, photos, the lot. The management had brought the wondrous Diana Boddington, a stage director known as 'the heavenly Bod', from London to oversee everything. She was meticulous. If there was a shadow of a doubt about any area of the production, she was onto it like the head beagle in a foxhunt.

We had commenced rehearsal at 9 a.m. and dragged our exhausted bodies out of the Plymouth Theatre at 5.30 p.m. I fell on my bed as soon as I reached my room after pulling the blinds down on a crepuscular New York sky. I promised myself vaguely that I would get up later, when it was dark, to eat something. I awoke to the telephone shrilling urgently near my bed and reached out to answer it, cursing whoever was calling for not granting me some respite.

'Where are you?' shouted a furious voice on the other end.

'Who's that?' I croaked.

'It's Diana Boddington, your stage manager. You were supposed to be here with the rest of the cast for the last session of notes with Harold Clurman and Bob Joseph.'

'But I just left . . . I thought that was tomorrow afternoon, before we open.'

'Are you out of your mind? You have just half an hour before the half-hour call for your opening night. You'd better get it together and jump in a taxi or they will have your guts for garters.'

I threw myself into the shower and leapt into my clothes. My body felt as light as a dandelion seed parachuting through the air. Nothing was real. I had fallen out of time. The whole world had changed because something had clicked a switch and twenty-four hours had disappeared from my life. I had no time to marvel at how such a thing could have happened. I just felt as free as a swallow and unconcerned. Not even the slightest nervousness entered my sphere of total consciousness . . . or was it a dream? I was Alice in Wonderland and I had fallen down the rabbit hole.

All through the evening, this extreme state of being disengaged but completely calm and in charge persisted. I did not question it. I went on the stage and after my first scene with Paris meeting Hector a roar of approval greeted my exit. Even this did not faze me. I was neither elated nor depressed. I was present. So, this was what all those months of walking around the stage culminated in. This was the state Yat had described. If I had to miss twenty-four hours of my life every time it happened, I wouldn't mind. I would perform every second day.

At the curtain, there was a standing ovation. Michael Redgrave was overjoyed, as were the director and producer. Everyone had been magnificent. Barbara Jefford and I, who shared a dressing room on the first floor, were forced out onto the fire escape by the crush of people trying to get into our room to congratulate us.

No-one who has not experienced the first night of a New York smash hit can comprehend the orgiastic lengths to which the first-night public goes to register their adulation. In actuality, they are celebrating 'success' – but not so much for the personalities involved, although all the talent comes under the umbrella of their worship. They are celebrating the fact that, against all odds, these actors, singers and dancers, in a combined effort with the writer, director, lighting people, choreographer, composer, costume and set designer, have brought off a galvanising work of brilliance and unprecedented delight. The money that will pour into the box office once the reviews have come out is another great turn-on and nowhere in the world are these reviews awaited with such expectation and apprehension as in New York. The ritual of Sardi's restaurant, where the cast must appear to be applauded or, in the case of a flop, shunned and ignored, is well known.

After such a first night, all of us had to review our plans. We were to run at the Plymouth for over a year and I was to receive the coveted Critics' Choice Award. Walter Kerr of the *New York Times* was to say about me: 'Her Helen sweeps nations into dustbins at the lowering of her eyelashes'. Even so, I didn't think the success of *Tiger at the Gates* was to change our lives forever.

Sadly, I never again experienced going to sleep one day and waking up twenty-four hours later. I would dearly have loved for it to happen again but this phenomenon does not seem to be commandable. I have achieved the same feeling of floating, of impervious bliss since then but not until much later in my life and it required an entirely different sort of effort to achieve it.

The immediate outcome of our success was that offers came flooding in. I did a television play with Laurence Harvey called *The Small Servant* for *The Alcoa Hour*, a major sixty-minute live drama series on American TV, and played Bianca in a classic production of *The Taming of the Shrew*, with Lilli Palmer and Maurice Evans.

Meanwhile, Andrea and I sent each other sad, passionate little recordings with recovery pauses and proclamations of undying love. His mother, the Contessa Elza, came to stay with me for a week now that I was eminently acceptable, being the toast of Broadway. Life began to take on a rhythm once I had found an apartment up on the west side near the Hudson River.

I went to all the benefit performances of other plays on Sundays, our only free night. The entire cast of *Tiger* 'observed' at Lee Strasberg's Actors Studio, where Shelley Winters, Marlon Brando and Marilyn Monroe, amongst others, were students. I remember going to see Shelley in a Sunday-night performance of *A Hatful of Rain*, one of the earliest improvisational plays from the Actors Studio about drug addiction in New York. She had insisted on appearing at the actors benefit even though she had broken her leg skating with her little daughter at the Rockefeller Center ice rink. I sat next to that monumental doyenne of British theatre, Gladys Cooper, mother of Robert Morley, grandmother of Sheridan. In the interval, I asked her what she thought of Shelley's very realistic mumbles and fluffs. Gladys drew herself up to her full height and, looking down her nose imperiously, uttered the immortal line: 'Miss Winters' leg is very well cast.'

That year was a vintage one for Broadway hits. Though we were

the first, we were followed by *My Fair Lady*, with Rex Harrison and Julie
Andrews; *The Matchmaker*, with Ruth Gordon; Joan Littlewood's *The
Hostage* by Brendan Behan; *The Chalk Garden*, with the aforesaid Gladys
Cooper; and Kurt Weill's *The Threepenny Opera*, with Lotte Lenya. A long
list of extraordinary works was on view that year and it was a time when
a great deal of socialising went on amongst actors from various casts.

Within walking distance of the theatre there was a place known as
Birdland. Over the door was a sign that read:

Through these portals,
Walk the *most* mortals.

We did not get out of the theatre until midnight, after visitors and
showers to scrub off the body make-up, but the witching hour would
find a group of us 'most mortals' descending the stairs into Birdland to
partake of the best evening to be had in New York City or anywhere else,
I contend. I became addicted to Count Basie on my first visit. After the
finesse of this great jazz master and his gentle ivory tinkling, one was
slammed across the room by the visceral attack of the big band sound.
Trumpets blared, saxes wailed and, under a deep-purple pin-spot that
turned his features into a molten indigo sculpture, the marvellous Joe
Williams belted out his numbers like no-one else I have ever heard.
I was thrilled and flattered when Joe, seeing me walk in every night,
would break his set and purr into the mike, 'Hey, girl, is that pussy still
at the gates?'

The place was always jammed with people from every country and
every milieu. Barbara Jefford and I once sat a table with a group of
Mafia hoods who not only dressed the part but also talked about their
exploits just like characters out of *The Godfather* films, except that
those films hadn't been conceived of yet. They were as fascinated by
a couple of foreign actresses with funny accents as we were by them.
I heard one of them ask Barbara what part she would like to play most

if she had a choice. She replied that she would like to act the role of Nina in *The Seagull* by Chekhov. For some reason, they all thought this was hilariously funny, but after they stopped laughing, one of them thought for a long moment and said seriously, 'I bin a seagull. It's nuttin'.'

The weeks sped by and Andrea was becoming more remote on the telephone, our different worlds becoming harder and harder to talk about. The cast was growing stir-crazy never getting out of New York City. I hardly ever woke up until well into the afternoon and my routine was to get myself together and walk the whole length of Broadway to the theatre, occasionally detouring into an art gallery or park if the fancy took me. I would not eat anything until late in the day, usually one of those famous giant Broadway sandwiches. Sometimes, I would forget to eat even that. I was propositioned by various gentlemen who were anxious to add me to their list of conquests, the fact that I was married seeming to add to my attraction. Inevitably, I was beginning to think of New York as home again.

About nine months into a run, unless the stage manager or director keeps an eye on the production, there is a slackening of energy and inattention creeps into performances. About this time, I went through three weeks of absolute torture on the stage every night. The whole thing came about in the most innocuous way.

In the latter half of the play, there is a scene between Andromache, Hector's wife (played by Barbara Jefford) and Helen. Andromache begs Helen to go back to her husband Menelaus and thus avert the war, playing upon Helen's womanly instincts and her responsibility to peace. Sobbing on her knees in front of Helen, who stands high on a rostrum above her, she pleads for the world for the sake of her unborn child. 'Fill it with pity!' she cries.

One night, perhaps because of a slight lapse of attention, Barbara sobbed with utter conviction, 'Fill it with putty, Helen!' After an initial moment of shock, the sheer idiocy of the statement set me off and

I could not stop laughing. It was painful. Though mortified by my inability to take command of myself, I was nonetheless overcome by the image of what she had just said. Barbara was lucky. She could mask her merriment by muffling her face in her robes but I was fully exposed on my rostrum for all to see. It was humiliating but, at the same time, liberating. Every night for three weeks, I actually dreaded going into the theatre, knowing that we would arrive at this same moment, a *Groundhog Day* nightmare in which Barbara would have difficulty getting her line out, stifling laughter as tears, and I would be seized by giggles that I could not control.

In the midst of this storm in a teacup, Jimmy Fraser telephoned from London to tell me that Sir Alexander Korda had died and that British Lion had been sold off to the British Government. I was very sorry that neither Sir Alex nor I would ever know whether he would have been frightened of me in ten years' time. Technically, I was now a civil servant and Andrea was jobless. This news focused my attention remarkably and I began seriously to count off the days until my return to London.

I arrived back in Britain to find a very depressed Andrea and a melancholic Sicilian maid, Rosa, in the flat at Roland Gardens, both bemoaning the leaden London skies. I immediately set about altering their mood by changing the habitat. I bought an apartment in a new block on the Bayswater Road called Caroline House. Large, with a lot of light, it overlooked a garden and had a parking area at the back.

Buying furniture and decorating could not dissimulate the feeling that Andrea and I had become two very different people since my departure. There was an unspoken rift between us. Andrea told me nothing of what he had been thinking or doing and, ominously, his mother arrived to stay. It seemed he had returned to the family fold in my absence. Elza informed me with great satisfaction that Andrea had only left Italy in the first place because he wanted to escape doing his military service. Any woman who marries an Italian must accept the undeniable fact that she has also married his mother.

British Lion, now a government concern, was anxious to make up for all the time I had spent in *Tiger at the Gates* in the USA, so they insisted that I work continuously. I was obligated under my contract to do any film they decreed and I found myself being shuffled into unsuitable parts in dreary projects with no guidance from Korda's entrepreneurial hand. I was determined to buy myself out of my contract at the earliest opportunity.

This was the watershed moment in my career when the choice of my next part was immensely important. It was finally decided that I should play the lead in a West End production of Max Beerbohm's *Zuleika Dobson*, to be mounted by Donald Albery as a musical. Fittingly, undergraduates from Oxford had adapted the novel and written the music for this tale of the wicked Zuleika, who breaks the most hardened of hearts at that hallowed university. It had initially been staged as an amateur production by the undergraduates themselves, and all the London producers had scrambled for the rights. There was one fly in the ointment. The contract with the two young writers stipulated that they retain the right to veto any director whom they thought was not presenting their work as they wished.

I recommended working on movements with Yat as soon as I returned from New York and it was with high hopes that I began rehearsals, aiming to live up to the lines of the opening number:

There's no girl in the world like Zuleika
There's no-one so lovely as she
All the world is in love with Zuleika
All the world has good reason to be

There's no creature so fair as Zuleika

Every feature so rare and refined

The Cleopatras of the past

Will be forgotten at last

She has left them completely behind

The rehearsal period in London was beset with disguised traps. For instance, our maid Rosa, who was a loyal creature, became a gibbering wreck each time Elza would sweep away the dishes she had taken all day to prepare and replace them with delicacies purchased at Harrods Food Hall. The apartment was filled with the sounds of sobbing and Sicilian invective, which Andrea and Elza completely ignored.

Then, every time I thought we had blocked a scene or set a song at rehearsals, the young writers would veto the director, who would be sacked. Each time a new director was appointed the entire musical had to be re-directed, as none of the previous director's work could be included; if it were, he would have to be paid for the rest of the run.

What's more, the management asked me to ensure that Andrea and his mother did not come and sit in the stalls during rehearsals. Like most Italians who have no theatre etiquette, they talked loudly and laughed at inappropriate moments. This upset the actors and infuriated the writers. Elza and Andrea spent their days walking around Bond Street and Burlington Arcade buying expensive items and popping into Brown's or Claridge's for lunch. It was fun to end their day in the stalls of the theatre waiting for me to finish, and they were astounded when I told them what the management had said.

'But you are the star!' Elza exclaimed. 'They can't say that to you.'

They still came every day, though they were slightly less strident.

I recognised that we were in deep trouble with *Zuleika* after the sixth director was fired (one of whom was Peter Hall). While outwardly trying to stay calm, I could feel panic taking over inside. Our latest director, Alfred Rodriguez from the Royal Ballet, managed to block the entire play before the young writers were able to sack him. It had become clear to everyone in the cast that these two were going to keep on vetoing directors until they were the only ones left to take over and save the play.

Rodriguez nursed me along with tenderness, suspecting that I was near breaking point. I had actually begun to feel I was getting somewhere with the difficult job of making the character of Zuleika come alive, and we were approaching the time when rehearsals in London would lead to an opening in the provinces and a short tour for cuts and polishes prior to our opening in the West End.

Elza approached me to say confidentially that Andrea was very upset. He was intensely jealous of Rodriguez, she told me, and she herself was sure that the man was in love with me. He was far too familiar. They had talked it over and I must act upon their advice before the tour started and have him replaced. I could hardly believe my ears.

I found Andrea in a very dour mood. It was impossible to talk in the apartment, so we walked all the way to the river and sat in a bus shelter watching the sleet sweeping across the water and the icy wind stirring the trees on the southern bank. There, Andrea confessed to me that he had been having an affair with the Italian wife of one of Korda's set designers. Crying, he told me the affair was over, that he hated her, that she was older than he was, that she had seduced him. She had threatened to tell me about the affair, he said, and he didn't want me to hear her lies.

Once he calmed down, his mood changed. He attacked me for going away again, for flirting with my new director and for telling him and his mother not to come to the theatre during rehearsals, as they had only been trying to help by giving me tips about my performance. The unkindest cut was saved for last, although I had already been dumbstruck by his revelations.

'Oh,' he said, 'and when you make your entrance and they sing that song about Zuleika and how great she is, why don't you try to walk exactly like my mother when you come on? Watch her and you'll see how she moves . . . like a model on a catwalk. That's how you should do it.'

I ran off into the night. I could not look at him any more. Where was my old lovely Andrea? Who was this castigatory stranger intent on ripping me to shreds? I ran all the way home and went straight to bed. The next day, I had a long floor class with Yat and I could feel the shivering up and down my back that is the forerunner of a cold. Please, God, I thought, don't let me get one now!

Later, when Andrea climbed into bed next to me, we did not touch. There was an ominous silence – no deep breathing that betokens the evanescence of the worries of the day, no warm hand seeking out my left breast, just unspoken rancour in the darkness. Tangibly, I could feel everything falling apart, as though my head and limbs were becoming disconnected from my body. I was too numbed to feel sorry for myself or even angry with Andrea. I just wanted to sleep, hoping that when I woke up everything would be different. But the next day I was informed that Andrea and Elza had decided to return to Italy. They had arranged their tickets the day before, so there was nothing to say but goodbye.

They were gone and there was just Rosa and me rattling around the apartment. When Yat came, I did a strenuous class, throwing myself into every movement and exercise, stretching, straining and sweating out the beginnings of a cold on the blue carpet on my living-room floor. I was exhausted – body, mind and heart – and felt feverish by the end of the day. I packed for the tour and then went to bed. My cold took hold in the night.

The next few weeks of my life are a blur. I dosed myself with cold suppressants, which rendered me virtually comatose through the terrible grind of more rehearsals, the inevitable sacking of Rodriguez, his sorrowful departure, new moves, old tunes and a new director who could not understand at first why he was not allowed to direct without the continual interference of the boys. They now had the reins firmly in their hot little hands, and there was no-one to turn to for advice or consolation.

It was on a Saturday night in Oxford, after two ghastly shows, that I knew the game was up. I opened my mouth in the second show and all that came out was an inhuman squawk like the mating call of a pre-historic beast. Somehow, I got through the show, with the other actors covering for me and gargles with saltwater every instant I was off the stage. At the curtain call, I looked out at all the people clapping and knew with utter conviction that I would never appear as Zuleika again. It was over. I was done.

I went straight back to the hotel and ran myself a hot bath. There was a blank wall in my head but I remembered my dad reading the death of Petronius to me; how he sat in a hot bath and opened his wrists, having invited all of his friends to attend his death. Well, I had no guests but I slit my wrists under the water, not feeling a thing, just watching the vivid red gouts of blood flow out. Then, nothing.

The next thing I remember was the pressing desire to have a pee. I kept my eyes closed for a long time and it came to me gradually that dead people have no need to relieve themselves. When I opened my eyes, I found myself lying in a strange room. There was a screen around my bed and the smell of disinfectant, daffodils and Jeyes Fluid perme-ated the air. I pressed the bell that lay on the coverlet and a nurse came bustling in, all efficiency and bedside manner as she straightened the blankets and smiled encouragingly.

'So, you've woken up at long last. We thought you were going to be Sleeping Beauty and sleep for a hundred years.'

She seemed to know what it was that had roused me and helped me use the bedpan. My wrists were bandaged but I could recall nothing. It was very strange to know that people had been working on my body as though it were some piece of equipment that needed to be fixed. I was disappointed to find myself alive, but, at the same time, I had lost my attraction to oblivion. I just wanted to disappear where no-one knew who I was or could question me about what I'd done.

The first person who came to see me was Rosa, who held my hand as though it were made of filigree. Then Jimmy Fraser poked his head around the door, loudly proclaiming his presence. When he saw that I was not at death's door, he gave me a tongue-lashing, saying I was a stupid girl, irresponsible and blah, blah, blah. But where had he been when I needed rescuing from the impossible task of re-learning an entire show every few days? He expressed concern that the press would find out what had happened and make a meal of it. I could see that he was both angry and relieved, a man intent upon damage control. The drama queen in him loved every second of it.

Over the next day or so it was decided that I would travel to Naples with Rosa, as her sister, and then take the overnight ferry to Palermo in Sicily. Until we arrived in Palermo I was hardly present, but then, like a bear awakening to spring after hibernation, I smelt the mimosa and orange blossoms of the Sicilian *primavera*. I was Persephone returning after nine long months in the Underworld. I was Eurydice who had made it back across the Styx. I was a seagull. No, I wasn't . . . I was an actress. From the balcony of a hotel on the beach in Mondello near Palermo, I looked out over the Mediterranean with wonder, as though I had never seen blue before. How amazingly definite and clever nature is. Blood is so red and the sea so blue.

I only called three people from Sicily – my mother, my sister and Rodriguez. He had been telephoning me every night since his untimely departure from rehearsals and was the only person in the world who had understood my real state, how very near to collapse I had been. I wanted him to know how grateful I was for his support.

I had a secondary reaction to my act of attempted self-destruction, a sort of seismic aftershock, and had to take to my bed. Rosa had gone

118

off to visit her parents while I lay still, feeling fragile, in the fragrant Sicilian air, watching the curtains sway and the light move on the ceiling. One afternoon, there was a tap at the door and the room was filled with Rodriguez. He stayed for a few days and I got up. We laughed as we walked up and down the beach at Mondello, watching the stocky German matrons and their consorts trawling the sands for beautiful Sicilian beach boys. Everything seemed simple again and funny. On his last night, Rodriguez took me to a nightclub in Palermo. The band was a wondrous, time-warped, pre-war sextet. Dowdy but passionate Sicilian couples did Rudolph Valentino tangos, dipping, gliding and clutching at each other with a fervour unseen in London or New York.

Rosa returned to tell us that a reporter had come to her house asking where I was and offering to pay her money for information. It was time to move. I had already been away for ten days. I boarded the night ferry to Naples and was accosted on the deck by this same reporter, who began questioning me aggressively. I brushed him aside and rushed below to my cabin, dreading our arrival at Naples, where I would be exposed to the onslaught of the press.

At dawn the next morning, we docked. I was stunned to see Andrea waiting on the wharf. How had he known I would be on that boat? He looked sad and grey, scanning the deck, screwing up his eyes and frowning in the early-morning sun. Something inside me lurched sideways. I felt relieved of the burden that had weighed on my chest for weeks. Of course he could not have forgotten. Of course we were still lovers and friends. He must have heard what I had done and been upset, but how had he known that I was on this particular ferry arriving from Palermo on this particular morning? Surely, Rosa, Rodriguez or the press must have given him this information. I have never solved this mystery.

I flew off the boat and into his arms before the waiting press could do anything but take some quick snaps. I answered no questions and, in an instant, Andrea bundled my luggage and me into the car. We were on our way back to Rome. I could hardly believe our lucky escape.

119

As we hurtled up the motorway I had not the faintest inkling that I was being transported to a different sort of imprisonment from which escape was very difficult. Besides the Volpe family – Giovanni, Elza, Andrea, Ludovica, Mooma and Roberto Vaiano – the apartment in the affluent suburb of Parioli was also the abode of two maids who had been born on the family estate in Sardinia, a manservant/butler, a cook, his assistant and Andrea's old wet-nurse, Gianna, who came from another family property in the north. I suppose you could call these other inhabitants family retainers.

Apart from their usual duties, the two maids were on hand to tighten Elza's waspy corset throughout the day and serve as hairdressers. They had a horrid time. I had little to do with the cook and the butler, but it was Gianna, the former wet-nurse, who became the bane of my existence. With her low forehead, lantern jaw, wide nose and large hands, she was a perfect specimen of Neanderthal woman. She shouted rather than spoke, as though addressing a deaf person, and it made me quite faint to think of Andrea suckling at her massive bosom. I suspect she had been told that I was slightly gaga, being an *atricetta* (literally a little actress but also denoting a prostitute in Italian), and that I was recovering from a nervous breakdown. Gianna had been instructed to watch me and inform Andrea or his mother if I showed any signs of agitation, distress or the desire to run away.

It was a shock, initially, to wake up in the morning and find the great beast Gianna weighing down the bed mightily on one side, breathing heavily while she fed Andrea raw eggs mixed with honey and little almond *biscotti* from a silver spoon. She had obviously done this all his life. I got used to it after a while, but what I could never get used to was the way she seemed to think she had the right to examine my body. So familiar was she with Andrea's body that he hardly noticed her investigations and rubbings but I dreaded her heavy-handed touch. She used to feel my throat and neck, never leaving without a prying examination of my breasts to see if they had swollen or had any lumps. She knew exactly when I had my period and how long it lasted. I hated it. It wasn't a personal touch but rather the way a farmer handles his cows when looking for evidence of disease.

Life in Parioli was different from anything I had ever experienced, and it took me some months to get used to it. Because neither of my parents was rich and because they were happily wedded to their professions, I was conditioned to think of adherence to the work ethic as a natural state. I had never encountered a lifestyle devoted to anything else. While Elza had a salon of *alta moda* (haute couture), designing very smart clothes for friends such as Edda Ciano (wife of Count Ciano and Mussolini's daughter), her visits to the establishment were irregular. It didn't take me long to realise with a sort of astonishment that everyone in the family despised anyone who worked for a living. Elza's days were spent talking on the telephone, flipping through glossy magazines, having the pedicurist call in or visiting La Nonna Eliza, Andrea's paternal grandmother.

La Nonna Eliza lived in one of the most unlikely houses I have ever seen. It was right in the middle of the Villa Borghese and had been the home of a famous charioteer in Rome's glory days. There was still a vomitorium next to a fountain in the garden, where the charioteer was buried. Andrea's grandfather, the historian Giacomo Volpe, was a small, chirpy and charming octogenarian who had discovered that it is sensible to accept the vicissitudes of life and not worry. The antithesis of his son Giovanni, the Shrug, he smiled all the time. His study, an octagonal room on the roof of the main house, was filled with cages of birds and thousands of books. A hundred canaries sang their hearts out all day long. Giacomo loved feeding them morsels of apple and banana from a bowl on his desk. I wondered how he could concentrate on Horace or Ovid with that din in his ears all day long.

La Nonna Eliza, who weighed well over twenty stone, lay in a vast bed in a room below. Unable to get up any more, she was tended by a small army of women – companions, nurses and retainers who massaged her, anointed her with oils and unguents, cooed in her ears and listened to her airy-fairy little voice complaining about how painful life was. She was hand-fed tantalising little snacks throughout the day and night.

When granted an audience with Nonna Eliza, you had to approach the bed, kneel down and kiss the surprisingly elegant, tapered, bejewelled fingers extended to you from her bed. It was from her side of the family that the money had come. It was mooted that, from this very bed, she wielded such authority that her two sons were in awe of her business acumen. It was for this reason that visits to La Nonna Eliza were so important. Should she feel slighted or dispirited, she might change her will. When La Nonna Eliza passed away some years later, it took many burly men to lift her from her bed and several doors had to be disengaged from their hinges before she could be carried from the house.

The one time during the day that everyone met was at lunch in the dining room and the pattern of the meal hardly ever varied. The girls flattered their father, who regarded them with good-natured scorn, Elza downed her bird-dropping portions of food, Roberto Vaiano ate ravenously but remained skeletal and silent, and Andrea kept up social chitchat with his mother and me. Roberto was a communist and a painter. I liked him. He redressed the balance at the table somewhat by disregarding all the rules. He didn't try to flatter or even bother to make conversation. He was there for one thing only – to get his fill of food so that he could go on painting without interruption for the rest of the daylight hours. After dark, he went out to revolutionary meetings and sometimes came home ripped.

Andrea was a different person in Rome, as I am sure I was too, and our relationship had undergone some radical changes. We were now both dependents of the Shrug and, as such, had to follow the house rules. On paper, Andrea had been a law student for some years, which exempted him from the compulsory two-year military service. Italian university students can take exams when they're ready, and the result is recorded in a little book until they have enough points to take their finals. Thus, one can be a student for a long time before a degree is obtained. Yet Andrea worried constantly about when 'they' would catch up with him.

The daily regime was quite stultifying unless one was prepared to make things happen. I managed to read all the works of Pirandello, including the short stories, which I would never have done otherwise. I could not help remarking on the difference between the English translations done in the 1920s and '30s and the originals. Elza supplied me with clothes and, with Andrea, I became part of *la dolce vita*. We appeared with Federico Fellini and his wife, Giulietta Masina, at nightclubs and the opening of the fashion season. We went to the opera and met Luchino Visconti, who was a dear friend of Elza. I may have been decked out in the latest creations, but I felt trapped, like a bird in a gilded cage.

In Parioli, with nothing to do, I was beginning to have the same claustrophobic sensations as I did at boarding school. Was my fate to become a female clone in the dysfunctional Volpe clan, flattering the Shrug for the rest of my life? Then Jimmy Fraser telephoned. I was summoned to appear at the world premiere of *The Admirable Crichton* in London at the end of the month. British Lion was adamant that I should be there to do publicity. It was a godsend.

It was virtually the next day that Gianna, during one of her more intimate examinations of my body, shrieked for all to hear, '*Signora! Signora! Questa ragazza è incinta! Sono sicura, Signora . . . è incintissima!*'

Chapter Five

I left for London two weeks later. I was footloose and fancy-free, but pregnant.

At the 1957 premiere of *The Admirable Crichton*, I wore an unusual dress which was avocado and brown, and cunningly cut on the bias. It was one of Elza's creations, which she'd passed on to me after her fashion show, *Indubbio*, in Florence. I felt special in it and was thankful that there was no visible evidence of my impending parenthood. Jimmy Fraser and I had gone to the theatre in Leicester Square with Kenneth More, Sally Ann Howes, Cecil Parker and the other stars of the movie. *The Admirable Crichton* proved a crowd-pleaser, receiving rapturous applause from the audience.

Yet what I remember most about that night was the presence of a tall, funny actor with two gold eyeteeth, who leapt about firing off a barrage of one-liners in a broad Scottish brogue that was coarser than Jimmy Fraser's camp Inverness drawl. But this Scotsman was definitely not gay. He walked with the peculiar forward-leaning, slightly pigeon-toed gait of a body builder, and his thick eyebrows met between his eyes. He looked dangerous but fun.

'Who is he?' I whispered to Jimmy Fraser.

'Oh, don't you know? He's your new leading man, Sean Connery,' Jimmy informed me. 'You start work with him on *Anna Christie* next month.'

Anna Christie, a play by Eugene O'Neill, tells the story of Anna, a prostitute, her sea captain father and Matt Burke, a simple stoker below decks who falls in love with Anna, unaware that she is on the game. It's a well-crafted melodrama about the redemptive power of love and, like all of O'Neill's plays, has an enthralling theme.

There had been two film adaptations of *Anna Christie*, one in 1923 and another in 1931, which starred Greta Garbo in her first talkie, for which she received an Academy Award nomination. However, ITV, the original commercial British television broadcaster, had decided to produce a series of O'Neill's entire *oeuvre*. I was cast as Anna, while Leo McKern played the role of my father and Sean that of Matt Burke. Later, I would also play the lead in the two-part television production of O'Neill's *Strange Interlude*.

Leo was a short, thickset man with a craggy face and stentorian voice that became familiar to millions of viewers through his role as the crumpled, irascible British barrister Horace Rumpole in John Mortimer's TV series *Rumpole of the Bailey*. It's a voice that is produced exclusively in Australia, I believe, having a pronounced nasal twang in the crescendos of the upper register. The first meeting of Leo, Sean and I together took place in a pub. We stood at the bar and Leo bought the drinks. He tapped on his glass eye with a two-shilling piece, which startled us. Then he took his false eyeball right out of its socket and placed it next to his drink on the counter.

'Keep an eye on my beer,' Leo trumpeted as he trundled off to the gents.

For me, rehearsals are always the best and worst of times. They're about struggle and discovery – striving for new things. If you get on with the other actors, deep affective bonds are forged in one day. It doesn't matter if you make a fool of yourself, as it's impossible not to respect the audacity displayed by actors who take risks. Both Leo and Sean were such actors.

The contrast between the rehearsals for *Anna Christie* and those for

Zuleika was remarkable. There was no better way of healing the wounds of that period in my life than losing myself in a new role with supportive actors and, unlike *Zuleika*, just one director. The name of this young director was Phillip Saville, and because he was a first-time director we were equally supportive of him. In those days, TV dramas were broadcast live. Leo, who had done more TV than the rest of us, was full of technical suggestions and ideas for innovative camera moves. The fact that I had to chunder every now and again didn't seem to bother anybody. I tried not to reflect too much upon my marital problems and my life in Parioli. I knew that after *Anna Christie* went to air I would return to Australia to have the baby, but that's about as far ahead as I allowed myself to think.

On the Sunday at the end of the first week's rehearsal, Sean invited me to his mews house in St John's Wood for lunch. He was doing the cooking – roast pork. My sister Margaret and I followed our noses to the door and were ushered into a very small but cosy conversion with a sitting room and kitchen downstairs and a bedroom and bathroom upstairs. Like a stereotypical Scot, Sean had saved all his money from the yearlong *South Pacific* tour and put a down payment on the house as soon as he could. He was immensely proud of his acquisition and escorted us on a tour of the place as though it were the Chateau de Versailles. Victor Spinetti, who was on tour with him in *South Pacific*, told me that Sean had saved every penny of his travel allowance by riding between cities on his motorcycle and they shared digs to economise on rent. In the *South Pacific* company, Sean was known as 'the Jolly Green Giant'.

In the front room was a definitive collection of 78 rpm jazz records, which we listened to after lunch. I told him about Count Basie and Birdland, while he introduced me to Bix Beiderbecke. As we lay on the floor, he told us outrageous stories about his childhood in Fountainbridge, an industrial slum area of Edinburgh. Margaret and I both found him extremely funny and liked him a lot. It was a relaxing day, and we decided to do it again the following Sunday but, this time, at my place in Caroline House. There was no question of romance, as I was pregnant and about to disappear to the Antipodes, but we had an easy rapport and he seemed to hold me in high regard.

After the second Sunday lunch, Sean lay on my blue carpet and told us how he came to be called Sean instead of Tommy, the name by which his family knew him. It seems that Tommy Connery had a milk run in his teens, driving his dray to houses in the more affluent suburbs of Edinburgh, where he'd occasionally stop for a cup of tea and a chat. One family was particularly friendly. When they asked him his name, on the spur of the moment he said it was Sean. Learning of his love for horses, they enquired if he had any tips on the races and he named the only nag he'd probably ever heard of. Of course, the horse came in. Afterwards, they assiduously followed his tips and, as Sean, he continued to pick winners for them. The family saw him as a sort of walking oracle, and he liked it. It became apparent to him that Sean was a talismanic fellow who could not only pick winners but who *was* a winner. Henceforth, Tommy became Sean, and it suited him. Of course, his mum and dad, Effie and Joe, always called him Tommy, and when they did I was aware that he felt diminished by his former moniker.

I took Sean to meet Yat Malmgren, knowing that he would benefit greatly from his movement classes. Sean and Yat were instantly compatible and movement lessons became part of Sean's life. Although he had no formal training as an actor and still moved as a body builder, Sean possessed an enormous store of emotional energy, which he reserved even from himself. He was instinctive and intelligent but, at the same time, not confident enough to control what he was doing as an actor. Even then, I knew he had a powerful presence and burgeoning talent.

My apartment was to be let for the time I would be away in Australia. This was accomplished before we shot *Anna Christie*, so I stayed at a hotel in Chelsea for the last few weeks before my departure. One night, a young woman came to see me. She identified herself as Julie

Hamilton, the daughter of Jill Foot, wife of Michael Foot, the future leader of the Labour Party. Sean had talked a lot about his left-wing political proclivities and about Michael Foot as a potential prime minister but he had never mentioned Foot's stepdaughter. Then it all came flooding out. She told me how Sean had become monosyllabic and withdrawn, how he'd made it clear to her that their relationship was over and how the cruelty of unrequited love had caused her to suffer so much heartache. She wanted my assurance that I was not taking him away from her. I didn't know what to say, except that I was about to leave for Australia to have a baby and that she and Sean would have a great deal of time to sort it all out when I was gone. She left disconsolate. I didn't think I had the sort of relationship with Sean that would permit me to broach this subject with him, so I didn't.

In the meantime, Sean had bought my Vespa and every morning would turn up to take me to rehearsals on the back of my old familiar machine. He was so much larger than Andrea that I had the impression, when riding behind him with my arms tight around his waist, that I was being carried off by some valiant knight protector who would deliver me to a mysterious destination of which I'd never dreamed. Perhaps that sensation was not so very far from the truth.

Back in Australia, where the *The Admirable Crichton* had made me a star, my family protected me from the press. My mother was eager to train me in her tried and true techniques of natural childbirth. I was encouraged to run up and down sand dunes at the beach, pick beans in the garden and practise panting like a dog for the third stage of labour. The weather became hotter as we approached the end of the year. I used to bribe my brother David to go out and buy me bottles of sarsaparilla, but the moment my mother caught me pouring the lovely black fluid down my gullet she would reproach me sternly.

'D, how many times do I have to tell you that too much fluid in the last months of pregnancy will make the baby's head swell up and harden? You'll have a horrible time pushing it past your pelvis. Don't do it!'

My mother kept a careful check to see just where the baby's head was and whether it had descended. She was triumphant when it did. 'Not long now, darling. Not long now,' she told me.

I returned to Mooloolaba to do the honours at a new surfboat-naming ceremony and stayed in my mother's Butterfly House, which my brother Carl and I had built. It was further down the beach than our former house that had toppled into the sand. My dad and I bought an old Queenslander nearby and I gave a Black and White party on the beach in front of the house. Black Velvets (Guinness and champagne) and White Ladies (gin and ice cream) were served, plus a great deal of XXXX beer, the local Queensland brew. It was so hot that guests had to retire to the surf to cool off.

The final month of my pregnancy, November, was the hardest. Suddenly, from hardly showing at all, I swelled to behemoth proportions. In the last week of that month, the Frizzos, an Italian family who owned and operated a wonderful wayside stopping place on the way to Mooloolaba, hosted a celebration for the Cilentos. It was a traditional Australian daytime party to mark not only my return to Australia and my dad's birthday but also the commencement of school holidays. Long trestle tables had been set up outside under the gum trees, where barbecues sizzled and beer and soft drinks were being imbibed in abundant quantities. Mamma and Papa Frizzo, with their countless offspring and grandchildren, were rushing around and shouting. My dad was beaming, children were riding ponies, men were telling old bushie yarns and rude jokes to each other, women were exchanging recipes or baby stories and kids were playing cricket in the dusty car park. Then, suddenly, the cry went up . . . BUSHFIRE! BUSHFIRE!

An open truck carrying ash-blackened men came crashing into the car park, scattering the young cricketers. They were shouting that the fire was still about a mile down the road but heading, with the wind, in our direction. If one of those hot-air balloons that film major sporting events had been in place, it would have recorded throngs of people, like an army of ants, on the move. The Frizzos were no strangers to bushfires. Hessian sacks were doused with a power hose, as were all the buildings; trucks and motorbikes appeared out of nowhere to transport reinforcements to the fire scene and an ominous blue haze began to fill the air.

My mother wouldn't let me go with the firefighters, so we sat under the trees at a deserted table where flies had already begun to swarm over discarded cakes and half-eaten sausages. The distinctive smell of burning eucalyptus hit our nostrils. I remember the new, cream-coloured Chinese blouse I was wearing. I caught my mum regarding me with an amused look on her face.

'What?' I asked, squirming uncomfortably. 'Do I look funny? I can't help it if I'm getting huge.'

'No,' she answered, now giggling openly. 'I was just thinking of something a patient said to me yesterday.'

'What? About me?'

'Yes, well, it was quite amusing. This patient asked me, "What do your daughter and Phar Lap have in common?" '

I waited for the punch line but she was silent.

As any Australian knows, the two most revered sporting icons are Don Bradman, the legendary Aussie cricketer, and Phar Lap, the phenomenal racehorse from Down Under, who dominated the racing scene during the early 1930s. After winning the world's richest race, the Agua Caliente Handicap, in 1932, Phar Lap was sent to Menlo Park, California, where he succumbed to a mystery affliction that many thought was the work of the Mafia. The equine hero was restored to his former glory by a team of ace American taxidermists before being shipped back to his native land, where he now stands majestically in the Melbourne Museum.

'So,' I asked my mother, 'what *do* I have in common with Phar Lap?'

'Well,' she said smiling, 'you both came back to Australia stuffed.'

As funny as I find it now, I didn't laugh then. I got up, went to the toilet inside and vomited. I didn't want my mother to know how upset I was. It felt humiliating. Just those few words had turned my whole pregnancy and coming child into a seamy joke.

One week later, on the way back from Mooloolaba, I went into labour. Needless to say, with all the physical exercise and training that my mother had insisted upon, I was like a champion athlete in the Olympic baby blocks. After a period of excruciating pain that defies description to anyone who hasn't experienced it, there occurred what is called a precipitated birth. In other words, the baby shot out like a bullet from a gun.

Amid the shock and disbelief felt by all present, my mother included, another person had made an entrance in the room – a diminutive, dark-haired girl with perfectly delineated features. There she was amongst us, all five pounds of her. I never had a chance to put the three well-rehearsed stages of breathing into use. Her lungs expanded and it was she who practised the first stage of breathing, accompanied by some lusty bellows, with no rehearsal at all.

I was overwhelmed with a sense of relief and accomplishment. I could not stop looking at her. She was so much herself, this tiny separate being who had lived and grown inside me but had now been brought to light. I couldn't get over it. I don't think anyone ever does. It's a miracle that happens millions of times a year all over the world but is no less phenomenal for that. I was grateful to my mother for making me stay conscious throughout.

When I imparted the news to Andrea over the telephone, I detected a short pause of disappointment when he learned the gender of the baby. I have never met an Italian man (although there may be exceptions to prove the rule) who did not crave a son. Daughters won't do.

'What shall we call her? What about Elza,' he asked hesitantly, 'after my mother? We said that if it was a boy we'd call him Giovanni, after my father.'

I certainly was not going to call the baby Elza or Eliza or even Phyllis. The feminine form of Giovanni is Giovanna and I liked the roll and roundness of the name. She would be nothing like 'the Shrug'.

'So, what about Giovanna?' I put to Andrea. 'Giovanna Margaret, after your dad and my sister, okay?'

'Giovanna d'Arca, the maid of Orléans . . . or Giovanna La Pazza, the mad queen of Naples . . . Giovanna Volpe . . . okay!'

Where my mother found Mignonne Clutterbuck I don't know but she appeared when the *Women's Weekly* was doing a cover story on me and I was feeling flustered. Mignonne was about six feet four and the baby fitted into one of her massive palms like a kitten. Literally, she had the situation well in hand. She spent a week with us, showing me how to bath, burp and change Giovanna. Her big nimble fingers had a light, calming touch and she foresaw every contingency. In an ideal world, every new mother would have a Mignonne.

My mother, who must have delivered thousands upon thousands of babies, believed that many babies do not become attached to this world during the first few days of life, and that sometimes the new life has to be encouraged to take an interest in what's going on here. In Australian Aboriginal culture, an elder of either sex will take on the task of 'singing' a baby into life.

My mum wrote notes on all her confinements, keeping a log of how many children of one sex were born consecutively. Her record was nine boys born in a row just after World War II. She used to make tests to determine how coordinated each baby was. One such test consisted in watching how much air it took in at the sides of the lips when it sucked and another in seeing how quickly the baby was able to follow a moving light, even if it hadn't focused its eyes yet. She was a natural researcher, my mum, and for all that a superlative doctor. Until she lost

132

the strength in her fingers through arthritis, she could manipulate a foetus inside the womb, turning a breech baby's head around to allow for a normal birth.

A few days after the confinement, I was lazing in bed when my mum said that she had to examine me. She was practical and impersonal as she slipped a finger into the inner labia of my vulva.

'Now, see if you can squeeze that,' she said.

'Why?' I queried.

'Because, my dear, most divorces are caused by prolapse. Think about it and practise!'

Giovanna wasn't quite a month old when we left the torrid, sub-tropical Brisbane summer and headed back to Rome. It was so cold there that I was terrified the baby would be unable to cope with the radical change of climate but, of course, I didn't know then that babies are extraordinarily resilient, especially when breast-fed and nurtured like this baby was.

The return to life in Parioli verged on culture shock. I had forgotten the oppressive presence of Gianna, who was waiting to pounce upon the baby and transport her to the frilly pink nursery replete with a wet nurse, who just happened to be Gianna's niece. As I unwillingly surrendered Giovanna to her great grasping hands, so different from Mignonne's, Gianna shouted, '*Questa non è una bambina; è un'angeletta!*' ('This isn't a baby; it's a little angel!')

I declined the wet nurse and insisted upon changing the baby's nappies and bathing her myself. This was greeted with stunned dismay. Why would I want to do that? I must be a masochist or mad. Gianna was outraged. Each time I suckled Giovanna she marched up and down in front of me, scrubbing my breasts with a large sponge and muttering curses in her guttural northern dialect.

Andrea wasn't particularly interested in the baby, as she did little but eat, sleep and soil her nappy, but the whole family attended the baptism at St Peter's. Pink-coated almonds were provided, as is the custom at christenings of baby girls, and Elza insisted I wear a daringly décolleté black evening dress, which was entirely inappropriate. It only took about three days for me to feel as though I was in prison again.

While I'd been away, Andrea's position in the family hierarchy had hardened. He was now completely dependent upon his mother for money and, having no job, was treated by his father with a sort of sneering disdain. Although Andrea desperately desired to be acknowledged by his father as a man of merit, neither of them seemed to possess the ability, or inclination, to budge one inch from their entrenched positions. The damage that fathers and sons wreak upon each other is unbearable to witness on a daily basis.

In Rome, Andrea wasn't the same person who had sailed around London on the Vespa. I could sense the distance between us growing as the glacial winter days passed. In his eyes I was now a 'wife' and 'mother', which he resented. He wanted his actress girlfriend back, someone he could show off, someone who thought of no-one but him. Now there was a baby who demanded more than half of my attention, and I wasn't the same person who had sailed around London on the back of the silver Vespa either. I found our relationship bewildering. How could my London Andrea have vanished so completely? I was fearful that our marriage would mirror that of Elza and Giovanni.

All the time I'd been in Australia, Sean had been sending me funny screeds written in huge childish calligraphy, with about ten words per page. I began to look forward to these communications like lifelines thrown to someone trapped down a deep well. Then came the short-term answer to my prayers. British Lion demanded my return to London to do another film under my contract and Jimmy Fraser had given a tentative nod to a play to be directed by John Dexter in the West End. At first, there was some brouhaha over whether Giovanna should stay in Italy but, of course, this was impossible as I was still breast-feeding her.

I have a vivid memory of arriving at the airport in London wearing a shocking-pink wraparound blouse, the latest fashion that Rome had to offer smart, young, lactating mothers. To my horror, an excess of milk had spurted out, staining dark splotches on each breast. Sean was there to meet me and was much more excited about Giovanna than Andrea had ever been. I was desperately embarrassed about my ruined blouse and held the baby close to cover the stains all the way home. In hindsight, I can't imagine why I was so concerned, but I was.

Back at Caroline House, the first thing I had to do was find a nanny – one as unlike Gianna as possible. She arrived in the person of Mary Moody, a buck-toothed blonde with a wry sense of humour, who immediately bonded with Giovanna without any fussing or fiddling about. It was a great relief to have the confidence to leave the baby in hands that would not be wrapping her in swaddling clothes or sticking strange medieval devices in her mouth to keep her quiet.

And so I began another intensive period of work. Sean was my constant companion, whether we went to lessons with Yat or to Cic Berry for vocal work. Cic was a wonderful instructor, whose revolutionary ideas on voice production have become legendary throughout legitimate theatre in the English-speaking world and beyond. At that time, the red-headed Cic lived in a ramshackle house in Kensington with a husband called Harry, a ratty old dog and several children. Her unconventional methods included sitting on your chest if you weren't breathing properly. I believe the excellence of British actors' voices in both the Royal Shakespeare Company and the National Theatre is directly due to her passionate dedication.

The British director Frank Hauser and Greek-born director Minos Volanakis were running the Oxford Playhouse and were anxious for us to work there. Having just read all Pirandello's plays in the original Italian, I suggested we do a new translation of one and present it in the season. I had already made a start on *Vestire gli Ignudi* (literally 'to dress the naked') in Rome. Minos and I decided to create an anagram of our names, Minos becoming Simon and Diane becoming Nedia, and thus the translation would be by Simon Nedia. I'd play Ersilia Drei, Sean would play the Italian Consul to Smyrna and Minos would direct. We called the play *Naked*.

It is so different undertaking a project of your own initiative with artists you know and respect. We tinkered with the translation as we went along, and by the time we opened, it was a commendable and polished piece of work.

Naked has a classic Pirandello plot in which nothing is ever quite as it seems. Ersilia Drei, a young governess previously in the employ of the Italian Consul in Smyrna, returns to Italy destitute and in disgrace. In the prelude, we learn that she has ingested poison in a public park. When the play opens, she has been discharged from hospital and is befriended by a writer/reporter who is intrigued by her story. The pernickety middle-aged bachelor unadvisedly takes Ersilia back to his lodgings, much to the indignation of his landlady, where he offers her accommodation in return for exclusivity to her story. Slowly, Ersilia's story starts to unravel and it is very different from the one the writer had anticipated. We discover that the Consul was the girl's lover and that the baby in her charge had fallen from the roof to her death while they were making love. Later, when the Consul arrives and confronts Ersilia, the writer is witness to the terrible scene that ensues.

Frank Thornton, from *Are You Being Served?*, was quite wonderful in the role of the writer, but for Sean it was a completely new experience to be acting the part of an aristocratic Italian diplomat in a morning suit who, during the course of the play, is given to an explosive emotional discharge of operatic proportions.

On the opening night, when Sean arrived at the moment of this powerful scene, he was wearing a formal wing collar held in place by an old-fashioned stud. His whole neck must have swelled with the enormity of his emotion because, during a pause, there was a loud PING! and his collar stud flew out in a great arc, landing noisily halfway into the stalls. The explosion hushed the audience into total silence as they hung on in suspense. Unforeseen moments like these make live theatre so much more thrilling and rewarding than movies. No-one ever knows what an actor will do. Will he feel for his throat and rip off the collar in a fit of fury? Will he lose his lines and leave the stage in humiliation? Will he break into laughter or burst into tears? Or will he stand his ground and allow the event to become part of the action of the play? That's exactly what Sean did and the audience stayed with him, transfixed. To Sean's credit, he never lost his concentration for an instant. Whatever he'd done would have been memorable. It's the hazard and humanity of live theatre that makes us prefer it to any other form of entertainment.

Sean and I did several more plays at the Oxford Playhouse. I played Inez in Henry de Montherlant's *Queen after Death* with, again, the lovely Leo McKern and an actress of sensational beauty by the name of Yvonne Furneaux, who had been at RADA with me. Sean undertook the extremely demanding role of Pentheus in the Greek tragedy by Euripides, *The Bacchae*, with Yvonne Mitchell as his mother, Agave. During the course of this play, Sean had to disguise himself as a woman. He met the challenge without any of the coyness that generally attends macho actors who get into drag.

It was around this time that I first met Sean's dad. He had travelled to London as the spare hand for the removalist he worked for, sitting in the passenger seat as he didn't drive. Joe Connery was an energetic little man with a Scottish accent so thick that I could barely understand anything he said.

We went to a pub at Shepherd's Bush, the cavernous one on the southern corner. As we sat there, I saw Sean pass his dad some money under the table. It was obvious that this was some sort of ritual. As soon as Sean went to the gents, his father looked at me and winked conspiratorially.

'How long have you known Tommy?' he asked.

I told him that we'd met when we'd done *Anna Christie* together more than a year ago.

'But ye've never met Neil, have ye?'

'Who?'

'His wee brother, Neil. Well, he's no' so wee the noo. He's in the army. He's the *one*, ye know.'

'What do you mean?'

'Well, once you've met Neil, you'll never look at Tommy again . . . and he's nine years younger than Tommy, too. Have you noticed he's going thin on top?'

When Sean returned, I looked at him and his father and felt a profound compassion for Sean welling up inside me. I wondered if he knew how derogatory his father was about him behind his back. Perhaps he resented the fact that Sean had walked away from his impoverished past in the underbelly of Edinburgh or maybe he felt compelled to say something in the light of my seeing Sean give him money. Who knows?

What I do know, however, is that when I eventually did meet Neil some months later, I found him utterly unremarkable. He turned up at Sean's mews house with, of all people, my brother Raff, who was doing a post-graduate course in neurosurgery at Edinburgh University.

When I think about how Sean and I were then, I see us as a pair of Ulysses butterflies flying helter-skelter through a towering rainforest – sometimes together and sometimes splitting off, only to rejoin each other in an airborne dance in another part of the forest. We were like that. We'd come together with relief and delight, skitter about, compare notes, dance, eat, go to class, have fun and then flit off in opposite directions to do a new show somewhere else.

I seemed to be filled with irrepressible vigour at this time in my life, which propelled me onwards in every situation. I hardly ever slept, considering it a waste of life, but people said I never looked better. I smoked heavily and tippled Pernod and ice in copious quantities.

I had a hacking cough and my voice was progressively acquiring the deep, rich, bass tones of Paul Robeson. When I finally did find myself horizontal in bed, I felt as though a lump of lead had been lowered onto my chest. Pole-axed, I slept like the dead, unable to rise again without double-strength coffee and a few fags. The signs of imminent disaster were plain to see and I should have heeded them.

Like a Roman candle, I produced showers of sparks and the occasional conflagration wherever I went. Then the brilliant bursts came to an end and I was all but snuffed out. It happened in New York City. I don't remember exactly why I'd gone there, although I know I did a screen test for a film, during which I had to cough to simulate consumption. It was to star Burt Lancaster and I was assured of the role. Afterwards, I went to the opening night of *West Side Story* with Hal Prince, the director. We had a date to take to the water in a private yacht but an enveloping fog had caused the excursion to be rescheduled.

We were staying with actress Sally Ann Howes and her husband, Richard Adler, who wrote the music and lyrics (with Jerry Ross) for the Broadway hit *Damn Yankees*. I recall that I went to sleep in a strange bedroom, and had no idea where I was when I awoke in the darkness and felt that the whole of my chest was wet. I managed to get the bedside lamp lit to discover that the wetness I could feel was blood. I looked aghast at my bloody hands and nightgown. The bedclothes looked like something out of the second act of *Macbeth* and my first thought was how mortifying it was to have made such a mess in someone else's home. I had some vague idea that a blood vessel had ruptured in my throat, but as soon as I coughed again I realised that the source of the haemorrhaging was somewhere deep inside my chest. My lungs seemed to be trying to exit through my mouth. This wasn't *Macbeth*; it was the final act of *La Traviata*. I was genuinely consumptive.

I was rushed to the Medical Arts Hospital on 57th Street, near Carnegie Hall, and placed in intensive care, where my left lung completely collapsed. I sank into a euphoric state in which everything was immensely clear and nothing was important. I was dying and it was not unpleasant. The separation from my body I experienced allowed me a freedom that I'd not known since my childhood days on the beach at Mooloolaba.

As I drifted in and out of consciousness, my family and husband were informed. My father arrived on the earliest plane; Andrea remained in Rome, convinced that I was playing a practical joke on him. My life hung in the balance for some days. Had the haemorrhaging spread to my right lung, I would have drowned in my own blood.

I saw Sally Ann Howes and others standing at the foot of my bed, careful not to come too near because I was extremely contagious. As I gazed into their worried faces, I felt nothing but detached compassion. I seemed to be looking through them into their innermost disillusionments and was constrained to try to explain succinctly to Sally Ann Howes what was wrong with her performance as Eliza Doolittle in *My Fair Lady*, the role she'd taken over from Julie Andrews on Broadway. She must have hated me.

I surrendered to my impending demise and felt only grateful for the release. My dad, however, was determined that I would not die. He arrived wearing his beret, which gave him the air of an ageing roué. It would have disappointed him terribly if I had refused to survive. As soon as I saw him, I knew I could not die. He made me smile as I watched him turning the arc light of his irresistible charm onto my American agent, Gloria Safier. Gloria's notorious bull-dyke persona was feared throughout the entire New York theatre scene, but, somehow, she was instantly transformed into a coquettish Broadway babe and the two of them went off to lunch hugging each other like a couple of teenagers.

My father stayed for two weeks, until he was certain I was out of danger, his protracted lunches with Gloria continuing until he left. There was a nurse – a Thelma Ritter character – who basically saved my life. She'd turn me over at all hours of the day and night when the adhesions forming on the walls of my lungs became unbearably painful.

To find oneself consigned to a hospital in America with no medical insurance is the quickest way to go broke, and thus it was that, after six weeks in the Medical Arts Hospital, I'd done my dough. I was taken by ambulance to the *Andrea Doria*, placed in the ship's infirmary below the waterline and so set sail for Italy.

Ironically, we docked at the very same port of Naples where Andrea had waited for me more than two years earlier when I returned from Sicily, but this time he was accompanied by his mother, the Contessa Elza. I'll never forget the shock on her face when she saw me. I weighed less than seventy pounds. Andrea's only comment was that it was a very interesting disease and that it had made me look 'like an alien'.

The next six months of my life were spent in an extremely unlikely place for a girl from Oz with no discernible religious inclinations. I was X-rayed at the Volpe apartment in Parioli, the equipment having been carted in for the event, and then transported to the Clinica Morelli in the Vatican. This was to be my home from November until the following June of 1959.

Behind the vast, imposing square of St Peter's Basilica, with its monumental steps and legions of Swiss Guards, there was an entire village. One could look down at a small filling station and watch the wine-bottlers, with whom the then Pope, Giovanni Ventitresimo (Pope John XXIII), was said to sit and gossip on summer evenings. The Clinica Morelli, which took up one of the buildings in the village, was a TB hospital for returned soldiers and members of Roman society afflicted by the illness. It was run by a fiery old *mangiapreti* (literally a priest-eater or rabid anti-cleric) named Professore Morelli, a septuagenarian with shoulder-length white locks and the operatic manner of Gabriele d'Annunzio, whom he closely resembled. Small and wiry, he moved about in his white coat at a remarkable speed, spearheading an entourage of young doctors, nuns and male nurses who raced around after him, sniggering at his jokes and taking notes on his pronouncements.

I was assigned a lovely airy room with a balcony overlooking a garden where the less seriously ill patients played *boccia*, a game similar to petanque or indoor bowls. I was surprised when another bed was placed in my room and even more astonished when the Contessa Elza announced that she would be staying with me in the clinic. She had made much ado about my hugging Andrea and baby Giovanna, as I was still meant to be exceedingly contagious. She and Professore Morelli seemed like old lovers, so effusive was their banter. She referred to me as 'my daughter' in front of him, while stroking my forehead and pushing my hair back for him to see my emaciated face. When Andrea visited they both fussed over me like mother hens. Such behaviour was peculiarly out of character for them but I felt cosseted with their attention and appreciative to be with family in such an unfamiliar place.

Tuberculosis is a curious disease in that one experiences the most extraordinary extremes of energy – one moment electrifyingly bright and the next plunged into a deep torpor. I couldn't sleep for the first week at the Vatican. I lay bristling with unspent excitement, listening to Elza's staccato snores and awaiting the approach of the night sister, Sorella Lamberta, with whom I'd made friends on my first night in the clinic. She was a large, pneumatic but gracious woman with a beautiful generous mouth, which was perpetually turned up in a smile, and the parchment skin of a nocturnal person. I immediately loved and trusted her, and we'd engage in whispered conversations while she sat on my bed. I told her about my life in the theatre, while she related what it was like to have been on night duty for eleven years with no breaks. I called her Sorella 'Lambretta' for at least three months before she gently informed me that her name was Lamberta and that she had not been named after a motor scooter.

It didn't take long before the reason for Elza's attention became apparent. In part I am doing her an injustice, because I'm sure she was very concerned about me, but after a few days she invited all her friends, smart Roman matrons like herself, to attend a cocktail party in our room. She had her chef prepare lobster and asparagus *amuses-gueules* and little delicacies of all descriptions, which were served with champagne. Slinking about in clothes made by Elza's couture salon, all the ladies were in a ferment of excitement to be partying at the Vatican, which was a real cachet in Roman society. It was just the sort of amusing experience that Elza was famous for providing.

The Contessa held court like a queen, with her coterie of ladies clustered close, hanging on her every word. I simply sat in the middle of my bed, the showcase invalid, allowed only one sip of champagne and no rich nibbles lest they make me cough. Everyone is cast in a role in Italian families – the joker, the melancholic, the intellectual and the perpetual invalid, whom everyone calls La Povera (the Pitiful One). I had no intention of playing the role of La Povera Dianetta for the rest of my life.

One of the Contessa's elegant friends remarked that Elza had not even tasted the delectable morsels on offer, but she waved her away.

'*Ma io non posso mangiare niente! Quasi mai . . . niente! Non so perchè,*' she trilled, holding up her little finger in exact emulation of the Nonna Eliza. ('But I can eat nothing! Nothing . . . hardly ever! I don't know why.')

'It's because your corset is too tight,' I said in English.

'What did she say?' the elegant lady enquired in Italian.

'And it gets worse when the maids tighten it all day long,' I added.

Elza was not pleased. She quickly led the group away from my bed towards the terrace. '*Ma che bella giornata è oggi!*' ('*Such* a beautiful day!') I heard her shrill as she left.

Because my lung had been collapsed for such a long time, adhesions had formed on the wall of my chest, which began to give me agonising pain, especially at night. Inadvertently, I had discovered a way of transferring the pain from my body. There was a wardrobe set high in the wall directly in front of my bed, and I would study the knots in the wood with every ounce of consciousness in my being. My object was to shift my pain to the wood, and I found that it worked. Unwittingly, Elza would often interrupt my concentration and I would lose the thread and be plunged back into pain again in a flash. I became bad tempered with her and wanted none of her solicitations.

One night Sorella Lamberta came to me shaking her head. She sat down on my bed, took my hand and, with her other hand against my cheek, spoke to me as though I was a child of ten.

'Dianetta, why are you so unpleasant to your mamma? She is so upset! She says you snap at her and don't appreciate what she is doing for you. You don't realise what she is giving up for you. You know you only ever get one mother.'

I was amazed. 'But she's not my mother,' I protested. 'She's my *suoccera*!'

The term *suoccera* (pronounced 'swotchera') is one of the ugliest words in any language and the fact that it means mother-in-law, with all the baggage that word carries, does not add any lustre. It was Sorella Lamberta's turn to be amazed. She heaved a long sigh and, rising slowly from my bed, softly said, 'I didn't know. But that is no reason for you to be so unpleasant to her.'

I don't believe that Elza ever forgave me for my rejection of her at this time and I still feel remorse that I treated her so badly. She left in a huff and I didn't see either Elza or Andrea for weeks.

Life at the Clinica Morelli settled into a regular routine of injections, baths, walks in the garden and reading. For the first time in many months I was able to settle down and read without the interruptions of the telephone, Giovanna to attend to, rehearsals or anything at all. It was the first time in my life that I had time for deep introspection. Someone gave me a copy of *The Light of Asia* and I was thrown into a state of intense confusion by what was described as 'Buddha's first ecstasy'.

When young Prince Siddhartha (Buddha's name in his youth) stops by the side of a creek, he watches a tiger killing a deer. He sits down to contemplate the event and sees with blinding clarity that, all around him, everything is in the process of eating or being eaten. Birds are eating insects; fish are eating flies; snails are eating moss; and moss is clinging to the earth, taking its sustenance from the goodness of the soil. Each is occupied in searching for food from the species lower down on the food chain. There is nothing – not even man – that is left out of this condition of life on earth. Instead of trying to save things from each other's hunger, Buddha had his first ecstasy at the order and symmetry of the universe.

To a child brought up on Walt Disney cartoons, this was unfathomable. What about Tom and Jerry? Tom never *ate* Jerry. What about the good guy rescuing the baby deer from the jaws of the wicked tiger in the nick of time? Where were the good guys? Who are the good guys? How can life be so cruel? It turned my world upside down. And what does man produce that is eaten by what is above him? Is it true that it is the drop of nectar produced by man when he manifests unconditional love?

When the nuns asked me what religion I followed, after long reflection I told them it was Buddhism. They were horrified and I noticed that their treatment of me changed significantly. 'But Buddha is a black beast,' they would say as they furiously flapped my sheets or jabbed a crooked needle into my bottom. When asked if I'd had a profession before my illness, I told them that I was a dancer (the Italian word for actress, *atricette*, being synonymous with prostitute). They gathered around me and patted my hand in sympathy. Smiling sweetly, one of them uttered the fateful pronouncement, 'What a pity, *cara*. You'll never *ever* dance again.' Something snapped shut in my chest. I smiled back as sweetly as I could but a voice inside me said, 'Oh, yes, you WILL!'

It was decided by Professore Morelli that the time had come to have my adhesions burnt off if I were to make any sort of recovery. I was taken upstairs to the theatre, where there were some extremely terrifying shiny saws, forceps and bone snippers. They made my teeth chatter with apprehension. I was allowed no anaesthetic or soporific, as I had to be conscious to breathe exactly as they told me. Four nuns held me down while the doctors cut two holes in my armpit – one to look into my lung and the other to insert a long tube with a small electrical device on the end, which heated up and burnt off the adhesions.

It was excruciatingly painful. Added to the fact that I could smell my own flesh searing like steak, I had to follow precise breathing instructions – pant, expel breath, inhale deeply – just like my training for natural childbirth. I screamed out 'O God! O God!' quite often and the nuns who were restraining me nodded sagely to each other and said, 'You see, no Buddha now. She calls out to our God when she feels the pain.'

After my ordeal, I lay in bed for a long time, hurting. I had tried futilely to break my adhesions by playing *boccia* left-handed. What a ludicrous idea. I was never so aware of how little control I had over my body or my life. I was determined that this would change, that soon I would recover, hug my daughter whenever I chose to, be a great actress and see Sean again.

Sean provided a kind of lifeline at this time by writing letters, as he had when I'd returned to Australia to give birth to Giovanna. I managed to speak to him on the telephone once or twice and found his warm Scottish voice a great comfort. I began to plan my escape from Italy and illness.

It now seemed like eons ago, but when I was still in my Ulysses butterfly stage in London I had played Carol Cutrere in a production of Tennessee Williams' *Orpheus Descending* at the Royal Court Theatre in London. Originally called *Battle of Angels*, the play had opened in Boston in 1946 but had been withdrawn as obscene and had not been attempted again until Tony Richardson decided to revive and update it at the Royal Court fourteen years later.

Orpheus Descending is perhaps the most seminal of Tennessee's works, having all the elements of his later plays. Val Xavier, a young guitar-playing man, a free spirit, drifts into a repressive small town in the American Deep South and into the arms of a passionate Italian woman called 'Lady' Torrance. She has been jilted by the local nabob, David Cutrere, but has established a romantic roadside nightspot for lovers. Val, who plays guitar in the bar wearing a snakeskin jacket, tells her about a bird with no feet that never alights on the earth until it falls from the sky in death.

In my role as Carol Cutrere, I was the crazy but fascinating daughter of the town's pre-eminent family, the Cutreres. She has broken all the rules and becomes enamoured of Val. When, inevitably, the local sheriff and his police hunt Val down with dogs, the play concludes with Carol appropriating his snakeskin jacket and taking over from Val as 'the bird with no feet'.

As Lady, Tony had cast an Italian actress, Isa Miranda, who had a very loose grasp of English. She had appeared in some Italian pictures directed by her husband but, by then, had left him to try her luck elsewhere. She played Lady with enormous conviction, full throttle, but the headline in the London *Evening Standard* read 'PURR VIT NO FIT'. This was drama critic Milton Shulman's approximation of what 'bird with no feet' sounded like coming out of Isa's mouth.

I had been quite intoxicated by Tennessee Williams. He arrived at rehearsals looking rather rumpled, speaking in his slow, deliberate but dreamy Southern drawl, as though he had just crawled out of bed with a hangover. He probably had. Tennessee came to all the later rehearsals and rewrote bits of the play as we went along. His great friend, Maria Britneva, was playing the part of a filling-station attendant, and we spent a few 'gaudy nights' drinking and 'jookin'. This was my character's way of describing what she did which, in today's terminology, would simply be called 'hangin' out' in some wayside inn, up to NO GOOD, as Tennessee always used to say when we asked him what he'd been up to.

I believe Tennessee changed the state of the generation that came after him in the United States and possibly the Western world. He was the first real American poet/playwright, whose loving exposition of what he called 'the fugitive kind' – the misfit, anti-hero, free spirit – spawned the Stanley Kowalski/Marlon Brando prototype. It is a role model that has been re-created by Hollywood with variations a thousand times since. The upheaval of the 1960s that brought with it hippies, drugs, rock 'n' roll, Bob Dylan, Joan Baez, human rights and black protest was set in motion by the public acceptance and celebration of Tennessee Williams' work.

I received wonderful notices for *Orpheus Descending*. Tony Snowdon (former husband of Britain's Princess Margaret) took some photos of me as Carol in the basement of the Royal Court on opening night. They appeared in the national papers the following day and we played to packed houses for the rest of the run. After the brouhaha had died down, Tennessee spoke to me about another play he was writing, saying that he thought I should play the young girl in it. It was to be called *Suddenly Last Summer*.

It was after my operation that Andrea came to tell me that my agent, Jimmy Fraser, was frantic to find out whether I was well enough to tackle work again. When Andrea enquired if he had anything specific for me, Jimmy said that Tennessee Williams was asking for me to do his new play *Suddenly Last Summer*. Jimmy insisted that he knew I would never be given insurance for a film but, as this was to be a theatrical production, insurance wasn't critical.

Professore Morelli laughed uproariously when I suggested work. Did I think I would not be a health hazard to my fellow actors being so contagious? Why did I think I was not allowed contact with my own child? Did I think I was different from the other TB patients? Besides, he'd heard that I'd been very, very naughty.

This last remark clearly referred to an incident that had the whole clinic buzzing and that made the nuns regard me as a beast as black-hearted as they considered the Buddha. It concerned the Australian actor Frank Thring (also known as Dank Thing). Outrageously camp, witty and fastidious, Frank was a gay icon in his native land, Melbourne's answer to Oscar Wilde. He had been a friend ever since my *Tiger at the Gates* days and he now found himself in Rome filming.

Having heard that I was ensconced in the heart of the Vatican, Frank decided to come and cheer me up. Armed with several bottles of Louis Roederer's best champagne, he presented himself at the Clinica Morelli's reception desk clad in a floor-length cape of purple velvet edged in ermine. When asked his name, he replied in Italian, hampered by an undershot jaw and a blatant Australian accent.

'Io sono Ponzio Pilato,' he rasped darkly. It was no lie as he had played Pontius Pilate in the 1959 American epic *Ben-Hur: A Tale of the Christ*. 'I've come to see la Principessa Cilento!'

After much consternation, with Frank bellowing his request repeatedly, they capitulated and he was escorted to my room by a bevy of nervous nuns. They stood inside the doorway preventing him from closing it, but Frank was having none of that. With a deft flick of the wrist and a pivot on his heel, he managed to oust the nuns, fling the door shut and have the top off the first bottle of bubbly in one orchestrated movement.

We could still hear the nuns whispering outside. After embracing me for real, Frank continued to make lewd kissing noises into the air, giving me a huge wink.

'*Mmmmmmmmm* . . . Yes, darling, yes, I love it! Do it again. *Ooooooh* . . . lovely, sweetheart. Oh, *ooooooooh*, yes, that's *soooo* good,' he began to pant. 'Oh, please keep doing it, darling. Ugh! Ugh! Ugh! I think I'm coming! I AM! YES! Agh . . . Agh . . . *Ahhhhhhhh! Mmmmmmmmm.* That was so good.'

It didn't help matters that I could not stop laughing helplessly at his wicked performance. I knew all the nuns standing on the other side of the door were beyond outrage at the imagined scenes of debauchery taking place within. Frank couldn't resist jerking the door open. He offered champagne to the flustered nuns, who fell into the room, but neither of us was surprised when they scuttled out, shaking their heads and muttering invocations. One or two even crossed themselves. I knew with deadly certainty that there would be a few more rusty needles in my already bruised backside before the week was out.

Of course, these goings on were reported pronto to Professore Morelli and the rest of the clinic with embellishments. I became the scarlet woman of the establishment. It felt very like being in trouble back at Glennie Memorial School for Girls again, only in Italian.

As the much anticipated, glorious Roman spring began to announce itself in the warbling of birds, sweetening of the air and lifting of hearts, I was allowed to take little trips into the world outside the Vatican. I had not realised how weak I was or how quickly I tired. At Frank Thring's instigation, and probably hearing his account of what a hoot it had been in the Vatican, many actors filming in Rome began phoning to ask whether they could take me to tea, to the trotting races at Villa Glori or to Cinecittà. I came back late from a hilarious outing with the Welsh actor Hugh Griffith to find a note from Professore Morelli on my pillow. I remember it to this day. It read: '*L'uccellino è fuggito dalla sua gabbia. Dove sei? Tuo marito è molto preoccupato! Anch'io.*' ('The little bird has escaped from her cage. Where are you? Your husband is very worried. I am, too.')

The very next day, it was decided that I should be taken out of Rome to Cervinia, up in the mountains on the border of Italy and Switzerland, where Andrea's family had a holiday house. I was not being given the anti-tubercular drug Isoniazid (Pasinah) as the Professore did not believe in it. Too modern. I knew I was not really improving much.

In Cervinia, I was to have my left lung collapsed every three or four days to give it a rest. This process, called pneumothorax, entails puncturing the wall of the lung and pumping air in, thus removing the vacuum that causes our lungs to fill with oxygen in ordinary breathing.

The entire family, including my daughter Giovanna, now a toddler, and the dreaded ex-wet-nurse Gianna, were there. I was so happy to see Gigi, even though I was not permitted to hold her. Elza was very strict about any tactility, especially with Andrea. We had managed a few quick embraces at the clinic, but in Cervinia it was difficult. Either Gianna or Elza was always in attendance playing watchdog. Our only time together was in the car coming back from my trips to the Dottore, down the mountain in Cervinia. After these passionate embraces we would inspect each other minutely for any telltale signs of our frenzied encounters.

The pattern of my life changed again. I had a small 'nun's' room into which no-one but myself and one of the Sardinian maids entered. In the morning I was allowed to play with Gigi on the floor, where her playpen was, but I could not lift her up, cuddle or kiss her. Before lunch, I would go for a walk on the mountain and inhale the thin air that made me breathless and slightly dizzy. After lunch, I would have a nap and then, in the evening, we played card games or Monopoly. Sometimes, at night, I would hear men's voices singing peasant songs that I seemed to recognise. Occasionally, they would break off and shout in unison but I could not make out the words. It was coming from somewhere very near and beneath me. It didn't sound like a radio, so I asked Andrea whether I was hallucinating.

'No, no,' he said. 'It's the Sicilians who live under the house.'

'Where?' I asked.

'Just under the house – in the open. They come up from the South for nine months every year to work for my father on his construction sites. He lets them sleep under the house. They love it. It saves them money.'

'But where do they eat? Where do they wash?'

'Oh, they only eat pasta with oil and chew garlic during the week.

They cook that up outside. If they wash, it's in one of the streams, I suppose. On Sunday, they go into Cervinia to go to church, and to eat and drink lots of vino. They go back to Palermo when it gets really cold at Christmas and their women have another baby every August.'

I had visions of joining them for a singalong but I never did. Not far from the house I had found a network of beautiful, narrow, swift streams rippling down the mountainside. I'd lower myself down beside the water and lie along the verge, watching the minuscule creatures that bustled about. There were serious water spiders zipping around in mysterious patterns, red and blue dragonflies, miniature green grasshoppers and bumble bees buzzing in the clover. Sometimes, looking intently into the reeds that were bent downstream by the pull of the hurrying water, I would see a trout dart out from its cover and expertly gulp down a fly that had been foolish enough to tarry too long in its sights. I began to collect flies and dig up worms. Staying low, I would quietly insert them into the water just upstream from where I knew a trout was hiding. Often, the tidbits just floated down the mountainside, but sometimes the trout could not resist. It would streak out of its safety zone and swallow the worm whole. Then, with one swerve of its body, it would be back in its place, awaiting the next mouthful of food to come into view.

The first time I saw the trout, I mentioned them at the lunch table, asking if anyone ever fished for them because they looked to me to be a good size for eating. There was a long pause. Everyone looked towards Giovanni, the Shrug, to pronounce judgement on trout fishing. With his usual gesture, still chewing his *saltimbocca alla Romana*, he uttered the last word on anyone stupid enough to try to catch a trout in a narrow mountain stream.

'No, it's a waste of time . . . not possible. The trout is too crafty. It can see the fool sitting there silhouetted against the skyline. Nobody I ever heard of has managed even one fish. I told the men I would give 100 000 lire for the first trout caught and 50 000 for each trout after that. No-one ever took me up on it.'

It sounded like a good deal to me. As I couldn't go swimming or participate in tennis or skating or any of the other sports that everyone else was rushing off to play, I decided that I would take up the Trout Challenge and maybe make enough money to get back to London. There I would be given proper drugs, like Isonazide, and get better. Otherwise, if I didn't get them soon, my recovery would be interminable. I was terrified of becoming fixed in the disagreeable role of La Povera Dianetta, the Volpe family's Permanently Ill Person.

There has to be a variable in every good equation and it wasn't long before I discovered that the Dottore in Cervinia, whom I visited every third day, had written two papers. One was on Chopin, in relation to the incidence of TB in the artistic confraternity, and the other was entitled 'La Vita della Trotta' ('The Life of the Trout'). I asked him to give me copies of both these tracts and he was flattered to comply, but it was 'La Vita della Trotta' which I read first and with great attention. Plans for my escape were beginning to take shape.

In retrospect, I picture my sojourn at Cervinia as an early Roman Polanski movie. To begin with, the Dottore turned out to bear an uncanny resemblance to Donald Pleasance at his most moist-lipped and sinister and, as I had to be bare breasted to undergo the pneumothorax procedure, I was not at all surprised that he availed himself of the opportunity to become over-familiar with my upper anatomy. I had been in Italy too long to expect otherwise. When I told Andrea that the Doc was a dirty old man, he vehemently insisted that it was impossible as the Dottore was an old friend of his father. I didn't bother to argue but when we were driving home I suggested that he pull over at the crossroads going out of town, where I had spotted a public telephone.

I phoned everybody from that callbox – Jimmy Fraser, my father, my sister Margaret and then Sean. Fatefully, Sean was the only person I managed to get through to. I impressed upon him my desperation and my urgent need to get out of Italy to avert the 'La Povera Dianetta' label, to obtain more modern treatment and to wrest Giovanna from the hairy hands of the gargoyle Gianna. I asked Sean to alert Jimmy Fraser and my sister that I was coming home. I told him that I would give him a number when I called again and that he should ring back immediately as I had hardly any money to feed the phone. All this accomplished, the die was cast and I ran back to join Andrea, who was impatiently sounding the horn of his mother's Maserati.

I didn't feel disloyal. To me, Andrea's complete capitulation to his former life of mummy's boy dependency and resignation to take his place in the inevitable line-up of competition for his father's approval made him seem like a quitter. I felt sorry for him. He was locked into the deadly tussle between his parents but prepared to play their game because it would keep him in funds without having to do any actual work. As his wife, I was caught in his slipstream and expected to play the game too. I just could not do it. This was not what I had spent my life preparing for.

My resolution hardened with every hour as I lay in my nun's bed in the big house on the mountain, listening to the men below singing out their defiance. Sometimes, I would creep down the stairs and stealthily enter the nursery to watch Giovanna while she slept. I went over and over how I would catch the first trout, just as though I was rehearsing a play. I called upon all the trout spirits in the cosmos to let one of their number be sacrificed to my resolve and, more practically, obtained a hand line and some trout-sized hooks and sinkers from the Dottore.

Each day as the summer advanced, I spent several hours observing where every trout in the surrounding streams was located. I did not attempt any line-in-the-water tactics until I was certain what their habits were in the morning and evening, when they were the hungriest, and what was their food preference. I practised lying down beside the stream, holding the line and pulling it at the same time. I even experimented with goggles and placing my head underwater but discovered that it was a very bad idea for someone with my illness.

I never imagined that there could ever be such a moment of sheer elation as the one when I landed the first trout. I thought of Buddha having his first ecstasy at the symmetry of the universal food chain. My ecstasy was as the predator fulfilling my destiny, hunting for sustenance, the tiger stalking the deer. I had done it, captured the prey, and here it was, my pearly victim, swimming around in a bucket, the most expensive trout in the world.

I had learned ultra patience, quite out of character, to snare my beautiful fish – waiting, hugging the earth, watching like a cat, completely still, utterly focused, anticipating the moment when greed could be repressed no longer and the silver body would flash forward to swallow the bait. We were synchronised to perfection and I felt the galvanic electricity of his being the instant he moved. It shot through my arm, and I jerked the line mightily. I knew I had him.

I caught two more fish that day and carried them back to the house, trying to contain my excitement. Everyone was quite flummoxed by my feat, none more so than my father-in-law. His eyebrows flew up and his mouth turned down. At first, he was very suspicious that Andrea and I had colluded and bought the fish to trick him out of his money. In the end, he grudgingly paid the full price of 200 000 lire, which was not bad for a day's work, and Elza's chef cooked the fish with crunchy sliced almonds on top. I relished the one mouthful I ate. It completed the entire undertaking and tasted just like money. By the end of the month, Giovanni had paid me 400 000 lire – enough to set Giovanna and me on our way. I was exhausted.

There followed a time of intrigue. Clandestinely, with Sean's help, I was in touch with Jimmy Fraser, who received advice from Arnold Goodman (Lord Goodman, the most adept lawyer in London). One-way airline tickets were arranged from Torino Airport to London Heathrow, and I hired a taxi to take Giovanna and me all the way to the airport. I ingratiated myself with the Dottore to procure a letter which stated that, in his opinion, I needed medication, specifically Isoniazid, to make a complete recovery. The addendum stated that it was unlikely that I was still contagious.

It was only after all these things had been accomplished that I went to Giovanni Volpe and informed him that I was leaving, taking Giovanna with me. If I had gone to anyone else, there would have been a monumental upheaval akin to an eruption of Vesuvius. Going to the Capo precluded dramatic scenes, tantrums, squabbles and machinations between Elza and Andrea about who would tell Babbo (Big Daddy) the distressing news.

It is the only time I ever had a satisfactory talk with my father-in-law. We discussed my illness and the fact that my recovery was hampered by not having proper medication. I backed myself up by producing the letter that I intended to show the doctor in London. He flattered me by saying that I had '*sangue dei pionieri*' (pioneers' blood) running in my veins and that his family could use such an infusion. I said that I didn't have any to spare at that moment.

We did not discuss Andrea or Giovanna at all but it was decided that, after six months, he would send an attorney to London to determine if I would return to Italy or seek a marriage annulment. Thus it was that I arrived back in London with my daughter, to be met at the airport by Sean and to recount the improbable stories of trout fishing in Cervinia and life backstage at the Vatican.

CHAPTER SIX

*I*t was with enormous relief that I settled back into Caroline House. I sat behind Sean on my old Vespa while he whirled me off to a doctor named Lee Lander. It was rapture to put my arms around his strong, warm back and breathe him in. He smelt so good – not just of man but of safety, protection and devotion. I hadn't experienced that heady aroma for a long time.

My feelings for Sean at this time were tempered by a strong sense of gratitude for his staying power through the vicissitudes of my turbulent life. Before that summer we had kept up a sort of wise-cracking, jovial intimacy, which had strict boundaries. I had relied on him, but was not in love with him. Now, although we never spoke about love, in some strange subliminal way our relationship had changed. Somehow, I knew he was to play an integral part in my future.

In order to get better, I had to take twenty-four lozenge-sized pink pills every day and visit the Brompton Chest Hospital twice a week. At first, I tried to take too many pills at once and couldn't keep them down. They stuck in my craw, causing me to cough, but I finally mastered the art and they went down accompanied by a bit of dry retching and some good gulps of red wine.

I had arrived in the middle of one of those memorable English summers that occur every ten or eleven years, when the temperature soars and the sunny days seem to stretch into infinity. People rush to Kensington Gardens or Regent's Park, turning bright pink and then various shades of brown so that they don't look English any more. Elderly people in stuffy houses perish of heat exhaustion while the lucky ones get out of London and fill up the coastal holiday resorts all over the country.

By some unknown convoluted process, a group of us had been lent Lady Duff-Cooper's seaside residence at Bognor for the remainder of the summer. I'd never been to Bognor before. In fact, I'd only ever heard of Bognor as reputedly being one of two words uttered by George V as he lay on his deathbed at Sandringham House. To rally his royal patient, the King's physician suggested that His Majesty would soon be well enough to visit Bognor, his favourite retreat. 'Bugger Bognor,' the King barked and promptly died.

Lady Diana was selling her house and wanted it to be filled with young people while potential buyers were inspecting. Her maid Waddle (a very Restoration-comedy name for a domestic) lived in the gatehouse and ensured we weren't trashing the place. It was a gorgeous property with a wide, walled garden that ran right down to the water. There were two buildings joined by cloisters, a comprehensive library containing some very instructive, beautifully produced pornography and a master (or rather mistress) bedroom decorated with seashells and hands. The bed was a great scallop shell inspired by Botticelli's *Birth of Venus* and I sank into its depths, a piece of grit, hoping to wake up a pearl.

Coming from the sub-tropical climes of Queensland, where the sun beats down on a different tonal variety of greens, I'd always found England's verdant, lamb-filled fields too picturesque and cloying. True to my origins, I disdained the centuries of cultivation that characterised the European countryside. There seemed something smug and staid in the precision of a million miles of stone fences.

Yet the beauty of the garden at Bognor could not be denied. It was an unparalleled marvel of a hundred years of care and genius. Graduated in size running back to the ancient russet brick wall were a profusion of pansies, giant orange poppies, pink peonies, larkspurs, delphiniums, wallflowers and golden rod. Its opulence was almost overwhelming, as though it had been waiting for such a summer to show off to us colonials what a resplendent thing an English country garden can be. It was the perfect place for a convalescent.

That summer, Giovanna and I stayed down in Bognor all week long, swimming in the sea and getting to know each other again while the others went up to London to do their various jobs. Then, at the weekends, there would be a convergence of young actors, dancers, designers and friends scurrying out of the city and ending up at Bognor – Sean, Gary Raymond, Delena Kidd and her sister, Keith Baxter-Wright, Peter Kerr and a host of others. Even Yat Malmgren turned up and we had an impromptu floor class on the lawn.

In the evenings we played charades as well as some wonderfully spooky games of Murder, using both houses. There were great feasts in candlelit areas of the garden, where an assortment of food brought by weekenders was laid out – sausages, caviar, éclairs, smoked salmon, passionfruit, pumpkins and lots of drink. I was never out of my red bikini except to deck myself in whatever silks and flowing robes I found scattered around the house. I began to feel my strength coming back and was not coughing so much, although I still had to rest in the afternoons and didn't accompany the others when they went on pub crawls or to the pier.

One torrid afternoon I was having a vivid dream in the scallop bed, during which I had thrown off my bathing suit. I could hear hundreds of voices whispering in my ears. A crowd of people was looking for me, shuffling along the passages somewhere near. I could hear them calling my name. Somehow I knew I was in a cubicle within a maze of rooms and that the place was a bordello. I was excited and terrified at

159

the same time, and tried to burrow down under the sheet but a high-pitched female voice said intimately in my ear, 'Don't worry, dear, it's only Huntley and Palmer's Biscuits.'

I awoke and stood up in the bed in one movement, clutching the sheet. The room *was* filled with people. It wasn't a dream at all. Silhouetted against the light was a throng of dark spectres ready to pounce and I heard an upper-class English voice say something like, 'You see, I told you so, darlings. It's Venus on the half-shell. Come along. Let her go back to her slumbers.'

With that, the spectres all filed out. They weren't as fearsome when I looked closely at them as they passed through the door, just some gentlemen in bowler hats casting sideways glances at my nudity and ladies fanning themselves with real-estate brochures pretending I was part of the furniture. They were being ushered by the lady herself, Diana Duff-Cooper, splendidly costumed in a dark blue, double-breasted naval officer's outfit glinting with gold buttons. I could hear her voice trailing off down the corridors as she pointed out views of the sea and the delights of sunken bathtubs. For a long time, I could still feel my heart thumping with the abruptness of their appearance and swiftness of their departure.

Years later, I was told by my great friend Bumble Dawson, the best dinner party hostess in London, who lived near Lady Diana in Little Venice, that Lady Diana actually inhabited an alternative reality of her own invention. Bumble cited as evidence the night Lady Diana was going to the opera to see *Tosca*. As she and her companion were about to leave the house, two men with stockings over their heads burst in and overpowered them.

'Take that silly thing off your head, Nigel,' shouted Lady Diana. 'It makes you look exceedingly ugly. I know it's you. You're being a very silly boy and I shall tell your mother!'

Her outburst was greeted with much Cockney grunting and scoffing.

'And it's no use putting on that gutter accent either. I've known you since you were in nappies. You can't fool me, Nigel! You always were a little tyke.'

By this time, the two intruders were getting very annoyed indeed but Diana kept up her barrage, threatening Nigel with disclosure to various relatives. The two ladies were finally bound up, Diana shrieking that if they must have their fun, they should tie the knots loosely lest they be late for the opera. When the robbers left, taking some jewellery and other items, Diana freed herself in a few minutes, phoned the police and was ready with a description of her assailants as the Old Bill walked through the door.

'Can't miss the murder of Scaprio. It's my favourite moment in the whole caboodle,' she cried, waving to the fingerprint men as she left. Needless to say, neither of the thieves was called Nigel.

One weekend during that summer Sean and I went to Scotland to visit his parents in Fountainbridge, Edinburgh. Joe and Effie Connery had lived in the same hideous building for over thirty years. The squalid stairway that led to their fourth-floor walkup, worn into scallops by countless feet, was quite a shock but Sean proudly showed me the 'back green' where he had played as a boy. I misunderstood what he said and thought it was called the 'black green' as a joke because it was a strip of tarmac ten feet wide squeezed between the dismal Victorian edifices.

It was easy to see where Sean got his looks. Effie, who was a good head taller than Joe, had huge brown eyes under winged brows. Her delineated features were of a dark beauty seen in illustrations of Celtic fairytales, though she seemed to be entirely unconscious of her striking appearance. Effie called me 'hen' straightaway and launched into stories of naughty behaviour in the rubber factory where she had met Joe. I could only understand every second word she said, but I liked her strong self-esteem and assertive manner. Without a doubt, she wore the trousers in that family.

161

There was also a subtle suggestion in the way Effie treated Joe that she had married beneath her station. She was a Maclean while he was the son of a tinker who had come from Ireland to trade horses and call around at backdoors to mend pots. But Joe Connery was an ebullient little man who loved telling jokes, which I found incomprehensible. He did a mean James Cagney impersonation, hitching up his trousers with his elbows and snapping the brim of an imaginary hat while standing splay-legged on the balls of his feet. 'Ya dirty rat,' he'd say in that high-pitched Cagney delivery. 'I'll blow ye away.'

Sean had a profound reverence for his parents, as attested to by the tattoos he bore on his arm. Amid scrolls and flourishes, one read 'MUM & DAD'; the other proclaimed 'SCOTLAND FOREVER'. They were legacies of his time in the Boys' Navy. Sean told me that Effie had kept a packed bag under his bed after the birth of his brother Neil, who was nine years younger, threatening that if her elder son played up on her any more she would send him off for some discipline in the Navy. Sean went to Whale Island, Portsmouth, and probably would have become an old Scottish salt had he not been invalided out of the service three years later with stomach ulcers, for which he received weekly medical benefits for years.

It's difficult for those who haven't experienced a particular era to imagine its peculiarities. At the beginning of the sixties there were strict social mores in Britain pertaining to many things we take for granted today. Homosexuality was still firmly locked in the cupboard, although screaming to come out. Censorship was being tweaked by Kenneth Tynan but D. H. Lawrence's *Lady Chatterley's Lover* could only be read by those who had smuggled in a copy from the Continent. And no serious actor would be seen dead in a TV commercial.

Undoubtedly, those of us who lived through that incandescent time in London look back and are still astonished at the craziness of it all. Quite suddenly, the inhibitions that had been packed down tight into the British psyche since Queen Victoria came to the throne were thrown out the window. Dionysius rules OK became Dionysius rules UK, and the more outrageous we could be the better. A generation of little Lord Byrons had been spawned, who took pleasure in being 'mad, bad and dangerous to know'. The combination of LSD, marijuana, mescaline, the pill, peyote, Carlos Castaneda, the Goons, the Beatles and Carnaby Street blew away all the old concepts of the past and left us breathless.

Personally, I did not find Mary Jane to my taste. It dried up my throat and gave me back my nasty hacking cough that was so reminiscent of my Vatican sojourn. Instead, I experimented with Alice B. Toklas hash brownies, which were wondrous . . . but not too often. They destroyed one's timing on stage and finally I found being 'stoned' basically boring. I was aware that there was a threshold for alcohol and dope – for all addictions, in fact – a threshold beyond which it could harm or even kill you.

I was now no longer a convalescent, and so began a phase of rushing back and forth across the Atlantic. Lists of archaic productions and names of obscure thespians are what make actors' obituaries often so tedious, so I shall elaborate on some of the more interesting of my adventures and fellow actors in the extravaganzas that ensued.

First, I was off to New York to do *Heartbreak House* on Broadway with Harold Clurman directing once again. George Bernard Shaw wrote *Heartbreak House* as a pungent diatribe against British Imperial culture. Prophesying, with anger and despair, what was in store for England after World War I, Shaw's mouthpiece, Captain Shotover, screams at the end of the play, 'We are all headed for the rocks!' I appeared as the spirited ingénue Ellie Dunn for the play's limited season, which inaugurated the Billy Rose Theatre on 42nd Street.

Our company was crammed with larger-than-life actors. One of my all-time favourite actresses played Lady Utterword; I had seen her in my student days in *The Lady's Not for Burning* by Christopher Fry. She was a fascinating, fey, red-haired beauty called Pamela Brown, and I was immediately smitten by her sense of the absurd and wry humour. I still have a digitally sharp image of her in my head at a costume fitting we attended together. She is standing nude in front of a full-length mirror, contemplating her body with absolute candour and no hint of bitterness. One round pendulous breast is much higher than the other and one of her hips protrudes horribly, twisted with arthritis. Holding up her misshapen fingers, which she always manages to hide so cleverly onstage, she asks with a mocking smile, 'Do you think this look will ever come back?'

For a short time, during the run of the play, I became besotted with American football. The reason for my infatuation was a New York Giant. He was everything the American hero of that moment was meant to be – tall, crew-cutted and soft-spoken, with a jaw and a build like Superman's. What more could a girl desire? Pamela Brown put paid to the courtship with one short sentence delivered as a gentle reprimand after she met the gentleman.

'Yes, very nice, dear . . . but afterwards, what do you *talk* about?'

Sam Levene played the role of Menken, the industrialist, with the same abandon he did everything. It was full-tilt, no-holds-barred acting, which demanded reciprocal energy. I loved Sam. He lived in a hotel on 57th Street, opposite Central Park, with only a pet canary for company but he had ordered his life with such precision that he enjoyed every instant as though it was his last.

Then there was Dennis Price, the former darling of British films, who had played the lead in the unforgettable *Kind Hearts and Coronets* with Alec Guinness. He was, by now, an undischarged bankrupt, alcoholic and outdated heartthrob, though still superb, wandering the streets of New York every night in search of romance . . . and drink. He played Hector Hushabye, the swashbuckling husband of Hesione, which part was encompassed by the redoubtable Diana Wynyard.

Diana was considered all her life to be a great beauty, and she carried about that special inner regard which all great beauties have. Unfortunately, this envied breed seldom have any vestige of humour, especially not about their own physical appearance, and Diana was no exception to the rule. This trait invited one of the most disastrous practical jokes I have ever witnessed.

Maurice Evans, co-producer with Billy Rose, was our boss and fellow cast member, playing the part of Captain Shotover. Unkindly called the poor man's John Gielgud, Maurice had come to the United States from Britain in 1935 to understudy that great actor's Hamlet but stayed on to forge a formidable career as one of the best-known British classical actors on the American stage. It was Maurice who perpetrated the ill-fated practical joke on Diana.

It was my habit to slip into Pamela's dressing room when I came into the theatre and then again just before the curtain. She opened the play lying indolently in a hammock and I was intrigued by her extraordinary knack of holding a full swig of cognac in her mouth until the very last moment before she spoke the first lines of the play. She did it perfectly and with such nonchalance that I was taking lessons.

One night, Maurice tapped on her door and came in with his assistant/boyfriend to ask us in a conspiratorial tone if we would lure Diana in the next evening after she had made her nightly visit to the loo at the half-hour call.

'Why?' we asked in unison.

'Because we're going to switch her wig while she's out of her dressing room.'

'Oh, God! Don't *do* it,' said Pamela firmly.

'Why not?' asked Maurice, hardly able to contain his delight. 'We found this disgusting old balding red wig I wore as Macbeth twenty-eight years ago. It'll be a hoot. She'll love it.'

'Diana? You must be mad,' Pamela retorted, though I could see a secret smile forming behind her eyes. After that, she held her tongue.

The next night, Pamela called Diana in on her way back to her dressing room and we had a brief conversation about the curtain calls, which had been getting ragged. Then Pamela doled out a thimbleful of cognac to each of us to prime our vocal chords. We toasted one another and off Diana toddled to get into costume and call her dresser, Doreen, to help put on her luxuriant red wig.

There has never been a human sound quite like the one which issued from Diana Wynyard's dressing room that night. It could easily have been on the soundtrack of *Jurassic Park*. There was an ominous silence and then all hell broke loose. Some high-pitched squeals interspersed with guttural yells resounded throughout the theatre, before a voice shrieked,' DORR . . . EEENN! YOU BITCH! DOR–REEN! HOW DARE YOU? I'M AN O–B–EEEEEEE!'

Diana then appeared in the corridor, waving her arms and sobbing. Her head was bound up ready for the wig but mascara was streaming down her cheeks. She was Lady Macbeth in the midst of the mad scene. Diana was certain that her dresser, Doreen, had vandalised her wig to spite her and nothing could persuade her otherwise. Even when a timorous Maurice Evans tried to explain that it had all been a joke and that the genuine wig had been restored to her wig stand, she refused to listen.

Meanwhile, Doreen had quite sensibly ducked out the stage door onto Broadway and didn't return during the performance. My dresser had to double up and change Diana as well. The curtain was held up for at least twenty minutes while Diana repaired her make-up and calmed down but she gave an extremely paranoid performance that night, looking over her shoulder continuously and muttering under her breath. She clearly believed we had all been complicit in the affair, and it didn't help matters when I mistook my line in the last act, describing 'Hesione's beautiful hair' as 'Hesione's beautiful wig'. I could have bitten my tongue off. Diana didn't speak to any of us for two weeks. She also insisted on a new dresser and large locks were fitted to her dressing-room door. Maurice never quite admitted that it had been his idea of a 'jolly wheeze'.

Later, when I recounted the story to Noel Coward, he laughed uproariously and made me tell it all over again with embellishments. Then, wiping tears of mirth from his eyes, he quipped in his inimitable way, 'Poor, poor Diana. She wouldn't crack a smile if a kipper flew out of her cunt!'

Billy Rose owned the very first stretch limo with smoked windows that I ever rode in. He used to pick me up after the show to watch me wolf down egg foo yong and lobster Cantonese at his favourite Chinese restaurant (he always ate earlier), and then his chauffeur would drive me home. It was a peculiar courtship.

Once he arrived unannounced at my apartment on Manhattan's Upper West Side at lunchtime. The door was opened by my friend Rufus, a black actor from the Living Theatre, who happened to be holding my daughter Giovanna in his arms. Giovanna was by now a gorgeous child of almost four, whose golden ringlets and rounded downy cheeks gave her the look of a Renaissance cherub. I could see that Billy was nonplussed.

'Oh,' Billy remarked, looking at Giovanna, 'a Ty-pollo angel!'

'What?' asked Rufus.

'You know, Ty-pollo, the artist.'

'Oh . . . Tiepolo!' we chorused.

'Yeah,' said Billy, eyeing us with undisguised displeasure. 'Dat's what I like about you kids. Ya got class!'

That afternoon, Billy took me to the David Belasco Theatre on 44th Street, which had been converted into television studios. A private elevator at the back of the theatre took us to a magnificent apartment in the uppermost part of the building. It was decorated in the same deep red velvet as the theatre and you could open a curtain to look down on the handkerchief-sized stage miles below. As we watched a skeleton crew rehearsing *The Ed Sullivan Show*, Billy explained that this had been David Belasco's hideaway from where he could keep tabs on the actors and, at the same time, entertain in private. He winked, saying that he admired David Belasco above all men for his style – except for Bernard Baruch, for whom he had worked in Europe. He had always wanted to own the Belasco Theatre, Billy told me, and now it was his.

'Here's the deal,' he explained. 'I'll rent this apartment to you for a dollar a month, no strings attached, just so you let me come round whenever, play with the Ty-Pollo angel and watch them shooting *The Ed Sullivan Show*.'

I looked at this diminutive dapper man with mournful eyes and suddenly saw Sean standing in his place. It was no contest. Poor Billy just wasn't my cup of tea. Besides, my mum was about to arrive and I knew without a shadow of a doubt that her approval rating of Billy Rose and his apartment would be zero.

But Billy was a hard man to dump. I suspect he went through the same routine with all the young ingénues in his productions. His next ploy was to take me to his mansion after the show. We drove a long way up the West Side and stopped outside a massive, sombre edifice which backed onto the Hudson River. I have never been in a more extraordinary private house.

Directly in front of you as you entered was a bar that was papered – ceiling and walls – with hundreds of sheet-music scores and publicity stills of Billy standing next to every name in world affairs and entertainment. Of course, he pointed out that he had written most of the songs himself, including the prominently displayed 'It's Only a Paper Moon'.

An enormous party room opened up behind the bar, the walls of which were covered with delicately painted panels of shepherds and shepherdesses on swings, frolicking in the pastel spring sunshine of rural France. The panels looked like genuine Louis Quatorze, except that all the original faces had been effaced and the features of every famous showbiz personality painstakingly painted in. The toothy grin of the comedienne Fanny Brice, Billy's first wife, twinkled up at Clark Gable's dark majesty. Spencer Tracy, Kate Hepburn, Ethel Merman, Bogie, Stan Laurel, Oliver Hardy, Sydney Greenstreet and Charlie Chaplin looked like lunatics flouncing about in their frills and mop caps. Billy was immensely proud that he'd found some impoverished Polish genius to re-create the style perfectly.

He led me downstairs to an equally large basement where Salvador Dali had been encouraged to go mad. Surrealistic hippos and elephants lumbered along the walls, while deserts and jungles filled with grotesqueries were meant to represent every aspect of the entertainment industry. A hidden door led outside onto a walkway where Henry Moore sculptures were tastefully lit. One empty plinth had obviously held the bust of G. B. Shaw, which now graced the Billy Rose Theatre foyer.

Back in the house, we climbed a fretted oak staircase and arrived in the study, at the entrance of which stood a superb model of a schooner in full sail. Ticker tape encoded with the world's stock prices clicked out of an old-fashioned glass dome and fell in spirals on the floor. The master desk was immense and the leather sofas, with their gleaming buttons, looked as though no-one had ever sat on them. Beyond, sliding doors opened onto a long verandah overlooking the Hudson River.

'Ya gotta see this,' said Billy, moving to the end of the deck.

He seemed to pull a lever, although I couldn't quite see, and like magic an entire island lit up some distance downstream in the dark water of the Hudson River. I was not convinced. It seemed so unreal.

'Did *you* do that?' I asked in amazement.

'Sure I did. Do ya wanna see it again?'

So, we stood there while Billy flipped the switch and his island flickered out of sight only to light up all over again at his touch. It was impossible not to be impressed. Expressing admiration has never been easy for me but I tried to convey my wonder at what he had done, telling him how incredibly talented I thought he was to have brought off such a bewildering variety of winners. I truly believe that's what Billy wanted to hear more than anything else.

'Okay . . . Okay . . . Enough already,' he said, holding up his hands while his eyes urged me to continue. 'You'll be giving me a swollen head soon. Hey, kid, I got one last treat for you. I'm gonna show ya my bedroom.'

I had dreaded this moment all evening and began stammering about how I had to get up early the next morning to go to the airport to meet my mother, who was arriving from Australia. Billy laughed and gave my shoulder a little punch.

'Hey, kid, I'm not gonna jump ya. I'm just gonna show ya where I sleep.'

Warily, I climbed the narrow staircase to the top of the house, but there was no immense bed piled high with cushions of myriad shapes and colours, nor a four-poster with black satin sheets and seductive lighting, nor even a mirror on the ceiling. Billy slept in a single, iron-framed, trundle bed in a small monastic room with no decoration of any kind.

'Ya didn't expect that didja, kiddo?' he chuckled as he helped me into the limousine. 'So long, honey. Stay well. You're a very cute gal and you've got class.'

And thus ended my romance with the illustrious Billy Rose.

William Makepeace Thackeray's heroine Becky Sharp in *Vanity Fair* is a character I love and I had always wanted to play her. When I heard that a major television company had asked for me in the role, I jumped at the chance, even though it meant doing two jobs a day. I was making up for all the months of idleness that my illness had enforced, and my mum was on hand to help with Giovanna.

Two things about that production of *Vanity Fair* stand out strongly. One was the fact that the sponsor of the show was a brand of shampoo, so I was constantly being coiffed with new and ever more elaborate hairstyles that seemed to take more time than the acting. The other remarkable feature was my meeting with the man who had adapted Thackeray's book, who was another sort of American hero, a brilliant young academic. Such a clever wordsmith was he that he'd been chosen to ghost many of John F. Kennedy's speeches and documentaries. I was transfixed by his tales of Kennedy's cold, calculating blue eyes and being locked into rooms in Washington hotels, where he'd been forced to remain for days until he had finished the work to the satisfaction of both Robert and John F. I was tapped into the source of the words that emerged from the President's mouth. It was heady stuff.

I'd hardly had time to catch my breath after we wrapped *Vanity Fair* when I was made another offer I couldn't refuse. It was called *The Good Soup*. André Barsacq's original production of *La Bonne Soupe* had been a *succès fou* in Paris, with Jeanne Moreau and Marguerite Moreno playing the same part as the younger and older Marie-Paule. What was proposed by David Merrick, the producer, was that I play the young Moreau part and Ruth Gordon play Moreno's role as the older Marie-Paule. Garson Kanin, Ruth's husband, would direct, keeping the same moves, costumes and lighting that had worked so well in Paris, and the play was to open at the Plymouth Theatre after a short tour.

The setting is a casino in Monte Carlo where the older Marie-Paule goes in the afternoons when business is slack. She tells her life story to the croupier, while the audience sees each scene enacted by the young Marie-Paule. Then, in a dazzling moment of theatrical brilliance, youth and age meet centre stage, a coffee pot changes hands and youth backs into the darkness, to disappear forever.

A huge cast was assembled, as there were about forty speaking parts. Of course, some actors played three roles, which meant that there was much changing of costumes and leaping about in the wings. Sam

Levene came with me to the production of *The Good Soup*, playing the salacious Odilon; Mildred Natwick played my mother; Ernest Truex, a veteran of a hundred early movies, played Monsieur Gaston; and the greatest of all comic actors I have ever encountered, Zero Mostel, rehearsed the role of the croupier.

It was a delight to be in a production with Zero. He was truly epic. Every day he would show us fresh evidence of his genius. I shall never forget watching mesmerised as he stitched all his fingers together in mime, meticulously tying the knot and biting off the thread. Then he attempted to play the piano with sewn-up fingers. No-one, not even the great Marcel Marceau, could equal Zero's credibility quotient. You would have sworn he'd actually sutured his digits together. He had a big rotund body like a Jewish Buddha, despite which he seemed to be able to move with extraordinary agility. Sadly, in the third week of rehearsal, Zero was run over by a bus on Broadway (an inauspicious omen boding ill for things to come). Though no bones were broken, he had to remain in hospital for months and so, as the show must go on, he was replaced by another classic Jewish comic, Jules Munshin.

As I was playing the youthful Ruth Gordon, I paid particular attention to her voice patterns. She had an explosive laugh and a penetrating, rather raspy voice that could be heard right at the back of the gods. I endeavoured to bring the beginnings of these vocal identities into my deliveries. Marie-Paule was the first part I ever had difficulty in learning – perhaps my brain was in overload with all the different roles I had been playing.

We travelled to Philadelphia, the city of brotherly love, where we were to open and iron out any of the wrinkles. Opening night went well and the audience loved it, applauding wildly at the end. Both Ruth and I were called back many times. I went home exhausted and slept like a baby.

We were called for rehearsal the next morning and the whole cast (except for Ruth Gordon, who was said to be resting) gathered in the large bar area under the foyer of the theatre. The reviews were laid out for all to see and I gasped as I spotted my name in one of the headlines. I was being hailed as a great new find, a star in the making. I was thrilled.

Garson Kanin came in and greeted the cast with gravitas. He sat down in his usual fashion, high on the chair with one leg tucked under the other in half-lotus position. 'Well,' he said, 'you did very creditably for a first outing but what was abundantly apparent from last night's performance is that the play is far too long. We're going to have to make some cuts. Now turn to page six . . . Diane.'

The whole cast groaned in unison. He then proceeded to gut and fillet my part. All the really good laugh lines went. It didn't make sense except that, of course, it did. It was to be Ruthie's triumphant return to Broadway and he couldn't allow someone else to steal his wife's thunder. I was devastated and could hardly contain my tears. The murmurs of sympathy and exclamations of horror from my fellow actors were of little comfort as I saw all my best moments disappear and thought of all the horrible rehearsal time that would be needed to patch up what was left. In fact, the whole cast was dejected at the end of that savage pruning. As we were about to leave, Garson called us all back.

'We had hoped that the author of this work, Félicien Marceau, would be joining us on tour and staying for the opening in New York but there's been a little hitch. Félicien has not been granted a visa to enter the United States. As you know, Félicien is from Belgium. Before the war, he worked as the director of an arts program on the radio. When the Germans invaded Belgium, he did not forsake his job but stayed on, using the program as a means to deliver many messages to the Allies under the guise of dramatic works. The problem is that the immigration authorities here are saying that he worked for the Nazis during the Occupation. It's rubbish, and I'm sure it will be worked out soon. Oh, by the way, I'd rather you kept this news under your hats for the time being, thank you. I'll see you all at eleven o'clock tomorrow morning, when we'll begin implementing the cuts.'

I rushed to the loo, where I locked myself into a cubicle and had a good blub. When I came out, everybody had left. I went to the telephone box to call my mother in New York to tell her the wonderful and the terrible news but it was already occupied by one of the minor actors, who was shouting into the receiver. He was repeating the Félicien Marceau story saying, 'I tell you he worked for the Nazis in Belgium. Yes, he's Belgian . . . F-E-L-I-C-I-E-N . . . Yes, M . . . No, not N . . . M for Mary A-R-C-E-A-U. That's it. And that'll be fifty this time. Yes, I said fifty! And the same to you!'

He put down the receiver, turned, and almost jumped out of his skin when he saw me standing there staring at him with my mouth open. 'Oh,' he said, 'I thought you'd all gone.'

'No, not me,' I said. 'I've got to call my mother.'

'Yeah, well, I was calling mine just now. I'm sorry about your part,' he said, sidling around me uneasily, and he was gone.

I was only mildly surprised the next day when the headlines in the Broadway rags screamed the news that some prominent Jewish theatricals, namely Ruth Gordon, Garson Kanin, Sam Levene and Jules Munshin, were appearing in a play written by a Nazi and that the prominent Jewish producer David Merrick planned to open this 'insult to those who died in the Holocaust' at the Plymouth Theatre in March.

What did surprise me was the furor that ensued. The misplaced ire generated by Félicien Marceau's innocuous job at a radio station in downtown Antwerp was frightening. Jewish societies, with millions of dollars' worth of pre-bookings, cancelled immediately. When we got to New York, dead flowers were sent to the actors and we were picketed outside the stage door every night by hordes of enraged people brandishing signs and swastikas. They made us run the gauntlet as they prodded us with umbrellas and shouted insults in our faces. The actor who was responsible for the whole episode never made it into the theatre on opening night. Someone hit him on the head with a placard and he was carried off to the hospital, never to be seen again. I never told anyone about his act of treachery nor the measly fifty Judas bucks he'd been paid for the story.

Needless to say, the cuts to my part were still implemented and I was having a hard time containing my bitterness at having been so deprived. I spoke to Garson Kanin after the show at the end of the first week. He sat down in my little dressing room on the third floor, listening as I tried to explain that this was not the part I had signed to play. I asked him how could he have seen the play in Paris, with Jeanne Moreau performing my part, and not realised that it was an equal leading role. I requested to be released from my contract.

'What did the bitch want?' I heard Ruth's rasping voice demand as I passed her dressing room on my way out of the theatre.

My mother's reaction to the whole thing was very interesting. In the second week of the run, when I came home cursing my fate, she took me by the arm. 'Come here,' she said, leading me into the bedroom where Giovanna was asleep. She stood me in front of the mirror and held my head steady.

'Look,' she said.

'What at?'

'Look at your eyes.'

'What about them? Are they a bit bloodshot or something?'

'No,' she said. 'They're filled with hate. I haven't been a doctor for thirty years not to recognise that look. It's the look that manufactures poison in your blood. You must learn to stop making poison inside yourself or you'll get sick again.'

Then she held my head again as I sobbed, and when Giovanna woke up crying we all had a good cry together. After that, I felt much better. The play was withdrawn after only twenty-one performances. I rushed back to London and fell into Sean's arms with a riven heart.

CHAPTER SEVEN

I suppose we chose Portugal because of Inez de Castro. We got hold of a little blue car, a Fiat I think it was, and drove across the Channel to Biarritz on the Spanish border in southern France and, after a quick surf, on through the hinterland of Spain. Our destination was Coimbra, the serene cathedral city where Inez is buried.

Henry de Montherlant's *La Reine Morte* ('Queen after Death') was a play that had haunted me since I'd played Inez at the Oxford Playhouse. Her story is unique. She was brought to Portugal as the lady-in-waiting to the Infanta of Spain, who was to marry Pedro, heir to the throne of Portugal, thus uniting the two countries. The young prince fell passionately and irrevocably in love with the beautiful Inez and, with the collusion of the Infanta, who also loved Inez, he secretly married her instead of the Infanta. The couple already had one child and were expecting another before word of their 'arrangement' reached the ears of the king. He flew into a titanic rage and had his son seized and thrown into prison.

While the prince was incarcerated, the king brought Inez to his court to interview her. He too became entranced by Inez and decided to accept her as his daughter-in-law. However, two of his advisors convinced him that his only recourse was to have Inez put out of the way. The order was given for her execution, and while he was travelling from the court her murderers caught up with her and she was decapitated.

The king died of a stroke within hours of her assassination.

When the prince heard of her death, he was so grief-stricken that he lost all reason. Having escaped from prison just as news of his father's death reached him, he made his way to the court, where, it is said, he ate the hearts of the two advisors. The prince then summoned every noble family in Portugal to join a procession from Lisbon to Coimbra bearing the body of the embalmed Inez.

She was set on the throne as queen in all her regal garments, a crown was placed upon her head and each of the aristocracy came forward to swear allegiance to the throne, kissing the ring on her lifeless finger. Inez was then interred with a thousand jewels in a magnificent tomb on the right side of the cathedral, feet facing the nave, while a matching tomb was prepared for Pedro on the left side. His feet would also face inwards so that on Judgement Day, as he said, 'We can arise and look each other in the eye.'

After the death of Inez, Pedro ruled the country with a heavy hand, becoming known in history as Pedro the Cruel. He left a deathless edict that, should anyone desecrate her tomb, they would find no peace from that day forward and would die like dogs. It was Napoleon Bonaparte who broke the curse when, desperate for money to finance his campaigns, he allowed his troops to rob the tomb of Inez. It is said that he never won another battle after this flouting of fate and suffered an ignoble death as a prisoner on an obscure island.

We entered Coimbra at night in the moonlight and found a room with a long balcony overlooking the river and a bridge. As Sean and I sat outside in the lemon-scented night, I looked down imagining the long procession of nobles dressed in their finery solemnly bearing the dead queen to her last resting place.

I told Sean about the night I was playing Inez when Leo McKern's glass eye fell out onstage. The set had a raked stage so that when the eyeball hit the floor, it took a long time to gather momentum before rolling down to the footlights, where it made a loud pinging sound.

Leo had just put his head down at the end of the speech in which he expresses his disgust at each relentless new spring. I saw him try to catch the eye as it slipped out of the socket and then his shoulders began to heave. I only managed not to laugh myself by picturing the eye as a huge petrified tear that had dropped out of his head.

The next day Sean and I visited Inez and Pedro in the cathedral. The space was immense, stark and slightly sinister. Their tombs were held up on the backs of dwarves, gargoyles and deformed creatures, while the whole cathedral had a tragic atmosphere, as though worshippers were constrained to acknowledge Inez and her death before they got round to God.

I was still feeling somewhat battered after *The Good Soup* and Sean, too, had been bruised by countless knock-backs in London. It seemed that he was too tall, too old, too young, too dark or too rough for every part he was sent up for. The time we had in Portugal was a break from the pressures of performance, a time to reflect on where we had got to so far, and we held each other tightly, as if to reassure ourselves that it was all worth the effort.

We were gentler with each other than we had been in the past, and less jokey. Subtly, we knew that things had changed. We were very special for one another and would remain so forever and ever, no matter what happened, like Inez and Pedro. Still, I had no wish to marry again. I felt fiercely passionate about Sean's career as an actor, as well as my own, and desired with all my heart to help him.

We drove on until we came to a place south of Lisbon and there we stayed. Fishermen lived in geranium-covered huts, made from driftwood and bracken, right on the beach, where the smell of sardines cooking over open fires pervaded the air. It was exactly the spot for two slightly jaded young actors to retire from the rat race, far removed from agents, auditions and telephones.

We could not altogether dismiss the fans, however. It seems odd, considering what was to occur in the not-too-distant future, but I was much better known than Sean at this time. It did not take long for the gawpers to arrive, and when they did, they came to look at me.

We returned to London reinvigorated and reinforced for the fray. The first fray I leapt into was *The Condemned of Altona*, a play by Jean-Paul Sartre about post-war German guilt. In it, the son of a wealthy German shipbuilder returns from fighting on the Russian front and shuts himself up in the attic of the palatial family home in Altona, a leafy suburb of Berlin. His only contact with the outside world is his sister, Leni (played by me), who is also his incestuous lover.

The cast included Kenneth Haigh, following his success as the original Jimmy Porter in *Look Back in Anger*, Claire Bloom, Nigel Stock and Basil Sydney. On the opening night, the whole audience stood up when they heard a chorus of the 'Horst Wessel Song', blissfully unaware that it was the Nazi rallying anthem. They thought the German ambassador was in the house.

The set was an even greater challenge than the rakes and ramps of *Tiger at the Gates*. Designed by the ingenious Sean Kenny, it was constructed of strips of burnished copper that reflected the action in distorted shadows. Centre stage, there was a virtual Jacob's ladder up to the attic, which I had to negotiate with amazing speed and agility so as not to slow the pace of the action. One critic devoted most of his column space to a description of my multifarious climbing techniques.

During the run of this play, Claire Bloom (affectionately known as Miss Tinpants) was being courted by Rod Steiger. Sean and I often dined with Claire and Rodney, as she called him, after the show. Nigel Stock taught me the importance of an actor's ability to do *The Times* crossword puzzle, thus filling in boring off-stage waits, while Sean Kenny allowed me to assist him in throwing projections of old Charlie

Chaplin films onto the walls of the Establishment, the new nightclub opened by Peter Cook in Soho.

The next fray was when George Devine called me into the Royal Court Theatre and propositioned me. Nothing could have given me greater pleasure because what he was suggesting was very dear to my heart. I was commissioned to translate three Pirandello plays from the Italian – *Naked* (which I had already done under the pseudonym of Simon Nedia), *Il Gioco delle Parti* ('Rules of the Game') and *Enrico IV* ('Henry IV') – which were to be produced at the Royal Court.

I was lucky enough to have found the perfect nanny to take care of Giovanna and me. She was called Nanny Foreman and was a bona fide treasure. Although not at all stiff or starchy, there was a distinctly no-nonsense set to her blue-grey bun and corseted form. A terrific bonus was that she was a keen cook. Lovingly prepared meals were set before us after the theatre and she enjoyed nothing better than when I brought home some actor whom she had seen on TV. Occasionally, I would hear her on the phone excitedly telling her son Ian about the Irish stew she'd cooked for some celebrity.

Nanny Foreman allowed me to spend time working on my new projects and I hired an assistant named Rosamund Waxing to help research and collate the translated pages. I still lived at Caroline House on the Bayswater Road and Sean remained in his mews house in St John's Wood. We'd painted his house together – a bright Rickett's blue, much to the dismay of his neighbours. It was a piece of tropical sky in the midst of the London gloom. Sean had housed his jazz collection in the downstairs room, where we would lie on the floor and listen to records for hours.

When the run of *The Condemned of Altona* finished, I went immediately into *Castle in Sweden*, a play by Françoise Sagan, the sensational French author who'd shot to literary fame at the age of eighteen with her 1954 blockbuster *Bonjour Tristesse*. For my first entrance, I was dressed in thigh-high hunting boots, with a great cape swirling around my shoulders, and carrying a real hawk on my wrist. I was so modish, the epitome of Swinging London with my boots and my bird of prey.

Jill Bennett, Alec McCowan and Gary Raymond, all good mates, were in the cast playing various lovers or brothers but I'm afraid I have absolutely no recollection of what the play was about. What I do remember is Kessie the kestrel. As there was no bird wrangler, I had to feed her, fix her jesses (long leather leg thongs), keep her on a stand in my bedroom so that she could bond with me and put on her little feathered headgear. I also had to wear a sturdy leather wristband so that when I carried her she did not claw my flesh.

There are some drawbacks to travelling with a bird of prey. A house-maid at the hotel in Brighton was bailed up shrieking in my bedroom when Kessie left her stand and flew at her as she tried to turn down my bed on the first evening I arrived. The management was not amused and I found myself sleeping in my dressing room at the theatre after Kessie had an unpleasant skirmish with the hotel cat. It was not very comfortable and I wondered at my bizarre life, ending up in Brighton playing nursemaid to a kestrel while the rest of the cast snuggled into their plush duvets in one of the lovely hotels that grace the waterfront.

But all was forgotten when I took Kessie out on the Downs and flew her. It was so thrilling when she actually returned to my wrist after an amazing swoop out of the sky. Sometimes, I felt as though I was in her body looking down on the sea and the sweeping uplands. I hated putting the mask over her eyes at the end of such a flight.

It was when we got to Portsmouth that I found out I was pregnant. I had gone to the hospital to have a check-up and to ensure that my lungs were clear. I wondered why I'd been feeling a bit queasy, but as soon as I saw the doctor's face, I knew instinctively what he was going to tell me. The world dipped sideways but I quickly recovered myself and resolved instantly not to tell anyone. I knew that whatever I decided would change the course of my life, so I stopped thinking altogether. Until the limited run of the play was over, I allowed my days to glide by in the routine of performances, flying my bird, walking by the sea and eating oysters after the show.

When the play closed, I lay in bed with the curtains drawn for a whole day, contemplating what I was going to do. I knew for certain that this baby wanted to be born. I could feel its spirit inside me, urging to be brought into the light. I could not deny that yearning. Unlike my previous pregnancy, when I had spent at least six hours a day throwing up, my body seemed to be undisturbed by the presence of the embryo and I could detect few signs of the impending event.

For months, I had been listening to George Devine, John Osborne and Tony Richardson planning the film of *Tom Jones*, the Fielding classic, which their company, Woodfall, would co-produce with an American company. Albert Finney was to play Tom and I was to be naughty Molly Seagrim. George Devine, Dame Edith Evans, David Warner, Hugh Griffith, Joan Greenwood, John Moffatt, Wilfrid Lawson, Rachel Kempson (Vanessa Redgrave's mother), Peter Bull, Susannah York and many other Royal Court stalwarts were enlisted in this spectacular stellar production.

George Devine's new love, Jocelyn Herbert, was the designer, Oscar Lowenstein was producer, Walter Lassally and Des Desmond, who were to become acclaimed as lighting cameraman and director in the future, were both secured and Tony Richardson was our intrepid director. The entire picture was to be shot in Dorset over the summer.

I planned to travel to Spain with my sister Margaret and Giovanna immediately after the shoot to see out the rest of the gestation period in the sun. The baby was due in December and I dreaded the miserable cold of London. While I was in Spain, I could continue with the translations of Pirandello and escape the watchful eyes of the paparazzi.

And then I told Sean. Being a canny Scot, he did not whoop or throw his hat in the air but I detected a deep satisfaction in him that had not been there before. We melded together as an alloy, and I felt his love envelop me even without words – especially without words.

I still had no intention of marrying again, but once Sean knew about the baby we devised a plan that he should buy a largish house in an inexpensive area of London and we would do it up. I would pay for the interior decoration and furniture and he would take care of structural changes. There we would live together and bring up the children but not impinge on each other's lives. Other actors would come and go in a sort of loose community of artists, which had worked so well in Bognor. In retrospect, the plan was wonderfully optimistic but about as practical as putting snake eggs under a duck.

Momentous things began to happen in quick succession. First, Sean was given the James Bond books to read and received a call-back for an audition with Cubby Broccoli and Harry Salzman. He gave the books to me for my opinion. I found the dialogue stilted, the character of Bond relentlessly awful unless he was given a sublime sense of humour, and the violence, or 'licensed to kill' stuff, could only be brought off if it was accomplished with a sort of ritualistic absurdity and fun. Sean carried these ideas back to the boys, who were evidently very impressed.

Not so Ian Fleming, the author. In his eyes, Sean was far removed from his Bond character. Ian was the product of the old school brigade, who are trained in snobbery without their even realising it. He simply could not see his beloved Bond, with the 'curious question mark of hair falling over his forehead', being played by a tenement boy from Fountainbridge. Fortunately, Broccoli and Salzman overrode his misgivings. Without the edge that Sean brought to the role, James Bond would never have attracted the international acclaim that has kept the Fleming estate in millions over the years.

The next momentous event was that my marriage was annulled. Giovanni Volpe sent a little Torinese lawyer to England to gauge my feelings about returning to Rome. I took him to meet Lord Goodman at his apartment near Victoria Station. He perched unhappily on the edge of one of Arnold's commodious armchairs while Goodman slumped deeply into his. He looked like a monumental Easter Island figure in repose and the little Italian was clearly intimidated. With alacrity, he agreed that as Andrea had never acknowledged the marriage in Italy, and had always written his marital status as *celebe* (bachelor) on forms, the marriage must be deemed to be invalid. He assured Arnold in suitably accented English that a papal annulment could be arranged within weeks.

Another momentous event was that I finally bought myself out of my contract with British Lion and stopped being a 'civil servant'. Now that I had recovered from my illness, the Government was anxious to start making money out of me again but I was determined to end the arrangement. As usual, the only way out was to pay them off in the amount of thousands of pounds. It was infuriating but I had no choice. So it was that, for the first time in five years, I was a free, single woman again . . . if being with child can ever be called being free.

There are some summers in the British Isles that become landmarks in memory. People say, 'Oh, do you remember the summer of '39 when the war broke out? Wasn't it fantastic? Day after day of glorious sunshine. We thought it would never end.' Others reminisce, 'We sat outside in the orchard every night during the summer of '59. The stars shone down, a huge red moon rose through the branches and we slept outside on blankets.' The summer we shot *Tom Jones* in Dorset was such a year and was probably the most enjoyable experience I ever had making a film.

Movie magazines invariably try to portray film sets as places of merriment, mischief and debauchery, but this is pure fantasy. Not only are film sets fraught with fear and loathing but they are generally quite smelly and uncomfortable. Tempers flare, people refuse to come out of their dressing rooms, and the producer–director relationship is often reminiscent of two male dogs circling around trying to sniff each other's rear ends before the snarling starts. Assistant directors become apoplectic, shouting curses at anyone who dares to cough or sneeze during a 'take', and if the film is going over budget the atmosphere is tense, with a frenzied urgency accompanying each new set-up.

The set of *Tom Jones* was the opposite of all that. Perhaps it was because everyone had worked together at the Royal Court Theatre or perhaps it was the weather. It could have been the beauty of the location, our mutual respect for each other's talent or the jollity of the material we were engaged in transferring from its classic literary form to the silver screen. Maybe it was a combination of all these things. Whatever the reason, the making of *Tom Jones* is an experience I will always relish.

The entire cast was farmed out in private houses throughout the countryside around Weymouth in Dorset. There was no room service, front desk or smell of Jeyes cleaning fluid. I was billeted in a heritage house with Oscar Lowenstein and family. My secretary came too and I drove down to Dorset in my new wire-wheeled blue Austin Healey convertible with the top down, the wind whipping my hair into a mass of tangles that took me hours to comb out.

Tony Richardson had just married Vanessa Redgrave, John Osborne had eloped with Penelope Gilliatt and then married her, and George Devine had lost more than three stone and looked particularly handsome on the arm of his great love, Jocelyn Herbert, our designer. The huge cast met in an ebullient mood. Imbibing champagne from the crates that filled the trunks of the fleet of fifties Cadillacs at our disposal, we were aiming to make the whole shoot into a summer celebration. Locations had been carefully chosen from the farmhouses, cottages and castles that abound in the area and it was with great delight that we used these architectural treasures as our own during the lulls that are inevitably part of filming.

I was honoured to be sharing a caravan with Dame Edith Evans.

Having made her professional debut in 1912 as Cressida in Shakespeare's *Troilus and Cressida*, Edith possessed the fruitiest voice in the business, which was imitated by everyone, including me. Her Lady Bracknell in *The Importance of Being Earnest* was legendary. To be allowed such proximity to an idol was somewhat overwhelming, especially as I kept remembering the famous story of her constipation during the run of *The Chalk Garden* in New York. This tale has woven its way into theatrical folklore and been embellished with each telling. One more recitation will do no harm.

As a Christian Scientist, Edith was implacably against any form of medical intervention and, although the theatre staff and actors in *The Chalk Garden* were aware of her continuing problem, she could not be persuaded to seek help. It became difficult for her fellow actors to be on stage with her without cracking up. The play was full of lines like:

'But she hasn't been for years.'

'Do you think she'll ever recover from this agonising wait?'

'She has no idea how big it will be when it finally comes out.'

'The whole thing may blow up in her face.'

Edith was hardly able to drag herself around when the management stepped in and a meeting was held in her dressing room after the show. Binkie Beaumont and the American producer insisted that she should be taken to hospital, assuring her that a month's rest would improve her health. She was not to worry, they told her, as another actress, who had been privately rehearsing the role, was ready to take over straightaway. There was a deadly hush as Edith took this in. Then she gathered her strength and pulled herself upright in her chair.

'WHO?' she boomed.

'Er . . . We thought you'd approve. It's your great friend . . . er . . . Dame Gladys Cooper.'

In the silence that followed, Edith stood up to her full height. The air crackled with electricity and then she spoke.

'Gentlemen, would you mind waiting outside?'

LEFT: My parents as young doctors with baby Raff on Mum's lap BELOW: Me as a toddler BOTTOM: Summer with my siblings. From left, Ruth, me, David, Raff, Margaret, Carl

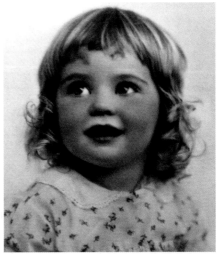

ABOVE LEFT: Wearing my circus outfit in *The Woman for Joe* (1955)

ABOVE TOP RIGHT: An early publicity shot ABOVE BOTTOM RIGHT: Posing with

a cigar in London OPPOSITE: Away from the studio

OPPOSITE: The actress as starlet ABOVE TOP LEFT: *Picture Post*'s 'February Personality Girl' ABOVE TOP RIGHT: Studio portrait ABOVE BOTTOM: With Kenneth More in *The Admirable Crichton* (1957)

OPPOSITE TOP: With Peter Finch in *Passage Home* (1955) OPPOSITE CENTRE: With Albert Finney in *Tom Jones*, for which I was nominated for an Oscar for Best Actress in a Supporting Role (1963) OPPOSITE BOTTOM: Dress rehearsal ABOVE TOP: Singing in the lion's cage after their mating marathon in *The Woman for Joe* (1955) ABOVE BOTTOM LEFT: Sir Michael Redgrave as Hector and me as Helen in *Tiger at the Gates*, for which I won the Tony Critics' Choice Award (1955) ABOVE BOTTOM RIGHT: Arriving at a premiere with Sean, long before Bond

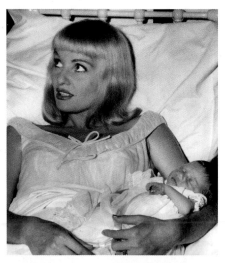 

ABOVE: Our London backyard with Jason and Giovanna OPPOSITE, CLOCKWISE
FROM TOP LEFT: The birth of my first child, Giovanna; Even when she was small
it was clear that Giovanna was a gifted child; With Jason in the garden at Putney;
Together with Jason and Sean; Holding on to Jason while he practises his golf swing
at the airport en route to Rome; Changing tiny Giovanna's nappy in my parents'
Queensland home

ABOVE TOP: Playing Caterina de Medici, the love interest for Charlton Heston's Michelangelo, in *The Agony and the Ecstasy* (1965), with my hair dyed black ABOVE BOTTOM: With Paul Newman in *Hombre* (1967) RIGHT: A Hollywood studio shot

TOP: Meeting the Queen ABOVE BOTTOM LEFT: In the limelight with Sean ABOVE BOTTOM RIGHT: Arriving in Australia with Sean and Jason OPPOSITE: Cruising on Sydney Harbour with Sean and Jason; the Opera House is still under construction in the background

OPPOSITE TOP: J. G. Bennett supervising Gurdjieffian Movements at Sherborne
OPPOSITE MIDDLE: With Christopher Lee in *The Wicker Man* (1973) OPPOSITE
BOTTOM: Tony and I were married under a flowering bauhinia tree in the garden
at Karnak on 22 June 1985 ABOVE: A pensive moment

TOP LEFT: Graduation day for Sir Raphael as a barrister-at-law (Qld) in 1939

TOP RIGHT: Sir Raphael and Lady Cilento at the time of their presentation to the Queen during her visit to Australia in 1954 BOTTOM: With my mother

She stood imperiously as they backed out the door. Nobody quite knows exactly what happened in the No. 1 dressing room while they stood outside nervously smoking, but after a considerable time the unmistakable sound of a fully flushing toilet was heard throughout the silent theatre.

'You may return, gentlemen!' came Edith's triumphant cry. 'There will be no need for dear Gladys to learn all those tiresome words. The problem has been solved!'

Nobody ever quite knew whether Edith's recovery had been effected by the mention of her great rival's name or whether she had acted out her recovery to reinforce the management's belief in the power of Christian Science.

Most of my love scenes with Albert Finney in *Tom Jones* were shot outside and it was a bit disconcerting to have Lord David Cecil, from the grand house in whose grounds we were filming, astride a shooting stick drooling lasciviously about ten feet away from our noses while we were wrestling around in the grass.

Once the outdoor seduction scenes were finished, one major indoor scene remained – the discovery of wicked Molly having it off with the curate (John Moffatt) in a barn. Tony held this scene back, so I just lazed about the locations laughing, watching the scenes unfold and listening to tall tales for most of the shoot. I exalted in my sobriquet 'the WC' (Weather Cover). If it rained, John Moffatt and I would be ready in a flash to get our gear off and maul each other in the hay of the indoor barn.

Helicopters were used in an innovative way to shoot the hunting scenes, hopping hedges and flying so low that they were practically part of the melee thundering across the countryside. They buzzed like hornets, shooting the whole mess from close quarters – flying clods of earth, baying hounds frothing at the mouth and real-life hunters hanging for dear life onto their steeds in full pursuit of the 'uneatable'.

Albert and I persuaded the helicopter pilot to fly us up to Cerne Abbas to have a picnic one day and we ran up and down the monstrous phallus of the Cerne Abbas Man while he filmed us waving out of the top – two minuscule spermatozoa waiting to be ejaculated. We inserted the clip of this into the rushes, causing a maelstrom of memos from the producers in Hollywood. They thought we might be shooting a porno film in tandem with *Tom Jones*.

On midsummer's night there was a great celebration. A whole boar had been slaughtered and prepared with great festoons of herbs and liquid marinades. It took many hours to roast on the spit over a huge fire, during which time the crew drank barrels of homemade cider and various other liquid refreshments. The cast of Royal Court actors went up to George Devine and Jocelyn Herbert's place for fun and games, and in the midst of the festivities Sean arrived with a small bakelite suitcase looking like a refugee from Eastern Europe.

I knew just how he felt, a stranger in a strange land, as he walked into that closely knit gang of Royal Court rowdies – actors who fancied themselves as the crème de la crème of British Theatre. With a few tipples inside them, thespians can become very competitive and stand-offish with an outsider, and I stayed riveted to his side to create a force field should he be subjected to too many snide remarks or offensive behaviour. It must be remembered that Sean was not yet James Bond.

Tony challenged Sean to a game of chess, as bystanders watched, expecting that the big daft Scot would be trounced in a matter of minutes. Not so. It took about a quarter of an hour and a little help from his friend to prove them wrong. There were a few raised eyebrows as Tony turned his king over and hunched up his shoulders like a disappointed vulture.

Everyone was clamouring for some game . . . but not charades. We had charaded ourselves out and, anyway, everybody was too good at it. Then I remembered a Chinese story I had heard from Ken Tynan about a woman crossing a bridge. It was a Zen puzzle, which actually had no answer but showed the participants what set of beliefs determined their behaviour in society.

There were strict rules as to how this game was conducted. All players were given a piece of paper and a pencil; they had to listen to the story without asking clarifying questions and were not allowed to confer before they had written their answers. A diagram was drawn of the geography of the place, with a list of the main characters, which the players could consult whenever they wished. Once all the players had been issued with paper and pencils, the story began.

There is a Woman who lives in a house beside a river in China. She has been discovered by her Husband crossing the bridge to visit her Lover, who lives on the other bank. He warns her that should she go back across the bridge to visit her Lover again, he will kill her.

One day, the Husband goes to market on his donkey and the Woman crosses the river to see her Lover. She tells the Lover what her Husband has said. Some time later, the Woman is looking out of the window when she sees her Husband in the distance riding his donkey slowly back from the market. She rushes out of the Lover's house and runs to the bridge. On the bridge stands a Bandit with a gun. He stops the Woman and tells her that no-one is to cross the bridge that day or he will shoot them.

The Woman explains that her Husband has also threatened to kill her if she crosses the bridge and that she fears for her life unless he allows her to get home before he arrives. The Bandit refuses, so she runs downriver to where a Ferryman plies his trade and tells him that her Husband will kill her if he finds out she has crossed the river to visit her Lover. The Ferryman tells her to jump in. Once she is in the boat, he says, 'That will be three yen before I cross.'

'But I have no money,' she replies.

'Then jump out,' says the Ferryman.

The Woman rushes back to her Lover and reiterates that she has to get home because her Husband has threatened to kill her. She tells her Lover how the Bandit with the gun is preventing anyone from crossing the river that day, and begs him for three yen to pay the Ferryman.

189

'No,' says the Lover, 'I will not give you three yen. Stay here with me. I will protect you.'

But the Woman panics and runs out of the house and across the bridge. The Bandit shoots her in the back as she gets to the middle of the bridge.

That is the story as the participants hear it. Immediately, they must each write down in order, one through five, whom they feel is most responsible for her death, without comment or question. Then they must read out their answers, explaining why they put that particular character where they did. Everyone listens to the answers, without any word of explanation from the conductors of the game.

Of course, it's obvious that, by law, the one who is responsible for her death is the one who shoots her – the Bandit. Yet, on that Midsummer's night in Dorset, there were only two people in a room of about thirty who put him first – Sean and Tony Richardson. Everyone else had imaginative answers filled with fanciful scenarios and conspiracy theories. It's astounding how the same story heard by many people at the same time can evoke so many different reactions.

The fracas that followed was similarly amazing. It began calmly enough but, perhaps fuelled by the abundantly flowing champagne, a fierce argument broke out as everyone attempted to prove that their explanation of who was responsible was the only valid one. Soon, the Woman had become symbolic of the Japanese victims of the atom bombs dropped on Hiroshima and Nagasaki. Big Van (as Vanessa Redgrave was known to one and all) was standing on the stairs raving about injustice while tempers flared and blows were exchanged below her. They were loving it. It was exactly the right game for the small 'l' liberals and the covert hawks to thrash out their differences. After a while, Sean and I escaped into the velvet night under a blanket of stars that lit our way. The next morning, he left for Jamaica to begin shooting *Dr No*.

There were many more memorable moments during the filming of *Tom Jones*. Hugh Griffith spent much of his time in a competition with Wilfred Lawson, who played my father, to see how much grog they could pour down their gullets. They locked themselves in Wilfred's room at the George Hotel, Weymouth, much to the consternation of Tony's lovely assistant, who was locked in with them at the time. She had been charged with the unenviable job of getting them to the set on time and sober enough to perform. It was a hopeless task.

One day, I accepted Hugh's offer of a country pub lunch in one of the wonderfully cosy snugs that have played host to countless drinkers over four or five centuries. Hardly had I got into Hugh's new blue Jaguar when he asked me to open the glove box and pass him what was inside. No wonder the car had been transformed into a sort of sardine tin flattened on both sides. Hugh was tippling brandy and sherry together as he drove like a demon down those narrow West Country lanes, bouncing off hedges like a dodgem car. Still wearing his elaborate eighteenth-century wig, which he continually used to wipe his mouth, he asked the ample-breasted mistress of the house what the white flowers were called that decorated her bar.

'Yes, aren't they beautiful?' she gushed, 'They're Annunciation Lilies, the flower that the Angel Gabriel gave to the Virgin to let her know she was going to have Baby Jesus.'

It took Hugh some time to take in this information, along with a good slurp of his deadly drink, now supplemented with cider, but when he spoke, it was a twelve-decibel Welsh shout that came out of his mouth, frightening the poor lady out of her wits.

'NOT MANY VIRGINS AROUND HERE, MOST LIKELY, IS THERE, MISSUS?'

This was orchestrated by bawdy, eighteenth-century guffaws and the turning of his wig sideways on his head. The incensed woman disappeared to fetch her innkeeper husband as we wisely left.

Finally, well into September, it rained and my barn scenes with John Moffatt were shot – but not before I had been persuaded to put on a red wig and play a prostitute in the crowd at Tom's execution by hanging. The crowds of extras hung about while a passionate argument broke out between the British producer, Oscar Lowenstein, and Tony Richardson, the director.

Oscar, a political idealist and rabid Leftie, was adamant that the crowd would deplore Tom's imminent death and scream their defiance at the powers that be. Tony, a pragmatist from birth, said that this was historically incorrect, that execution crowds traditionally bayed for the blood of the murderer, standing for hours in rare high spirits to catch a glimpse of the last juddering of the dying man's legs. His research had led him to believe that they hushed only to listen to the wretched man's dying words, and then let out a deafening triumphant hoot when he was pronounced to be lifeless. After much heated debate, it was shot both ways and I have no idea which version made it to the final cut of the film . . . probably bits of both.

The only mishap I experienced during the shoot was when I fell off a horse. I was in agony for a full night and a day but my fears of having a miscarriage proved unfounded. I found it amusing that Tony made me wear two false pregnancy stomachers, as he thought one was not noticeable enough. Yes, Molly gets pregnant in the film too. When at last it was over, we all parted ways and I went back to London brown and healthy, with rosy cheeks and a small bump representing six months of pregnancy.

In those days, Marbella was a little-known destination in the south of Spain, whose only claim to fame was the fact that a prince named Hohenlohe had built a club by the sea, where yachties and aristotrash stopped off for R and R and a spot of golf. There were some villas loosely attached to the Marbella Club named after colours – Rosa, Azzurro, Blanco. I chose Amarillo. It faced the water and was so newly built that it still smelt of wet cement. It was here that my sister Margaret and daughter Giovanna and I settled down to await my confinement.

The basic plan was to have the baby in Gibraltar. This would ensure that it was born with a British passport so we'd have no difficulties bringing it back to London. We all drove to the Rock, showed our Australian passports at the border and were told politely but firmly that, as Australians citizens, we could have two more entrances through the border but, after that, could only enter Gibraltar by sea from the port of Algeciras.

I went to have an examination at the big, scrubbed naval hospital halfway up the hill and was nonplussed when the doctor, who was a surgeon, measured me up and informed me that, as it was my first child and because my pelvis was narrow, I would probably have to have a Caesarean. I told him that I'd already had a child. He did not believe me, so I said I would bring the child to the hospital and he could see for himself.

When I got back to Marbella, I rang my parents and told them what the doctor had said. My father was quick with a possible explanation, 'Is he a surgeon?' When I answered in the affirmative, he said, 'You must never forget that surgeons have sets of scalpels and they like to use them.'

I told them that this surgeon was not very observant, as he had thought this was my first child, even after an examination. 'Oh dear, D, I don't want you to have a Caesarean section,' said my mum, the gynaecologist. 'They cut right through the abdominal wall, and it's never the same again.'

Life in Spain was very dozy after the hustle bustle of London and Dorset. The golden days slid by as we picnicked on deserted beaches and drove up the treacherous mountain roads to Ronda to visit the bridge where the martyrs were thrown off. I floated on my back in the gentle Mediterranean every day, watching my bump grow and forgetting all about Caesareans and surgeons. My sister was painting, Giovanna found children to play with, and a delicious calm descended on me. I stuffed myself with food at the long Spanish lunches that lasted until four in the afternoon, and then I slept, sometimes until the next morning.

It was during one such marathon sleep that I had a veridical dream. I saw a mountainous sea, more frightening than any I had ever witnessed in the natural world. The waves were fuming and incandescent, giving off spumes of blue and orange lightning like flames. The crashing sound seemed to fill my entire body, which shook with the force of the thunderous waves and wind. And then I saw him. It was Sean marching resolutely through the ocean. He was wearing an Australian lifesaver's harness around his chest and there was a thin rope trailing back into the sea behind him. Taking no notice of the waves breaking around him and over him, still he came, his glistening eyes fixed ahead of him to where I was.

I woke up panting, not knowing whether I was terrified or elated. I was shivering and sweating at the same time, and sympathetic contractions began to make my stomach as hard as teak. I hoped I was not actually having the baby. Gradually, by lying absolutely still and breathing as deeply as possible, my body calmed and I fell into a sort of lucid coma. I was completely conscious but paralysed. Distantly, I could hear the telephone ringing, but could not answer it. It was Sean, calling to say that he was arriving the next day.

It was well into December when he came, and we went through the border to Gibraltar for the day to celebrate. I was getting very tired of being pregnant and carrying around such a mound, so we decided to play golf – not fairway golf but just silly clock golf by the side of one of the roads that lead up to the Rock. It was fun, and I thought that if I walked up and down picking up golf balls a lot, maybe the baby would get annoyed and decide it was time to bale out. We'd only got to the fourth or fifth hole when the contractions began, so strongly this time that I was glad. I thought, 'This is it. The waiting is over. What good timing. We're here in Gibraltar, a stone's throw from the hospital. No Caesarean. Great!'

I was booked into hospital but when a nurse had a look at me she sent us home. 'Not this time, dear,' she said. 'Braxton Hicks contractions they're called.'

So back we went to the Villa Amarillo by the sea. Giovanna and Sean sat on the edge of the bathtub laughing as they watched the acrobatic efforts of the baby. It was always most active when I had a bath, the distinct outline of a bottom rising up and descending rapidly when they gave it a little smack. Sometimes it seemed to be standing on its head, waving its arms around.

It wasn't long before we realised that I had used up my three border crossings into Gibraltar. I'd completely forgotten a Christmas shopping trip that I'd made before Sean's arrival.

'Well, that's it,' Sean said. 'This is getting stupid. You can't drive to Algeciras and wait for the ferry that only comes twice a day while you're in labour. You'll have to get a British passport and there's only one way to do that. We can go into Gibraltar, me by car and you by boat, meet up and get married and then they have to give you a new passport . . . Gibraltarian, probably, but British.'

And so it was planned, the most romantic wedding of the decade.

Early the next morning, we got up and drove to Algeciras in time for me to catch the morning ferry. Sean, unshaven and rather haggard, left me on the dock and headed off to the border crossing. He was to meet up with me at the other end, having arranged two witnesses and a Justice of the Peace or some dignitary who could perform the ceremony.

I stood on the wharf feeling uneasy in my brown leather coat, which covered my swollen stomach. All the workers were milling about, jostling for positions near the gangway. I was pushed out of the way and a man approached me, saying that I could come and sit in his shop until the boat was ready to leave. I went with him along the wharf to a jewellery shop set back from the bustle of the dock. He unlocked the door and ushered me in. It was only when I looked at the display cabinets that I realised that Sean and I had completely forgotten about rings. I asked to see some of his wares.

195

He was only too pleased to comply and rushed to open the display tops, bringing out trays of rings, earrings, bracelets and lucky charms. He must have gone over to lock the outside door while I was engrossed with the rings on the counter, and when he came back he brought with him several mantillas and a brightly coloured headscarf. He must also have put on some music because, suddenly, the deafening sound of castanets and 'Olés' filled the small shop. I didn't notice anything unusual until he tried to put the headscarf around my shoulders in a too-familiar way. I shrugged him off brusquely and picked up a largish gold ring that I thought might fit Sean's finger.

'*Que costa esta?*' I shouted above the wailing and stomping.

Without reply, he pressed close behind me and leaned against my body, squashing my stomach against the cabinet and blowing his garlicky breath into my hair. 'Eh, Rubia, h'you like Espanish musica, h'yes?' he mouthed into my ear.

I could hardly believe this was happening to me. I reared backwards and elbowed him in the stomach with all the strength I could muster. I was incensed beyond measure. I don't think I have ever been so angry. He grabbed me around the waist, coming into contact with the baby. For an instant, he released me and then there was an unseemly tussle before I escaped to the door, which, to my dismay, I found to be locked. Grabbing an umbrella from the stand, I tried to break the glass door while simultaneously slashing out at him whenever he tried to get near me. I could hear my hysterical voice, shouting and cursing, above the gypsy music.

'Let me out of here! You creep! I'm PREGNANT! Can't you SEE, you filthy little man! I'm getting MARRIED! HELP! SOMEONE . . . HELP!'

I saw a few surprised faces staring back at me through the glass door, and I shouted even louder. The man instantly changed tack and the music abruptly stopped in mid-cadenza. He went to the other end of the window, spinning his finger around against his head like I was crazy and mouthing words in Spanish while pointing at me all the while.

He was indicating to the people looking in that I was having some kind of psychotic episode but that he could handle the situation.

The people moved on and he walked very tentatively to where I was standing by the door with the umbrella in my hand. He held his hand above his head as though to ward off any blow I might inflict upon him and pulled the key out of his pocket with the other hand.

'You go now! NOW! Go, *rubia* . . . OUT! I will not tell them how you were stealing my rings.'

He grabbed the umbrella just as I was bringing it down on his head, unlocked the door and shoved me out onto the dock. Then he quickly locked himself inside again and disappeared behind the postcard stand. I looked around, not knowing how long I had been in the shop, when my worst fears were confirmed. The gangplank to the ferry had been lifted, the retaining ropes thrown off and the hooter was wailing as the boat slowly pulled away from the wharf.

'WAIT! WAIT!' I shouted, running to the water's edge as fast as I was able. I knew it was useless, even as I ran, and finally I could do nothing but stop in disbelief and dejectedly watch the aft of the vanishing boat disappear into its own wake. Whimpering and dishevelled, in a sudden burst of terror, I rifled through my handbag. Thank God it was still hanging around my neck and my passport and money were intact.

I went to the loo and threw up. After that, I felt better. I was still quaking inside at my unfortunate encounter but I had no intention of taking my complaints to the harbourmaster or anyone else, being aware of the attitude of Spanish authorities towards young foreign women who had suffered indignities at the hands of their compatriots. Instead, I walked as far as I could to the end of the dock, where there was no-one, and sat down to look at the sea. Expanses of water have always calmed and mesmerised me.

For three whole hours, I hardly moved. I knew that when the ferry arrived in the city of Gibraltar and I was not on it, Sean might think I'd got cold feet. Having seen me buy my ticket, he'd be both furious and worried. I also knew that if I told him what had really happened, he would bash the man's head in. Finally, I envisaged myself having a fainting fit in the loo. I'd explain to him that by the time I'd recovered, the boat was gone. I stopped thinking about anything then and dozed, with my face towards the winter sun.

When I opened my eyes, the ferry was quite near and, leaning far out on the prow, was a figurehead like a piece of carved teak on a privateer. Sean, frozen-faced with fury, scanned the docks for my presence. He didn't see me until I flailed my arms and flew down the dock to where the boat would berth. He was first down the gangplank and I saw that his face was covered in little cuts. I rushed into his arms and clung to him as though we hadn't seen each other for four years rather than four hours.

'What happened to you?' he demanded, anger making his voice higher.

'What happened to *you*?' I countered, touching the cuts on his chin.

'Nothing. No soap. Just shaving in the toilet on the crossing. Couldn't keep a steady hand.'

'I can't really explain what happened to me but I'm very sorry I missed the ferry. Maybe this is telling us something. Do you think we should really do it?' The baby gave me a nasty kick.

'Yes,' he said emphatically. 'I'm going to buy myself a one-way ticket now and you're coming with me and this time you won't miss the boat no matter how hard you try.'

I cannot say that from that moment everything went smoothly on our wedding day, because it would not be true. In fact, once we were disgorged in Gibraltar and went to the Register Office where the ceremony was to be performed, we found that the witnesses Sean had lined up had left. Added to that, my divorce papers and passport were not in order. I have vague recollections of running through tunnels under the city and arriving at an underground dairy to swear out documents before a Justice of the Peace. He was in charge of milk distribution throughout the whole of Gibraltar, and the sounds of shouting and breaking glass reverberated throughout the cavernous factory like audio effects in a murder movie. Out into the bright Spanish sunshine again, we went to a proper jeweller this time and picked the ring. I bought Sean a silly hat.

It was late in the afternoon before we grabbed two taxi drivers off the street and paid them to stand up for us as witnesses. Both of us were practically hysterical by the time we finally became man and wife. To top off the day, we decided to drive up the Rock as far as the military barrier would allow and then walk on further towards Europa Point to glimpse the famous apes. It is believed to bring good luck.

We stood close together to take in the spectacular sunset but soon darkness fell. It wasn't long before we had lost sight of the sea, lost our bearings and had to admit we were hopelessly lost altogether. By that time, everything we attempted seemed doomed to disaster but, to us, it had all become absurdly funny. We stumbled about, falling over rocks, bumping into barbed wire, lighting matches, laughing and swearing until we were spotted by a patrol of British Tommies, who escorted us off the military no-go zone and back to civilisation. We never did get to see the apes.

My ultimate memory of that demented day was having trouble keeping my eyes open at dinner in the shabby hotel where we took a room for the night. A lady in a fuchsia dress with long lampshade fringes sang popular opera arias slightly off key while accompanying herself on the piano. She winked suggestively at Sean each time she finished one.

The next day I became the proud possessor of a British Passport (Gibraltarian) and we re-crossed the border into Spain, confident that any time the baby decided to be born we could zip back to the hospital in style. When we arrived back in Marbella, there was a message from the surgeon at the hospital requesting my presence for a check-up the next day, so back we went to the Rock and I presented myself for his further examination at the appointed hour.

'Well,' he said, 'I've got some good news for you. I can just squeeze you in before I go off on my annual leave. Isn't that fortuitous?'

'How do you mean?' I asked stupidly.

'A Caesarean is such a wonderful procedure these days. You won't feel a thing. You'll just go off to sleep, and when you wake up the baby will be there, all clean and sweet and waiting for you to hold. If you can get your things together on Wednesday, we'll admit you in the evening, prep you up early Thursday morning and I'll deliver the baby at 9 a.m. How's that?'

He looked at his watch and patted my hand in a well-rehearsed bedside manner. Had he known I was the archetypal dissenting doctor's daughter, he wouldn't have bothered.

'Sorry,' he said, 'I'm playing golf at two o'clock. Hope you don't mind if I dash. See you Thursday morning. Not to worry. *Mañana por la mañana. Adios.*'

As we drove back slowly past the rolling green hills and sandy inlets to the blue Mediterranean, I could not stop thinking of the scalpel cutting into my abdominal wall, the words '*Mañana por la mañana*' ('the day after tomorrow') echoing in my ears. The next morning, I went and lay in the sea with Sean for solace but it was no use. There was something very wrong with the whole deal – too little action, too small a baby to be a health risk, too much breeziness, too much bedside manner and definitely too much golf. In the afternoon, I called a little conference with Margaret and Sean.

'But do you think they'll let you travel nine months pregnant?' Margaret asked.

'I'll be wearing my Empire-line brown leather coat. No-one can tell I'm preggers with that on. You'd be surprised.'

I looked down out of the plane as we circled over the Rock and wondered what golf course the good doctor would be playing on. I didn't care that London would be freezing. It was better than cold surgical steel biting into my belly.

The moment we got back to the Bayswater Road, Sean had to leave for Italy, where the publicity machine for the first Bond film, *Dr No*, was cranking up. He was required to go to the main casino in San Remo, decked out in Bond wig and accessories, and win £100 000, the casino management being in on the game. As soon as the press had disseminated the story worldwide, Sean would give the money back and come home. Picture opportunities with bevies of beautiful Bond girls, bottomless champagne, martinis shaken not stirred and staged encounters with nymphs in luxury hotels were the publicity prerequisites of Sean's life now, and would be long after he had finished playing Bond. In those early days, funnily enough, he hated it.

While he was away, on the coldest day in living memory, the eleventh of January 1963, the Thames froze over and Jason Joseph Connery was born in a nursing home in London. He weighed less than six pounds and had reddish stubble on his head. Shirley Bassey was my first visitor and I thought she looked a bit startled when she looked at him. To me he was unbelievably beautiful, even though his features resembled those of a robust elderly gentleman. Sean put it better when he returned and got his first sight of his offspring.

'Shove a cigar in his mouth and you've got a dead ringer for Winston Churchill,' he said.

There it was. Jason had received his first review.

CHAPTER EIGHT

It wasn't long before baby Jason morphed from his Churchillian persona into a wondrous blond munchkin with disturbingly candid eyes reminiscent of my dad's. In no time at all, he learned how to flirt his eyelashes so that, wherever we went, he was cooed over and chucked under the chin by every female he encountered.

We took up residence in an old Victorian house in Acton Park that Sean had bought for eight thousand pounds. I knew at once that this was the home that had featured in a recurrent dream ever since I could remember. It was a strange, solitary structure in a cul-de-sac at the end of a pathway through Acton Common, which had been owned for some years by an order of Spanish nuns called the Adoratrices. Apparently, one of their number must have been an electrical genius because the whole place had been hard-wired to the mains so that any short would have caused instant fulmination. There was a large yard next door where hundreds of ladders were stacked. These were rented out from a front office on the Uxbridge Road and were to prove a perfect convenience for fans who fancied invading our house at the height of Bondmania.

At first I was stunned to find that the house was so familiar to me but soon I forgot my dream and thrust myself into the joyful task of transforming it from a ramshackle wreck into a home where we could experience warmth and beauty of our own making. In true sixties style,

I had curtains with bold ochre, scarlet and orange splotches made up for the L-shaped sitting room. This front room, with twenty-foot ceilings, was on the first floor looking through to the back garden. A narrow staircase led down to the cork-floored kitchen and dining area, while on the second floor was our bedroom and the guest room. On the very top floor of the house was a sanctuary for the children, two bedrooms with a kitchen and roof garden, which was Nanny Foreman's domain.

I haunted Heal's, Habitat, Whitley's and Harrods, picking up a mad selection of furniture, crockery, vases and pictures. In classic Scottish fashion, Sean bought an unusually weighty piece of Victoriana known as a Robinson's Powder-Proof Safe, which was installed amid the eclectic bits and bobs that adorned the front room. That safe was to prove a magnet for thieves.

Looking back, I would say that my initial attempt at interior decoration was probably a pretty crude one but I was nothing if not enthusiastic. Like typical new parents, we settled down to sleepless nights of baby colic, teething and weaning. We jubilated at Jason's toothless grin and Giovanna's first faltering ABCs. Our marriage, Jason's birth, a house to renovate, a large German shepherd called Harry Hotspur and a profound mutual trust and love for one another had melded us into a cohesive unit. We faced the future just like any other young couple hoping to make it together . . . except that we were not like any other young couple.

Overnight our lives changed. *Dr No*, the original Bond film Sean had shot in Jamaica, opened to worldwide acclamation. A genuine international male icon was born and, suddenly, Sean wasn't Sean any more. He was James Bond, 007, licensed to kill. I, too, ceased being Diane Cilento, the cool young star of British flicks, and became what's-her-name, wife of the macho idol of the Western world. I was arguably the most envied woman alive, but, alas, I was so naïve that it took me some time before I realised that I was an embarrassment to the publicity department. After all, I was a *live* Mrs James Bond. Anyone who has ever read Ian Fleming's *On Her Majesty's Secret Service* knows that when Bond does actually get hitched, his wife, Contessa Teresa 'Tracy' di Vincenzo, is shot dead in his arms within hours of their nuptials, rendering our hero even more captivating by dint of his tragedy.

At first we were both elated by the overnight success, not comprehending the full extent of what it meant. All Sean's hard grind – movement classes with Yat Malmgren, Cic Berry voice production, playing lousy parts and tedious hours of learning lines – had paid off. The enormous boost it brought to his wounded youthful ego was vindication for all the years of being underrated.

We both knew that James Bond was just a role, one that had been carefully constructed, like a racing car that has been specially engineered to make it unbeatable, but there was surely something more to it than that. The character hit a special nerve at a special moment in time, when men ached for identification. It was time to come clean and admit what lay behind the façade of real blokes. Isn't it every man's secret dream to be the object of feminine desire, to be the one man whom women of every age, denomination, race and creed fantasise as their lover when they lie in bed next to their boring husbands? It is fascinating to analyse the peculiar combination of masculine traits which make the Bond character so irresistible to both sexes.

Basically, Bond is overtly sexual. He is unsentimental and amoral, a daredevil who kills with a wisecrack, beds every woman who comes within his orbit, dresses like a gentleman and behaves like a connoisseur of the finer things in life but who would have been called a cad or a swine in Victorian times. He defies class by disregarding every decent reaction of a gent, and, lastly, he is a spy, someone who operates in the covert world of international politics. In this undercover world, he is 'licensed to kill', outwitting his most powerful enemies and surviving whatever dangers are thrust in his path. Therefore, he's the envy of just about every man I have ever met.

In fact, no-one was less like the Bond character than Sean Connery.

In some ways, being cast against type was very good. It gave him the freedom to play the part as a completely different person, disassociated from himself by everything but age, while at the same time using all his physical attributes and intelligence to realise the potential of such a character.

In real life, Sean wore lumberjack flannel shirts with large checks, loathed anything but loose fits around his loins, never wore jeans or ties, and preferred beer and single malt whisky to anything either shaken or stirred. Like many Scots, he had a diffident attitude towards women, teasing or being confrontational in a roguish rather than ribald way.

Sean loved Giovanna and was besotted by his baby son. He revered and loved his mum and dad and had held as firm as a rock throughout our relationship, which, by then, spanned more than six years. He liked nothing better than watching soccer and eating big home-cooked roasts and never bothered to hide his broad Scottish burr in public. The two things he hated most about playing Bond were wearing the hairpiece all day, because by evening it had become very itchy, and having to have his back shaved for love scenes. I used to do the job in the bath about every three weeks.

It had been our habit for some time to go to Richmond Golf Club to play with the likes of Stanley Baker, Emlyn Williams' son Brook, Percy Herbert, Robert Shaw and many other 'hell-raisers'. We all played incredibly badly and everyone cheated quite openly, but after Bond entered our lives Sean began to take his golf more seriously. It afforded him refuge from the overwhelming attention of fans, who had begun to dog his every move. He played much better when it was raining and became known as 'the Water Buffalo'.

Sean and I had long discussions in bed at night about how he must *insist* on playing other roles in major films so as not to become altogether identified with Bond. We talked about how to take the unpleasant edge off the character by giving him a wicked sense of humour (which Fleming left out of the Bond mix) and how to make him move from 'strong and flexible in movement to light and sustained in vocal delivery' (Yat's terminology). These features would define the quintessential 'cool dude' figure replicated in countless films since *Dr No*.

It was shortly after the opening of the first Bond film that Sean had his first run-in with the producers, Cubby Broccoli and Harry Salzman. These two made an unlikely couple. Cubby Broccoli, whose family had given their name to the vegetable when they crossed rabe with cauliflower, was an Italo-American with Mafia connections. A big, cuddly, teddy bear of a man who laughed a lot and was reputed to be a serious gambling addict, it was difficult to dislike him. Harry Salzman, on the other hand, probably assumed the 'bad cop' role consciously but it suited him very well. He was squat, dark and hairy with a background, it was said, in Canadian circuses as well as some other more dubious ventures into the skin trade.

The two men realised that the success of the Bond film was largely due to Sean's presence in it but that didn't deter them from refusing to alter the original contract to let him in on the deluge of money that would fall on them from Bond merchandising. There was a long legal wrangle, which entailed lawyers, agents, flaring tempers, shouting and a lot of aggravation. Fortunately, Sean's agent was bargaining from an impregnable position of strength so it was only a matter of time before a compromise was reached and equilibrium restored.

Effie and Joe Connery came down from Edinburgh to stay, and we were all invited to dress up and go as guests of the management to Crockfords, London's oldest and most prestigious gambling casino, situated off Pall Mall. In another publicity stunt, Sean was to win thousands of pounds without raising an eyebrow, just like his cinematic alter ego. All the attendants at Crockfords were decked out in eighteenth-century satin costumes, complete with knee breeches and powdered wigs. Impossibly thick carpets buffered any vulgar yelps of triumph from winners or groans from losers as we watched in awe as the 'have mores' placed their thousand-pound chips and covered the green baize tables with enough money to buy a couple of counties in Scotland.

Joe, particularly, was not his usual ebullient self. With his mouth agape, he watched Dana Broccoli, Cubby's femme-fatale spouse, lose thirty thousand pounds in ten minutes. I could see his face flush and then, quite suddenly, he erupted in a violent stream of Scottish invectives. Incensed at seeing more money than he'd probably ever earned in his lifetime being thrown about by these self-indulgent twits, Joe shook his fist and cursed them all. Strangely enough, none of the staff took much notice of his outburst. He calmed down on the way home, though he still couldn't understand how Cubby Broccoli allowed his wife to squander so much money without giving her a 'good clout around the ear'.

The great actor Joseph Wiseman (who had appeared with Marlon Brando in *Viva Zapata*) was cast as Bond's counterpart, the villain in *Dr No*. Joseph had an amazing face and a vulnerable passion that simmered just below the surface of his skin. I admired him greatly and was thrilled when he accepted one of the leading roles in the first of the trilogy of Pirandello plays that George Devine had commissioned me to translate for the Royal Court. It was the very same play, *Naked*, which Sean and I had done at the Oxford Playhouse. As this was to be my return to the stage after having Jason, I was very excited.

I decided to put my own name to the translation instead of the nom de plume of Simon Nedia (the anagram of Minos and Diane), which we had used in Oxford. George Devine was very helpful with the casting. We sat in his little office at the back of the circle at the Royal Court and went through *Spotlight*. I can still see him wielding one of those thick octagonal red pencils as he rifled through the pages. He came to a Danish actor called Morgans (pronouced 'Moans') Veita, whom we had been considering for the part of the Consul but who had recently died. 'Sleep sweeter, Moans Veita,' he sang cheerily to the tune of the Bournevita ad, as he struck through Morgans' face with his red pencil.

I felt a sudden shudder and wished he would stop doing it. It is a very unlucky thing to mock the dead, and so it was to prove. On the opening night, two terrible things happened. The first occurred before the curtain had gone up. The whole cast had gone down to the stage just before the half-hour call to practise curtain calls but, when Joseph Wiseman returned to his dressing room, he noticed immediately that his wallet had been removed from his make-up table. Someone must have climbed up the fire escape and nicked it in those few minutes when both he and his dresser were absent from the room.

What upset Joseph wasn't the loss of the money it contained but rather that the wallet held the only photo he possessed of his son, who had committed suicide only months before. He was thrown into a crying fit with the shock and grief, so we held the curtain for ten minutes to let him regain control. All through the first act, I could see tears forming in the corners of his eyes and felt such compassion for him that I was distracted, though still trying to use the emotion somehow.

But the real coup de grâce, the ultimate horror that every actor prays will never happen, took place right in the middle of my big scene. Someone died in the second row of the stalls. It appeared at first that the old gentleman had only fainted but soon, with the awful, unmistakable sound of the death rattle, it was apparent that his life had deserted him. There was nothing to do but wait until his body was removed, passed with difficulty along the row by theatre patrons and stage staff. It was a devastating situation. We had to decide whether to abandon the play altogether or to get on with the scene as best we could. Somehow we struggled on, but it was an impossible task. I will never forget the desperate feeling of impotence I felt that night, as though the world had come to an end and the glittering prize had been snatched from my outstretched fingers and hurled into a black pit.

Harold Hobson, that wizened little *Times* critic whom everyone feared, wrote that it was a pity Diane Cilento had not used Simon Nedia's translation. I was too shattered to protest that the translations were identical and, mercifully, the rest of the limited run went smoothly. I was flattered when Dame Peggy Ashcroft came to see the play twice, assuring me that it was the best piece of acting she had seen all year. It was edifying, too, when theatre critic Sheridan Morley gave me a much-belated guernsey. In a 1998 review that appeared in the *International Herald Tribune*, Morley pithily wrote:

> In an entirely understandable desire to sell as many advance tickets as possible, London theatres are beginning to operate a 'Year Zero' policy that would have been the envy of Pol Pot himself.
>
> Virtually any show that has not had a major West End revival in the last twenty years or so is routinely hailed as an 'amazing rediscovery' with seldom any reference to any earlier rediscoverers: theatrical history is simply ceasing to exist.
>
> Thus at the Almeida, Pirandello's *Naked* gives no program or other credit to the pioneering work done on the play here by Diane Cilento at the Royal Court in a much more Pirandello-hostile climate of the 1960s.

Sean had not been present at my traumatic first night, although he sent a telegram saying 'Here's to a warm hand on your entrance!' It was in reply to my telegram sent when we had stayed in bed and he had missed his plane. It read: 'Procreation is the thief of time'.

Sean had started shooting the second Bond film, *From Russia with Love*, in Turkey, and I joined him there as soon as *Naked* was finished. Istanbul was simply the most exciting and extraordinary city I had ever visited. What made it all the more enjoyable was the fact that Ian Fleming and his bodyguard, the mammoth Mustapha, were my companions when Sean was working and we were all treated like royalty.

Terence Young, director of both *Dr No* and *From Russia with Love*, had a son called Sean, so he called my Sean 'Junior', which always sounded a bit odd. Though born an Irishman, Terence had cultivated the veneer of an English gent, with a mid-Atlantic accent and slicked-down hair. Determined to eradicate Sean's plebeian Scottish ways, he somehow managed to get Dom Perignon to send us a case of champers every week and Turnbull & Asser shirts turned up at regular intervals. He had also arranged that, every night like clockwork, a young Turkish waiter would arrive in our suite bearing a magnificent silver tray on which an open tin of Beluga caviar glistened. Another tray came covered with mounds of egg yolk, egg white, minced onion and lemon with which to mix the delectable roe. The champagne glasses were always frosted to perfection, the roasted pistachios arrived still warm to the touch and the room was filled with clusters of fresh violets and lilies of the valley. I wallowed in every minute of it, although I hate to admit that too much caviar too often can make one blasé.

Nearly every morning, a black limo turned up to collect me for a day of discovery and delight. At the wheel was Mustapha, a 300-pound Turkish wrestler who wore all the wages he'd ever earned in gold in a money belt around his ample belly. Thus, he moved ponderously, walking with his knees wide apart like a toddler who has just dirtied his nappy.

Ian Fleming was a tall, impressive man who began every morning with a massive hangover, which rendered him grey and miserable until we had stopped for a bracer of vodka steeped in cracked pepper. I used to watch the blood creep up his neck and cheeks until the little veins in his nose turned from waxy white to bright crimson.

Pedro Armendáriz, the great Mexican actor who had become an international star in the classic 1947 film *The Pearl*, often accompanied us on these jaunts. Pedro, who was playing Bond's ally Kerim Bey, discovered in the middle of the shoot that he was suffering from terminal cancer. Instantly, the entire film schedule was changed so that his scenes were shot first in case he died before they'd been completed. I learned later that Pedro's cancer may well have been attributable to his work on

The Conqueror, which was filmed in 1956 near a nuclear testing site. Over the next two decades, an inordinate number of cast and crew members, including John Wayne, Susan Hayward, Agnes Moorehead and Dick Powell, succumbed to various forms of cancer, ostensibly caused by the nuclear fallout that contaminated the location and film sets.

With the intensity of someone who knows he may be looking his last on the beauty of this world, Pedro was determined to gorge every sense in the moments left to him. He carried with him a supply of small round chillies and, without a pause in the conversation, he would pop one of these into his mouth, crunch it with relish, swig tequila and make jokes while his eyes scanned the horizon in case something of interest got past him.

I have an image of the four of us on the top deck of a ferry going up the Bosphorus. The sun is high overhead and Pedro has bet me a hundred dollars that I cannot ingest one of his little fireballs. Stupidly, I put the thing in my mouth and, within seconds, my eyes are streaming while they are laughing their heads off at my grotesque expressions of torment. I win the money but have to go down and wash my mouth out as it is not asbestos-clad like theirs.

Within a year they are all dead. Ian Fleming has a fatal heart attack playing golf near the drying-out place at Hove where he has been for some weeks; Pedro shoots himself in a Mexico City Hospital, the gun having been smuggled in by his son when his father's pain becomes too unbearable; and Mustapha drowns in a collision between two ferries exactly like the one we are travelling on now, his golden hoard carrying him straight to the bottom of the Bosphorus.

But, for the present, I adore being with these three wonderfully contrasted men. I feel proud to be the only woman taken with them into the inner sanctum of the harem at the Santa Sophia Mosque as guests of an ancient Ottoman prince, to drink silted-up Turkish coffee out of tiny silver cups. They dress me up in concubine robes and watch as I try to teeter about in a pair of the wooden platform clogs that ladies wore to the baths. We visit the spice markets at the Galata Bridge, where Mustapha knows everyone and Ian spends hours writing down various herbal remedies described by a vendor.

Like John Osborne, Ian Fleming carried a small black notebook around with him everywhere he went, noting down expressions or anything that caught his fancy. He asked me for some Australian descriptions of a hangover and I recall that he particularly liked 'a mouth like the bottom of a cocky's cage'. Every year he would travel to whatever city hosted the Interpol Convention, where police chiefs, the secret service and law-enforcement officers from all over the world came together to discuss and update methods used against organised crime. He recorded everything meticulously and gleaned plots for his Bond novels from these authentic sources.

Mustapha, who had been the star wrestler in the city where the sport originated, organised a special evening when the British stunt-men challenged the Turkish wrestlers to a contest. When the Turkish team turned up, we laughed at their pear shapes and lack of fitness. They were all flabby, with bald heads, double chins and big moustaches. Sitting upstairs in an exclusive circular venue once used by the Ottoman emperors to view the Whirling Dervishes, we looked down on the contestants from above. The Turks, through their guile and expert knowledge of how to use their weight strategically, just leaned on their adversaries, weakened them and then struck mercilessly. They won every bout. The stuntmen retired humiliated, having been tossed around like marionettes, but that didn't stop everyone from having a marvellous knees-up afterwards.

It was at this testosterone-fuelled event that Robert Shaw, with his side-kick and 'trainer' Percy Herbert, challenged Sean to a foot race. I had known Robert Shaw for many years, ever since he'd played one of the sailors in *Tiger at the Gates*. Cast as SPECTRE's arch villain, Donald 'Red' Grant, dispatched to kill Bond, Shaw had been training like an Olympian for months. He had even dyed his hair platinum blond for the part, to formidable effect. Robert was a born competitor and loathed losing more than anything in the world, and so the stage was set for this rare spectacle a week hence at the railway track just outside Istanbul where they were shooting. Everyone, including Lotte Lenya (Rosa Klebb in *From Russia with Love*), Ian Fleming, Mustapha, Pedro and the wrestlers, promised to be there.

Percy Herbert had appeared in hundreds of British war films, almost always as the ugly mug standing behind the star, egging him on in the rumbles. All week, Percy and Robert were seen at every spare moment running, practising flying starts and talking tactics in corners of the park below the hotel. It was deadly serious stuff. Sean, however, seemed to disregard the whole thing.

When the day of the race dawned, we set off for the location late. A buzz of anticipation greeted us as we got out of the car and Robert was there already, warmed up and sporting magnificent new running shoes for the occasion. Sean was wearing his clumsy old bovver boots. 'Okay, let's go,' he said tersely, walking towards the starting point further down the tracks.

'God, aren't you going to change your boots? You must be crazy!' said Percy, rubbing his hands together and winking at Robert.

Sean didn't bother to answer but took a swig of his stand-in's coffee as he went past. They lined up like two pros and Percy produced a pistol from somewhere. BANG! . . . and away they went.

If it had been a hundred-yard dash, Robert would have won by miles. He streaked off like a greyhound out of the traps, leaving Sean behind, but he began to tire at the halfway mark (or maybe he believed he didn't have to try any more). Slowly, Sean's longer legs began to make up the ground, his heavy boots pounding the grey stones between the railway lines until poor old Robert was overtaken and passed, with yards to spare. I could see money changing hands as Sean went off to get changed. He made a daft face at me and took another swig of his stand-in's coffee as he passed.

'Stupid fucker!' I heard Robert shouting at Percy. 'These fucking shoes are no good on sharp stones. I should have worn *boots*, you wanker!'

There was a litany of reasons why *From Russia with Love* went over schedule: Pedro Armendáriz having to be shot out of sequence; Daniela Bianchi, the female lead, having an accident and bruising her face; and Terence Young crashing into the sea in a helicopter (though emerging unscathed with his assistant, Michael White). It all added up to £200 000 over budget and some very edgy producers. Then, when they found they couldn't shoot the speedboat scenes in Turkey, the entire crew of seventy-two, plus wardrobe, stuntmen and baggage, were airlifted to the unlikely spot of Argyllshire in Scotland, where the final stunt sequences with powerboats were shot on the Firth of Lorne.

Here, I walked along the empty romantic shores of the loch and discovered acres of lovely fresh mussels. As a fitting culmination to the filming, Cubby Broccoli sent me to Oban to visit the fish-holding tanks and buy a mountain of lobsters. Together, we cooked up a classic pasta marinara, with fresh mussels and lobsters, for the entire crew. After an arduous struggle, there was great relief when the film was finally in the can. But who can argue that it wasn't worth it when the film finally came out? Some people think *From Russia with Love* is the best Bond film of them all.

When we got back to London, there was hardly time to settle in and cuddle the kids before we were off to Majorca for Sean's first big non-Bond film, *Woman of Straw*, with Gina Lollobrigida. Soon, having secured the house and farmed out our dog Harry Hotspur, the whole family joined him. By this time, I was beginning to understand what Mirabell Millamant, in William Congreve's *The Way of the World*, meant when she said, 'If I continue to endure you a little longer, I may by degrees dwindle into a wife.' It was another way of describing the condition of being a camp follower.

Still, the sun was warm and the sea was as clear and blue as only the Mediterranean can be. We frolicked on the beach and ate luscious paellas under moonlit skies, so there was absolutely nothing to complain about. Ken Adam (the production designer on the Bond films) and his wife, Letizia, were already ensconced at the same resort. Letizia and I used to loll about together on the beach with the kids in the day and go dancing in the open-air nightclub in the evening. It was on just such a night, while the music played and we danced under the stars, that Gina Lollobrigida arrived, dressed for Buckingham Palace, encrusted with diamonds, and alone.

In the early sixties, as in each particular era, there were specific dress and behavioural codes that had to be observed. At that time, it was the fashion to wear stockings held up by suspender belts, to have one's hair perfectly in place, to have one's lipstick appear as though it had been applied with an air-brush and to never allow one's false eyelashes to look like they were stuck on with cement. In other words, women were required to look like Barbie dolls, however uncomfortable it made them.

Gina must have been between husbands because she was travelling with her hairdresser only. Hairdressers have always played an important role in the movie industry, both as confidants and as couturists, especially in Italian studios. They knew all the age-concealing tricks, such as gathering the long hairs around the temples and plaiting them into thin lengths. These plaits would then be pulled together tightly and tied up on the top of the head, thus stretching the face upwards to produce taut, wrinkle-free skin and almond eyes. A wig would then cover the unsightly topknot and, presto, one effectively had a facelift. This accounted for the presence of Gina's hairdresser. Of course, the same result is more commonly achieved today by cosmetic surgery.

Gina's almond eyes scanned the scene and fixed on Sean, who was dancing with Letizia. She undulated across the floor on impossibly high heels, accosted him as though his partner did not exist and, thrusting her body forward, began to dance sensuously towards him. It was clear she meant business. Sean stopped dancing immediately and brought both women back to the table.

'This is my wife, Diane Cilento,' he said.

Gina turned her false-eyelash-fringed orbs on me, taking in my straight, uncombed hair falling over my face, which was without make-up, my bra-less brown body clad in the sari that Letizia had lent me, my bare legs and shoeless feet (I had kicked off my sandals under the table), and shuddered visibly.

'Oh! . . . This is your wife?' she gasped in disbelief.

'*Ciao*,' I rejoined. 'Care for some sangria?'

'*Straordinaria! Madonna!* . . . *Buona notte*,' she muttered, waving over my shoulder to an imaginary friend before, without looking at either of us, disappearing.

Sean sat down and we all laughed.

'That was what you'd call a cameo performance,' he said flatly.

During the shoot, Sean had to slap Gina, which gave rise to the usual tawdry stories in the press. Every trained actor knows that making slaps and punches look real without actually injuring someone is very much an art. Actors spend hours practising the old stage method of putting a hand up to the cheek very quickly, just before the open hand of the adversary hits the face. Hence, the full slap is taken on the hand rather than the cheek, producing a loud, effective sound. Jerking the head back at the same moment gives the impression of a thunderous blow. As with everything in the theatre, it's all a matter of timing. In films, it's more difficult, but still possible, to fake a slap, even if the camera is in close-up. It is the business of stuntmen to choreograph fights and they mostly do so superlatively well.

For some reason, perhaps because they hadn't rehearsed enough, when Sean slapped Gina during a scene in *Woman of Straw*, she must have turned her head away slightly, dislodging her wig so that the plaits tied up on the top of her head came adrift. One whole side of her face suddenly collapsed. She rushed from the set and was not seen again for the rest of the day. Of course, the press announced that Sean had hit Gina in the mouth and cut her lip. She was very gracious about it when Sean telephoned and apologised later in the evening.

This was a time in our marriage when I felt most cosseted and confident. I had the absolute certitude that Sean and I had found the equilibrium of one soul in two bodies and that nothing would ever sunder us. Even if Sean had to make love to countless women every week on the screen, he would never betray his love for me or his loyalty to us as a family. He had helped me through so much and I loved him for it.

I've since found a rather embarrassing quote, which I am supposed to have made at the time, although I don't recognise myself in these words at all:

Men have always been interested in me. I've always taken it for granted. But it's dangerous to be obsessed with your own good looks. Beauty-conscious women seem to miss so much of life. They are forever worrying if a nail breaks or wasting the best years under a drier. Sean likes me to be natural. After all, he knows me. He doesn't want me to be an ornament and neither do I. He has good taste and that means plain taste . . . elegant but not flashy. And I understand him thoroughly. I buy all his ties for him, play golf with him and do most things that he does. I can even do judo with him.

I *know* I didn't say that last sentence! Being too smug can sometimes prove to be a deadly mistake.

It was when we returned to London that a great surprise was awaiting me. *Tom Jones* had opened to rapturous notices and received several

Academy Award nominations, including my own as Best Supporting Actress for my part as Molly. For the very first time, I had my name up in lights at the big cinema on the corner at Piccadilly.

I was ecstatic, and so was my agent, Jimmy Fraser. The moment an actor receives an Oscar nomination, the phone never stops. Offers began to pour in, and Sean was not pleased.

Ever since we had married, Sean had become progressively more disapproving of my working. I expect that, without knowing it, he had an image of what a 'wife' should be, and one of the things that did not fit the picture was a competitor in the fame stakes. I assured him that it was very unlikely that I would actually win an Academy Award, as three actresses from *Tom Jones* had been nominated – Dame Edith Evans, Joyce Redmond and me – and it would be very difficult to show preference for one above the others.

I did not listen to Jimmy Fraser's urgings to cash in on the many offers that the nomination had spawned, but flew off to Los Angeles with Sean and Jason, leaving Giovanna, who had started school, with Nanny Foreman. We rented Sammy Davis Jr's house for the duration of the shoot of Alfred Hitchcock's *Marnie*, in which Sean was starring with Tippi Hedren.

As opposed to our ex-convent in Acton, my bet is that Sammy's pad had never housed a nun. The downstairs room contained a huge, semi-circular black leather couch that reeked of orgies, and at the touch of a button a screen would descend on which one could watch any sort of erotic film imaginable. Outside the sliding doors from the orgy room was a swimming pool and patio area without a fence, ready for a toddler's tumble, and a garden with a profusion of cacti waiting to prick small fingers.

By this time, Jason was about eighteen months old and had already shown himself to be something of a homebody. He fretted coming over on the plane and then cried for the next two days. The only way we could get him to sleep was to drive him around in the car until he was lulled by the rhythm of the engine. As soon as we stopped, he would wake up and start screaming again. We were at our wits' end until, in some sort of Eureka moment, we devised a way of floating him in the pool and dragging him around in the water, his little legs kicking with all his might. Sheer physical exhaustion finally overcame him and he slept for about ten hours. When he woke up, he was back to his gurgling, good-natured self. It was bliss.

The making of *Marnie* was fraught with frustrations. Hitchcock was in the midst of an ongoing battle with Tippi Hedren, the female lead; there was continuous argument about the script; and Alma, Hitchcock's inspirational wife, who was once his editor and now his most trusted advisor, was less than happy with the way things were going.

Despite all this, Alma and Hitch were nothing if not convivial. When we went to dinner at their house, Hitch showed us a massive freezer in the basement filled with frozen samples of every memorable dinner he had ever had. He kept them there and sometimes treated himself to little bites of venison from his daughter's wedding feast or maybe a spoonful of raspberry mousse from some former epicurean orgy. He was proud of being a gourmand.

He also told incredibly filthy anal-fixated jokes extremely well and spoke slowly through pendulous lips with a lugubrious Cockney accent. He was mesmeric when recounting stories of the practical jokes he had played, especially on actors who took themselves too seriously, and what made these tales so irresistible was the pure pleasure he derived from telling them. I have always remembered the one he told about the time he hosted his famous 'Blue Dinner'.

No expense was spared in the preparation of this savage lampoon. First, in great secrecy, he went to Central Casting and auditioned fifty or more actors to impersonate foreign royalty, their families and their blue-blooded companions. The chosen actors were drilled in etiquette and the history of their various kingdoms, outfitted in sumptuous clothes and adorned with much real jewellery. Next, he sent out gilt invitations. Places at the dinner cost thousands of dollars. Then he hired the best chefs in town to prepare a fantastic array of dishes, all of them coloured blue: the bread rolls were blue, the cream for the coffee was blue and the azure champagne flowed like water.

His guests were the crème de la crème of Hollywood – stars, male and female, with their agents, producers, directors, as well as an assortment of multi-millionaires and tycoons. He arranged the tables so that the 'aristocracy' intermingled with his guests and a servant was positioned behind each person's chair. Unbeknownst to the guests, he had set up cameras to cover all the action at the tables. What ensued was hilarious, classic *cinéma-vérité*.

I would love to have seen some of that footage. The evening ended when Hitchcock stepped in, halted the proceedings and announced the real names of the 'monarchs, princesses and queens' – but not before his guests had gushed, grovelled, pretended to adore the grotesque blue food and set up deals or romantic rendezvous with the exotic 'luminaries'. The evening provided Hitchcock with enough blackmail material for a lifetime.

Hollywood was very seductive, and I had a lovely time being alone with Jason and teaching him to swim, but sometimes I longed for our own bed, for Gigi, Nanny Foreman and Harry Hotspur. Even awful old Acton and the Uxbridge Road were attractive at a distance. I had fallen in with Sean's image of the 'wife' but I could not help feeling horribly constrained as a camp follower. My tolerance for creative inactivity and playing 'the little woman' was very low. To make it worse, Jimmy Fraser rang me every day with new prospects but I stopped telling Sean about them because his antagonism towards my working was growing every day.

Finally, while I was still in Hollywood, I accepted the leading role in *Rattle of a Simple Man* opposite Harry H. Corbett, who was another client of my agent. Harry had become famous as Harold Steptoe, the son in the popular BBC sitcom about rag-and-bone traders, *Steptoe and*

Son. It had been the top-rating show on the box for several seasons and Harold's adenoidal Cockney catchphrase, 'Ooooo-er . . . You dirty old maaaan!' was repeated by imitators throughout the Western world. As Harry wanted to escape his Steptoe image, the character of Percy Winthram, a football fan from the North of England who comes to London for the Cup Final and loses his virginity, seemed to fit the bill. I was to play Cyrenne, the tart with a heart of gold who teaches him about life. For me, the added attraction of *Rattle of a Simple Man* was that the whole shoot would be in London, so I would be able to live at home throughout. I had begun to feel guilty about leaving Giovanna and not being there to cook dinner every night.

Sean's next Bond film was to be *Goldfinger*, but while we were in Hollywood there had been a major controversy about the authorship of the projected fourth Bond movie, *Thunderball*. Following litigation that reached the British High Court, Kevin McClory, whom I recall as a stuttering Irish chancer with incredible chutzpah, received a substantial out-of-court settlement of his claim to have written the book in collaboration with Ian Fleming. Consequently, the Broccoli-Salzman company, Eon Productions, had to make a deal with McClory to secure the film rights to *Thunderball*. It was a strange situation. So much money was being thrown about but Sean was still getting paid only peanuts. He resolved to change the state of play and did so, but not without a lot of fur flying. He and his agent, Richard Hatton, cut a separate deal, which increased his salary to fifty thousand pounds, a percentage of the films and some payment out of the merchandising. In comparison, I was the one who was being paid peanuts now.

The moment a newspaper article appears stating that someone has been paid or has inherited a large sum of money, three things are bound to happen in rapid succession. The first is the sudden attention of the Inland Revenue in the persons of eager, long-snouted taxmen; the second is that one is visited by many people who claim to be related; and the third is a spate of robberies. There's another feature of the fame game, notably that tradesmen either charge double the price for any work or nothing at all if they're fans.

As soon as it was announced that Sean's salary had reached epic proportions for a British movie actor at that time, the sequence was set in motion. Taxmen emerged from nowhere and Sean spent much time with his accountants. The relations were headed our way but they took a little longer than the spate of robberies.

We were lying in bed one morning in the big front bedroom on the second floor in Acton when we heard the engine of my little blue Mini Cooper turning over and chugging into life. It was parked out in front of the house as there was no garage. Sean jumped up and went to the window in time to see some guy who had hot-wired the car climbing into the driver's seat. He flew down the stairs and out the front door with nothing on. Seeing Sean belting down the street in naked pursuit, the culprit must have lost his nerve because he slewed the car sideways, crashed it into the curb and leapt out. There was a race out into the Uxbridge Road until the man disappeared into the traffic and Sean gave up the chase. I shall never forget the view of Sean's bare buttocks jiggling down the street like two white moons receding into the morning light.

We had no security personnel to guard us and the house in Acton was very vulnerable. One hot summer's day, I was out in the back garden (which backed onto Acton Common), wearing a bikini and trying to make a border garden against the wall, when a low drone began quite close to my ear. The volume increased until I could make out words. It was a Dalek voice.

'Are . . . you . . . receiving . . . me . . . Mrs Sean . . . Connery? . . . I . . . have . . . a . . . message . . . for . . . Mrs . . . James . . . Bond! . . . I . . . am . . . coming . . . to . . . get . . . you! . . . Be . . . prepared!'

I retreated to the house and peered out from behind the curtain of the sitting room. A group of beefy bovver boys were huddled against the fence, one of whom had his mouth pressed against the palings making the Dalek sounds while the others clustered behind him and egged him on.

I went down to the kitchen, where Harry Hotspur was snoozing on the warm cork floor. Harry was a gentle giant of a German shepherd who would have been a tightrope walker had he been a person. We used to watch him negotiate the top of the brick wall that separated our garden from the ladder-hire place next door. He would run along the mossy bricks like a dog dancer; it was his way of greeting tradesmen. He also allowed the children to sit on him, though I was careful not to let them get too near his nether end as he became rather sensitive to little fingers prying about in his private parts. Perhaps it was because the poor dog was a monorchid (that is, he had only one testicle). We resisted the idea of renaming him Harry Hitler. He was altogether a singular dog.

I roused Harry and ushered him out the sliding door and into the garden. Then, as we neared the fence, I shouted 'Sool 'em, Harry! Go get 'em, boy!'

It was all that was needed. Harry barked like the hound of the Baskervilles and leapt up on the fence, scattering the crew behind it. Harry was definitely the answer to the interloper/pest question.

We lost Harry in a singular way. It happened like this. An Irish nightwatchman came to guard one of those little holes in the road that appear and disappear all over cities. It was covered by a small tent and was situated at the end of our street on the Uxbridge Road. He used a frying pan to cook up sausages on a primus stove every evening at about 11.30 p.m. When the seductive aroma of 'snorker' drifted up to the house and reached Harry's nose, he would stir himself from his usual comatose state and ask to be let out.

Making his way along the back wall on tippy-paws, Harry would drop noiselessly into the street and saunter up to the tent to get his sausage. The nightwatchman and the dog would sit in comradely silence all night until the first rays of sun lit up the chestnut trees. Only then would he come back through the garden and bark briefly at the back door to be let in.

One morning, he didn't come home. There was no barking at the door, no Harry. I looked out into the Uxbridge Road and saw that there was no tent, no night watchman and no more hole in the road. Our theory was that the Irishman had fallen in love with Harry, decided that he couldn't live without him and had taken him off back to Ireland or to some other building site far away.

We were all very despondent about Harry, believing we would never see him again. Then, one day, months and months later, he crawled in. He was hardly recognisable. He was covered with mange, his fur lifeless and falling out. His paws were a terrible mess, calloused and bloody with nails ripped out. But he was our lovely Harry and we hugged and kissed him. It was so heartening to see his yellow eyes laughing and to hear his moans and snorts and the children's shrieks of pleasure. Sadly, he had contracted some fatal disease on his long trek home and no amount of begging the vet would change his firm belief that Harry's life would become more and more miserable. Reluctantly we agreed to let him be put to sleep.

As for the other effects of instant wealth, for me they meant that I had to learn fast how to cater for the increasing hordes of people who invaded our house, as neither Sean nor I wanted to employ servants. The large contingent of golfing chums who would come back with Sean after a game were invariably ravenous and thirsty. Golf had become something of an obsession with Sean since our carefree days at Richmond. His dentist, Ian Caldwell, was the amateur champion of Great Britain and he had arranged for Sean to have special lessons. There is a notable scene in *Goldfinger* when Bond plays Auric Goldfinger (Gert Fröbe) for five thousand pounds at the famous Stoke Poges golf course and beats him, albeit by foul means, and Sean wanted to make his golfing prowess look genuine.

It was in August 1964, while Sean was shooting the golfing scenes for *Goldfinger*, that Ian Fleming suffered a massive coronary and died. Earlier, when I'd been night shooting *Rattle of a Simple Man* at a location in a Soho street, Ian used to come and visit me. We'd sit in my caravan talking about his life while he took little nips of cognac from his flask. A driver was always waiting to transport him back to the all-night club he'd come from but Ian confided that he was going to get serious and renounce the demon drink. He told me he was going to a special drying-out place near the coast where he could think, write and sort himself out. He'd read all the books he'd missed out on and play golf when he felt fit enough. His plan was to go back to Jamaica and stay at Golden-eye, the house that had featured in many of the Bond books, where he'd discovered an old volume on birdwatching by a certain James Bond. Like a magpie he had appropriated the name.

True to his word, Ian had gone to the drying-out place near the coast and had not touched a drop of alcohol for weeks before his death. Perhaps the shock was too much for his system. I felt that I had lost a true friend and was amazed to read in his obit that he was only fifty-six years old.

The subject of 'friends' was becoming a point of contention at around this time. Sean contended that I was mixing only with gay guys, listening to their prattle and relying on their professional judgement. He didn't want to come home, he told me, to find a house full of queens. The object of his ire was a man called Neil Harvey who was working with me on *Rattle of a Simple Man*. Neil was very quiet and professional, encouraging me without trying to be bossy. He watched me like a hawk, giving me back-up and supervising my accent and clothes, etc. Sean didn't like his influence over me.

I didn't tell Sean that the reason I had a lot of gay friends was because they provided protection. It seems weird, but many of Sean's dear 'friends' (with some noted and appreciated exceptions) tried to play the poacher with me the moment his back was turned. I knew that I wasn't batting my eyelashes at them or flirting in any way. I thought back to my marriage to Andrea. No-one had tried it on with me then. My only conclusion was that his so-called 'friends' had some peculiar subconscious idea that if they could have *me*, they'd be more macho than James Bond, having cuckolded him in the person of Sean. I still ran around cooking and catering for golfers and comedians, but there was an uneasy atmosphere.

As an actor, I had been harbouring a dream for a long time. The idea had come to me many years before, when I'd first signed the contract with Sir Alexander Korda. I wanted to make a film in Australia. It must be remembered that the only feature films that had been made in my mother country were populated with American stars in the leading roles, like *On the Beach* with Ava Gardner and Gregory Peck, and *The Sundowners* with Robert Mitchum.

I dreamt of finding a book by an Australian author that would make a good screenplay, and of having enough clout to produce a feature film on location with an almost all-Australian cast (including myself and Leo McKern, and with Sean). I was sure I had found the right one when I was sent a copy of *Call Me When the Cross Turns Over* by D'Arcy Niland (author of *The Shiralee* and husband of Ruth Park, who wrote the Australian classic, *Harp in the South*). Sean was looking for a part as far removed from the suave 007 as possible, so why not an Irish–Australian rodeo rider in the Outback? It *must* be a contender. I was fired with enthusiasm and showed the book to Sean. He was cagily interested but a trifle leery of finding his way into the notoriously difficult Australian accent.

Immediately, I embarked on meetings with Ruth Park and D'Arcy Niland. I had talks with Leo McKern, discussions about directors, finance and all the other exigencies of getting a film up. This pre-pre-production process has been known to take decades but I had the stomach for it and my spirits soared at the thought of going home to accomplish such a project.

'Call me when the Cross turns over' is an old bushie's saying, which refers to that time just before dawn when the stars of the Southern Cross constellation turn themselves over and disappear below the horizon. The Australian press was informed of the impending shoot and anticipation grew as the script took shape. The producer, Doc Merman, renamed the film *Big Country, Big Man*, convinced that the book's title was too obscure.

In the meantime, I had not forgotten my promise to George Devine to translate two more Pirandello plays in time for the next season at the Royal Court. The one I was working on was *Il Giocco delle Parti*. It is nearly always called *Rules of the Game* in English but I thought its more subtle and true translation, *The Game of Roles*, was a better title. George agreed and I tweaked him about coveting the leading role.

'I'm not just going to covet it, I'm going to *play* it!' he stated unequivocally. 'So get a move on.'

I didn't mention to him that I was spending whatever free moments I had after being mum, wife, chief cook and bottle-washer, gardener, actor and film star, trying to coordinate the raising of money for a movie to be shot twelve thousand miles away. I must have been mad.

These years of my life were so crammed with events – rushing around the globe making films, evading the press and fans alike, being hustled in and out of buildings – that I became rather muddled about whether I was a wife or a diva or both. For Sean, the schism between his public and private lives was even more significant. He was expected to behave like 007 in public and in private to be the 'Jolly Green Giant' Scottish laddie with a wife and kids.

The dynamics of our relationship had changed radically since our marriage. Sean demonstrated his opposition to my working by stating categorically that if I continued to do so, he would give me no money for housekeeping. I found it difficult to believe that I should be castigated for practising my profession, a craft I'd honed throughout all of my adult years and which had been the reason we'd met. He knew I was a serious actor.

Without creating too much discord by discussion of the matter, I chose to accept work when it was attractive and lucrative. However, Sean really hated it when the studio chose a splendid villa for me in Rome for the shoot of *The Agony and the Ecstasy*, directed by Sir Carol Reed. I was playing Caterina de Medici in the big-budget film about Michelangelo, opposite Charlton Heston and Rex Harrison. My father and mother came over to stay, the children were there with us and we even acquired a marvellous dog that looked exactly like one of those antique hunting hounds in old medieval tapestries. We had palatial quarters and a swimming pool in a grotto. Ludovica, my ex-sister-in-law, arrived to inspect the set-up and was duly impressed. The children were in ecstasy, with no agony in sight.

Yet it was hard to ignore Sean's discomfort at the fact that I was the star of this particular film. He and Charlton Heston were instant antagonists, whereas Rex Harrison became a firm friend and golfing partner. At that time, Rex was married to the Welsh actress Rachel Roberts, who was desperate to have a baby. I can recall one spectacular Sunday lunch with the Harrisons at our villa. The day stretched into a glowing Roman evening as we ate leisurely and lazed by the pool with the kids. My mother spent hours in deep consultation with Rachel, advising her about conception, gestation and childbirth, while my dad, Sean and Rex hooted at each other's outrageous stories. Later on, we all played a wicked game of croquet. The visit terminated when Rex's dog, a lumbering basset hound called Homer, had a heart attack after chasing our speedy bitch around all day.

An odd thing happened that afternoon. I was lying on the lawn next to the pool dozing while my fingers absentmindedly picked at the sweet-smelling grass beside me. When I sat up, I found that I had a four-leaf clover in my hand. Even with our professional dissension looming ominously in the background, I supposed it was pronouncing that I was one of the luckiest women in the world.

Sir Carol Reed, famed British director of *The Third Man*, had a hard job trying to balance the subtlety of Rex Harrison's Pope Leo with the more blunted approach of Charlton Heston to the part of the great master of the High Renaissance. Michelangelo di Ludovico Buonarroti Simoni is described as a man of small stature with bandy legs and a broken nose. Michelangelo produced several uncompromising self-portraits in his later years which show all these attributes to be true. While lamenting his own ugliness publicly, he just as publicly celebrated male beauty in his work, such as his statue of David. Despite the fact that Michelangelo was a noted and devoted homosexual, Hollywood chose Charlton Heston, a six-feet five-inch right-wing homophobe to play the part. Heston refused point-blank to play Buonarroti as anything but stolidly heterosexual and I was employed in part as the 'love interest' to fortify Chuck's theory that Michelangelo was straight. I had my hair dyed black for the role and was in awe to be working in the real Sistine Chapel. I adored the costumes but the shoot was marred somewhat by my having to wear enormous wooden platform shoes to come anywhere near Chuck's towering height.

There was no more Chianti under the stars or Roman sultriness when we arrived back in Acton. It was two rounds of golf a day for Sean, if he wasn't working, and much scouring, cooking and dog washing for me. I didn't hate it but I knew it would never be enough to hold my attention for long. I accepted to do a TV spectacular with Denholm Elliot and a host of other stars in an adaptation of *Camino Real* by Tennessee Williams.

Everyone of a certain generation remembers where they were when JFK was assassinated. I was on the roof at Acton having tea with Rigs

O'Hara and the children. We had just come back from a rehearsal of *Camino Real*, in which I was playing the Eternal Virgin, the one who sleeps with a new man every night but who is miraculously restored to a *virgo intacta* every morning. 'Highly unlikely,' I hear you say. The role entailed a great deal of dancing and Rigs, a small, leaping leprechaun of a man, was the choreographer. We had been teaching Giovanna the Time Step when the news came through on the radio. Rigs, who had come to the UK via New York as a dancer, burst into tears. For a moment I thought he would thrust himself off the roof but both children began to cry in sympathy and rushed towards him. I joined in with the nanny and we all held each other and sobbed on the roof until the light faded and it got cold.

So many tears must have been shed in the days that followed that fateful death which altered the atmosphere of the whole world. Somehow, we had lost our innocence, but unlike the Eternal Virgin I was playing, it was never restored. I was astonished to read years later that the last film John F. Kennedy saw before his assassination was *Tom Jones*.

I cannot move on from this dramatic year without recording one jewel-like day that Sean and I spent with Rachel and Rex Harrison. It was after we had returned to London from Rome and we'd decided to spend the day together. The air was balmy, so we planned to finish our round of golf, have a late lunch and a leisurely scrub-up before a night out at the Old Vic where *The Royal Hunt of the Sun*, Peter Shaffer's masterpiece about the conquest of the Incas, was having its London debut. All those things duly happened but in such a way as to make them unforgettable.

We were happily hacking our way though the second nine holes, miles away from the clubhouse or any shelter whatsoever, when one of the most violent freak storms I have ever lived through hit us with no warning at all. Suddenly, trees were bent to the ground or swaying like drunken sailors and branches were whistling through the air above our heads. The flashes of lightning instantaneously followed by crashes of thunder told us that we must be very near the centre of the perturbation. The howling gale made shouted communication impossible. We were all urging each other in different directions like demented traffic cops, fearful of sheltering under the swaying oaks but anxious to find some refuge.

Hail began pelting down on our heads, and that did it. I can't remember who started it but it was infectious. Soon we were all rolling about covered in mud, hugging each other and oblivious to whatever the elements hurled at us. 'Sexy Rexy' and '007' were no more, the ungentle rain from heaven having leached out of all four of us saturated souls what remained of our pride or pretensions.

We staggered back to the clubhouse, dragging our drenched belongings, before squelching our way to the car and speeding off, still giggling like idiots. A voracious craving for hot food and liquor overcame the four of us once home, showered and attired in clean dry robes. I proceeded to crush garlic and place planks of succulent, massaged steaks under the grill while Rachel peeled saucer-sized field mushrooms and tore up lettuce. Sean and Rex opened bottles of Dom Perignon and lager, tasting them together in a ritual act of male bonding.

Once our appetites had been sated, there was a collective hum of appreciation, followed closely by the desire for a post-prandial nap. We lay where we fell and slept like old dogs. Later, refreshed, dressed and fortified with another drop of remedial champagne, we were driven in Rex's Rolls-Royce to the theatre, where Robert Stephenson gave a sensational performance as Atahualpa, last king of the Incas during the invasion of Peru by the Spanish conquistadors. Backstage, I asked him how he managed to stand naked and frozen in space for twenty minutes at the outset of the play, and then move with the agility and grace of a puma thereafter. 'Yat,' he said, and there was nothing else he needed to say.

Who could have guessed that if we fast-forwarded my life a few years, I would be standing under a flowering bauhinia tree in Far North Queensland marrying the playwright's identical twin brother?

CHAPTER NINE

The way events in one's life come together is truly amazing. The very same Uxbridge Road butcher who supplied the sumptuous steaks we'd enjoyed after the storm whispered to me the name of the person who was committing the robberies that had plagued us since the announcement of Sean's upgraded salary. There had been so many break-ins that I'd lost count. We knew it must be someone who was well aware of our movements and Sean had sworn to break the hands of the person who was making our lives such a misery. The butcher uttered the name of the thief's brother first, a well-known British pop star.

'Who?' I asked, flabbergasted.

'No, not *'im*. It's 'is bruvver who's bin doin' your place over. 'e took a room on the second floor next door and 'e watches out the window wiv binoculars. When you go out, 'e goes in, wiv a mate sometimes. I reckon 'e does it 'cause he's jealous of 'is bro. 'e's only a lad.'

The initial robbery was a botched affair. While attempting to carry the Robinson's Powder-Proof Safe down the back stairs, they dropped it. They left it there on its side but took my wedding rings and all my jewellery plus a new twelve-bore Purdey shotgun that had been given to Sean, along with five hundred rounds of ammunition. The police were extremely concerned about these last two items but appeared indifferent to anything else. They knew it wasn't a professional job, nor were the ones that followed, but the robbers had succeeded in denuding our house of most of the precious bits and pieces we had collected.

I was thrown into an awful quandary. I knew it would be dangerous to tell Sean, so I turned to Fred Vallachi for advice. Built like a main-event wrestler, which he may well have been at some time in his life, Fred had become a fixture at Acton. He was a member of Cubby Broccoli's entourage, who massaged Sean and did some gofering and chauffeuring. Fred had frizzy red hair, a flattened nose, twice as many teeth as most humans and enormous forearms like Popeye, which were covered with hair and freckles. He talked in a very loud voice with a heavy Bronx accent. Cooking and eating pasta were his favourite pastimes and his awful jokes and laughter made him irresistible. He became a member of the family and the children adored him. Fred's response to the information I imparted to him was classic. He looked sideways at me and said meaningfully, 'Ya mean ya want me to *lean* on him some?'

I assured him I did not. I just wanted to stop the robberies and to reclaim what had been stolen without involving Sean, who would fly off the handle.

'Okay, foist thing you do is get in touch with the guy's brudder and tell him what his liddle bro is doin' . . . then you tell the cops, but quiet, wit' no fuss. Ask the top guy to come here, meet me, then we talk about it.'

The meeting between Fred, me and the local police superintendent took place in a secluded corner of the back garden. We sat at a small round table drinking tea while the serious British policeman made it clear very quickly that he would tolerate no Mafia-type violence on his patch and that he knew about people like Fred's methods of persuasion. If he thought he was going to ruffle Fred's feathers, he was wrong.

I explained the situation, stressing that, if word got out to the press, there would be a media feeding frenzy. 'POP STAR'S BABY BROTHER ROBS 007 OF HIS GUN' was amongst the sensational headlines that came to mind. There would be recriminations, court cases and possibly real violence. The inspector concurred and a plan was hatched whereby he would approach the pop star and inform him of his brother's activities. The pop star would then persuade his brother to confess to where the missing items had been sold and would pay to retrieve them. At this point, the inspector would step in and arrest the boy. Being underage, he would appear in Juvenile Court and receive a caution. Sean would only have to know that the thief had been apprehended and that the stolen goods had been retrieved. End of story.

The first part of the plan worked well, except that although the gun and ammunition were returned, I never saw my wedding rings or jewellery again. Then, at the Juvenile Court, the judge insisted that the young offender (who had several other convictions) be sent to a corrective institution. The young man leapt up and started shouting that the police were liars and that this was not the deal, while Fred stared balefully at him and made some ugly gestures with his hands. I do not know whether this had any salutary effect whatsoever but the culprit was sent to Borstal and we heard no more of him. In all, he had entered our premises seventeen times.

Goldfinger opened in Leicester Square to enormous crowds who broke through the reinforced plate-glass window in front of the theatre. One hundred policemen braced themselves while the shrieks of crazed fans and the wail of Shirley Bassey's voice repeating the refrain 'He loves only gold' filled the air. With a box-office gross of $124 900 000 internationally, *Goldfinger* was the most successful Bond film up until that time. Yet, paradoxically, the more successful Bond became, the more insecure Sean felt. He was convinced that he would never feel safe until he had a million pounds in the bank.

It was around this time that I met a man called R. D. Laing, an iconoclastic Scottish psychiatrist and author of an astonishingly astute book called *The Politics of Experience*, which he was in the process of writing. In it he describes a radical new method of helping patients through times of stress without endless hours on the couch. I talked to him about Sean, and then I talked to Sean about Laing. They were fascinated to meet each other, though Laing laid down stringent rules for the consultation. He demanded a great deal of money, complete privacy, a limo to transport him to and from the meeting and a bottle of the best single malt Scotch at each session. After his initial shock at the sum of money, I knew Sean was pleased at the arrangement. He knew no-one could ask for that much loot without being sure of his skills.

On the first encounter, Laing gave Sean a tab of pure LSD, taking about a tenth of that amount himself. It was his standard procedure with patients he felt were emotionally blocked. No-one was privy to what happened over the next six hours but I believe that, with his enormous reserve and armouring, Sean resisted the drug. As a consequence, he had to go to bed for several days to recover.

Still, it seemed that this initial trip opened a Pandora's box. Suddenly, Sean began to remember challenging childhood scenes with his mother or father. Buried anger, victories or defeats came tumbling out without warning. I recall him suddenly telling me and a fascinated Millicent Martin (my friend, who was the wife of Ronnie Carroll) how he used to hide sweets, comics and chocolates, which he'd nicked, under the coverlet when he pushed his baby brother Neil's pram around the shops with his mother. One day she flipped back the blanket and uncovered the stolen goodies. After a public belting in the street, Effie dragged him back to the shop by his ear, forcing him to apologise to the shopkeeper and replace the lot. Sean also started to think a great deal about why so many Scots leave their native land. He spent much time trying to tease out this knotty problem with Laing, although Laing laughed and said it was simply a question of boredom and Celtic constriction.

I have never known whether the intervention of Laing and his sessions with Sean affected the way things began to unfold in this next period of our lives together. Even though we had been working on the film of *Call Me When the Cross Turns Over* for months, and there was so much expectation and anticipation in Australia of our imminent arrival to begin major shooting, Sean suddenly pulled out, making a unilateral statement to the press, saying, 'Diane and I are often asked why we don't make a film together. Frankly, it would be a bloody disaster. I don't go along with husband and wife double acts. I want a wife to go to bed with, not a script conference.'

He was making his opinion public and there was nothing I could do or say. After my initial devastation, I did some serious cogitation. One night I sat down and began to write a book instead, inspired by the mad and memorable few weeks I'd spent at the Acapulco Film Festival in Mexico in 1960 with John Osborne and Penelope Gilliatt (who had just eloped together), Tony Richardson, Billie Whitelaw, Mary Peach and Oscar Lowenstein. We'd made up the British contingent but there had been many avant-garde filmmakers present from France, Italy and other countries. The action of my book, *The Manipulator*, takes place over twenty-four hours and has as its central theme the interaction of the locals with the jaded sophisticates of the film world.

When I had written forty pages, I showed it to Hodder & Stoughton, who liked it. They gave me an advance and a date to hand in the completed novel. That was it. I had a new career. I got stuck very often and came to know the wretched despair of sitting in front of a virgin sheet of paper without the twinge of an idea moving in my brain. It was a very different experience from anything I had ever known. Picking up a script with all the words in black and white staring from the page, the camaraderie of rehearsals and the guiding hand of a director seemed easy in comparison to the loneliness of an author.

The novel was my attempt to comply with Sean's ardent wish that I accept no work away from home, but like anything one commits to, writing cannot be undertaken without bringing all of oneself to the act. Clearly, it's a very demanding job, easily as absorbing as acting, and it has one glorious plus: unlike mounting a play, which costs a fortune, a writer can describe the most outrageously elaborate scenes at no cost whatsoever, except to the imagination of the reader.

The film Sean chose to do instead of *Call Me When the Cross Turns Over* was *The Hill*, an uncompromising exposé of the sadistic practices carried out in British army prisons during the North African campaign in World War II. There were no women in the film and it was directed in black and white by the illustrious Sidney Lumet, who chose to film in Spain at the height of summer in a place called Almeria, north of Málaga.

Running in full pack up and down a steep man-made hill in temperatures well over a hundred degrees Fahrenheit was the draconian punishment endured by the prisoners and, consequently, the actors who played those parts. Compared to the horrifying images of the abuses of prisoners in Abu Ghraib prison near Baghdad, *The Hill* would hardly raise an eyebrow today, but at that time it was shocking to question the integrity of British officers or their basic compassion. Many of the actors (the chubby Roy Kinnear for one) collapsed in the heat and others, including Jack Watson, Ian Hendry, Ossie Davis, Alfred Lynch, Harry Andrews, Norman Bird and Ian Bannen, developed thirsts worthy of camels traversing the Sahara desert. All these actors were from that exalted fraternity of thespians equally at home doing Shakespeare at the National Theatre as playing yobbos, criminals or soldiers in movies or on TV.

All of us, except Sidney Lumet and his wife, Gail (Lena Horne's daughter), stayed in a newish three-star hotel on the coast. I can only remember two other wives being present, Janet Munro, wife of Ian Hendry, and Jack Watson's wife, Betty. Most of these jerry-built hotels had been thrown up to cater for the massive influx of film crews who came to Almeria to film spaghetti westerns and any movies with desert locations, like *Lawrence of Arabia*. It was noisy and crowded, and the atmosphere amongst the cast and crew was thick with testosterone. Furious games of table tennis or any other competitive sports were devised by men bored with the tedium of life, going from dull desert location to hotel and back again with no women. The drinking was similarly competitive and therefore excessive. Unlike any other set I had been on, the violent and oppressive nature of the film spilled over into ordinary life at the hotel I was staying at with Sean. It was against this backdrop that our lives together began to unravel.

One weekend, towards the end of the shoot, the hotel hosted a large local wedding party. All the male wedding guests were slicked up with hair oil and wearing finery that almost outdid the females' gaudy outfits. There was music, clapping, the cicada-like clicking of castanets and the incessant hum and crash of Spanish guitars. The noise was interspersed with the raucous laughter and bawdy jokes customary at wedding parties. The film crew and actors mingled with the guests and became part of the celebrations, the liquor flowing down throats as fast as the army of waiters could serve it. The actors were introduced to a deadly drink, Fundador, the fiery Spanish brandy that's known to take your tonsils out. The guys were drinking it with beer as a chaser.

I found myself at the centre of a group of excited young Spanish hidalgos, none of whom could speak any English. My glass of sangria seemed to be bottomless and my Spanish became more fluent, however faulty, the more I drank. I can vaguely remember being whirled about and bent backwards before a crowd of stamping, clapping men, whose mouths all seemed to be open and shouting. I was learning to dance the flamenco, while the crew clapped and cried, 'Go, girl, go!'

Then the music and dancing stopped momentarily while mountains of food were served. I looked around but couldn't see Sean anywhere. I went searching for him at the snooker table and out on the terrace overlooking the sea, but he was nowhere to be found. Yet, later, I could strangely recall seeing his face scowling at me through the blur of faces, although I couldn't be sure.

It was late when I climbed the stairs to our room. I can't remember if I had a key or if the door was unlocked. I was a bit drunk. Once inside, in the darkness, I felt a blow to my face and was knocked to the floor.

I remember screaming, and I think we were both shouting. I got to my feet and tried to fight back, but another blow sent me flying. I managed to get through the bathroom door and locked myself in. I spent the rest of the night sprawled on the bathroom floor, covered with towels, whimpering. In the end, I must have slept.

When I woke at dawn, I dragged myself to my feet and looked in the mirror. With disbelief and utter horror I viewed the stranger staring back at me. I looked appalling and I felt sure my face would never be the same again. Something lurched inside me.

Hopelessly, I tried to collect myself and think what I should do. I felt that the whole thing was my fault and I was filled with shame, desperate that no-one should see me in this condition. I had to hide from the actors, the crew and, above all (horror of horrors), the press. One photo of me in this state would open the floodgates. We would be hounded until they'd squeezed the story dry. The only solution was to get away quickly so that no-one would see me until I looked like myself again. I thanked God that really large sunglasses were in fashion.

Collecting the few things that were scattered around the bathroom – my bathers, purse, sun hat, towels and toiletries – I slipped out the door. I could not even look at the bed where Sean was sleeping. The only people I saw were Jack Watson and his wife, who had just come up from a morning dip. Neither sun hat, hair nor goggles could hide my face, so I mumbled something about going down the coast to visit relations, collected the keys of the hire car from the front desk, and sped off, travelling south, away, away from all of it, with never a backward glance, wailing and cursing both of us.

I was so unnerved that I kept driving the car on the wrong side of the road and was nearly hit head-on several times. I was truly exhausted by the time I reached Málaga. Holing up in a little *pensione* by the sea,

I slept for the rest of the day and through the night. The next morning, I apprehensively faced the mirror again and was overwhelmingly relieved to find that the swelling had subsided. I still didn't want to have to think about what had happened, so I lay dozing for the rest of the morning before driving further south to my old stamping ground of Marbella in the afternoon.

As I drove, I allowed myself to think back in time and try to make sense of our present situation. There had been so much pressure on both of us in the preceding months. It is no use my trying to describe what it's like to be oppressed by public fanaticism, although some people think it's the price paid for fame. I once heard a man tell Sean he'd give his left testicle to be James Bond. I hated it. After the initial surprise, to discover that everyone is crowding in, wanting to touch, wanting to worship, it becomes frightening. You never feel safe, knowing that some stalker might do something crazy. Not only is the invasion of your space incessant but crowds of avid fans can knock you down and trample you to death, with no knowledge of what they are doing.

I knew with certainty that the house in Acton couldn't provide protection from a clever interloper. Only a week or two before we left for Spain, a young woman had taken a ladder from the hire place next door, propped it against the back wall and had been climbing through the window of the guest room when my dad had barred her entry. He'd escorted her from the house with stern warnings. 'If I'd been twenty years younger, D, it might have been different,' he quipped, but I didn't think it was funny. Several of the robberies had occurred while the children were sleeping upstairs. It was unthinkable that they should be drawn into the dangers and media maelstrom that surrounded iconic figures like Bond and the Beatles. The Fab Four were luckier than Sean; there were four of them and they were known by their real names. Anyone would suffer from an identity crisis if continually addressed by someone else's name.

The pressure on Sean had been overwhelming but I, too, was heartily sick of answering the same ghastly query, 'What is it like being married to James Bond?' Every day, the conviction had become more deeply rooted: we had to have somewhere to get away from the torment of living in such a frenzied fishbowl.

There had clearly been a build-up of fury and frustration in Sean; it had been fermenting just below the surface for months. Of course, we should have talked it through but we did not. We had allowed the pressure to get out of hand, stupidly and irresponsibly, our only excuse being that there was no precedent. No star had evoked such a reaction in Britain since Henry V after the battle of Agincourt – and he had his army to defend him from fans.

I could hear my mother's voice in my ears – 'There's nothing less attractive than a moaning, whining woman, Diane' – and some obdurate part of me stopped me from going to a doctor or calling up my sister. I simply could not have explained what had happened over the phone or even attempted to put it into words. All I knew was that something had been irreparably damaged. Thinking about it now, I would say that my unequivocal conviction that Sean was my loyal protector forever, the one person who had always made me feel safe in the midst of whatever crisis, had been shattered. Although I still loved Sean deeply, he would never be quite the same person I had trusted unconditionally. I felt a stinging pain in my heart for something lost that I would never find again and, at the same time, I was filled with mortification – not only for myself but for him. In today's world, one would have recourse to counselling but I was unaware of such possibilities then and I was mightily confused.

When I rang Sean that night to tell him where I was, I said nothing at all about my feelings and I did not cry. He was businesslike when he told me the shoot would be over in a week and that he would join me then. Neither of us mentioned what had happened.

The event that had occurred in our hotel room in Almeria was a taboo subject, too painful to touch upon. It lay between us like a blind boil that has not been cauterised; the infection lingers on but becomes isolated – a damaged part of one's being.

I never spoke about it until years later when I read the following quote from an interview Sean had done with David Levin for *Playboy* in 1965.

Playboy: How do you feel about roughing up a woman, as Bond
             sometimes has to do?
Connery: I don't think there is anything particularly wrong about hitting
             a woman – although I don't recommend doing it in the same
             way that you'd hit a man. An open-handed slap is justified – if
             all alternatives fail and there has been plenty of warning. If a
             woman is a bitch, or hysterical, or bloody-minded continually,
             then I'd do it. I think a man has to be slightly advanced, ahead
             of the woman. I really do – by virtue of the way a man is built,
             if nothing else. But I wouldn't call myself sadistic.

When I read this inflammatory quote, I was incensed by what I felt was a tacit agreement to violence to all the males who used Sean as a role model. The old saying 'A woman, a carpet and a walnut tree, the more you beat 'em, the better they be' is wrong. In my case it was more than that – I was once beaten, twice shy.

I drove through Marbella towards Estepona that afternoon, and as I passed the green sloping hills that climbed gently towards the mountains beyond I felt drawn into their serenity. I turned up a narrow roadway near a place called San Pedro de Alcantara. There were no houses that I could see but fig trees lined a driveway and I could smell the pleasant, musty odour of their leaves on the breeze that blew down from the hills. Something about the place seemed familiar and friendly, and so, on a whim, I found a place to stay nearby. The whisper of an impulse moved me to enquire whether there was some land with a farmhouse for sale in the area.

Following the instructions of a local, I found myself driving back up the narrow road near San Pedro de Alcantara. I had been informed that an Englishman owned the seventeen-acre *finca* and was thinking about selling it. This time, I turned into the long driveway with the fig trees, passed a small white farmhouse on my right and arrived at the main house that overlooked the sweep of countryside, with the sea in the distance. To the south, on the coast, was a large and beautifully kept golf course attached to a large new resort hotel.

Major Brassey-Thorn and his good lady trumpeted a welcome as I alighted from my car. They were an archetypal British couple who'd been in India all their lives ('British Raj, dontcha know, couldn't stand the climate back in Blighty, came here to make the most of the pension, couldn't live without the servants'). It was impossible to imagine them being called anything other than 'Brassey-Thorn'.

I explained that I'd been in a car accident, and that I was on the mend and anxious to look at properties in the area with a view to buying. They were only too happy to show me around. The main cottage was a typical Andalusian farmhouse, pristine white inside and out, with a jutting fireplace thigh-high from the floor, large warm terracotta tiles and a long terrace at the front. Opposite the house was a honeysuckle-covered arbour with table and chairs and a barbecue, perfect for eating out in hot weather. There was an airy master bedroom in the front and several smaller rooms for the children.

The other cottage was almost a replica of the main house, where guests could stay and be completely autonomous, but it was when I saw the orchards that ran up the hill to the highest part of the land that I knew the property was for us. There were apricots, figs, plums, melons, tomatoes, onions and peppers in beautifully tended gardens surrounded by lawn paths bordered by irrigation channels leading back to the long rectangular dam that fed the system and which doubled as a swimming pool.

I met Rafael, a small man with whiplash black eyes who was the master gardener, and his son Pepe, a large youth with a shock of black hair and a bad limp, the consequence of childhood polio. By the time I left, I was convinced that I had stumbled upon an answer to the problem of finding 'somewhere to get away'.

I believe fervently in the ideas put forward by R. D. Laing his book *The Politics of Experience*. Oddly enough, Laing was writing this very book when Sean had his sessions with the eminent doctor. Laing states under the heading 'Experience as Evidence':

> I see you, and you see me. I experience you, and you experience me. I see your behaviour. You see my behaviour. But I do not and never have and never will see your *experience* of me. Just as you cannot 'see' my experience of you . . . *Only* experience is evident. Experience is the *only* evidence . . . The relation between the evidence of experience and behaviour is the key stone that builders reject at their peril. Without it the whole structure of our understanding is not there and our lives may collapse.

Apart from the evidence of my experience on my face, I felt I understood in some part why something so sudden and brutal had happened. It was the result of months and months of pressure, unlike any that either of us had ever experienced. That was the keystone of our behaviour. For me, after the event, it took the form of an imperative desire to get away from the pressure of exposure. I could not exist in that sustained oppressive atmosphere. I had to escape and breathe the air. That was my experience of the way our lives had been. I could only imagine that Sean's had been the same.

Like an instinctive animal, I had run for cover, away from the relent-less gaze of people and the press, and at that moment nothing could have persuaded me to return.

I telephoned Sean from the Ayalaya Park (the brand-new hotel with the golf course next door to the *finca*) and described my find. I invited him to come and see for himself as soon as he had wrapped up the shoot the following week, and then I went back to the Brassey-Thorns to make a deal.

Sean did not look at my face when we met but it was an enormous relief to me that the farm met with his instant, unqualified approval. The terms of sale were agreed upon quite quickly and we returned to Acton with renewed vigour and hope. It was sheer joy to be reunited with the kids after what seemed like an ice age of darkness in sunny Spain.

Even so, the controversy about my accepting acting jobs still hung between us like a bad smell. Anyone who dared broach the sub-ject or propose doing a joint theatre or film venture was treated with the utmost derision by Sean. I was still working on my translation of Pirandello for the Royal Court and on my book, *The Manipulator*, but even these stay-at-home occupations irritated him. It seemed that Sean wanted me to do nothing but wait on him and dote on his every word like some sort of trained robot, a Stepford wife. How could he possibly have believed that I could turn into that sort of woman overnight?

I used to cook enormous Sunday lunches while Sean played golf, watching the goggle box until the arrival of the horde of ravenous mates he'd bring home. Every Sunday it got later until, at 5 p.m., I would be trying to resuscitate poor dried-up barons of beef and potatoes baked into oblivion. I spent much of my time with tears welling behind my eyelids and a sinking feeling in my chest. I was the worst sort of cliché: a golf widow.

Then, quite suddenly, I could hack it no more. There had been an ugly scene when Sean had thrown my entire manuscript across the room and I'd sat on the floor trying to match up the pages, fuming. I still feared Sean's fists but I'd had enough. So, one day, contrary to everything that has ever been written, I found a little house in Moscow Road. It has always been reported that it was Sean who left, as it would have created a bad image for Bond had the girl walked out on the mighty macho man, but this was not so.

Apart from the housekeeping, cooking, cleaning and other wifely duties I was supposed to perform, I had a deadline for turning over the manuscript of my book to Hodder & Stoughton, the publishers. On top of that, I simply couldn't afford to remain at Acton because, true to his word, Sean had stopped paying any housekeeping money. The most effective means to curtail anyone's freedom is to prevent their access to money. Even though I wasn't working at my profession of acting, he didn't reinstate the weekly cheque. The result was that *I had to work*, and I took parts in two films to earn quick money. One was *The Third Secret*, with Richard Attenborough and Stephen Boyd; the other was *Once Upon a Tractor* with Alan Bates, Melvyn Douglas and Jean-Pierre Aumont, in Rome.

The house in Moscow Road was a snug little haven away from the madding crowd, and I knew all the shops because it was just behind my old apartment in Caroline House. I didn't think our marriage was over for a second. I left because I refused to be treated as a doormat wife; I was able to earn a living and I was determined to ply my trade without guilt or oppression. Inevitably, Richard Hatton, Sean's agent had to deny rumours of a rift while reporters were like slavering wolves, waiting to get their teeth into our marriage and rip the life out of it.

It all came to a head one Sunday when I had invited the young Mexican director Raul Martinez-Ostos to have lunch at Moscow Road. George Devine had proposed Raul as a possible director of the Pirandello plays and we were discussing actors who were to be considered for the main parts. Raul had come to London to work as an assistant director at the Royal Court Theatre, and our friendship dated back to the

Acapulco Film Festival. Sean must have been sitting in his car watching the house because he suddenly came through the door, thundering, 'It looks like he's EXPECTED and I'm NOT!'

'That's right,' I said, 'but you're welcome to stay for lunch if you wish.'

He stormed out, but I knew it was only a matter of time before we would settle our differences – or at least that is what I fondly hoped.

As a complete novice in the writing business, my governing priority was to finish and hand in my manuscript by the prescribed date. I sat up all night writing, my theatre training having conditioned me to believe that lateness is a sin only marginally less grievous than murder. I didn't know then that writers, unlike reporters or actors, don't respect deadlines and hardly ever finish their books on time. In fact, some writers never even complete them. Thus, publishers are forced to become very patient people. But, for me, it was unimaginable that I would fail to finish my book by the due date.

I can remember quite clearly the panic I felt as the completion date grew nearer, being still unsure of how to end the novel and stopping only to walk Gigi to school or rush Jason out for a quick ride on the slippery slide in Kensington Park. I had no time to worry about Sean, the paparazzi or anything else until it was done. Reading the end of *The Manipulator* still makes me cringe. Hodder & Stoughton were somewhat astonished when I panted into their offices on the required date and threw the bulky package down on the desk. I thought it was finished but I hadn't yet encountered editors with large blue pencils.

While all this angst and mental activity was going on in Moscow Road, the fourth and most controversial Bond film, *Thunderball*, had commenced shooting at Pinewood Studios. I couldn't identify the strange emotions that were troubling my sleep and making my waking hours so fraught. I kept thinking that there was something really important I'd left behind in Acton but I didn't know what it was. It wasn't until Sean rang to say that he was leaving for Nassau on location that I realised what it was. It was *him*. I was missing Sean badly, and so were the children.

There is a photo in *Time* magazine of us all meeting at the airport in the West Indies. On our arrival, we were whisked away from prying eyes to Jasmine Cottage, Love Beach, in a place called the Garden of Eden. I now know that these seductive names were thought up by the real-estate confraternity to induce wealthy fools to spend a lot of money on their fantasies – before being developed, the place had probably been called Mosquito Bay at the Tip End – but here we were together again in the warm tropical sunshine, reunited in our common desire to make a go of it. We began to really talk again about finding a new secure place to live, about Spain and what we could do with the land.

Thunderball was a tough shoot, with all-night filming and a lot of aggravation. Once again, the director was Terence Young, the one who always called Sean 'Junior', but he was now treating him very differently, like Russian royalty, possibly haemophilic. One night a scene was being shot at a swimming pool, in which Bond had been given a small oral device by M that allowed him to breathe underwater. Every time the take was over, Sean would climb out of the water and leave the device on the diving board. A nurse would then come along and remove it to be sterilised before the next take.

For some reason, every time 'Action!' was called, something would go wrong and they'd have to do it again. Sean was getting pretty tetchy, quite rightly, and the atmosphere was becoming poisonous. Sound was blaming Camera, saying there was a hair in the gate or the focus-puller was out of synch. Somewhere around Take 30, the nurse, a lovely jokey lady who was a favourite with everyone on the set, left the breathing device on the diving board. She was busy gossiping with the make-up man when Terence Young pounced.

'You haven't sterilised it, have you?' he screamed at her, holding up the device and shaking it in her face. 'You can get off this set and never come back, you lazy bitch! Sean could be infected with a fatal disease and you would be responsible! You are not only lazy, you are a stupid fat cow!'

He went on and on, reviling her until she ran away in tears, never to return, while a stunned crew mumbled and looked at their boots. There had to be a scapegoat for the mistakes and she was it, someone expendable. I was surprised that Sean hadn't interceded on her behalf but he did not; he just stood there as though Terence was perfectly justified in behaving like a rabid mastiff. It was the first time I had seen Sean impervious to the plight of a fellow worker. In the face of an inflamed emotional scene on set, he had arrived at a state of virtual catatonia. It was a very telling turning point.

This incident happened in the magnificent grounds of the residence where Sir Harold Christie held court. Every evening, when the cast and crew were night shooting at his place, Sir Harold would appear, immaculately attired in evening dress with a wide red cummerbund encircling his generous waist, to play host with graciousness and affability. We took a shine to one another, perhaps because I am a sucker for a storyteller or perhaps because neither of us was actually involved in the work-at-hand.

Sir Harold and I swapped yarns about glorious vistas of coral cays as compared with the wonders of the Great Barrier Reef. He was full of tales of bygone days when he was a boy and sailed around the islands with his father, an evangelist and self-appointed Poet Laureate of the West Indies. He mentioned with pride that his mother, Margaret, had endured twenty-one pregnancies and had lactated throughout her marriage while her dreamer husband, Henry, avoided work by disappearing on preaching excursions. I said I thought she must have been a very extraordinary woman to have put up with twenty-one pregnancies and he agreed.

Sir Harold was immensely proud of having turned the family fortunes around, and he invited me to join him the following day on a tour in his Duck, a compact little aircraft that could land on both land and sea. Off we went next morning, carrying ridiculous supplies of picnic goodies and champagne on ice. Heiress Bobo Sigrist, wearing lounging pajamas and a picture hat, together with her husband of the moment, Kevin McClory, the co-producer and best chum of director John Huston, came along for the ride.

It was the perfect jet-set fantasy, riding around the skies looking down on little coral atolls in a turquoise sea, then swooping down to land, if the fancy took us, to march up and down white-hot beaches examining the possibilities for house sites. There were tiny pockets of detritus where stunted palm trees managed to push out of the ground, but the atolls were actually minuscule deserts in the middle of the deep blue sea.

'Wouldn't you like to have one of these getaways of your own?' asked Sir Harold, as I realised why I'd been invited to come and view the prime H. G. Christie Ltd real estate.

'Not really,' I replied. 'You couldn't grow anything here.'

'What do you mean?' he quizzed me, his eyes gleaming in the sun.

'Well, they've got no soil, no topsoil.'

'Shhhhhhh,' he whispered. 'Don't shout it out, you cunning girl. I'm trying to make a sale. As soon as they commit, I arrange for a whole shipment of Grade A topsoil to be shipped in from Trinidad. Costs just about as much as the island. That's how it works.' He tapped the side of his brown beaky nose and winked at me. 'And what would you grow if there *was* topsoil?' he asked. 'We've got far too much sugar cane as it is. We want resorts, playgrounds for the weary wealthy. Look what we're doing at Lyford Cay in New Providence or Windermere Island on Eleuthera.'

'I reckon I'd put in some passionfruit vines,' I told him. 'Passionfruit is great.'

He chuckled as we went back to the Duck and wagged his finger at me. 'If you don't tell them about the topsoil, I'll find a little island paradise for you and bring you some earth for free. Then you and Sean can plant passionfruit all day long if that is your pleasure.'

The film crew were still night shooting at Sir Harold's mansion when he invited a small group of Nassau's elite to dinner to watch the filming. It didn't take long for his guests to discover (as many have before them) that one of the most tedious exercises in the world is watching films being made. The party retired upstairs to nibble on seafood canapés and imbibe copiously. If I remember rightly, Sir Harold recited some of his father's poems, someone sang and we played a few desultory hands of poker until, finally, Sir Harold asked if anyone knew a game we could play that everyone could take part in, as we had to keep things going until the film crew had their break at midnight. Then, we would all eat together.

I thought it might be amusing to introduce them to the Zen Buddhist story about the Chinese woman who crosses the river that had so disrupted the party when *Tom Jones* was being shot in Dorset. Of course, this was an entirely different place with a cast of characters who couldn't have resembled less that madcap bunch of actors and directors. Foolhardy as always, I plunged in, passing out pieces of paper and pencils, drawing the diagram of the river, the houses, the husband on the donkey, the ferryman and the lover's house in relation to the bridge, taking care to mark a cross on the bridge where the woman is shot in the back by the bandit.

I gave considerable attention to relating the story dramatically so that no-one could miss the crucial points. During the middle of my performance, I noticed a certain *froideur* had fallen over the room. The faces of my audience, 'the weary wealthy' as Christie had called them, weren't weary any more; they were worried, aghast, and one might even say fearful. They turned from me to look towards Sir Harold at regular intervals. There was a stony silence when I asked the final question: 'So who, in your opinion, was most responsible for her death?'

No-one moved. No-one spoke. They just stared at me in disbelief and then back at Sir Harold. He stood up and threw down his paper. 'What a silly game,' he said vehemently. 'It's obvious! The husband is the only guilty one. He *paid* the bandit to shoot her. No question! End of story.'

With that, he downed his drink and strode off. Everyone began to talk about something else – sailing, golf, real estate, anything other than the puzzle of who was responsible for a hypothetical murder in China. Fair enough, I thought. The game was probably a bad idea anyway. I slipped off downstairs to see how they were making out on the set. There was sudden silence followed by hubbub as I left the room and I wondered what I could possibly have done to incur such a virulent reaction.

It didn't take me long to find out. I heard from the cleaning lady the next day that the buzz around Bahamian breakfast tables that morning was all about how I had tried to rumble Sir Harold about the Oakes murder. She said my ears must be burning and that I must be either very brave or an idiot. I had never even heard of the Oakes murder so she related the story with all its gory details. It seems her old auntie used to work for Lady Eunice, Sir Harold's wife. 'Not *this* Sir Harold,' she qualified, 'the Sir Harold who was murdered, Sir Harold *Oakes*.'

Below is the verbatim account from the Sangerville Library website of what transpired on that rainy night of 8 July 1943 when Sir Harold Oakes was murdered:

His close friend, Harold Christie, who was later fingered as the culprit, told authorities that when he went to wake Oakes at his Nassau estate, he discovered his skull had been shattered by four blows behind the ear. The body had been partially set afire, possibly to disguise the true nature of the crime, which still remains unsolved. Christie, who reportedly slept in the next room that night, claimed he never heard a sound.

What followed was one of the most disastrous and incompetent police investigations on record. Important evidence was ignored or discounted. Oakes' autopsy was so botched that the plane carrying his body had to be recalled in midair for new photographs. According to the autopsy, death had been caused by a blow or blows from a blunt instrument. An odd conclusion, some said, considering that on the mastoid bone just behind Oakes' right ear were four holes arranged in a square.

Suspicion was focused immediately toward Oakes' son-in-law, Alfred de Marigny. Oakes had been seen arguing with him, and de Marigny was frowned on by the locals. He arrived in the Bahamas with a playboy reputation, with two marriages behind him, and in 1942 had married Oakes' eldest daughter, Nancy, only three days after her eighteenth birthday. He had embarrassed Bahamian society by becoming successful in several businesses without their help, treated blacks as equals and particularly irked the socials when he often won local yacht races. Oakes' son-in-law was arrested and charged with murder the day after Oakes' death. De Marigny stood trial and, in less than two hours, the jury returned a not guilty verdict. The case was never reopened.

Years later, Alfred de Marigny went public and claimed he found one of the missing watchmen who were at Oakes' estate the night of the murder. He insisted the man told him that, on the night of the murder, he and the other watchman were sheltering themselves from a sudden storm in a shed when, just after midnight, a sedan pulled up to the house. Two men got out and went inside. They heard three or four gunshots and minutes later flames could be seen in Sir Harry's bedroom. The two strangers ran out of the house and left in the car. The two watchmen fled in terror. The car had contained a third man, the driver, whom they said they saw clearly. It was Harold Christie, they told de Marigny.

The next day, Christie tracked down the pair and paid them each £100 to leave Nassau and never return. Danger to do otherwise was heightened when they heard that the local harbormaster, an experienced diver, had been found floating in the harbor, reportedly drowned. He had been the only witness to the arrival of a mysterious boat about midnight.

According to de Marigny, Christie avoided investigation because any competent inquiry would have revealed that Oakes, Christie and the Duke of Windsor had conspired to smuggle millions of dollars out of the Bahamas in violation of currency regulations. The Duke, then the Governor of the Bahamas and former King of Great Britain, possessed the power to reopen the investigation. But he never did.

Harry Oakes left a personal fortune valued at slightly over $12 million, not counting his shares in Lake Shore Mine or his numerous houses. What happened to the rest of his fortune, estimated to be at least $200 to $300 million? No satisfactory explanation has ever been offered. And who killed Sir Harry? The official autopsy declared Oakes was killed by a blow to the head. De Marigny insists a Nassau doctor told him Oakes was shot to death, which fits the watchman's account. If de Marigny is correct, there are four small-caliber bullets in Harry Oakes' skull. But that lies with the rest of the remains in the millionaire's crypt in the East Dover cemetery in Dover-Foxcroft.

It was generally believed throughout Bahamian society that, the previous night, I had set Sir Harold Christie up in the same way that Hamlet set his trap for Claudius, except that I had used a game. 'The play's the thing wherein to catch the conscience of the king.' It would have been truly fantastic if I had, but Sir Harold's reaction was unique, to say the least. I wrote a diary of the events of that evening as I had an idea in the back of my mind that it might be worked into the plot for a thriller one day.

Almost a year after we returned from Nassau, I received a small basket of passionfruit from Harrods with a card bearing the Bahamian flag. The fruit were dark and wizened by the time they arrived in Putney, where we then lived; they had been delivered to Acton months before but not sent on. They could only have been a belated offering from Sir Harold Christie. I sometimes see his face staring out of the television, as repeats of *Unsolved Murders* are shown quite often on cable TV. He took the secret of the Sir Harold Oakes crime to the grave with him. Oddly enough, Sean and his present wife, Micheline, live to this day at the exclusive Lyford Cay, Providence, the first big private resort built by Sir Harold Christie.

CHAPTER TEN

*O*n our return home from the Bahamas (after yet another break-in in Acton), Sean and I decided to take the children and try the waters on the other side of the Atlantic in the US of A. It was with a sort of rueful sadness that we put Acacia House on the market. We'd had to keep the curtains drawn all day for months, as spectators regularly took their places in the street outside for a good 'stickybeak'.

Sean was scheduled to do a film called *A Fine Madness* with Joanne Woodward in New York while I was to shoot *Hombre* in Arizona with Joanne's husband, Paul Newman. We moved into Julie Andrews' old house in LA, a cosy mock-Tudor mansion with a big garden and lots of trees for the kids to climb. It was a great contrast to the Sammy Davis Jr sex pad of our last visit.

Sean threw himself into the part he was playing of the free-spirited Canadian poet who falls foul of the law and is chased around Manhattan by an army of cops. He wore old brown corduroy trews, sported a large moustache, revelled in sloppiness and was given to outbursts of uplifting poetic claptrap. He was about as far away from James Bond as Lassie is to King Kong. We laughed a lot and listened to classical music in the mornings if we weren't working, especially Sibelius, Beethoven and Schubert. It was that kind of house.

Yet a strange thing happened which made me question this house's beneficence towards us. One afternoon, we were playing a game. Sean was chasing me with a broom while the children screamed with laughter at our antics. As I streaked through the doorway to run outside, my wedding ring somehow caught in the hooked door handle to the terrace. I was pulled right off my feet but the ring didn't break. It was jerked backwards so that all the flesh was torn off my finger, right down to the bone.

Sean turned ashen and nearly fainted while the children were frightened that my finger was about to fall off. They didn't want to be left alone, so we all went downtown to the outpatients department of the local hospital. Fortunately, no-one recognised us. Despite the excruciating pain, it was rather lovely to be just an ordinary young family – Dad worried sick about his wife, a couple of snivelling children trying to make Mum feel all right again, and Mum sniffing and smiling through her tears. The fact that my wedding ring had been ripped off so viciously didn't strike me as odd until much later.

After talks with Marty Ritt, the director of *Hombre*, I decided to dye my hair red. Elmore Leonard wrote my part as a feisty, free-thinking woman. She takes no nonsense from anyone, is practical and self-sufficient but has burning emotions she keeps tamped down in case they get her into even more trouble. The passion has to come out somewhere, so why not her hair? Besides, I fancied being a 'bluey' for a change.

Locations for *Hombre* were Old Phoenix, a ghost copper mine called Glory fifty miles away in Death Valley National Park (the lowest point in the United States) and the top of a hill in some rugged terrain. The pick-up shots were done back in Los Angeles.

The cast and crew all lived in a retirement complex on a Native American reservation, the original home of the Pima Indians. It was a strange life, out in the middle of nowhere in a multi-storey apartment block inhabited by the incapacitated and the aged. They used to line up every morning to watch us leave for work. There was a full department store and deli in the basement, and food could be delivered to one's room at any time of the day or night.

Also in the basement were sauna baths and workout gyms for the health conscious. Paul would get the caretaker to turn on the sauna every morning at 5.45 a.m. precisely. He would then spend an hour and forty-five minutes roasting himself in the sauna and twenty minutes under a cold shower until 8 a.m., when we would leave the complex. The dehydration and cleansing effect left him free to drink beer for most of the day and a large restorative jug of mint julep at night, but he had been warned to take it easy lest he sweat off all the subcutaneous fat in his body. Paul looked very lean and mean, but with his sapphire-blue eyes (which he called his 'baby bloodshots') he could never have been mistaken for a Native American.

To research his part, Paul lived with the Pima Indians, watching how they walked, held themselves and chewed sunflower seeds. He saw their natural reserve and easy silence and incorporated all these things into his role. The 'hombre' he played had been inspired by some old daguerreotype photographs taken 'on the trail' in the late nineteenth century; these same photos were used in the title sequence. A young blond boy had been found on the trail and brought up by Native Americans. He resembled a white man, but was not. It was a difficult part to bring off.

Marty Ritt, the director, was a rotund man who was said to be the prototype for the film *Marty*. He always wore a pale blue jumpsuit with a little silver buckle belt. By popular standards he was very ugly, but he was also wonderfully attractive. Marty had used his extraordinary talents to tide him over the hard times he suffered when he was accused of un-American activities during the McCarthy era. One of his occupations was horserace handicapping and the other was teaching 'timing' to drama students. This he did using ball skills – rolling a ball along the ground, delivering the speech, walking beside the moving ball and timing the speech to end at the same instant as he picked up the ball. I admired him greatly. He was a master craftsman and had won an Academy Award with Paul when he directed him in *Hud*.

The cameraman on *Hombre* was a legend in his own right, Jimmy Wong Howe, known as 'the Fortune Cookie' or 'the Laundry Man'. A consummate artist, Jimmy was a veteran of some 132 films. He worked in his own time, making the director and cast wait if he had not set his lights exactly where and how he wanted them. He insisted on re-shooting two sequences in *Hombre*. The producer was tearing his hair out at the additional cost but Jimmy had spotted that Richard Boone, the bad guy, had a head the size of a pumpkin. This fact was inconsequential in itself, but when he was sitting next to Paul in the stagecoach it made Paul look like a pin-head. The other sequence we had to do again was the meeting of the passengers in Old Tucson, which is a pretend cowboy town that has featured in nearly every western ever shot. Jimmy didn't feel that he had attained the oppressiveness of the place, so back we went.

The other members of the cast were American actors I was honoured to appear with and fascinated to meet. Fredric March had been a fantastic leading man in early films and had won two Oscars, one for *Dr Jekyll and Mr Hyde* in 1932 and the other for *The Best Years of Our Lives* in 1946. He was married to an actress whose name was also legend, Florence Eldridge. She accompanied her husband to Arizona and was a huge asset to our oddly assorted community. Then there was Richard Boone, famous for his many years in one of the most successful TV series ever, *Have Gun Will Travel*. Richard was a great big man with a voice to match, who drank copious amounts of bourbon whisky and was a tireless practical joker.

Marty Balsam was never less than exceptional in every part I ever saw him play. Who will ever forget him as the detective in *Psycho* or as Arnold Burns in *A Thousand Clowns*? Cameron Mitchell, Barbara Rush and Maggie Bligh – in fact all the cast – became fast friends during the making of *Hombre*. It would have been awful had it been otherwise, as we were thrown together for unconscionable periods of time – so many hours on mountainsides, so many days sitting in the sweltering stage-coach when we hardly got anything in the can.

One of Richard Boone's practical jokes held up production for a day or two. It was so hot and dry on top of the hill where we were stranded that Richard decided to import a swimming pool. At great personal expense, vast amounts of water were carried up the hill and a large above-ground pool was constructed for our comfort. It was called 'Boone's Lagoon'. We arrived for work the morning after its inauguration to find that the road up the hill to our location was impassable. Boone's Lagoon had sprung a leak in the night and was running down the only road up the hill, turning it into a veritable quagmire. From then on, it was known as 'Dick's Folly'. In fact, Richard was delighted. He loved getting up the noses of the 'bosses' – so much so that we wondered whether he had not assisted in the debacle.

And then the film closed down entirely for two weeks. All we heard was that Paul had 'desert fever', a malady that occurs when the body can't stabilise its own temperature. It's either up around the early hundred degrees or sinks into the eighties. Joanne Woodward was flown in, Warren Cowan, Paul's PR man, arrived and, yet again, we all waited. Ugly rumours abounded, perhaps incited by the fact that my stand-in, a foxy lady who drove a black Mustang and was covered in jewellery, had disappeared. It was said that her brief on *Hombre* was to get Paul into a compromising situation with herself and another male partner – with photos. Twentieth Century Fox would then be made an offer they couldn't refuse and the 'compromising' photos would not be printed in a gay porn magazine called *Hombre*. God knows what the true story was.

At last we cranked up again. Paul's temperature went back to normal and the whole caravanserai was transported to Las Vegas, Nevada, where we were night shooting in Death Valley. It was amazing to arrive back in the dawn light, bleary-eyed and sleep-deprived to find gamblers we had left the night before still playing, riveted to their tables, totally uninterested as the bunch of filthy actors in nineteenth-century rags dragged themselves through the gaming rooms. We envied Barbara Rush, who stayed at Frank Sinatra's private apartment. She was a special friend, a sort of honorary Rat Pack member, and was high on Hollywood's social register.

Here, I must record the only time that I ever won any serious money in my whole life. I fronted up to a blackjack table at the casino, having only ever watched what in Europe is called 'vingt-et-un', and began to play. At first I was hopeless, but after some coaching from the dealer, I began to win, and win and win some more. When I got up from the table, elated at my pile but weary from all that hard work, two employees of the casino came up and asked me what my name was and where I was staying. This is standard practice if you get up with all your winnings and prepare to leave.

'Babs Huzzi-Buzzi from back of the burnt stump,' I told them for a laugh.

'How d'ya spell that?' one of the guys wanted to know, with no humour in his voice.

In the end, I was allowed to depart with my big bundle of Monopoly money, which I immediately went off and spent on a swag of Mexican turquoise and silver jewellery to give to all my friends back in London.

Generally, however, when the children were not with me, I felt very lonely and isolated. I read voraciously – Turgenev, Tolstoy and Dostoevsky, all the Russian heavies, marvelling at their power and realising how much I still had to learn about construction and characterisation in writing a novel.

I think the reason for my depression was what happened when Sean came to visit. On the set, a photographer took a still of me standing between him and Paul. The photo appeared in the press worldwide, bearing the caption: WHICH ONE WILL SHE HAVE TONIGHT? Beneath the picture was a short paragraph saying that my marriage to Sean was probably heading for the rocks, as I had fallen madly in love with Paul Newman during the shooting of our new film *Hombre* while on location in Arizona.

Sean was infuriated, fit to be tied, but then he became suicidal and wretched. I felt guilty again, enraged and astounded. How could they get away with saying that in print? To make it worse, some 'dear friend' sent a copy to my mother, who called me from Australia to ask, 'What's going on, D?' I could hear the uncertainty in her voice.

'Nothing. Absolutely *nothing*, Mum.'

'Yes, but D, it's printed in the *paper*!' My mother was of that generation who believe that if something is in print then it must be true.

'Well, I can't help that. It's just *not* true,' I insisted. 'They're always printing things that are not true! They insinuate something and then everyone believes it. It's horrible.'

My mother and Sean were mad about each other. They had an instant empathy from the moment they met in London. I think she secretly loved it when her patients greeted her as James Bond's mother-in-law, though she disapproved of certain aspects of the character. I recall with great affection when, at a private showing of *Thunderball* in a cinema in Mayfair, she backed both Harry Salzman and Cubby Broccoli up against a wall in the foyer. 'Yes, but *who* licensed him to *kill*?' she wanted to know. 'Was it the *Queen*?'

Harry muttered something about national security but my mother cut through with, 'Well, I can't see that the Queen can have made a judgement like that. She's the head of the Church of England and she must know that nobody's licensed to kill anybody else except in times of war.' No wonder Harry and Cubby couldn't wait to get away. My mother was not called 'Indomitable Mum' for nothing.

By now she was worried that my marriage was in jeopardy and that I was guilty of grave impropriety. She would never have thought that Sean could have been at fault. She gave me a lecture on a wife's duty to her husband and responsibility to her children. Then, I expect, she went back to bed and probably nudged my dad, who was certainly fast asleep. 'Can't stay out of trouble, that girl,' were most likely her last words on the subject.

In the film industry (and in many other big business consortiums) there are always extremely powerful men who remain in the shadows. Businessmen. The public has seldom heard of them but they make crucial decisions, know where all the bodies are buried, have access to massive amounts of money, decree who is hired or fired and are privy to all the secrets of the company. They are the éminences grises, the fixers, the big wheels who hardly ever go to their offices but spend a great deal of time in Palm Springs. Though generally less than impressive physically, they have been married to some spectacularly luscious ladies, perhaps three or four. Recently, the press has begun to winkle them out but the public still thinks they're boring. They are.

One such man was Warren Cowan. He was known as the Godfather of Public Relations but PR was not his only concern. When at last the *Hombre* cast returned to Los Angeles to do the pick-up shots, Warren asked me to go to lunch with him. It was a formal request, so I knew there must be some kind of proposition in the air. Warren never did anything for nothing.

As we sat at a quiet table in the Studio Commissariat, Warren pushed a new sugar substitute across the table towards me. 'You see this?' he said in his quiet, ingratiating voice, as though he was talking to a backward child. 'I can make everyone in the United States taste one of these ... once.'

He paused for dramatic effect, turning the little sachet over in his hands. 'I can make 250 million people taste it just once, but, after that, it's up to the product. If they like it, they'll go on buying it. It can get to be as big as Coca-Cola. But if they don't want it, it's gone. You'll never hear of it again.

'I can do that for *you*,' he continued, opening the sac and pouring the contents into his coffee. 'I can make them taste you big-time but it's up to you whether they want some more.'

He stirred his coffee delicately, watching me all the time while I squirmed a little at the blatancy of his analogy. 'Think about it,' he told me. 'Let me know soon whether you want me to work for you.

I know you could be a great star. It's just how much you want to put yourself out there. I can help you to do that.'

These are the sentiments that every young actress wants to hear but I was profoundly uneasy. I knew that I could not present myself to the American public to taste from the UK. My mum's lecture had driven home the point that I had to consider Sean and the children as my most precious commission and priority, not being a silly actress reading Russian novels to ward off loneliness in the middle of the desert.

I shook my head. It had taken very little time for me to know that I wanted much more from life than Hollywood fame but what it was I yearned for was still hidden from me, a mystery.

'I'm sorry, Warren, but I just can't shift the centre of my whole life. I can't disregard everything my instincts are telling me. It's incredibly seductive to think of starting a new life here, getting offered all the best parts for huge sums of money, and I'm immensely flattered but . . . we . . . No, I don't want to be a new brand of sweetener, however well it's packaged.'

Warren didn't look discouraged or even disappointed. He just smiled his deprecating little-boy grin and sipped his coffee. 'Well, don't tell me later that I didn't make the offer. I take it you would not like another one of these,' he said, reaching for a sweetener and waggling it at me.

I suspect that what I'd just heard was a well-rehearsed tape about sweeteners he switched on whenever he approached any actress with a representational pitch.

That interview with Warren Cowan marked the end of our sojourn in the United States, as well as the end of my aspirations to be a Hollywood megastar. Warren obviously wanted to represent me, as he did Paul Newman and a host of other celebrities, but I had no desire to become a commodity marketed to the world. I'd seen the other side of the moon, where all the dead seas, burnt-out wrecks and dangers lurk. I'd had a bellyful of languishing in caravans on desert hillsides and playing the role of the gushing, accommodating actress. It was apparent to me that my boredom threshold was incompatible with acting full-time in movies. Many film offers were made, all to be shot in Hollywood, and when I called my agent, Jimmy Fraser, he came straight to the point in his imitable camp Scottish manner.

'Well, the word is out on you!'

'What word?' I queried.

'That if anyone employs you, Sean will never ever work for them again.'

'That's nonsense. Sean's already discussing doing *The Molly Maguires* with Marty Ritt.'

'I didn't say directors you've already worked with,' Jimmy stipulated. 'I mean any new ones.'

I chose to disbelieve him, and when we returned to the UK I turned my attention to the lovely Victorian house on Putney Common we moved into after Acacia House was sold. It had a walled garden, with a rock pool where the children could keep guppies, and there were heavy Victorian doors, a huge kitchen with a fireplace and a basement with enough room to build a gym. Again, we decided that Sean would take care of any structural alterations while I would undertake the interior decoration. A household account was opened at the bank in Putney High Street and I settled down to some serious nest-making and mothering.

The property in Spain was also my focus of intense refurbishment. I established a working relationship and great respect for Rafael, the gardener, his son Pepe and Anna, who kept the house as clean as a new pin. We went on expeditions into the hinterland with the kids seeking out wild asparagus. Nothing can compare to the taste of a wild asparagus omelette after a morning on the mountainside. Alarmed quail would fly up at our feet while birds of prey soared above our heads and the wind blew up from the sea. We would return ravenous to breakfasts of monumental size and delectability.

I made many trips up the winding mountain roads to Ronda, scavenging for remnants of Conquistador art. I found a set of hand-carved chairs, a *bibliothèque* and a table with an unusual motif of flying breasts and gargoyles. Ronda is still a romantic, historic town famed for its high bridge from which members of the Republican Army were thrown during the Spanish Civil War. Each year, a *corrida goyesca* (a Goya-esque bullfight) is held in the ancient Roman amphitheatre where the legendary Ronda-born matador Antonio Ordóñez was initiated into the bullring. In his last published work, *The Dangerous Summer*, Hemingway immortalised the brutal series of bullfights that pitted rival toreros Antonio Ordóñez and his brother-in-law, Luis Miguel Dominguin, against each other.

We watched the astounding sight of a young boy dressed in full eighteenth-century costume run up to the bull, which was in the act of goring a fighting horse, and try to drag the beast off by pulling at his tail. He showed no fear and the crowd went mad with pleasure. Needless to say, little blond Jason became a favourite with the old *banderilleros* who hung out at the back of the bullring. Giovanna was more self-contained, with her hair plaited and framing her heart-shaped face. She always had been.

She was a special child, Giovanna. That sounds like the ravings of a doting mum, but it is not. Already, at six years of age, she had demonstrated an uncanny knack of putting together Rubik's Cubes in a matter of minutes. At first, we thought it was a fluke and marvelled that one so small could stumble upon complex solutions, but, after a while, it became apparent that Gigi was gifted. This proved the case when, a few years later, she was tested by the prestigious Millfield School in Somerset and found to have an IQ of 173. On the strength of this, they offered her a full scholarship.

Before that, however, we sent Giovanna to the Montessori school at Ibstock Place in Roehampton, where they introduced her to non-competitive play. There were cubby-houses to build and real little shops where they learned money and maths in a practical fashion. Jason joined her there when he was four years old. The delightful thing about my children, and a genuine boon for any parent, is that they have a natural affinity. They adore each other and are far enough apart age-wise not to be in conflict for attention.

Meanwhile, Hodder & Stoughton, the publishers of my book, *The Manipulator*, sent a very tall young man named Gillon Aitken, armed with a large blue pencil, to edit and polish the manuscript prior to printing. Gillon, who was somewhat underwhelmed by my spelling and grammar skills at that time, was indispensable in the assembly of the book.

Sean went down to the basement one day and arrived back upstairs carrying an amazing painting he'd done, which depicted a figure being crucified upside down with a blazing sun behind him. This became the cover of the book. All the rancour that had remained within me since the incident at Almeria was dispersed by this reconciling, gracious act and I felt a great surge of love for this complicated man who had such a hard time expressing his emotions. I dedicated the book to him.

This was a time in Sean's life when his creative urges soared like wild birds, frequently alighting in unusual places. He wrote a ballet, a sort of psychological *Swan Lake*, which he showed to an impressed George Balanchine of the New York City Ballet, and he directed a documentary in Scotland called *The Bowler and the Bunnet*. This work came about through his friendship with Sir Iain Stewart, who was a member of St Andrews (the golf Mecca of the world) and a melancholic, dyed-in-the-wool conservative 'Boss'. Sir Iain and Sean had opposite backgrounds but these two unlikely bedfellows came up with an idea for a film about the Glasgow shipyards. Sean asked me to do up the smaller farmhouse at the property in Spain for Sir Iain and his son, who came to stay with us every year.

Some unspoken tragedy concerning his wife was the purported cause of Iain's melancholy. Sean was always introducing him to various ladies who might jolly him up and make his life less bereft of female comfort. One such person was novelist Edna O'Brien, who lived down the hill in Deodar Road, Putney. She was addicted to the company of men, preferably famous/rich or sexy/literary ones. Her book *Girl with Green Eyes* was being made into a film at the time, and she was incorrigibly romantic, as only the Irish can be. Sean thought Edna might be just the person to bring Iain out of his shell.

Accordingly, she was invited early one evening for a drink when Iain was our houseguest in London. She turned her dazzling wit and seductive face towards him with such power that Iain was quite knocked out, but before he could impress her, the whole melting pot of Putney personalities descended upon us. There was Stanley Mann (scriptwriter of Sean's film *Another Time, Another Place*, which also starred Lana Turner) and his wife Delphine (they lived next door), Ted Allan (a Canadian playwright, also of Deodar Road), Georgia Brown (the original Nancy from the musical *Oliver*) and her husband Gareth Wigan, the film producer . . . and somehow French director Roger Vadim (ex-husband of Brigitte Bardot) got himself into the party.

We all swept off to the Richmond Rendezvous, that icon of Chinese restaurants, to eat Peking duck – wafer-thin pancakes wrapped around crispy, hot duck skin, slivers of shallot and cucumber, and oozing with plum sauce. I could see that Iain was having a hard time as he called the waiter and ordered a knife and fork. Afterwards, hot toffee bananas sprinkled with crunchy sesame seeds were served. Could any dinner have been more gastronomically erotic? For Iain, it was a torment and so was the company. He found nothing in common with these jet-set glitterati and retired within his grey armour.

By the time the party returned to Putney, everyone was exuberant, noisy and ready for whatever turned them on. This being the sixties, any new substance proffered was acceptable, and our guests had come prepared with a great choice of turn-ons. A chasm opened between swinging London and stern Caledonia, and as Edna flew off into the dawn, hotly pursued by a salivating Roger Vadim, I brewed a cup of hot cocoa for Sir Iain. Sean and I fell into bed, sighing with relief at being horizontal. Playing host and hostess was hard yakka in the sixties. The rules had not been set and so it was a situation of 'anything goes' – and mostly it did. For a passionate observer like me, there was never a moment when the pace slackened and I relished the interplay between stitched-up conservatives and dope-crazed weirdos.

I was aware that our friends were very different. One night I'd be cooking dinner for a mob of British comedians, including Jimmy Tarbuck, Eric Sykes, Eric Morecambe, Benny Hill and Bruce Forsyth (all far more edgy and self-centred than any actor I have ever met), and the next we would be entertaining the Berliner Ensemble or Rudi Nureyev. The comedians, like Sean, were wedded to golf and would sit around the table outdoing each other with awful jokes – some side-splittingly funny and others outrageously obscene.

It's interesting that wives of comedians either shut up or talk amongst themselves, having heard all their husbands' jokes before. When a trophy bride arrives in their midst and sits, gorgeous and monosyllabic, staring at the men, the other wives make her life a misery until she conforms and huddles with the women. The one comic who was universally loved and admired was Tommy Cooper and his wife, Dove. Though the funnymen were viciously scathing about each other, they never said a word against Tommy or Dove.

The next Bond film, *You Only Live Twice*, was being filmed in Japan. The screenwriter was Roald Dahl, who at the time was married to actress Patricia Neal. I knew them both from New York, although I hadn't seen either since Pat had suffered a massive stroke after the death of one of her children. I'd worked with the film's director, Lewis Gilbert, on *The Admirable Crichton* and Donald Pleasance, who was playing Ernst Stavro

Blofeld, was a chum, so there were many good friends converging in the Land of the Rising Sun.

We landed in Manila on our way to Tokyo. Hardly had we stepped off the plane when a wave of fanatics swarmed onto the tarmac and right over the top of me. I was extricated about ten seconds before death by asphyxiation and it is an experience which has left me with a real fear of maddened crowds. Still agitated by the incident, we flew on to Tokyo, where I was immediately separated from Sean and taken to an underground detention centre. Here, I was questioned about my birthplace, Australia, and about what my father had done in the war. The officials then informed Cubby Broccoli and Harry Salzman that I would not be allowed into the country without a visa. Since I did not have one, I was to be deported as soon as possible.

I could hear Sean raving upstairs, though I couldn't make out what he was shouting. Evidently, he refused to stay in the country if they didn't allow me my freedom immediately. I should think a great deal of money passed hands that night before I was finally escorted from the bowels of the airport and into the blaze of neon light that illuminates the great city. The thing that makes Tokyo so marvellous by night is that all the signs are in Japanese so you can't read any of them.

The next morning, literally thousands of reporters and paparazzi gathered as we were crowded onto the street. We had to walk down some steps in a park holding hands while looking at the beauty of bonsai nature. There is a newsreel of this in which I look utterly shell-shocked. We only had one night in Tokyo before we flew off to the filming location, but that soirée turned out to be a B-rated kung fu flick in need of some serious editing.

Scene 1. Night. Limo carrying principals pulls out from curb and travels only fifty yards before five waiting cars crammed with cameramen join the chase. Tyres squeal as flashbulbs explode, cars clash and the principals inside limo appear visibly fearful and unhappy.

Scene 2. Restaurant. Night. Principals are about to be served their *yakitori* when an ordinary customer suddenly morphs into a frenzied photographer, clicking at the principals as he approaches their table.

Scene 3. Enter small Japanese female ninja who slams the photographer with deadly accuracy. He is joined by another kamikaze cameraman, who is dealt with in the same fashion. Soon the floor is piled with men. And so it goes, all evening.

The proprietress, being the small, muscular, ninja woman, was quite wonderful. She confiscated at least ten cameras and was looking around for more photographers when we left. One of them even followed Sean into the Gents and climbed up the wall to try to get a shot of him peeing. Next morning, with relief, we flew off to the southern island of Kyushu.

It was a beautiful sub-tropical place with strange rocky protuberances around the coastline, which Alan Whicker characterised as 'instant Macbeth'. Alan was doing a story on the making of the Bond film for his British TV series, *Whicker's World*, with his co-producer and lover, Shell heiress Olga Deterding. The cast and crew of *You Only Live Twice* were housed in a remote holiday resort far into the hinterland. From this base, a helicopter ferried them to the location. When we arrived they took away all our clothes and gave us lovely cool kimonos. A new clean one was provided every day. I thought it was an ace idea.

From the start, Japan was like nowhere else I had ever been. Every day some bizarre thing would happen that showed us how extraordinary are the Nipponese. The very first problem we encountered in Kyushu wasn't mine. Not being tall, I didn't have to worry about the height of doorways, whereas Sean, Cubby Broccoli and Roald Dahl, all well over six feet, were forever walking into big headaches. Almost every time they entered a house, they bumped their heads on the doorframe, as the standardised height of a Japanese dwelling is five feet nine inches.

For the Japanese, the novelty of the great height of these men was surpassed only by the amazement they felt when observing the amount of hair growing out of their torsos, limbs, ears and noses. They stood back and gawped, pointing out to their children that they were indeed witnessing one of nature's wonders. In fact, shaving Sean was a production not unlike Gulliver being administered to by the Lilliputians. The squat little barber brought his whole family with him, at least ten assistants, plus women and children crowding into our unit. Sean lay on the floor propped up on cushions, while Dad barked out guttural orders like one of the seven samurai. Boiling water, towels and a razor strop were carried in and a major ritual began. The diminutive man proceeded to sharpen his cut-throat razor on the strop with long frightening strokes until the blade glistened wickedly. Sean and I exchanged wide-eyed glances. Could we perhaps have met a Japanese Sweeney Todd, the demon barber of Kyushu?

Lather was applied with the same rigorous attention to detail. Then he took Sean's nose between thumb and forefinger and bent his head back so that Sean was completely supine. He could have been about to cut his throat . . . but no, sitting on the floor, he worked on Sean's face and cheeks, and cleared his nostrils and ears of any outcrops, all the while chattering to his assistants and singing little snatches of song. You could tell he was having the best time of his life and that he'd relate the story of how he shaved the hirsute Bondosan for the rest of his days. Afterwards, the whole family swarmed over various parts of Sean's body. Toenails and fingernails were trimmed and anointed and hot towels applied to his face. Strange-smelling Asian unguents came next. It was truly an inspiring sight to see the dedication with which they worked upon the large foreign body that lay before them, impassive to their combined efforts.

When at last it was over, a blind woman was pushed forward. She stood blinking and smiling in the light while it was explained to us in halting English that when a child of either sex is born blind or develops blindness, they are taught massage so that they will always have a gainful profession. It is also widely believed in Japan that the hands of a sightless person are more sensitive and can more readily discover areas of the human body that require attention. Sean declined the offer of the massage but told them he would remember her for any future needs. They left reluctantly and Sean instantly fell into a deep sleep. Maybe the unguents contained soporifics.

Peter Hunt had been the editor of all the Bond films thus far, but for *You Only Live Twice* he was entrusted with the job of directing the second unit, the one that does all the pick-up shots. This entailed numerous underwater shots of abalone collectors who, in the film, were meant to be women, but no Japanese women in the surrounding area of Akime wished to take to the sea. I offered myself as a female *awabi* (abalone) fisherperson, and was taken away by the make-up department and given a black wig and lots of extended eyeliner to turn me into an Oriental. A revealing but oddly cut swimsuit completed the transformation.

Abalone is an edible shellfish that attaches itself to rock faces underwater. Its shell is shaped like a large ear and the pearly interior is used to make jewellery, while the empty shell is often polished and makes a pretty ashtray. The collector's tools are a floating bucket and a metal lever to pry the live molluscs away from the rock. Back at the fishing village, where rows of drying octopuses are strung up in lines, the air carries the smell of rotting fish as the men wait at the jetty for the abalone collectors to return with their buckets of live *awabi*. Needless to say, abalone is considered to be a powerful aphrodisiac, especially when sliced thinly and eaten while it still squirms with life. I spent a couple of fascinating days learning how to be a proficient abalone poacher – and there are a couple of shots in the film to prove it – but I could never bring myself to ingest the still-moving pink flesh.

Meanwhile, members of the first film unit were running up against a lot of script problems and days were spent trying to hammer out an acceptable form for Ian Fleming's eleventh Bond book. Loud voices could be heard throughout the hours when work had finished and poor old Lewis Gilbert, the director, was worn out. One evening, he dragged himself into yet another script conference with Roald, Sean and other key figures from the crew.

'God,' he moaned pitifully, 'I can't keep this up. Can't I just have a few minutes' rest before we start on this shit again? Just five minutes, boys?'

Sean suggested that he should have a quick energising massage from the blind lady and she was summoned forthwith. She arrived smiling and blinking as usual and was told what was required – just a five-minute gentle massage to vitalise and refresh, nothing more, as Lewis was so frail. She shook her head, still smiling, indicating that she had no idea what anyone meant.

'Five minutes! Only five!' shouted Lewis in her ear while the lady continued to smile and shake her head. This went on for some time.

'Wait a moment,' Roald confidently interjected, 'I know how to handle this.'

He took her hand in his large paw and, holding one finger at a time, he folded her fingers into her palm. 'One . . . two . . . three . . . four . . . five! There . . . *five* minutes. You understand?'

He had closed her small brown hand into a tight fist. This time she nodded her head vigorously in agreement and Lewis laid down on his stomach ready for his session. We congratulated Roald.

Who would have thought that someone so meek and inoffensive-looking could pack such a wallop? She leapt upon Lewis, pummelling his back and shoulders with her piston fists before anyone could blink. Lewis was bleating weakly under the barrage of blows and it was much more than five minutes before she was literally physically lifted away from the target of her merciless fists. It took the strength of several men to prise her loose, but then they were weakened with laughter at the time.

Lewis turned over and sat up after his ordeal. He grimaced with pain and was given a stiff drink. After a while he pronounced himself much better and ready to get to work. 'I think maybe I should have one of those every night,' he said jauntily. 'She's very good, y'know.'

Each day, when we returned hot and sweaty from the location, there would be a female character out of a Kurasawa movie awaiting our arrival. Quite elderly but very wiry and strong, she was utterly disinterested in who we were. Her job was to wash us thoroughly before we got into our baths. This she did with the same purposefulness she would have applied to cleaning an old pair of boots. It is disconcerting to have a total stranger scrubbing away at one's private parts but that is the Japanese way and, in the end, it is merely their good manners not to make these intimacies personal. One felt almost like a paralytic, having to just give in and get used to the indignities. Baths were communal, naked males and females together. Afterwards, as a special treat, you could have a rub down with the fruit of your choice . . . even pineapple skin.

Roald Dahl wore his voluminous Bombay bloomers throughout his stay in Kyushu, even when we attended the Green Tea ceremony given in our honour. Instead of following the tradition of sitting on one's haunches and accepting the clay cup from a kimono-clad beauty who knelt in front of one, Roald chose to sit with his great long legs and dusty sandals extended in front of him so that no-one could get near him. It was the cause of great embarrassment to the Japanese, who kept bowing and swerving to exclude him from the proceedings.

Another day, Pat, Roald and I went out with the local fishermen. Pat Neal was still in the process of relearning basic information that had disappeared from her memory since her stroke. She was baffled by ordinary things and, to his credit, Roald was infinitely patient with her.

'Where does the sun come up, Roald?' she would ask.

'The sun comes up in the east, over in that direction, and goes down in the west, there into the sea,' he'd reply.

The fishermen gave them both lines and set them to fish on either side of the boat. Pat caught a good-sized fish within minutes, then another, and before long she had netted two more. She was as excited as a child but, to the Japanese men, this was not the way things should have panned out. Feeling that Dahlsan was losing face, they made Pat and Roald change places. As soon as this was accomplished, Pat threw her line in from Roald's former position and at once screamed with joy as she got a big bite. After a tussle, she hauled in a whopper. The fishermen moved Roald back to where Pat had caught the big one and threw a bunch of burley into the water to entice the fish. Then they moved Pat down to the stern of the boat and let her toss her line in our wake. No sooner had she done so than she was shouting with delight as yet another fish took her bait. After this, the men removed her line and we sat together holding hands, watching Roald hold his flaccid line in the water until the sun sank into the sea in the west . . . just as he had promised.

Another incongruous pastime practised by the local Kyushans was their own particular brand of golf, brought about by the simple fact that they did not have a golf course to play on. To overcome this disadvantage, they took their clubs down to the beach where markers had been set up in the sea at 300, 250, 200, 150, 100 and 50 yards. Taking their drivers, they hit out into the ocean, consulting a map of some famous international links for information about the first hole. The distance of the drive if there was a dogleg, how far they were from the hole, all would be noted. Perhaps a four wood was their next choice. They would chip up and, when they deemed themselves to be on the green, putt out on the sand. The card was carefully marked as to how many shots they had taken. If they deviated too far or sliced heavily, it was understood that they had landed in a sand trap. There was no fooling about; they followed the rules strictly, as best they could, and were anxious to complete the full eighteen holes before they called it a day. Small darting boys would dive for the balls at the end of the game. These were arguably the most unique golf fixtures I have ever witnessed, as each player arrived to play with a whole bucket full of balls and was aggressively competitive.

As a camp follower, I spent much more time with the locals than Sean did. I even began to have a smattering of conversational Japanese, an imperative if you are gambling. We played ferocious games of poker for money, drank Suntory whisky and, as the weeks passed, I began to be addicted to Japanese food. I had found raw fish unappealing at the beginning of our stay but soon the smell of deep-frying fat turned my stomach. It took me some weeks to get over my aversion when we came home to Great Britain.

For most actors, the rehearsal period of a play is an invaluable time not just to familiarise oneself with the text but to dig into the subtext and find out the underlying meaning the playwright is so intent upon serving up to his public. Often, the playwright is just as fascinated as the actors to discover what it's all about.

Plays that are written as a vindication or explanation of emotional events in the playwright's own life are different. They are very difficult to bring off because all the time the writer's aim is patently clear. He is justifying himself and subtly putting blame onto one or another of his characters. It unbalances the play and the audience generally sees through the subterfuge, coming to loathe the character the playwright is trying to make blameless.

The classic case is Arthur Miller's *After the Fall*, in which he justifies his part in his marriage to Marilyn Monroe and the subsequent disintegration of her life. I was offered the play but turned it down. It was obvious to me that in every scene (perhaps without his even being conscious of it), Miller is determined to demonstrate what a dreadful time he had and what an impossible creature Marilyn was. Well, sorry, but an audience won't wear it.

I have, in fact, appeared in two plays of the *After the Fall* ilk. The first was Arnold Wesker's *The Four Seasons*, which he wrote to explain away an affair he had carried on for one whole year. It was a two-hander performed by me and Alan Bates. *The Four Seasons* opens in winter, when the man meets a woman who corresponds to the season. She is catatonic with misery, frozen in a winter wasteland from which the man awakens her in a rebirth of spring. They wallow in summertime and move on to autumn, when she begins to sink back into her coldness. When they part, it is winter again. To me, the play said nothing except that Arnold was making known to the audience (and Dusty, his wife) what a hard time he had had trying to save this ungrateful woman from her despair.

Of course, it didn't work, even with all the Wesker wizardry, including one scene when Alan had to make a whole apple strudel on stage. By the end of the run, we were all strudelled out. Arnold blamed me because I was always asking him to make my character more credible but he didn't want that; he was after something else. He tried the play out again in Europe with a different cast. It still didn't work.

The other vindication play I did was directed by Sean and written by Ted Allan, our Canadian neighbour who lived down the road from Edna O'Brien in Deodar Road, Putney. With his sharp wit, Ted was garrulous and great fun but he was also filled with remorse. It seems that he had colluded with his mother to have his sister committed to a mental institution, where she was given electric-shock therapy and never completely recovered. The title of the play, *I've Seen You Cut Lemons*, derived from a real-life event. When Ted's sister, who adored him, accused him of being a basically cruel person, he asked her how she knew this.

'Of course I know. I've seen you cut lemons,' was her reply.

Ted Allan's hidden agenda in the play was to show that he was perfectly justified in having his sister committed, as she was a borderline psychotic about to become dangerous unless given treatment, and that his mother was the wicked manipulator who had forced him to betray his beloved sibling. I played the sister and Tim (Robert) Hardy assayed the brother's part. Tim was to become one of the best-known faces in

Britain after his masterly performance as Siegfried Farnon in the popular BBC series *All Creatures Great and Small*. We always knew *Lemons* was an unlikely crowd-pleaser, so we only undertook a limited season at the Fortune Theatre. Tim came to live with us during rehearsal and we worked night and day, enjoying each other's company both professionally and socially.

Most theatre critics are motivated by personal taste, political correctness and a love of the arts but they often harbour envy for those who have the talent and chutzpah to actually get up and *do* it. They spend hours thinking up bitchy verbal bombshells to drop on plays, actors, sets, music and directors, and like to think they have the power to turn theatrical productions into hits or flops accordingly. And they have – not always but almost always. Long before he saw the Orson Welles production of *Othello*, Ken Tynan had written his headline: 'CITIZEN COON'. Many of his memorable crits are quoted lovingly as gems of lyrical assassination (for example, when a well-known actress, who shall remain nameless, was singing for the first time in a musical, he wrote 'She shook her voice at the audience like a tiny fist', and of another unlucky thespian, 'He had the detonation of a falling marshmallow').

One critic called our play 'an emotional dustbin', whatever that means, and we all took a bit of a drubbing. Five years later, we might have been hailed as 'a breakthrough in modern psychological drama' or something of the sort. Of course, nowadays, nudity and incestuous sex on stage have become the norm, being so ordinary that they would no longer even raise an eyebrow, but in the mid-sixties no-one was quite sure what was beyond the pale.

For a long time, I had wanted to show Sean where I came from in Australia. We decided to spend Christmas at Mooloolaba with my entire family but in the meantime Sean had a movie to shoot. He had grown an impressive handle-bar moustache for his part as the cowboy in *Shalako*, to be shot in Almeria with Brigitte Bardot, old friend Stephen Boyd, golfing buddy Eric Sykes and ex-Olympian athlete, the giant Woody Strode. Though I wasn't too keen on returning to that particular location in Spain, I couldn't wait to get back to the *finca* in San Pedro di Alcantara, where I could continue my literary career and plant apricot trees.

My Pirandello translating had suffered a major setback when George Devine had died the year before. We had no formal contract for the translations and subsequent production of the plays I was still in the process of polishing. I'd had the same reaction as Anthony Quayle, who exploded on hearing of George's death, 'Dead? What do you mean dead? We've got a lot of unfinished business.'

Nonetheless, I had acquired a new project, one that I savoured. I had bought a Kafka short story while in New York. For ten thousand dollars, the Kafka Estate sold me *Report to the Academy*, the story of an ape who learns to speak and becomes a star of stage and circus, ultimately presenting a devastating report to a prestigious scientific academy about what it is like to become a 'man'.

My idea for the screenplay was to begin the action during the conflagration in the Belgian Congo, the ape being bought in Kinshasa as a dead carcass by a group of merchant seamen. They put the body in their mate's bunk as a joke, shove a cigarette into its mouth and wait for their drunken mate to return and find the body. But when he does, the cigarette is puffing. Of course, the ape is not dead and the mate falls in love with it, nurtures it back to life and begins its education. Instead of becoming a star of the circus, Rufus the ape conquers the world of TV ads and finally plays a classic Othello as the Ape of Venice and saves the National Theatre, while the merchant seaman becomes his chauffeur. I was having great fun working on the script.

My novel, *The Manipulator*, had been well received and, although I hadn't forgotten the struggle I'd had to finish it, I was game to have another go. An idea for a plot was stirring in the back of my brain. Most ideas take years to gestate and this one came from way back when I was crossing the Pacific as a teenager on the *Pioneer Star*. The ship had anchored off Pitcairn Island and a man carrying a guitar was rowed out. We watched as he clambered on board and begged to work his passage to America. He said his name was Urine (pronounced U-ryne) Thompson, and although his skin was a deep coffee brown he had bright blue eyes, a legacy of Fletcher Christian whose descendants, the mutineers of the HMS *Bounty*, had inhabited Pitcairn Island since 1790. He played a mean guitar with strange little old-world riffs, and when someone in the crew called him 'the blue-eyed coon' he replied that he was neither a coon nor a white man.

'What are you then, mate?'

'I'm a hybrid not a coon, maybe I'm a hybrid loon,' he answered coolly.

I looked the word up in the dictionary and read that hybrids are crosses between different varieties of crops or animals, which are often stronger than the original stock. It was a description I never forgot. I would call my book *Hybrid* and it would be about a blue-eyed brown man, though I would not call him Urine.

So life settled into a rhythm of writing and social events. One Sunday before we travelled to Spain, we were driving sedately back from lunch at Eric Sykes' place on the North Circular Road when a cop car began tailgating us. Sean was extremely careful to drive just under the prescribed speed limit. The car came level with us and we could see the policemen inside gesticulating and talking animatedly. They hung back for a few more miles and then inevitably the siren started wailing and they pulled us over. A young officer approached the car with a big grin on his face and said, 'You were over the speed limit, Mr Bond.'

I could feel Sean's blood beginning to simmer as the young cop took out his notebook.

'You know, my name is PC James Bond,' he informed us, as though we would be thrilled to hear the news. 'You were over the speed limit by five miles per hour. I've been waiting all my life to nick you. You understand that.'

I was amazed at his temerity. He was already rubbing his hands together, anticipating a front-page story in the Sunday papers. It was so unfair and there was absolutely nothing we could do about it. These cumulative little injustices are the downside of celebrity but they accrue until, finally, one anticipates the worst in every situation. Yes, the young policeman got his name in a front-page story and Sean was summonsed to court in his absence. The Magistrate observed to Police Constable James Bond that he thought he was making history. Those in court got a good laugh out of it and there was a fine of fifteen pounds to pay. It's all money.

Once, when I was about eight years old, my grandmother took my right hand as I lay on her bed next to her. She turned it over, squeezed it and spread it flat.

'Go on,' she said, 'open up your palm.'

When I did so, she flattened my palm against hers. I have always had rather over-extended joints so that the inside of my hand bends out like an Indian dancer's.

'Oh dear, I'm afraid, my girl, you're never ever going to be able to hang on to money. That's for sure. But there are some compensations,' she said, kneading my palm. 'You've got a lovely mount of Venus and your mount of Mars is prominent. You'll always stand up for yourself and you'll be a favourite with the opposite sex, so it's not all bad.'

At the time I had no idea what any of this meant, but I have had occasion over the years to ruefully remark how accurate my grandmother was in her prediction that I would never be able to hang on to money. Whatever you call it – spondulies, dosh, bread, shekels, moolah, green stuff, lucre – money has managed to slip through my fingers and off my palm with amazing speed, sometimes before I even knew it was there. Of course, I am not alone in this regrettable trait and I commiserate with all my fellow sufferers worldwide. Oddly, I have never been unduly distressed by this flaw as I learned to be frugal at an early age, to make do and be enormously grateful when some windfall arrived to see me through.

Sean on the other hand, being a Scot, was situated 180 degrees away from this position in the money stakes. After we returned from Japan, he came to me with a sheaf of papers in his hand, shaking them at me angrily and saying, 'Look at this! God, D, you are so ridiculous! We're overdrawn to the tune of five thousand pounds at the bank. How is it that you can make such a mess of things when it comes to money! You'd better fix it up as soon as possible.'

I apologised profusely, accepting that it was my fault, but I was confused. How could we be five thousand pounds overdrawn when I was sure that I had not spent more than that amount in the entire time we'd had the housekeeping account? I went to see the bank manager, who ushered me into his office, sat me down and shook his head at me as he must have done to ten thousand other overdrawn clients over the years.

'Well, what are we going to do about this, Mrs Connery? We've held off as long as we could but the time has come to put some money *in*. Our limit is five thousand pounds, you know.'

I was mortified and brought out my personal chequebook straight-away.

'Of course, you understand, we made a special allowance in your case, as no money has ever been put into the account.'

I was astonished. Somewhere in the dark recesses of my brain, I vaguely remembered Sean saying something about not giving me any housekeeping money if I continued to work. Did he mean if I *ever* worked again? It was a puzzle, as I had been camp-following and had not done any theatrical work for months.

In the end I did not say anything to Sean, as the quickest way to send him into a rage was to talk about money, especially as he was so derogatory about my shortcomings in that direction. I asked the bank manager to write Sean a letter, stating that no money had ever been put into that account and that I had paid the shortfall. I asked him to enquire whether Sean would remedy the matter of the joint account as soon as possible by depositing some funds for the future.

In reviewing the situation, I realised that the house in Putney and the *finca* in Spain were both in Sean's name and that, basically, I was a pauper. I had nothing of my own. Now that I was no longer working, I was beginning to feel financially powerless. I had turned down so many jobs that my agent was beginning to despair of me. It was simply ludicrous that in the midst of the deluge of money pouring in from the Bond films, I was feeling so vulnerable.

I was determined to use what little money I had left over from *Hombre* in a sensible way for once. I took to driving around Kingston-on-Thames, Putney and other greener areas on that side of the river, trying to get a plan together to maybe buy something and do it up – not to live in, just to let as an investment, a nest egg that would be mine.

Looking back on this period of our marriage, I can see that it must have been around this time that Sean and I each began to realise that the differences in our interests and attitudes to life were widening. It was golf that started the rot. I knew I would never be able to follow that little white ball around for the rest of my life. The sound of cleats on cement floors and gravel pathways has the same effect on me as scratching a blackboard with a set of keys.

What's more, I had no intention of joining the ladies in the changing rooms, where the talk was always about nail polish or some new bauble prised out of their respective hubby, boyfriend or father. On the course, I lost concentration after playing a hole or two, having started thinking about my writing or what I was going to cook for dinner. The only thing golf has to recommend it, as far as I'm concerned, is walking around outdoors smelling lovely fresh air.

Sean was now so deeply entrenched in golf that he was playing pro-am games with the likes of Stanley Baker, Charlie Drake, Les Dawson and Michael Medwin, as well as with professional golfers Christy

O'Connor and Harry Bradshaw. I once told him that his world revolved around a golf ball, and he was quick to admit it was true.

Had I been paying attention like a good compliant wife, instead of being as headstrong as ever, I should have *made* myself love all the accoutrements of golf – changing rooms, cleats, clumping around in ugly shoes, the lot. I should have learned to wax lyrical about the Golden Bear, Arnold Palmer, Gary Player and all the other golfing heroes of the day. I did go to driving ranges and watch Sean hit balls, even though the temperature was often below freezing, but after many attempts at all these things, I could not go on doing them. Basically, I could not get away from the impression that for people like me, who have no real desire to hit something endlessly, golf is a waste of life. Of course, Sean is perfectly justified in believing conversely that golf is a philosophy and, as he has said, 'a great help to somebody like myself who doesn't have a religion.'

And then, during one of my reconnaissance trips around the Putney area, I turned into a leafy grove. It was a small circular road that serviced a piece of lush, enclosed land on a gentle slope of Kingston Hill called Coombe Springs. This diversion was to mark the first of a number of meaningful coincidences that were to change my life forever. I knew it was the right place immediately and put down a payment on a plot set back from the road at the top of the hill furthest away from the entrance and main road.

Chancellor's Lane had a remarkably pleasant feel – quiet and private but lively at the same time. The developers recounted rumours that Cardinal Wolsey (the Lord Chancellor) had hidden his secret fortune at Coombe Springs after he was stripped of his wealth by Henry VIII for failing to secure Henry's divorce from Catherine of Aragon. More recently, it had been the grounds for some sort of school. I discussed the four possible sets of plans with the builders, made many adjustments and soon a splendid house began to take shape.

In the meantime, I was still camp following. The location of *Shalako* was that Mecca of spaghetti westerns, Almeria, the same fateful place where *The Hill* had been shot. This time, instead of the seedy resort on the sea that had been our digs, we were magnificently housed in a villa in the town. It was not an impossible drive down the coast to our farm and so the children, Sean and I commuted between our two Spanish destinations.

Brigitte Bardot turned up with her millionaire husband, Gunther Sachs, a blond German with ice-blue eyes. Brigitte evidently also travelled with an entourage of very young French jetsetters of both sexes. They took over the top floors of the best hotel in Almeria and spent their free time on the beach flaunting and frolicking.

Unfortunately for Gunther, he developed a mystery illness which precluded him from their sport and he stayed in bed lonely and undiagnosed for some days. It turned out to be unromantic lumbago and the gutter press got hold of the story. As usual, they turned his affliction into a personal attack, mocking the poor man for having an old man's disease of the lower back while married to 'the sexiest woman on earth' who, they wrote, was at that moment consorting on screen with 'the sexiest man on earth', Sean.

There must have been something else amiss in their marriage because, one day, Brigitte took all his clothes and threw them out of the window into the main street below. They were later collected and distributed to the poor people of the town. Gunther left soon after and, it is said, was never spoken of again in Bebe's company.

Oddly enough, the chemistry between Sean and Bardot was nonexistent. Who knows why? These things are so impossible to predict. On paper their co-starring should have sizzled the silver screen and sent temperatures soaring, but instead they seemed to cancel each other out so that *Shalako* is as unmemorable a film to see as was its making.

Jason and I had one glorious adventure while that film was being shot. Sean had gifted me an elegant western saddle inlaid with Mexican silver, but he was not present when a group of us set out on our marathon ride. Inevitably, Sean had chosen to play golf with Eric Sykes. I remember the scene of our departure better than the actual movie. The stunt men had all the horses used in the film ready at first light and we trotted through the town to music and cheers from bystanders.

A graceful, dancing Palomino pony, whose mane matched Jason's blond head, was chosen for the six-year-old boy. Huge and black, Woody Strode, wearing a black Stetson, was magnificent on a rearing black stallion while his monumental Hawaiian wife wore a scarlet mumu and dwarfed the minuscule donkey she rode by his side. Stephen Boyd, smiling but slightly uncomfortable, having tried to protect his inner thighs with sticking plaster, was mounted on a rangy seventeen-hand roan gelding. He said he hadn't been astride a horse since *Ben Hur*. One of the stunt men laughingly offered him a chariot. I was given a beautiful milk-white mare. She was docile and tractable and I felt utterly exhilarated to be on top of such a superb creature.

We rode into the hinterland up a wide dried riverbed. On either side of us were vast orange groves, their fragrance filling our nostrils and making the horses snort. There were no roads to the country we were heading for. Peasants had used the riverbed for centuries when they ventured into the outside world, which wasn't often, but the oranges were exported with no difficulty at all in the dry season.

We made a gaudy troupe of glamorous interlopers into that austere landscape as we rode along, singing and chattering, but by midday everyone was getting thirsty and peckish. Almost on cue, there appeared up ahead of us a small bunch of children waving and gesticulating. As we drew nearer, we saw that the little people we had seen from the distance were not children at all but a group of oddly shaped figures dressed in black. Several hunchbacks and dwarves, a gnarled old lady bent over almost double and a few children with crossed eyes were beckoning us excitedly to follow them.

They led us up a path to a collection of ancient houses clustered together and holding each other up. Piglets and mangy dogs scampered out of the shadows, jumping about under our horses' feet while a cacophony of sounds hit our eardrums – squeals, shouts, clapping and homemade tin trumpets. People ran out waving and nodding at us, as humans and animals alike celebrated our arrival.

We were about to dismount but the head stuntman, Bob, stopped us, saying it was probably better not to get mixed with so many over-excited locals. 'This is likely the first big visit they've had since Columbus was a little boy. Just sit tight, smile and say gracias,' he advised us.

It wasn't long before they brought out plates of luscious olives, jalapenos, pepitas and dark meat on skewers, piping hot from the fire, which had the aroma of wild thyme and garlic. They brought leather wine bottles and showed us how to pour the wine into our mouths. Woody Strode made his stallion rear up as he whooped with his first taste. 'Wow!' he shouted. 'This is gen-u-ine firewater! What *is* this stuff?'

'It's the local homemade Jerez,' Bob told him. 'Dangerous, probably fortified to about fifty per cent proof!'

Once Woody had tried the meat, he couldn't get enough of it. He crammed chunks into his mouth and chewed with gusto. 'This is the best tapas I've ever had,' he said. 'It makes that crap you get in Almeria taste like dog shit! What is this meat? I hope it's not horse!'

When Bob asked the locals what sort of meat we were eating, they shouted, '*Higado de cerdo . . . higado de cerdo!*' Bob was silent.

'Hey, Bob, what are they saying?'

Woody took another long swig of the sherry and gulped down a few more Spanish shish kebabs before Bob's Cockney accent cut through the babble of Spanish all around us. 'Pig's liver, Woody!' he shouted above the din. 'I'm pretty certain what they're saying is it's pig's liver, mate.'

Woody looked down thoughtfully at the filthy animals that swarmed in the dirt below him and then, quite suddenly, he heaved and a great arc gushed forth from his mouth. The entire contents of his stomach flew out in three involuntary spasms onto the crowd of people looking up at him with such awe. His horse reared up and whinnied in protest as a communal gasp of horror and curses rang out. Dogs ran in to get their share and were kicked, snarling and yelping, out of the way. I felt I was in the middle of a surreal scene from a Buñuel film as, in slow motion, Woody turned his giant steed around and gave him a touch of the spur. The great beast moved off smartly, kicking out at the vomit-stained mob. Bob jumped off his horse, took a wad of pesetas out of his pocket and ran around distributing money to anyone who held out his hand. By the time we left, they were all grinning and rubbing the stuff into their faces.

'*El hombre negro no puede beber mucho!*' was the jeer and the mob took up the cry. ('The black man can't take his drink!') We left amid catcalls and shouts but some of the children ran with us, laughing and hanging on to our stirrups until we got back to the riverbed again. The next day, none of us could walk very well but poor Stephen Boyd was incapacitated for nearly a week with raw welts on the inside of his thighs.

CHAPTER ELEVEN

By the end of the year, we were sweltering on the beach at Mooloo-laba, celebrating a good old-fashioned Down Under Christmas beneath the merciless southern sun. My mother was by now the doy-enne of female doctors in the land. Her articles on health, vitamins and diet had been collected and made into bestselling books, practical bibles for the housewives and mothers of Australia. So many people have approached me to say, as though we share a precious secret, 'You know, your mother brought me into the world.' She must have deliv-ered half the population of Queensland.

That Christmas, the Cilento clan gathered at the Butterfly House on the beach at Mooloolaba. It must have been overwhelming for Sean to be out of the clutches of the paparazzi and into the hands of a gang of noisy Australian rellies. Apart from the six children and their respective husbands and wives, there were twenty-seven grandchildren. It seems excessive but my brother Raff had produced eleven children from two wives, with more to come. He lived in America, being one of a steady stream of young Australian doctors, researchers, writers, actors, directors and musos who'd emigrated there.

There were picnics and barbeques on the beach in front of the house. Sean played golf up the coast at Coolum, a spanking new course in those days, and managed to hit one of the kangaroos that frequented the greens. Then he decided he wanted to learn to surf. An army of new brothers, sisters and cousins-in-law, Aussie blokes and sheilas were ready to oblige. He learned very quickly after a few dumpings and was soon catching the curlers with the best of us.

I think Sean was somewhat nonplussed that there were none of the trappings of wealth that he might have expected of a titled family in England – no servants, chauffeurs or silver service. It was all pitch in, but then Australians have a peculiar way of treating celebrities. They sneer knowingly and stammer brusquely in their presence, without ever making eye contact, or else they ignore the famous person completely. These reactions serve to show that they don't care who you are, that you're no better than they are and that you're more likely to be a bull-shitter or a phony. This attitude, known as the tall poppy syndrome, has supposedly come about through the residual memory of convict days when those in authority, or those who attained an elevated status, were treated with the utmost suspicion and were despised.

Jason caught chickenpox and was forced to stay out of direct sunlight, which could have damaged his eyes. He had to be cooled with sponge baths of chamomile lotion over his entire body so that he didn't scratch the sores and turn them septic. We thought there might be an epidemic with all the other children around, but I can't remember anyone else getting the disease.

Sean and I accompanied my dad up to the Barrier Reef where the entrepreneur Eric McIlree, proprietor of Avis Rent-a-Car, had purchased the paradisiacal Dunk Island. He was donating a half-acre surrounding the burial cairn of E.J. Banfield to James Cook University. As head of the Historical Society and the National Trust at the time, my dad was visiting the area to mark out the proposed area for the Banfield Memorial Centre. While we were there, McIlree offered Sean a half share in the casino he was planning to build but Sean declined. Sadly, poor McIlree's projections for the casino and Banfield Memorial Centre came to naught when he was blown up in a motorboat accident in Sydney Harbour shortly after our visit.

My dad was a terrific guide, walking us through rainforests, keeping us from getting tangled up in the moils and coils of 'wait-a-while', a vicious, prickly bamboo vine that can reach out, grab you and make you do just that . . . wait a long time while you try to extricate yourself from the thorns without tearing your skin off.

Dad told us stories about E. J. Banfield, who was a journalist with tuberculosis who had been given six months to live. In 1897 Banfield decided that, if he had to die, he would spend his remaining time, like Thoreau, living in a small cedar hut in the wilds of uninhabited Dunk Island. His hut was built with the assistance of his friend and mentor, Tom, a local Aborigine, and here Banfield and his wife created a self-sufficient farm where they lived for twenty-six years. Ten years into his life on Dunk Island, he wrote a lyrical book called *Confessions of a Beachcomber*, published in 1907, which became a bestseller and bible for would-be castaways and drop-outs who wished to live in paradise.

We toured some of the other islands, notably Palm Island, where some surly Aborigines brightened up amazingly when we spent the day listening to their stories. Afterwards we went to Timana Island, where we were greeted by an unselfconsciously naked man with a beautiful woman and a boy of seven, similarly unclad. He was Bruce Arthur, the ex-Olympian wrestler-turned-weaver, waiting for us on the sand with his wife and small son. Fabrizio, the boy, took us to his cubby-house – the carcass of a light aircraft which had crashed on the island. We marvelled at the untouched splendour of tropical North Queensland and I felt instantly at home, as I have never felt anywhere else.

At that time, neither of us entertained ideas of returning to the country of my birth on a permanent basis. Sean and I loved Australia's egalitarian atmosphere and wallowed in the freedom of its open skies and empty beaches but in the sixties the country was only just beginning to awaken to what was happening in the rest of the world. As far as we were concerned, it was still deep in the land of Nod and the tyranny of distance from big cities and places where we could earn our living seemed insurmountable. We returned to London refreshed but with no intentions of making professional forays Down Under in the foreseeable future.

Back in Putney, Sean's first engagement was the premiere of *Shalako*. I did not know that I had not been invited. Unbeknownst to me, it had been agreed that Sean would partner Brigitte Bardot so that the press could do their usual and get some mileage out of the inference that they were an item. Ergo, I was not to be seen or heard of. I had been sidelined without my collusion and it hurt. Not long before, Sean would have told the arrangers to take a running jump but now the work of the spin doctors was accepted without question. Even though he was not playing 007 in this film, he was still required to maintain the Bond image, despite the fact that he and Bebe didn't even like each other.

I had the uneasy feeling that I was in line to take on that most ghastly of all roles, the ghostly wife in the background, smiling mechanically in the face of hubby's blatant or pretended indiscretions. I was definitely not right for the part. We had some blazing rows about money at this time, about my working and my friends, but it wasn't really about any of these things. What was wrong was that Sean's criteria for the position of 'wife' didn't match up with mine. The perfect wife for Sean (a) would have to be as besotted about golf as he was; (b) would have to be a millionairess so she would never have to ask him for money; (c) should definitely not be a celebrity in her own right; and (d) should have no friends but his. I did not fit one of these criteria.

I accepted a part in a shoestring film called *Negatives* to be shot around London. The director, Peter Medak, was a young Hungarian refugee with eyes that looked as though he was about to fall asleep. He wasn't. Peter was as sharp as a tack and talented. This was his first film and we all felt sorry for him as the movie was on such a tight budget that there wasn't enough actual film stock to shoot some of the scenes. He went on to have a prestigious career directing such films as *The Ruling Class*, *Romeo is Bleeding*, *The Krays* and *A Day in the Death of Joe Egg*.

Our little flick was a quirky tale of obsession and sexual kinkiness, two qualities that attracted people mightily in the late sixties. Theo (played by Peter McEnery) and his lover, Vivien (played by Glenda Jackson in her first film role), engage in fetishistic dressing up during their love-making, with Theo impersonating notorious murderer Dr Crippen and Vivien taking on the sexual role of Crippen's wife or mistress. Reingard, a mysterious German lesbian photographer (played by yours truly), takes pictures of them having it off and becomes intrigued by the couple. Under Reingard's influence, Theo abandons his Crippen characterisation to assume the persona of German flying ace Baron von Richthofen, and tries to build a replica of the Red Baron's bi-plane on his terrace. I can remember no more than that, except that I wore a big-hair blond wig and a black jumpsuit. I felt pretty ridiculous but I liked Glenda and Peter, so it was fun.

Glenda never stopped moaning that she and her husband never did anything together except *The Times* crossword puzzle. 'Why don't you do a baby together? It's much more amusing, and it can be a talking point for you both for years to come,' I quipped. She must have taken me at my word because by the end of the shoot Glenda was with child.

I had also met up with members of the Living Theatre, an eclectic group of Germans, Italians, Americans and Asians – actors of many nationalities – who gave astounding performances all over the world, as far afield as Nepal. Amongst them was my old friend from New York, the African-American actor Rufus, now playing leading roles. We fell into each other's arms and it was decided that I would try to help them write a film script based on their arrest in Italy on drug charges when a member of their troupe was murdered.

Out of the blue, my agent Jimmy Fraser rang me and announced that Anthony Quayle had requested my availability for his new production of Dostoyevsky's *The Idiot* at the National Theatre. I had never read the book but the adaptation was to be done by Simon Ward, who was a wonderful writer in his own right. It was to be presented at the

National Theatre with a cast that included Derek Jacobi, Laurence Olivier, Anthony Hopkins and a full company of NT actors. I was to play Nastasya Filippovna.

'I don't suppose you'll do it,' Jimmy said rather gloomily. 'They hardly pay anything anyway, but when the play becomes part of the repertory you only have to do it two or three times a week.'

I was fully alerted by this possibility. How could Sean object to my being absent from my wifely duties for only two or three nights a week? I tackled reading *The Idiot* with enthusiasm. Once you begin one of these classic Dostoyevsky tomes you enter another world, and while you are reading them, ordinary life is the vague dream and *they* are the reality. I didn't emerge from *The Idiot* for some weeks, but by the time I did, I was hooked. I would have played the part for nothing.

There was a major kerfuffle at the National Theatre before I was actually offered the role, though, because Laurence Olivier was insistent that his wife, Joan Plowright, should play Nastasya. He gave in reluctantly after Anthony Quayle threatened to quit if she was thrust upon him and my great friend Bumble Dawson, who was designing the costumes, similarly put her foot down, telling him in no uncertain terms that Joan was 'ridiculous casting'.

Even then, Olivier had to see *Negatives* and I had a very uncomfortable interview with him in his office near the Old Vic. He spent most of the time telling me that he had been able to see my wig-join in the movie but, in the end, it was settled. I was to play Nastasya and I was truly excited by the challenge of such a difficult role.

Before rehearsals began, I spent a brief but excruciatingly unpleasant time in Pennsylvania while Sean was shooting *The Molly Maguires*. It should have been a wonderful reunion of old friends, with Marty Ritt, the director of *Hombre*, and old chum Richard Harris on hand, but I have rarely been less happy.

At first, we stayed in a motel where wailing women banged on the walls and chanted Sean's name all night and we had to run the gauntlet of the foyer every day, fighting off both fans and press. Finally, we rented a house way out in the boondocks where I was left with no transport in the hideous, flat countryside, unable to write even though I had begun my second novel, *Hybrid*.

When I got back to London, I didn't say anything to anyone but I vowed in my heart that I would never go on another location as a camp follower. The experience only confirmed my desire to free myself from the oppression of having to conform to my peculiar conjugal role and I could not wait to start rehearsals at the National Theatre.

Anthony Quayle was playing the lead in the two-hander smash hit production of Anthony Shaffer's *Sleuth*, and so wasn't free to rehearse on matinee days. It was a Herculean task he was taking on by directing such a large production while playing a demanding role in the West End. Added to this, the National Theatre was mounting a mammoth production of *Guys and Dolls* with Larry Olivier playing Sky Masterton, the singing and dancing lead. Cast members who were doubling in both productions had to take lessons every day, so rehearsals for *The Idiot* were interrupted continuously by actors rushing off to class or standing in for other actors who were missing.

Poor Tony Quayle was a beleaguered man, especially when both Larry Olivier and Anthony Hopkins sat in on our first read through and both proclaimed they did not want to take part in the play at all. Everyone said it was because Larry hadn't got his way about Joan. It was a body blow but we recovered and a young actor called Tom Baker was chosen to play Rogozhin, the lover and killer of Nastasya Filippovna (the part Anthony Hopkins had been earmarked to play). Tom went on to become a beloved Dr Who but this was his big chance and he was lucky to have Derek Jacobi, Ronald Pickup and Ted Hardwicke to coach him in the basic skills.

I had an instant rapport with Derek Jacobi, who has something of the beauty and innocence of a genuine God's idiot as well as a Dostoyevsky one. This was the first time he'd had to carry a play, even though he had been at the National for nine years. In fact, he had never acted on any stage other than the Old Vic. Immediately after this play, he took his courage in his hands and left the National to fall squarely on his feet in the part of Claudius in the brilliant BBC TV series *I, Claudius*, adapted from the classic by Robert Graves.

Obviously, our rehearsal period was protracted. It was many weeks before we got onto the stage for our first dress rehearsal, and when we did, it seemed like such a mess we thought the play would never open. The plan was that there would be a dress rehearsal every week until opening night three weeks hence.

Olivier had brought in Svoboda, an ace stage designer from Russia, to do the sets. He was renowned throughout Europe for building huge, impressive but unwieldy mechanical devices to fill the stage with magic. Some scenes were set on a rail journey, so Svoboda built a train with carriages, which seemed to fill the entire working area with railway lines that criss-crossed the stage, creating an obstacle course for the cast. Actors wearing their new costumes floundered about, tripping over the lines they spoke as well as the ones on the floor.

Olivier came to the first, deplorable dress rehearsal and afterwards demanded that Anthony Quayle cut the scene of my entrance. I was horrified, because it was a pivotal introduction. For the entrance of Nastasya, Bumble Dawson had designed possibly the most gorgeous costume I have ever worn. It was spectacular, made from period fabrics and laces that she had scoured London for. Both the director and Simon Ward, the writer, pleaded with Larry to reconsider and reinstate the scene but he was adamant. My beautiful costume ended up as a display piece in the window of one of Oxford Street's fashion houses.

By this time, we were all convinced that Larry was trying to sabotage the whole production for a number of reasons. If we had too much public acclaim it might take the gilt off *Guys and Dolls*, or perhaps he was still cross at losing the argument as to who played Nastasya Filippovna. I had learned to deal with adversity, and we soldiered on against all odds and finally opened to reviews that were enthusiastic but not as great as we knew they could have been.

Several weeks after our first night Larry Olivier suffered a major stroke, from which he only just survived. It put paid to the production of *Guys and Dolls* and his tenure as director of the new National Theatre. He had to content himself with an Academy Award nomination for the film version of *Sleuth*, playing Sir Andrew Wyke, the part that Anthony Quayle had created on the stage.

When I recounted the saga of Larry's sabotage of *The Idiot* to Noel Coward some time later, he became pensive for a long moment. When he looked up, he said, 'Did you know that Larry, by his own admission, possesses one of the smallest willies in the Western world? He used to call it his rosebud.'

'Really? You mean like "rosebud" in *Citizen Kane*, the last word Citizen Kane says before he dies? No-one could ever discover what "rosebud" meant but the audience knew that it was a little sled that burnt up when he was a boy . . .'

'Oh, no it wasn't,' Noel countered. 'It was Orson Welles being very naughty and causing a great deal of mischief which, incidentally, hounded him until the end of his life. I shall tell you, if you care to listen. "Rosebud" was William Randolph Hearst's pet name for Marion Davies' clit.'

Noel paused for effect. I was speechless.

'You know, short for clit-oris. Marion was his mistress for many years until he died. He doted on her. She was a very accomplished comedienne in early films, by the way, although she was always partial to a bit of a tipple. At some grand piss-up at San Simeon, the castle he built where they entertained lavishly, she told her old drinking mate, Tom Mankewitz, all about her intimate life with the richest tycoon of the day. Tom may have been legless at the time but he was not so far gone that he didn't repeat this juicy morsel of information to Orson Welles, who was beside himself with delight. They wrote the script of

Citizen Kane together, using the theme of "Rosebud", aware that Hearst would know that his secret was out. Hearst was so incensed that he tried to have the film withdrawn and his newspapers did a hatchet job on Orson for the rest of his life.

'It's fascinating,' he mused, 'how often, in perfectly normal conversations, one finds oneself discussing other people's private parts. Do you think it was always so? Do you think the pharaohs sat about comparing the size of their enemies' paraphernalia with their own? It's an interesting thought.

'Yes,' he went on, 'I think Larry is one of the most envious men who ever lived but it wasn't *you* he was after. It was poor old Anthony Quayle.'

While I was appearing in *The Idiot* at the National, Sean went to Russia to do *The Red Tent*. He was fascinated by the way people looked at him in that country. Peasants in the street had an unaffected candour and unabashed curiosity. Sean thought this unselfconsciousness had vanished from people in Western European countries. He had many stories to tell but no sooner was he back than he was off again to the States to shoot *The Anderson Tapes*.

So there we were, just Jason and I, rattling around in the big house at Putney, Giovanna having begged for and been granted leave to stay in Australia to attend school with her cousins for a year. I had begun to write seriously again, working on the Kafka script. Sometimes the crew from the Living Theatre would come over and we would make tapes of each person's recollections of their arrest and time spent in prison in Italy. Later, this material would be used to cobble a script together. When the work was over, we would cook up something delicious and eat together in the cosy back kitchen with the fire blazing, as it was getting very cold.

One night, I was at the stove cooking steak when Jason came in looking very strange and trembling. I thought he was just cold but he said to me in a voice I can remember to this day, 'Come and sit on your bed, Mummy, I have to tell you something.'

I stopped cooking immediately and turned the gas off. Instinctively, I knew that there was something very wrong here. We went upstairs but Jason would not say anything until I was seated at the bottom of the big bed.

'I went to Nigel's but he was asleep, so I went up to Wimbledon Common by myself to have a slide on the pool because it's frozen over. I skidded about for a while, but every time I started to come off the ice there was a man standing where I was going to be. It didn't matter which side of the pool I went, he would always be there.'

I could feel my mouth drying up but did not interrupt him. He started to speak and mumbled something I could not catch. I tried not to prompt him and finally he got it out. 'He pulled me . . . into the bushes . . . and then he . . . made me kneel down . . . I think you have to call the police.'

I held his little body and hugged him to me but he stayed rigid and did not cry. I could tell he was severely traumatised. When the Flying Squad came, which they did with the utmost speed, they brought a policewoman along with them. She sat Jason down in the front room and talked quietly to him about school, pets, anything, until he was more relaxed. Only then did she tackle the subject of what had happened on Wimbledon Common. He was able to give a detailed description of the man and what he was wearing, even down to the colour of his socks, which was ominous, but he always stopped short of saying what actually happened after the man had pulled him into the bushes. She didn't pursue it any further than he was prepared to go, which was merciful.

The actors from the Living Theatre were wonderfully supportive and made cups of hot soup for everyone. I was trying to stay focused but inside I was in shock, unable to handle the fact that such a thing could happen to my seven-year-old. I called Sean in New York City, where he was doing post-synching work on *The Anderson Tapes*. His voice came through in a business-like way from the other side of the Atlantic. I explained the situation carefully, but instead of a concerned dad on the end of the line, I got an explosion of anger from a furious husband.

'It's one of those no-hoper actors you've got there! That's who's done it!' he shouted. 'Just get those creeps out of my house as fast as you can. You're asking for trouble with those hippy slimebags around the place!'

I thought he must have missed the fact that Jason's attack had happened on Wimbledon Common. So, as calmly as possible, I went over the story again.

'Stanley told me those bastards have been in my house nearly every day since I left. I want you to get rid of them . . . NOW!' was his reply.

Now I knew what was going on. Stanley Mann, our next-door neighbour who had known and adored Sean since the early days when he wrote the script of *Another Time, Another Place*, the stinker Sean did with Lana Turner, had been keeping his friend informed as to who came to and who left the house. He had been at the window of his kitchen, watching the whole parade of people who came to eat and talk in my kitchen opposite.

It seemed that Sean, with all this souped-up information from Stanley, had associated what had happened to Jason with members of the Living Theatre and nothing would budge him from this conviction. I put the receiver down. Jason needed to talk to a male person, preferably his father, to whom he could relate what actually had happened and who would assure him that he was safe.

I sat with Jason until he went to sleep. The next day his friend Nigel came over and the two boys went off to play in the snow which had fallen overnight. I was working, keeping warm next to the fire in the back kitchen, when Nigel and Jason burst into the room, breathless with news.

'WE SAW HIM! WE SAW HIM!' they shrieked, 'He was at the Wimbledon Pond, just like yesterday!'

I was thrown into a panic to think that they had gone back to the Common by themselves without my knowledge.

Nigel shouted, 'AND HE SAW JASON! HE CHASED US ALL THE WAY HOME!'

In a flap, I called the Flying Squad again and they returned with the same policewoman to get the story from the boys. I took Nigel home to the flats opposite our house and kept Jason indoors for the rest of the day, as he was feverish. I was beginning to feel distinctly paranoid.

I called Sean again in New York and told him that Jason had gone back to the Common with Nigel and a few friends to find the man, and 'beat him up'. That was his reason for going, he'd informed me. Sean was still positive that the whole thing was a storm in a teacup and had something to do with the Living Theatre.

I reiterated that it was imperative that Jason should talk to someone, to have some counselling from a strong male figure who would reassure him. '*You*,' I said. 'When can you get back? It's important.'

'Why are you trying to get me to come back? What are you up to?'

'Sean, I'm not trying to get you back here for any reason other than that Jason *needs* you.'

'Did you get rid of those people?'

'I swear to you that they have nothing at all to do with what happened to Jason. I am merely working with them on a film script. I really like their company. You haven't seen any of their performances. They're so talented . . . and different . . . and really hard-working.'

The line went dead.

It was very uncomfortable in the ensuing weeks knowing that every time people came to the house, Stanley Mann would be watching, ready to inform Sean. I did not take guests into the back kitchen any more; in fact, I discouraged anyone coming to the house at all.

For several nights after the man had chased the boys home from the

Common, I noticed a blue car stopped on the road outside the house under my window. It remained there for twenty minutes at a time with the engine running, and I could faintly hear what sounded like a two-way radio. I went down into the garden one night to try to get a look inside but the car suddenly sped off, as though the driver was aware of my presence.

It was after this that I began to feel very scared and rang the number the police had given me. They assured me that they would re-route the patrol on duty in the Putney area to drive past my house every couple of hours. They said not to hesitate to call them if it happened again.

Then some oddly marked pages of magazines were dropped through the letter box. Pictures of children circled in red crayon. Chains were drawn round their ankles, and dollar and pound signs were etched round their heads. Interpreting these as some sort of abduction threat, I became even more terrified. I hardly allowed Jason out of my sight.

I could not understand why Sean hadn't comprehended the serious-ness of the situation. This was a time when the kidnapping of children of tycoons and film stars was reported in the papers every day. Sophia Loren had relocated from Europe to the United States, fearing that her children would be kidnapped. Why not 007's kid? When the press prints the sum a star is being paid per film, and that figure is well into the millions, it is liable to motivate desperate people to do unspeakable things. I felt sure that the man who had followed the boys home knew whose house Jason had run into and who he must be.

One Saturday night as I lay in bed, the unmistakable sound of a car engine and the faint echo of a radio reached my ears. The old blue car was back. I called the police number and lay back in bed tensely, wait-ing for their car to arrive. On cue, as the police car sped up the hill and through the Common, the blue car took off. I lay sleepless, listening all night, and through the long hours a plan began to form in my head. By Sunday morning I knew what I had to do.

It took at least twelve trips with the car loaded to the gills every time. Jason helped, thinking of it as an adventure, and by evening I was satisfied that most of the necessities had been transported. Even though it wasn't quite finished, that evening we took up residence at 9 Lord Chancellor's Lane on Kingston Hill. I locked up the house in Putney, took our dog, Stella Polaris, and cat, Tommo, and had the best night's sleep I had had in a month. It was as though I had slipped the traces and was free to fly again.

CHAPTER TWELVE

There are certain times in one's life when one must live from day to day. That is what I had to do in the time between my leaving the Putney house and Sean's return from the States. I felt that something irrevocable was happening but I was torn by indecision. The indifference shown by Sean towards the very real fear I felt for myself and for Jason during the past few months convinced me that he was no longer my protector. In fact, I did not know who he was any more. His 'taming of the shrew' policy was certainly not working as far as I was concerned. By showing his disapproval of my working as an actor, he had driven me far from that warm intimacy we'd shared when we were both struggling. Now that he had achieved stardom as Bond, anything I did became inconsequential.

I knew for sure that I could not live the rest of my life in the shadow of 007, and the evidence was weighing heavily on the side of escape. I loved the old Sean – I still do. Sometimes, when I see him today on some talk show, I catch a fleeting glimpse of my old love in the turn of his head or a well-remembered phrase and it still makes my heart turn over. But this is now and that was then. Neither of us was entertaining loving thoughts of one another at that time.

When our meeting finally took place, it was at my new house on Kingston Hill and there were no fireworks. We both knew that our disagreements stood sentinel between us like assassins with loaded guns.

We managed with difficulty to arrive at a sort of compromise, his main concern being that the press should not get hold of the idea that *I* had left *him* and not vice versa. I agreed that I would not say anything to them. He was stunned by the fact that I had actually vacated the house, walked out on the whole deal, left Mrs Bond and fame far behind.

Much later, it was agreed that Sean would sell the house and I would get half the money for it but that was *all* I would get, nothing more. I suppose I agreed because it was true that I *had* left him and I knew only too well about his money hang-ups. In my mind I had left *the house*, not Sean, but in Sean's mind it amounted to the same thing. He would set up a trust fund for Jason's education but not for Giovanna's. She was not his responsibility, he said.

It took me a while to get my bearings. The house needed decorating; Stella Polaris had to adjust to there being no fences; my Abyssinian cat had to learn new rooftops; and I had to learn a new route to take Jason to school. I also had a new secretary, Rosie McGechie, and was driving a new yellow MG. In Vietnam, the war raged on, that arch-manipulator Henry Kissinger ordered the bombing of Cambodia, man had walked on the moon, Woodstock and marijuana had gone mainstream, both Kennedys had been assassinated and I had begun to 'feel immortal longings in me'.

I went to Glastonbury, arriving in the middle of the night before the festival officially started. It was unforgettable. The atmosphere was charged with anticipation as, up and down the valley, different drums answered each other in the night. Fires were lit and wisps of smoke rose into the clear night sky. LSD tabs were passed out free to anyone who wanted them. The next day bands played and everyone was high. Nicholas Roeg, director of *Walkabout*, was directing a documentary of the whole affair, walking about with a cameraman who had a camera mounted on his shoulders. Several hippy exhibitionists followed them around, vying with each other as to who could get their gear off in front of the camera. I sat in a tepee meeting new people. I saw the sunrise when Melanie sang 'Lay Down (Candles in the Rain)' but after two days I left. The smell of excreta had become appalling.

It was in this post-Connery period that I experienced my first guided LSD trip, which had a profound effect upon me. It wasn't something I did just for kicks. I prepared very seriously by fasting for twenty-four hours, choosing music and rubbing avocado oil into my skin to counteract any dryness. Instead of the traumatic horror described by many people, I was taken up on a sweet trajectory that confirmed my belief in something beyond this material world. I saw energy, light, colour and life in everything around me, even those things deemed to be inanimate. I had no ill effects whatsoever from my trip because I was prepared and had approached it as a sacred matter.

I had recently met a young entrepreneur, Robert Whips, who'd worked with Michael Butler on the production of *Hair*, the archetypal musical of New Age breakout. *Hair* had taken the world by storm when it had opened at the Biltmore Theatre on Broadway in 1968. It was the first time an entire cast had stripped on the stage. Robert had taken part and he was now busy putting together the Living Theatre film. He read my Kafka ape script and fell in love with the idea. It was decided that, if he could raise pre-production money, he would be co-producer.

I had sold an option on the film to Arthur P. Jacobs, producer of *Planet of the Apes*, through my agent Jimmy Fraser for fifteen thousand pounds and there were plans afoot to cast Marlon Brando as the merchant seaman who is keeper of the ape. Jon Voigt was suggested for the part of the ape. There was one condition to the sale – that the story be relocated to New York and that the protagonists all be American. Robert thought we could work together on the script to transport the action across the Atlantic. Though I resisted the idea, this condition was non-negotiable if we wanted to get the movie made.

We had just started work when we heard that Arthur P. Jacobs had dropped dead of a heart attack and that all his assets, including the option on the ape script, were frozen, pending probate of his will. There was nothing to do but wait until the lawyers had finished their vulturine work.

That summer, Jason went to stay with his father in Ireland, where Sean was shooting *Zardoz* with John Boorman directing. As usual, I needed money badly, so I took a job away from England, in Denmark. The movie was called *Zero Population Growth*, co-starring Oliver Reed and Geraldine Chaplin (daughter of Charlie). It became a cult film known as *ZPG*. I don't know whether the group exists today, but in the seventies there were many ordinary couples worldwide who joined the Zero Population Growth movement and abandoned the idea of ever having children.

ZPG is set in the future, when the earth is entirely polluted, people are forced to live in specially built cocoon cities underground and no-one is allowed to have children as the world has become disastrously overpopulated as well as toxic. However, the public is invited to visit a fantastic museum to see a simulation of how people lived in the past (today) and couples can even purchase bionic babies to assuage their longing to produce a family. My character was the mother of a robot baby acting out life with her husband in the museum, while Geraldine Chaplin and Oliver Reed played the young lovers who dare to have a genuine baby so that the hunt is on to catch them. I thought the script could have been much more imaginatively handled but I needed the work. The film was sponsored by Seagram's Whisky (although I could never see the connection between Seagram's and pollution), and the cast and crew were accommodated in a huge SAS hotel right in the centre of Copenhagen for the duration of the shoot.

The commencement of principal shooting was on a set where a machine belched thick acrid smoke into the air to simulate pollution. Special Effects told us it was made with carbocyclic margarine, whatever that meant. Its only 'special effect' was that after a couple of days of exposure to the concoction we all became violently ill, coughing, retching and finally collapsing. Clearly, the simulated pollution was truly toxic and filling our lungs with margarine. To continue shooting would have meant the demise of a few good actors and an entire crew, so Management decided to close down the whole production for a few weeks while the problem was sorted, but we were not allowed to go home. We were forced to stay at the hotel with full board and keep, our per diems in our hot little hands, sampling the delights of downtown Copenhagen.

Our team was made up of me, Geraldine and her partner, the talented Spanish director Carlos Saura, Oliver Reed and his stand-in/bodyguard/stuntman, who had just emerged from the nick where he'd done time for GBH, and Don Gordon, the American actor who played my husband. We used to meet every afternoon in one of our suites at the hotel to drink tea or booze, eat delicious Danish pastries, smoke dope and relate what we had done the day before. In this way, we got to know each other very well and found out the best places to go in town – what was hot and what was not.

Denmark had a young innovative female Minister of the Arts at the time who, in an experiment to wipe out the alarming number of rapes, had lifted the ban on live sex shows and brothels. It was amazing how many executive conferences suddenly relocated to Copenhagen. The country was flooded with businessmen, especially Americans, doing all sorts of things other than business. Danish film companies stopped making ordinary films and shot exclusively porn – films like *Danish Blue* and *Scandalous Scandinavia* – and bookshelves throughout the country were festooned with well-known censored works.

Geraldine, Carlos and I went to a sex show where the Mistress of Ceremonies spoke a mixture of Swedish air hostess and BBC *Children's Hour* presenter. She was actually done up to look like a sexy air hostess and began her spiel in a dreamy sing-song accent as though we were pre-teens. 'Are you sitting comfortably? Then we will begin. Tonight, you will see the most beautiful act that two human beings can perform together, the sex act. Meet Hans. Hans is a University student and has not seen his girlfriend, Ebba, for two weeks. You see, Hans has been in hospital. Poor Hans broke his arm, his *right* arm. Hans has been longing for his love, Ebba . . .' she droned on.

Who can say why, but this speech sent us into paroxysms of laughter. Perhaps it had something to do with the way she emphasised 'his *right* arm' or maybe it was our proximity to the young couple, who looked undernourished and bored. We tried to stifle our mirth but the young man was aware of our giggles and snorts and found it impossible to achieve an erect state. We were admonished severely by the air hostess but the damage had been done. Poor Hans had lost it and it wasn't coming back. We were kicked out of the theatre for spoiling the performance.

Oliver Reed spent his evenings lining up glasses of schnapps at the long bar at the hotel, challenging anyone to match him glass for glass in a drink-off. Of course, he and his bodyguard/stand-in ended their nights pissed and in punch-ups but that was the way Oliver liked it. He would arrive at our afternoon teas bleary-eyed but still cheery, and I wondered why this incredibly talented actor was so hell-bent on destroying his body and mind.

At one of our tea sessions, which happened to be held that particular afternoon in my suite, Don Gordon, who had just appeared in *Easy Rider*, arrived with a blue book in his hand. He was in a filthy temper, and when we asked him what the matter was, he flew into an even greater rage and threw the blue book against the wall. It dropped behind the sofa and he didn't attempt to retrieve it.

'That fucking book is sending me crazy. I promised my old lady I'd read it before I got back to LA but it's scrambling my brain. I never got past seventh grade. Fuck, who needs it? It's freaking me out!'

I was clearing up the mess after they left when I noticed the book lying on the floor. Intrigued by what could turn a usually taciturn and passive actor into such a vessel of wrath, I picked it up. *In Search of the Miraculous: Fragments of an Unknown Teaching* by P. D. Ouspensky, the cover read. I leafed through it and discovered that someone had underlined passages carefully in red pencil until, a third of the way through, the red pencil abruptly stopped, perhaps hurled against the wall like the book.

It has been a habit all my life to read avidly, but I noticed quite early on that if I went to bed with a very boring book, or a crossword puzzle that I couldn't do, it had the almost instant effect of sending me into a deep sleep. It worked much better than any pill. I picked up the blue book that first night expecting a quick exit into unconsciousness, but I was still awake reading it the next morning. It turned out to be a heady mix of reportage by a White Russian intellectual called P.D. Ouspensky, describing his meeting and becoming a pupil of an extraordinary man known only as G. With some other refugees from the upper classes, he travels with this fascinating G for some years during the Russian Revolution. G keeps his small group of followers out of harm's way while battles rage around them. They spend their time in intense spiritual, emotional and practical instruction, and G uses the group's heightened sense of danger to instil his teachings deep into their essence. This mysterious G, as I later discovered, was George Ivanovitch Gurdjieff, a mystic and philosopher who also staged movements and dances of amazing precision.

Most of the book is taken up with the description of G's teachings, insofar as the author could remember them. Interspersed throughout are mathematical equations which defy description. I could understand why poor Don had thrown the book across the room – it was maddening to be unable to understand only half of what was written. The ideas were extremely challenging but iconoclastic and some seemed impossible to grapple with. I felt out of my depth, stupid, and yet I could not stop reading. In the days that followed, the book seemed to take over my life to the extent that I got a Danish director friend of mine to find me an apartment away from the hotel. Room service, housekeeping, actors and crew were always banging on my door at all hours of the day and night and I could not concentrate.

After some weeks, filming on *ZPG* resumed and this time there were few glitches. We were three weeks over schedule and I had to dash back to London to commence shooting an episode of a television series. This is where meaningful coincidences (synchronicities, I called them) began to pile up thick and fast. In the end, they could not be ignored.

I set out to drive to the UK from Copenhagen via a town called Esbjerg on the west coast of Jutland, the peninsula comprising mainland Denmark; one has to cross by ferry to get to it. I had been treated to a magnificent send-off lunch in a tavern in the woodland park of the city. Many toasts were drunk, 'skolling' done and choruses sung. In the late afternoon, I glanced at the time. I had an hour to reach Esbjerg. Undaunted, I set off at great speed but was pulled over by the police before I reached the ferry. The police admired my sprauncy yellow MG and, thank God, I was not breath-tested, but inevitably I missed the ferry to Jutland and arrived just in time to see the Esbjerg–Newcastle boat steaming off into the distance. The next scheduled crossing was in two days hence. There was nothing to do but hang out in the dreary port of Esbjerg, kicking up my heels.

I was in a state of revolt. I had promised myself I would not look at the cursed blue book again, so I took a room in a hotel in the main street, went downstairs to a bookstore and bought a pile of pornographic literature. I would read filth for two days and take the taste of the 'miraculous' out of my mouth. I persevered for the first day and a half but something snapped on the night before I was to leave. A feeling of revulsion for myself assailed me, for my lassitude, my ignorance and the ludicrousness of the whole human condition – the mindless adherence to fornication, eating and accumulating 'things'. I jumped up, and on an impulse threw all the books out of my window and into the main street. Then I went back to bed, purged of pornography, and slept soundly until morning.

The next day I put my car on the ferry and embarked for Newcastle. From the moment I woke up that morning I felt a change in my physical state, as though I had taken some psychedelic drug. I was filled with a spontaneous awareness of everything around me. I looked at the churning water in the wake of the ship and it was me churning inside. I was filled with anguish and yearning at the same time, but I did not know for what.

We docked at midday on the Saturday. I was to be at work at the television studios by seven on the Monday morning and I was bristling with anticipation to get back to London to see Jason and also Giovanna, who had returned from Australia in my absence and was ready to try out for a scholarship at Millfield School.

My car responded to my heightened state of excitement as I sped off down the M1 to London, going faster and faster. It seemed fitting that the road was empty of traffic all the way. Some catastrophe must have taken place, leaving an endless empty motorway with one little yellow bomb zipping along at breakneck speed. It was intoxicating. By late afternoon, I was home at Lord Chancellor's Lane and feeling a tumultuous enlargement of my heart at seeing my children again. There had been no disaster. It was a football cup final that had emptied the roads.

I remained in the same state of excitement all through the next day, and even a particularly difficult crossword couldn't help me sleep. In the early hours of the morning, I leaned far out of my bathroom window to take a picture of the trees in front of the house, silhouetted by the brilliant orange glow of the rising sun.

A few hours later I was sitting in the make-up chair looking at the back page of *The Times*, wondering how I'd word an advertisement in the Personals column for a scholar to teach me mathematics so I could better understand the dreaded book, when my eye was caught by an ad that read: 'Tonight at Conway Hall, Red Lion Square, a lecture by J. G. Bennett on Ouspensky's *In Search of the Miraculous* at 8 p.m. For tickets call 949 2526.'

At first I was dumbfounded, not just because of the synchronicity of the lecture being held that very evening but because my telephone number was almost exactly the same as the one in the paper – 949 2524. The organiser of the event must live very near me on Kingston Hill or thereabouts. I asked my secretary to call and book tickets, knowing that I would have to drive straight from work to the city if I were to make it in time. I knew vaguely where Red Lion Square was because my literary agent, George Greenfield, had his offices there. I showered, changed and dashed off to meet the theatre crowd head on, sitting in gridlocked traffic for what seemed like hours. At last I arrived, with enough time to spare to gulp down a restorative shandy in the pub on the corner. The first person I saw was George Greenfield, who seemed amazed to see me.

'What the hell are you doing down here?' he exclaimed.

'Going to the lecture at Conway Hall,' I replied.

'What, with all the freaks?' he said. 'Well, you'd better hurry up. They've all gone in already.'

There was a great crowd of people inside the hall. Once I had found my seat, I looked around to find myself surrounded by the most eclectic group of humans ever assembled under one roof. Ladies with lorgnettes rubbed shoulders with hippy girls carrying babies on their backs. There were Russians and Germans talking loudly across the aisles, men in turbans, women swathed in veils, children eating sweeties, tall, bearded, bespectacled students, cripples in wheelchairs and society matrons. Seated on the stage was a half-asleep man who appeared to be a giant by the size of his hands, which hung down limply over his knees. Amid the hubbub of a hundred voices, a baby began to bawl loudly and a young woman in the audience rose to shuffle along the seats to take it outside. A clear, incisive voice came from the stage. 'No, no . . . Don't take her away. We're going to be talking about her future.'

An instant hush fell over the room. Even the baby must have sensed the sudden quiet because she shut up at once. I wondered how the tall man on the stage had known it was a girl. With that, the man (whose face resembled one of the saints in Leonardo's sketches for *The*

Last Supper) began to speak. He didn't raise his voice but was audible throughout the hall. I adjudged him to be somewhere in his fifties, but in fact he was seventy-five. He told us that he was a mathematician and physicist, who had been sent to Turkey after World War I as 'Our Man in Constantinople', a diplomatic spy. It was there that he had first made contact with the hidden knowledge described in Ouspensky's book, *In Search of the Miraculous*.

After recounting his travels from the Middle East to France, Greece, India, Java and Nepal, tracking the sources of the Gnostic tradition, he told us that a monumental change was coming to the planet and that there would be an urgent need for people to wake up to the changes we were still utterly unprepared for. The reason for this lecture was to announce that he was opening a School for Continuous Education in Sherborne, Gloucestershire, where a select body of teachers would impart the rudiments of this knowledge. He had been on a lecture tour to many universities in the United States and was already assured of seventy students.

'Much work must be done before the building in which the school is to be housed will be fit for habitation, but already volunteers are living on site, slaving round the clock, to have everything in place for the commencement of the first-term studies at the end of the autumn. The course will last for a year and will cost a total of one and a half thousand pounds.'

I looked around me at the odd assortment of souls present and wondered which ones would be taking up residence in Sherborne. I knew for certain that I would not be one of them. I had been congratulating myself all through the latter half of the lecture on having so many valid reasons why it would not be possible for me to become one of his students. I had two children, a career, a dog and a cat all standing between myself and Sherborne, thank God. I also had an estranged husband who might not take kindly to my disappearance into the depths of the West Country with the kids.

After the lecture, as a sop to my conscience for already having decided not to commit myself to his poxy school, I picked out a book entitled *Witness* from the pile of literature on the table in the foyer. It was written by the lecturer, J. G. Bennett, and bore a picture of him on the front cover.

When I eventually got into bed that night, sleep still eluded me. I picked up *Witness* and leafed through the photos. I could not help but gasp. There in front of me was a full-page photo of the trees I had photographed from my bathroom window that very morning. They were unmistakable. Alongside them was a large wooden building with a caption that read 'The Djamichunatra, Coombe Springs'. This *was* Coombe Springs, but where was the building?

On an impulse, I grabbed the telephone and dialled the number I'd seen in the paper that morning . . . 949 2526 . . . a six instead of a four, I remembered. The phone was answered immediately and I recognised Bennett's voice.

'Yes,' he said, 'who is that?'

'This is getting to be ridiculous, more than coincidence,' I blurted out.

'There's no such thing as coincidence,' was his immediate reply.

I have no idea what came out of my mouth by way of explanation – a jumble of words about how I had built a house in Coombe Springs, how I had seen the picture in his book of the trees in front of my house and why was the wooden house not there any more? I paused for breath, knowing that I was not making much sense.

'There are only three houses built at Coombe so far. Which one is yours?' he asked.

'The one at the top of the hill.'

'Yes, that would be opposite where the Djamichunatra stood. Shall I come and see you?'

'Yes,' I said.

Bennett was some inches taller than Sean and filled the doorway when he arrived. The first thing he said to me face to face was, 'What do you want to know?'

'Everything,' I answered unhesitatingly.

'Well, that's a good beginning.'

Chapter Thirteen

When I presented myself at Mr B's residence in Brunswick Street at seven the next evening, the door was opened by a smiling woman with a knowing face who asked me my business. When I explained that I had an appointment with Mr Bennett, she seemed surprised and left me waiting at the door while she made enquiries. She returned with Mr B himself, who looked at me disapprovingly.

'When we met at Chancellor's Lane last night, you told me to come to this address at seven,' I began, flustered. Maybe the whole thing had been a mad dream.

'I told you to come at seven o'clock in the morning,' he replied testily. 'That's when we hold morning meditation.'

'Oh,' I said, 'I couldn't have come at that time. I leave for work at 6 a.m. I must have misunderstood you.'

'All right,' he continued, still put out. 'You'd better come in now and have a coffee. We've nearly finished dinner.'

I was on the point of walking out and putting the whole encounter behind me when I felt the warm hand of the woman on my back. Smiling benignly, she ushered me into a cosy sitting room where a fire burned in the grate. Coffee cups were set out on the table, which still bore the signs of their dinner. I was embarrassed and it took some time before I felt relaxed enough to talk about my reasons for being there at all.

Elizabeth Bennett, known as Mrs B, broke the ice by asking how I happened to have built a house at Coombe Springs. They had owned the property for many years and it had been a Centre for Esoteric Studies since before the war. I asked her what 'esoteric' meant exactly.

'It's difficult to explain,' replied Elizabeth. 'I suppose you could say it describes hidden knowledge, an oral tradition passed on over the centuries, but only to those who are constrained to seek it out, those who wish to become Initiates. It has been passed down through the ages in every country of the world.'

Mr B began to talk about 'Sufism' (Islamic mysticism), which I'd never heard of, and its many sects of dervishes. One in particular caught my fancy, the Mevlevi or Whirling Dervishes. He described the training they had to undergo for their 'turning' ceremony and how the ritual was a sort of meditation during which the sheikh, their teacher, took the place of the sun while the turners became planets revolving around him. The tradition had been passed down through Jalaluddin Rumi, the thirteenth-century Persian poet and mystic known as Mevlana, who introduced it in Konya, in Turkey. Mr B emphasised that, in our age, esoteric knowledge was being disseminated as the need grew more crucial.

'It's called being "raw" and then being "cooked",' he said. 'When you are "cooked", you become tasty. You individuate. Sometimes, it's just called "the Work".'

I cannot say that I wasn't suspicious of this towering man with the face of an early-Christian martyr. His vivid blue eyes could suddenly flash fury. I couldn't decide whether he was shaman, charlatan or sage – or a mingling of all three.

After coffee, Mr B showed me an exercise, which he made me do with him seated cross-legged on his sitting-room floor. It was a silent exercise, he told me, which could be done even in company. He then suggested that I should try to do it as often as possible while at work the following day, and that I should report back to him if I noticed anything different about my state.

The exercise, called 'blending', is like learning the ABCs of meditation, using breath control to correlate the three centres – intellectual, emotional and body centre – so that they vibrate at the same level. It requires utter concentration, especially in the effort to direct one's sensations to the various parts of the body involved. I was determined to test this 'esoteric' exercise while it was fresh in my mind to see whether all this grandiose rhetoric was not just a load of old cobblers. I set myself the task of remembering to do it assiduously at least twenty times during the next day's shoot.

At the end of the day, I was astonished. Instead of the weariness that enters the bones at around 4.30 p.m. on a usual day at the studios, when tea is over and there are still several hours' slog to get through before one is mercifully released, I felt a boundless energy inside me as though I had just leapt up from a great night's sleep. I rang Mr B when I got home and said I had something to report. He told me not to come that night but to turn up for morning meditation at seven on the first day I wasn't working.

The following Saturday morning, I arrived at his house a few minutes late but the door was open. To enter, I had to step over many people sitting cross-legged on the floor of the corridor apparently in a trance, all perfectly still as though asleep with their eyes half open. They were truly a diverse group – women in saris, a professorial type with crinkly grey hair, a young man who looked like an escapee from police detention, a lank-haired girl with a sleeping child in her lap and a very fat woman wearing pearls and a cardigan. At first I didn't notice Mr B but his voice came through clearly: 'Sit down and be still.'

All I can remember about that first meditation was feeling intensely impatient, wondering how long it could go on before I exploded from boredom and inaction. Covertly, I watched my fellow meditators and started thinking about what a good 'dining out' story it would make – me sitting on the floor of a strange house with an assorted bunch of nutters who behaved like zombies.

To finish the meditation, the whole group sang a note together with a sustained expulsion of breath that sounded like '*Huuuuuuuuu-uuu*'. Then they bowed their heads to the floor and stood up, with their eyes still unfocused. One of the group brought around glasses of water and, after desultory introductions, we all sat in a circle with Mr B at its centre. It appeared that every one of us had been given the 'blending' exercise and we were invited to describe our reactions to its practice during the week. I was a bit put out because I had thought that I had been special.

No-one seemed willing to break the ice, so finally I piped up, 'Well, I found its effects very surprising. I had thought it might make me go to sleep but it did exactly the opposite.' The tearaway young man said that it had made him thirsty and the lady in the cardigan told us that she had been able to work out her knitting pattern much more easily than usual. No-one else proffered any information.

Mr Bennett whistled gently through his teeth (a characteristic I was to get to know very well). He looked up at last and said gently, 'You see, it's all about energy – whether one has enough of it to make the extra effort outside the simple procedure of handling our normal physical requirements, like work, shopping, preparing meals and household chores. The 'blending' exercise allows the three centres, the intellectual, the emotional and the physical, to start working together, to become compatible. We get tired because one of the centres is being overworked and the others are not exercised at all. It is a question of learning to maintain equilibrium. People have very little concept of how to manage their energy.'

For the next few weeks, I used the exercise to maintain equilibrium and conserve energy. As a practical woman, I knew it worked. I was playing in an episode of the British television series *The Persuaders* at the time, starring Roger Moore as Lord Brett Sinclair and Tony Curtis as Danny Wilde, millionaire playboys reluctantly recruited as crime-fighters. It was mooted that in my role as Lord Brett's cousin Kate

I should become a regular participant in the show. However, I quashed the idea before it became fixed, as I couldn't envisage myself as the token bird in such a series. Roger Moore had a raft of feeble stories, which he repeated nonstop on set, and Tony Curtis (known as 'Sooty' by the crew) was hyperactive until he had one of his entourage burn some 'Lebanese Yellow' under his nose. After a little inhalation of LY, he was as docile as a lamb.

Before long, I imagined myself an adept at putting sensation into various parts of my body at will. I had a notion that if I had control of those centres through sensation, I could put myself into any state I wanted without the use of any outside stimulant, ingested, inhaled or smoked. I was determined to persevere and learn more.

One Sunday, my children and various friends joined me on a drive up the M4 to Bennett's proposed School of Continuous Education at Sherborne House in Gloucestershire. I wanted to inspect, first-hand, what was going on. We arrived in the midst of a late-summer shower that developed into a gale-force wind and driving rain the moment we stepped out of the car.

Sherborne House sat in solitary splendour on seventeen acres of lush meadowland. It was a monumental edifice, dating back more than a millennium. Various bits had been added on periodically, chiefly in Victorian times, until it had acquired a lopsided look. On that particular day, with the gathering clouds, my first impression was of an ancient, haunted prison. Certainly, it had a chequered history. Long before it became the ancestral seat of the Dutton family, it had been a Catholic monastery. When Henry VIII broke with the Papacy and began his destruction of monasteries in the sixteenth century, the monks entrusted their church and grounds to the Duttons until they could return to reclaim it. The Duttons, however, double-crossed them. As a punishment for their deceit, the monks put a curse on the family, which decreed that the property would never pass directly from father to son – and it never had. There were lurid accounts of the eldest son in each generation meeting with some disaster (one being squeezed to death by an anaconda in South America, one falling off a cliff in Spain, another being gassed in World War I), though most of these stories were probably fantasies concocted by the locals.

The remnants of the family had taken up residence in a small hunting lodge on another part of the estate and had leased the great house to a school. This school was immortalised in Lindsay Anderson's 1968 film *If...*, which was based on the true story of a revolt by the boys against a brutish Head Master and the pedantry of the British public school system. Using smuggled guns, they wrested control of the school from the staff, threw the Head Master in Sher Water, bashed in walls, threw furniture out of windows and virtually wrecked the whole place. In the end, there was an official investigation, the findings of which resulted in the school being closed permanently. This incident had occurred seven years before and Sherborne House had remained derelict ever since.

We got out of the car and dashed towards the main door, which was locked. It took twenty minutes of shouting and banging to get any response from inside. This came in the form of a frizzy-haired American hippy who said his name was Rick Margolis from New York City. He ushered us in to the long, forbidding foyer and invited us to look around. Sounds of the Grateful Dead echoed through the empty corridors.

We spent an hour wandering around the shambles inside this once-stately home. There was a massive ballroom which opened onto what had been the billiards room and library. There was an immense medieval kitchen whose paving stones were deeply indented by the feet of thirty generations. The wind whistled through gaping holes in the walls, and the sky was visible through the ceilings in most of the rooms on the top floor. All the staircases were sagging and treacherous. The place was in such a state of disrepair that it seemed the best thing would have been to gut the entire building and start again.

The smell of dope heralded the presence of the other occupants of Sherborne. Eight future students were camping out in one of the downstairs lecture rooms while trying to get the renovations organised. There seemed to be no plan of action and no-one supervising the work, although much banging and hammering was heard as we moved about.

Outside, the grounds and high-walled gardens were a jungle of nettles and dock weed, while the old Victorian greenhouses were barely visible under piles of dirt. Without an army of professional people – plumbers, electricians, roofers, carpenters, decorators and gardeners – it seemed an impossible task to make Sherborne House habitable by late summer, although Bennett had said that students were going to do all the renovation work by then.

'You can't ask people to live in *that*,' I told him at our next meeting.

'You, of all people, should not say that,' was his enigmatic reply.

I argued that not only did I think the place was uninhabitable but it would be very difficult for me to drop everything and spend a year at Sherborne without displacing my children and disrupting my already damaged career. Mr B just smiled. 'If you are going to come on the course, a way will open for you to do so,' he said with maddening finality.

My visit to Sherborne only served to strengthen my resolve not to be a student at the school. Like the answer to a prayer, my agent rang to ask if I would like to go to Greece to shoot a film with Christopher Plummer. I jumped at the chance. Giovanna had secured her scholarship to Millfield School in Glastonbury, so once she was settled in as a boarder I leased my house for three months to the Korean Ambassador, put my dog in kennels, gave my cat to Stanley Mann's wife Delphine to look after and flew off to Athens with Jason.

I knew that the film would take at least three months to complete, by which time the Sherborne course would be well under way. Returning from Greece too late to be a student, I would move back into my Coombe Springs house and have a tidy little nest egg from the rent as a bonus. I had it all figured out. However, my agent had failed to tell me that the money to make the film had not been secured and I was expected to assist the director/producer in his quest to get it. I spent the first few weeks in Athens chatting up bank managers and big businessmen with a view to finalising the deal. They all agreed that it was a terrific idea but insisted on a start date the following spring. It was very frustrating. There was no way I could go back to London as my house was let. I had to stay in Greece for at least three months until the Korean Ambassador found a suitable place for his family and vacated my beautiful new pad in Chancellor's Lane.

I cast about for something to do in the intervening time and hit upon the perfect plan. I would continue making Tarot cards. While still at the National Theatre, I'd had the idea of making huge psychedelic posters of the Higher Arcana of the Tarot. They were all the rage and the format we used was Agfa Contouring (an innovative photographic process). Annette Green was the brilliant young photographer/designer consigned to the work, and accompanied by actors from both the National and the Living theatres we set up our first shoot at Ockham Churchyard. A young German actor from the Living Theatre was strung upside down by one leg from a tree as card No. XII, the Hanged Man. Annette got her shots, but before we had pulled him down, the local police arrived and arrested us.

They had received complaints that a group of necromancers were doing some unholy witchcraft and desecrating the graves of suicides in the unhallowed ground next to Ockham Churchyard. Having come to investigate, they discovered us in the act of hauling the Hanged Man down from the tree. It took a good half-hour of explanations to convince them that we were not a coven of witches up to no good in the woods. Finally, we were let off with a warning and told never to be seen in the area again.

Next, we got hold of an enormous white draughthorse, a 'rosin-back' they are called in the circus. We put Jason up on its broad back, which was so large that his little legs stuck out straight on either side, put a swirling pennant on a pole in his hands and shot the naked boy on the white steed in Richmond Park to represent the Sun, No. XIX. Bumble Dawson made amazing costumes for the High Priestess, the Fool and an angel for the Lovers with an enormous wingspan and real feathers. We had completed all of these posters to our satisfaction before I left for Greece. Bumble had also done designs for an Empire-line gown of white silk jersey, which I was to wear as the Empress, No. III, as well as a superb snakeskin Greek outfit to be worn by whomever we chose to depict the Magician, No. I.

My plan to fill the months of enforced stay out of England was to bring Annette Green, the photographer, to Greece. She'd carry the costumes from Bumble with her and we'd use the great amphitheatre at Epidavros or the temple at Delphi as our locations for the Magician and the Empress.

Jason and I took an apartment at the seaside resort of Vouliagmeni and frolicked the days away on the beach. When Annette's boyfriend joined us, we did all the tourist things like breaking plates at bistros, eating mounds of moussaka, drinking retsina and dancing Zorba-like fandangos with the locals. Things went smoothly and enjoyably. I was pleased that I had side-stepped Sherborne so successfully.

In the second month, we travelled to Corinth to stay in a glorious villa by the sea owned by Sarah Churchill, daughter of the Marquis of Blandford and niece of Winston, who was married to a very attractive Greek playboy/antique collector named Theo Roubanis. Our hosts took us deep-sea diving to search for ancient Greek amphorae at the bottom of the wine-dark Mediterranean. With no discussion at all, Annette and I agreed that Theo would make the perfect Magician. Of the twenty-two cards in the Higher Arcana of the Tarot, the Magician is number one. He owns all the symbols – Cup, Sword, Wand and Pentacle – signifying his dominance over heart, body, mind and spirit. Ordinary playing cards omit the Higher Arcana but the suits are derived from the Tarot – Cups became Hearts, Swords Spades, Wands Clubs and Pentacles Diamonds.

Theo was photographed as the Magician on the steps of Epidavros, wearing Bumble's magnificent snakeskin toga. Mindful that every symbol was in position and every colour and number correctly shown, we placed his signs of power – Cup, Sword, Wand and Pentacle – at his feet. Jason, engrossed in the acoustics of the place, ran up and down like a blond whippet, whispering messages from the centre of the amphitheatre and making us go out to the rim of the stadium to hear what he was saying.

When we said goodbye to Sarah and Theo we travelled to Thessalonika, where we'd heard there was an extraordinary waterfall location to shoot the Empress. No. III in the Higher Arcana, the Empress represents the female principle of nature and wears a crown with twelve stars (the months of the year) on her head. Her gown is sprigged with green shoots and she carries a basket overflowing with flowers and fruit. At her back, waterfalls spill down and rainbows glint behind her head. Compassion and fecundity are the qualities she personifies. Bumble had done me proud. The dress fell in luminous white folds and I felt like a veritable queen when I climbed into it.

It took us more than a day's motoring into the hinterland of Macedonia before we found the location for the Empress. On the way, we stopped at the Temple of Alexander the Great to examine the carvings and mosaics. By noon on the second day, the camera was set up while I dressed. We shot all afternoon, using the rays of the dying sun to backlight the fine mist that flew out in a golden spray. It was perfect for capturing prisms and rainbows in the lens of the camera.

I could hardly believe it when, just as we were packing up, two police cars and some heavily armed soldiers arrived and arrested us. It was *déjà vu*. We'd been through all this before, but this time it was much harder to talk our way out of things. To start with, none of our interrogators spoke English and none of us knew more than a smattering of Greek.

Initially, they spoke to me in a language I didn't recognise but I knew it wasn't Greek. They took us to the station and questioned me for an hour, shouting at me in this unfamiliar language to try to get a reaction. I thought it might be Albanian as they kept mentioning Tirana, which I knew was the capital of that country.

Finally, an interpreter was brought in who spoke English. It seemed that we had strayed into a restricted area and were taking photos of prohibited installations. For some reason they thought I was an Albanian spy. I kept showing them my passport and repeating, 'Australian, not Albanian, Australian.' In the end, after some heated conversations on the telephone, they believed me and we were freed. They shook my hand and, astonishingly, didn't confiscate our film. I could at last get out of my damp Empress costume.

The three months were up, so I put through a call to my house in Chancellor's Lane, where the lease had expired and the Ambassador was ready to vacate – I hoped.

'Hello, this is Miss Cilento. May I speak to the Ambassador?'

'Miss Cirento not here,' came a Korean voice from London.

'No, I am aware of that. I *am* Miss Cilento. I would like to speak to your boss, the Ambassador, please.'

'Solly. Miss Cirento no here! She gone away!'

I thought I'd go mad after several of these repetitious exchanges. Eventually, I got on to someone who informed me that the Ambassador had decided to stay in the house until the Korean Embassy residence was redecorated the following year. It was a blow. I couldn't stay in Greece any longer and I had nowhere to go when I got back to London.

I rang my agent, Jimmy Fraser, who had just bought John Osborne's old flat in Ebury Street, to ask him if he would put me and Jason up for a week or two until we could find somewhere to live. He agreed that we could come for a week. Surely I would find somewhere in that time. We were both in dire need of a place to lay our heads for more than three nights at a time. I knew very early on that Jason was not a gypsy, and I, too, had had enough of hired cars and airports.

I rushed around in the ensuing days looking at dreary places, each one more depressing than the last. Jason was hating being cooped up in Jimmy's bijou flat watching endless cartoons, and Jimmy made the fatal mistake of asking him to come and sit on his lap during our first evening there.

On the last day before our week was up, I'd had enough. I picked up my dog Stella from the kennels, collected Tommo the cat from Delphine, threw all our belongings into the car and headed for Sherborne. I thought I would stay for as long as it took to get another job. In the meantime, I'd continue with my writing and only nominally take part in the course.

As I drove up to the main entrance, Bennett was standing at the front steps as though he had been waiting for me. 'Ah, it's you,' he said, signalling some students to help me with the luggage. 'We've been expecting you. Room 17 on the third floor has been made up for you. Did you have a good trip?'

I shall never forget the atmosphere of our first night at Sherborne House. Once we had stowed our gear in Room 17, we went down to the dining room where students were gathering for the evening meal. No-one spoke as we all lined up at a window through which plates of food were passed. I hadn't realised that all meals were silent. I looked down at what I had been served as the evening meal. There had been some attempt to make toad-in-the-hole, I suspect, but what rested on my plate could easily have been described as turd-in-the-hole. A horrible black thing protruded from some dark brown pastry and Jason's offering was an exact replica. I shuddered. So this was to be the standard of the food at Sherborne House. We looked at each other and nodded complicitly.

Back in our little room on the third floor, we sat on our beds to devise a plan of action. Luckily, I had two Mars bars and a croissant tucked away for just such an occasion and we devoured them hungrily. Stella and Tommo, who had been shut up in the room so they could get used to their new home, shared some crumbs of our frugal repast. Clearly, it was going to be a question of organisation. We would probably have to buy all our food and eat it in the room, which meant some sort of fridge and storage space. I got my notebook out. This was the classic 'LIST' situation.

For the next few days, I typed diligently in my room. Jason, who had discovered that there were twenty children at Sherborne and a school to go to, was settling in nicely. I had put butter on the cat's paws so that she was content doing her endless ablutions but I could not say the same for Stella. Had she been a woman she would have been Bette Davis. Every time I opened the door for even a second, she was through it and off down the stairs yowling. I'd have to follow her to the ground floor and into the lecture room where Bennett held his daily sessions. There she would lie cowering at Mr B's feet making loud moans. I would then put her on a leash and drag her away while the students fell about with laughter. Four times over two days I had to repeat this humiliating exercise. On the third day, as I reached over to affix the leash to Stella's collar, Mr Bennett leant down and whispered into my ear, 'Don't you think your dog's trying to tell you something?'

As a final blow, when I went back to the room I couldn't find any of the pages of the new novel I'd been typing. I searched high and low but they were gone. For a moment I suspected that there was some hideous plot afoot to thwart anything I tried to do, but then I saw Jason with some of the other children flying paper planes out of the window. 'Look, Mummy – they fly!' he shouted when he saw me.

That was the moment I surrendered. From that instant onwards, my revolt was over. I threw myself into the course like an Indian widow throws herself onto her husband's funeral pyre. It was impossible for me not to leap into the flames, even if it meant metaphorically losing my life.

For someone who always had profound difficulty in handling authority, I found the rigorous timetable of Sherborne House well nigh impossible. Rising for ritual ablutions in cold water at 5.30 a.m., a half-hour of meditation, breakfast of porridge and toast and ready for work by 8.30 a.m. precisely. The day was a whirlwind of lessons and activities. Bells rang and students rushed about the corridors so as not to be late.

Movements, History Studies, Theme Talks, Art, Carpentry, Readings and Kitchen Work were punctuated throughout the day by two more meditations, one at midday and one at 6 p.m. We had two days of indoor work and two days in the garden. Each day one of the students was chosen to be the full supervisor for everything that went on throughout the school, while two others became observers, taking notes and documenting his or her performance step by step.

I volunteered to be a chief cook (there were twenty in all), which meant that you had to run the entire kitchen for one day every two weeks. It was actually through a sheer desire not to repeat our toad-in-the-hole experience and try to produce some edible food once in a while. Everybody had to take a turn at being the lowest of the low in the kitchen as well, spending a day scrubbing huge pots, clearing slops and peeling vegetables. All meals except breakfast were silent. When dinner was over, we had Music and Talks, after which (sometimes until ten or eleven o'clock at night) we were obliged to paint and redecorate those parts of the building that were still uninhabitable.

I remember very little about those first few weeks except that my feet were killing me. It was my own fault. I was wearing thick, platform-heeled boots and the hours I spent wandering about, trying to find out where everything was, seemed endless. I fell into bed each night like a stunned mullet and knew nothing more until the infuriating bell clanged pre-dawn and we lined up in the ablutions block to wash. The

TOP LEFT: My sister Margaret's portrait of Andrea Volpe TOP RIGHT: Getting around London on my Vespa BOTTOM: Posing for the camera at Margaret's wedding to Geoffrey Maslen. From left, me, Geoffrey, Giovanna in front, Margaret, Sean

OPPOSITE TOP: Scot's Farm in summer . . .   OPPOSITE MIDDLE: . . . and in winter

OPPOSITE BOTTOM: Karnak Theatre from the front ABOVE: The Castle at Karnak, the largest one-bedroom house in the Southern Hemisphere

RIGHT: Jason in his *Robin Hood* days BELOW: Family life in Queensland. From left, me, Tony, Jason and girlfriend, and Giovanna OPPOSITE TOP: With Jason OPPOSITE BOTTOM: With my grandson Dashiell

OPPOSITE AND ABOVE: The Karnak Playhouse, from construction of the stage to completion

ABOVE TOP: Tony discussing the set design for *The Thing in the Wheelchair*

ABOVE BOTTOM: Cast and crew of *The Thing in the Wheelchair*

ABOVE TOP: The outdoor theatre at Karnak ABOVE BOTTOM LEFT: Tony Shaffer

ABOVE BOTTOM RIGHT: With members of the Kuku Yalani Community in *Creation*

OPPOSITE TOP: The Meditation Room at Karnak OPPOSITE BOTTOM: One of the stained-glass windows designed and made by my brother David for Karnak ABOVE: On a tractor at Karnak LEFT: With my dog Lazlo

ABOVE TOP LEFT: Wearing the *hijab* in Damascus ABOVE RIGHT: My mother, Lady Phyllis Cilento wearing her new opals ABOVE BOTTOM: With David and Kristen Williamson at Karnak OPPOSITE: At home on my verandah

OPPOSITE TOP: Jason and his wife Mia at the Premier of his new film *Shanghai Noon* OPPOSITE MIDDLE LEFT: Sean with Stella Polaris in our Putney backyard OPPOSITE MIDDLE RIGHT: With Molly and Max's puppies OPPOSITE BOTTOM: 'It takes one to know one!' – Dashiell and 'Ampa Oni', my grandson's special name for Tony TOP: Flying Granny at Floors Castle in the Scottish Borders LEFT: On the banks of my lake at Karnak

ABOVE: In my garden at Karnak

ritual ablution we followed was eyes and nose first, then one hand over the forehead while the other hand cleaned the ear as we repeated, either aloud or silently, 'Lord have mercy. Increase my knowledge.' Next, the other hand went to work on the other ear with the same supplication and then it was hands, genitals, underarms and, lastly, the tired old feet.

There was a roaring fire in the ballroom where meditation took place. The women sat with their backs to it, looking out the long windows on the other side of the vast room. The men sat facing the women and the fire. There was a grand piano at the northern end of the room, in front of which sat Mr B, between the men and women, so that we could see him while he introduced us to different morning exercises.

I needed to catch up. I had missed some exercises and vital pieces of information, which left me at a disadvantage. Sometimes I couldn't understand any of the references, so I spent every free moment questioning other students and reading back over any sketchy notes they had made. Of the hundred students, roughly seventy were Americans and they were a mixed group – whole families uprooted from small Midwestern towns, mathematicians from Ivy League colleges, ex-Vietnam soldiers, pop musicians, dope dealers, drop-outs and runaways. They all had amazing stories to tell about 'how I got to Sherborne', most of which included coincidences as remarkable as my own.

There was an Australian couple, some older Canadians who had been pupils of Gurdjieff in Paris, an Argentine, Africans from various countries of that continent, an officer from the Israeli Army, several Armenians, Turks and a token Scandinavian or two. Twenty children, from neo-natals to fifteen years of age, made up the rest of the inhabitants of the great house at Sherborne on that inaugural course and, contrary to my predictions, we were all housed more or less comfortably, if not elegantly.

The course had started in October and the weather was now getting very cold. Even so, we all got out in long lines with chippers and hand-hoed the fields ready for spring planting. We had to learn to do every type of task. One of the hardest things for me was using a double-handled long saw to cut firewood with a hard-nosed Yankee woodsman from Seattle, Washington, who nearly ripped my arms out of their sockets. Some days we were encouraged to do everything left-handed, some days were fast days and some days we were silent, the only communication being sign language.

It was on one such silent day that Sean came to visit with Giovanna. He hadn't telephoned to announce his arrival but just rolled up and asked for me. Of course, no-one answered him and he became angry and aggressive. None of the students recognised him, strangely enough, but they finally led the angry man to Mr Bennett, who tried to explain about silent days. I have a vivid image in my head of our meeting in a corridor at Sherborne, with Giovanna peeking out fearfully from behind Sean's back and Sean looking up quizzically into the face of J. G. Bennett, who was half a head taller.

When they left, Sean went immediately to his lawyer and told him that I had persuaded my fellow students at the school not to speak to him. He had secured the services of Oscar Beuselinck, the lawyer who became notorious as the model on whom John Osborne based his play *Inadmissible Evidence*. His plan was to prove that I was an unfit mother, too irresponsible and flighty to have custody of my children. Luckily, Mr Bennett introduced me to one of his older students, Norman Farmar, an astute lawyer who suffered from a chronic stutter. It could take him several minutes to finish a sentence, which sent his adversaries in court out of their minds.

Norman's stutter is noteworthy in that it relates to Mr B. Several years before he became my lawyer, Norman had suffered a massive stroke, which left him paralysed on one side of his body. Extensive hospital examinations revealed a large tumour lodged in his brain. His surgeons were consulted, who advised its immediate removal or it would paralyse him completely and, ultimately, prove fatal. His wife,

Betty, was unwilling to make such a crucial decision without consulting Mr B, Norman's closest friend and teacher, so she spent a day trying to telephone him in Australia, where he happened to be lecturing with the great Indonesian mystic, Pak Subud. Failing to reach him, she left a message for him explaining the situation but plans for the operation went ahead regardless.

On the night before his operation, Norman was lying in his hospital bed contemplating his probable demise when what he thought were powerful truck headlights lit up his room. He remembers thinking it extremely odd as he was on the third floor. Next, he heard Mr B's voice and Pak Subud answering in what seemed like a normal conversation. Suddenly, he told me, he was bouncing around in his bed. A powerful person seemed to be trying to change the sheets with him in it. The beams of light burned into his head and he passed out. He doesn't remember anything more until the nurse arrived in the morning with the doctor to give him his pre-op medication. The doctor examined his eyes, took his pulse and blood pressure, and then scratched his head. 'Something has changed radically since yesterday,' he announced. 'I think we'd better take you down and give you another X-ray just to be sure.'

Subsequent tests showed no sign of the tumour. After double-checks and arguments as to the validity of the original X-rays, Norman's operation was cancelled forthwith. As so often happens when there are physical changes in a patient for which the medical profession has no explanation, the doctors closed ranks. Norman was not allowed to retain, or even view, his original X-rays. They told him he was free to leave but that he would be paralysed and remain a cripple for the rest of his life. He walked out two days later and the stutter was the only legacy of the entire episode.

It didn't surprise me that Norman prevailed in the court case, after which Oscar Beuselinck actually invited him to become a partner in his firm of solicitors. Sean wondered out loud where I had managed to find 'that stuttering cunt' who had outgunned the sharpest and most ruthless lawyer in London. For his final victory, Norman managed to reverse Sean's previous edict and Giovanna's schooling was included in the package made up for Jason's education.

Of all the new challenges we were exposed to at Sherborne, I think the Movements were the hardest. We had a magnificent teacher, Anna Durco, a self-contained Russian woman with a chalk-white face who had amazing control of her body and mind. Anna, who had been with Gurdjieff in Paris, dyed her hair ebony black and it was whispered that she wasn't thirty years old, as she looked, but well over sixty. Unrelenting in her precision, she'd walk around the class watching every student like a cat stalking a room full of rigid mice, moving a finger here or a foot there, and she was scathing when a mistake was repeated too often. Again, I had to play catch-up as the other students had had a few weeks of practice.

The first Obligatory exercise had to be learned before anything else and I found it devilishly difficult to wait for the right beat. The music had been composed by Thomas de Hartmann and I was always jumping in too early, having to start again. I felt embarrassed and worried that the other students were irritated by my slowness at picking it up. I could see that the object of the exercise was the same as the 'blending' in meditation but in a physical form – an ever more complicated blending of the arms, legs and then head, all doing different things in time to the music. It could, and did, send me into a frenzy of fury against my recalcitrant limbs.

It took weeks of struggle and perseverance to arrive at that magic moment when I had enough faith to give the whole thing over to my moving centre. Suddenly and harmoniously the limbs respond without effort or direction from the brain, like learning to change gear in a manually driven car without having to think about it. Yet, once you feel you've mastered one exercise, you have to start all over again and learn another fiendishly difficult one. I noticed that the hours spent going over and over the maddening precision of the Movements had the effect of making us all more coordinated in everything we did. On the distaff side, there was always a gnawing despair that I would never be able to master the Movements at all.

We were taught History by Dick Holland, a colleague of Bennett's who had worked with him for many years at Coombe Springs. Dick's approach to the subject was completely different from anyone I have ever encountered. He didn't deal so much with dates or facts but rather with the 'expansion and contraction of ideas' that brought about certain events. For instance, we were asked to contemplate three men who lived more or less in the same era and to work out whose ideas had expanded into the future and whose had died like dodos. They were Napoleon, Rousseau and Bismarck, in his opinion the most powerful men of their time, whose influence over European thought extended from the middle of the eighteenth century to the latter part of the nineteenth and into the present. We were asked to write an essay on the effect the ideas of these men had on the contemporary world. Discussions of the essays became multi-dimensional and fascinating, not at all like the dry facts that had been taught to me in school. Dick also opened up the notion of different types of energy – material, reactive, conscious, intuitive, creative – not forgetting sexual – and the all-pervasive energy of unconditional love.

Each day the lectures and readings by Mr B opened new horizons that I had never before imagined. The more I learned from Mr B himself, the more I was astounded at the immense wealth of ideas and techniques that fifty years of searching had afforded him. I believe that he arrived at the zenith of his powers at Sherborne. It was the culmination of his life's work and there was a bloom about him even though he had passed his seventy-fifth year.

Sometimes, when Mr B could see that we were all dozing off in one of the lectures, he'd leap up and hurtle himself outside, calling upon us to keep up with him. Everyone, except the longest-legged and fittest, had to run, as he led us helter-skelter around the half-finished gardens and back again. He was a dynamo of energy, paradoxically extolling the virtues of patience and conscious effort. Once, during a lecture, he stopped speaking and was reflective for a long time. We had become used to this, but when Mr B finally spoke he said, very seriously, 'You know, if Adam had been patient, God would have *given* him the apple.' He was bewildered when we all screamed with laughter.

'Chalkie', as we sometimes endearingly called Mr B, had five children. His eldest, a daughter by his first marriage, was fifty-eight while his youngest daughter Tessa was eight. She had a sister, Hero, and two brothers, George and Ben, the latter a lanky youth of eighteen who was also a student on the course. Mr B doted upon Tessa, who became Jason's soul mate. He was devoted to all the children, and used to have them up to his study every afternoon for tea and games. He believed that children learn 'through their skin' and that these first Sherborne offspring were destined for great things.

Tessa and Jason worked up a small business together, running down to the shop in the village to buy Mars bars on consignment for hungry students. It is a well-known fact that people who enter seminaries or attend spiritual schools become fanatical about food for the first few months of their courses. This has something to do with the idea that they are being deprived of all the creature comforts they once held so dear – television, fast food, binge drinking and sex – so they cast about for something to take their place. It was no wonder, then, that the kitchen was broken into repeatedly in those early days until, sensibly, locks were put on all the fridges and pantries.

On 13 January 1972, we prepared a huge feast. The best of the students, wearing white costumes they had made themselves, did the Movements breathtakingly well. We drank straight vodka toasts to all the idiots in the world, especially ourselves, and music resounded throughout the old house. As I had been entrusted with the job of boning hundreds of kippers for a kipper pâté, I kept at a distance from guests that night. Even though I had spent a good half an hour scrubbing my fingers with lemon, I knew I still smelt like a fish market on a hot day.

The course at Sherborne was comprised of three stages: the Exoteric (beginning level), the Mesoteric (intermediate level) and the Esoteric (higher level when, hopefully, there would be some light at the end of the tunnel). This feast marked the completion of the first third of the course. Friends were permitted to come and stay for the weekend after the Exoteric to see that we weren't being mistreated, having a psychotic episode or gravely ill, as friends tend to think that something grave and irreparable has happened to chums who become inmates of esoteric schools. When my agent Jimmy Fraser came, he cried, but Bumble Dawson stayed over for three days because she liked it so much.

We had been asked not to read newspapers or listen to the news, as it would divert us from the intense concentration needed to assimilate the information we were being given. The course was promising to be gruelling work and no-one ever slept more than five or six hours a night.

Late one Saturday night I was standing under the glaring lights in the ancient kitchen, wondering when I would be able to cease guarding the mountainous piles of covered bread cut for the next morning's toast. It was always a bit of a meat market in the corridors on Saturday nights – shadowy figures embracing, outlines of people furtively entering and leaving each other's rooms. Old habits die hard. Often, couples trucked through the kitchen after some sexual encounter to filch a quick slice of bread and a hunk of cheese. You had to be vigilant.

By midnight, I'd had enough. Let them take what they wished, for it was up the stairs to Bed-fordshire for me. There were flickering hurricane lamps dotted along the stairs and corridors to light the way and save on electricity. I sat on Jason's bed and gave him a big hug. He mumbled and hugged me back in his sleep. It was too cold to sit around for long so I climbed into my bed, relishing the thought of the few hours of dreamless slumber I was about to experience.

The moment my head hit the pillow, I was aware that there was a light in the room. I thought I'd left the door open and that it was the hurricane lamp shining in, but when I got up to close it, the door was firmly shut. I climbed back into bed and the light was still pervading the whole room. If I shut my eyes, it was still there . . . and it was getting brighter every instant. I thought that the strip lighting in the kitchen, where I had been working for most of the day, had possibly affected my eyes. As the light blocked out sight altogether, I thought that I must be going blind. I kept opening and shutting my eyes to see if anything made any difference. Open or shut, there was only this light, which suddenly began to splinter into slivers of a million colours, fragmenting like breaking glass. In the centre, a garden took shape in which there were luminous trees and a stream. At first I didn't notice the figure in the scene. Then I saw him. Someone was facing away from me, whose back and posterior I could see. This person was prostrating himself, like we did at the end of meditation.

As the figure sat up, I saw it was a young man. He turned his face to look at me as though he knew I was watching him. Although he was in a garden and I was sitting in my bed at Sherborne, we looked at each other for a long time. I cannot say how long it was but I was filled with an overwhelming sensation of such wellbeing and rightness that it seemed I would sit there all my life looking at that young man's pale face, with its broad cheekbones and rim of dark hair framing the jaw-line. I never wanted to get up again.

With no sense of the passing of time, I remained still until the light splintered into a kaleidoscope of colours once again and the slivers began to obscure the garden. More and more light flooded in – the exact reversal of before. The garden and the man were finally effaced by the whiter-than-white light and my eyes were dazzled by its brightness. I wished we could have stayed longer. I don't know what happened then, whether I slept or just sat there. In what seemed to be no time at all, it was dawn, time to get up, run downstairs, stir the porridge, turn

338

those mounds of bread into toast for 120 hungry mouths. I couldn't understand why I didn't feel at all tired but I knew something very extraordinary had happened to me.

While I was flipping the toast with the other breakfast chef, a girl rushed into the kitchen. 'Mr B says you're to come at once to the Meditation Room. He says he wants everybody in Sherborne there this morning. I have to go round and see that there's no-one having a Sunday-morning lie-in.'

She dashed away and we turned everything off, so that nothing would be burnt, and went to do ablutions before we went into the ballroom where the entire school was gathered. I opened the broad heavy door, backed by green felt to minimise noise, and peeped in. The room was so crowded that I could find nowhere to sit except just inside the door, crushed up against the other late-comers.

I was aware that Bennett was speaking but I only half listened to his words. He was saying something about having received proof of the mandate to establish such an ambitious course. He had the approval of all those who had gone before him, he said. I was so busy thinking about how to tell him what had happened to me that I hardly listened to his words, although they must have filtered through somehow or I would not have remembered them. Later, when I was serving him his porridge through the hatch, I asked if I could speak to him after breakfast, before he went to church. 'Yes, but you'll have to make it quick,' he answered. 'I have a lecture to prepare this morning.'

I rushed to his flat, which was in the front of the building overlooking the main drive, and had to wait outside with the other students until it was my turn. When I entered his little study, I tried to tell him the whole story as fast as I could. I spluttered on about thinking that I was blind, the refracted light, the garden, the man's bottom in the air being my first view of him ... everything ... and then I stopped. It all sounded perfectly ridiculous. I expected him to clear up the whole perplexing incident in a flash by telling me I had been hallucinating, but he did not. I believe I am a sceptic, a practical woman not given to imagining fantastic phenomena. But it could not be denied. I had seen something and someone for which I had no explanation. Bennett was brusque and to the point. 'What was he wearing?' he asked.

'Not modern clothes, something loose, a shirt not trousers,' I replied.

'What colour?'

'Light, not dark . . . I can't remember.'

'Not green?'

'I don't think so.'

'Hmmmmmm,' mused Mr B.

'Who do you think it was, Mr B?'

Bennett whistled through his teeth for some seconds. 'You'll find out . . . You'll find out,' he barked, and then he was gone. He didn't tell me it would take sixteen years to do so.

For weeks, I read every relevant book I could lay my hands on, hoping to discover how and why I had seen what I saw. I went to bed every night expecting to see the dazzling light again and the man who'd brought to my chest the most palpable calm I'd ever felt. I was in a ferment of expectation, but the weeks passed and nothing happened.

We could now smell spring in the misty rain that fell over the meadows. The snowdrops were finished and crocuses and hyacinths were pushing through the damp soil. On the afternoon of a fast day in March, when we had been encouraged to take a long walk to clear the head of any toxins rising from our rumbling tummies, I was climbing a road when a barn owl flew up suddenly just over my head, startling me out of my reverie. With no warning at all, Mr B fell into step beside me and we walked abreast for some minutes in silence.

'You have to stop this,' he told me.

'What am I doing that I have to stop?' I asked.

'You're so busy waiting, expecting some cosmic clap of thunder or visitation from above. It's no good, don't you see? It puts you in the wrong time slot to receive anything.'

'I don't understand what you mean.'

'Well, you have isolated yourself with this fixed hope of another vision. When it does not happen, you are disappointed but still expectant. Nothing works if all you do is wait for something to manifest so that you can be amazed! Stop being a silly sensationalist. You must live in the present moment and forget about visions and such fancies. You will understand only when you are ready – and it will only be after you stop being surprised by these phenomena. It is only then that the *real* work begins.'

In April, Hasan Shushud Konevi arrived from Turkey and Mr B gave me the job of being his interpreter. Hasan was one of the most remarkable men I have ever met. Physically, he was small and insignificant but he possessed intense black eyes that could look into the most buttressed heart with ease. Hasan spoke only Turkish and French. It took me some time to decipher his speech in the latter language, as he pronounced 'd' like a 't', saying, for example, '*tans ce monte*' instead of '*dans ce monde*' (in this world). I believe he was one of Bennett's teachers. He had written a definitive book, entitled *Kwajagan Hanedani* ('The Masters of Wisdom of Central Asia') and was a direct descendant of Sadruddin Konevi, a great dervish sage who lived in Konya in the fourteenth century. The day I met him I was wearing a flowing lavender dress with flared sleeves and my hair was very long, hippy style. He stared when Mr B introduced me and asked quite genuinely, '*Etes-vous une fée?*' (Are you a fairy?) 'Yes,' I spontaneously answered, and from then on he always called me '*ma fée*'.

I would go to Hasan's quarters in the Stable block every day to translate for the stream of people who passed through. At the outset, I was embarrassed to hear my fellow students disclosing a raft of intimate and sometimes confused problems for me to translate into French but then I realised that I must become invisible and forget what I was listening to on a personal level. After that, it became much easier. Occasionally, Hasan would give active advice but he would always dispense 'baraka' (blessing) by blowing his breath onto their heads. At times, he would hold their hands or write something on a slip of paper. He would give them a protection to wear around their necks for a week or so, and he always listened with the utmost care that took in the entire person as he did so.

Hasan also had an infallible sense of the physical state of each individual who entered the room and would insist vehemently that some give up smoking or that others visit a doctor, if he deemed it necessary. Initially, I thought he was just an eccentric but a couple of days in his presence changed my opinion. I saw that he gave those people something very valuable that they desperately needed.

I don't know whether he had invented it, or whether it had been passed down to him for generations, but he claimed the '*zikhr-i-daim*', the Zikhr of Infinity, was the most powerful tool in his vast armoury of knowledge. This *zikhr* (incantation) is the repetition of patterns of breathing, using the number eight, until a moment arrives when it is held for as long as is comfortable. It has to be taught because it is quite difficult to perform without help and practice.

Some of us had been shown the *zikhr* privately but only by a member of the same sex. It was secret and special. When Hasan gave his dissertations, he would begin '*Cette zikhr*...' (this *zikhr*) and half the group would scratch their heads in puzzlement. Finally, I told Hasan that more than half the people in his audience had not even been given the Zikhr of Infinity and had no idea what he was talking about. I thought he would explode with fury. He went straight to Mr B and shouted, '*C'est pas a toi! C'est pas a toi!*' It was a salutary sight, Mr B submitting with humility to his superior. He was chastened and remorseful, and after that everyone was taught the *zikhr*. It was practised for half an hour privately each morning before we went to meditation.

One day I undertook the remarkable job of driving Hasan to London, where he was to stay for a few days, and I was obliged to take him wherever he required to go. His first stop was the City of London, where he purchased an ordinance map of the Sherborne area. Next, he explained to me that his son, who worked for Turkish Airlines, had recommended a good place for him to stay near Marble Arch, so off we went.

I was apprehensive when we entered a very seedy hotel in one of the back streets behind the big cinema at Marble Arch. Hasan demanded a room with windows facing the south and Mecca, and, taking charge, proceeded to open various doors without knocking to examine the interior. The place was clearly a brothel. Couples lying in bed were surprised when a small gentleman of Middle Eastern appearance entered, taking no notice of them, looked around and then, still without acknowledging their presence, left without a word. The Pakistani proprietor chased after us in a panic, throwing up his hands and waggling his head.

'Where did you pick him up?' he asked me, perplexed.

At last, Hasan found a long narrow room with a small balcony facing south at the end of an upper corridor and called for his bag to be brought up. After paying the Pakistani from a leather bag he wore round his neck, Hasan waited while they brought his belongings from my car. He seemed utterly oblivious to the fact that his son had chosen a brothel as the most suitable accommodation in London for his father. I wondered whether his son had a wicked sense of humour or was in revolt against his pious father.

As soon as his large suitcase arrived, Hasan opened it and asked me to wait. I watched in awe as he revealed two dozen single-serve packets of Kellogg's breakfast cereals, some chocolate bars and a number of copies of the Koran. I could see no clothes in his luggage but perhaps they were buried under the Korans. He then selected two beautifully bound books from the pile and we left with them wrapped in a long green silk scarf that he'd also produced from his bag. The proprietor was very relieved when the door closed behind us.

Our next stop was the British Museum, where Hasan had an appointment to meet some representatives of Islamic art and an Arabic scholar to show them the Korans. They pored over the volumes for a hour or two while I walked around the museum's Egyptian section. Though it is an unwritten law of Islam that no-one should *sell* a Koran, I think there was talk of the British Museum acquiring the books in exchange for some relic. Hasan emerged from the meeting looking depressed. '*Ma fée*, drive me to the River Thames,' he sighed. 'Take me to the river so I can throw these Korans into the water. I cannot continue casting pearls before swine.'

I took Hasan to the Chelsea Embankment, where he walked up and down for some time, but he didn't toss the books into the water. Instead, he came back to the car and stood beside it, wiping his face with a large white handkerchief while clutching the Korans under his arm. There were tears on his weathered cheeks.

Before returning to Turkey, Hasan gave me a real seahorse, which had been specially preserved so that it was impermeable. 'This is for you, *ma fée*, because it is your symbol,' he said. 'Seahorses are the only male creatures that give birth to their children and this is the talisman of the Fidele d'amore.'

Later, I had Hasan's gift set in gold and wore it around my neck for many years until one day, while swimming in one of the mountain streams in the Queensland rainforest, I lost it, so my seahorse returned to its watery abode.

All our teachers at Sherborne were nothing if not unusual. Dr Chandra Sharma had been sent from India to London to study medicine. His studies were paid for by the followers of Ramana Maharishi when, as a young man, it was recognised that he was a natural healer. Both an allopathic and homeopathic physician, he ran the first homeopathic hospital under Royal Charter, at Liphook. His classes took place at one in the morning, as this was the only time Dr Sharma had free. They were enthralling. He ascribed human personalities to therapeutic plants and enumerated their characteristics. Wind flowers, for instance, were timid people with fluctuating temperatures who blushed easily. Nux vomica, arnica, berberis and so many others were introduced to us as friends. I used to dig my nails into my wrist to try and stay awake in his lectures, too often failing in the attempt. The snores echoing around the room were testament that other weary students had succumbed but they never dampened Dr Sharma's enthusiasm and he concentrated on those few insomniacs who managed to remain conscious.

Bante Dharmawara always reminded me of a human hazelnut, with his small polished brown head and seamless face. An Ashoka Buddhist monk, originally from Cambodia, he taught us how to use a blending of different colours to eat correctly. He had been alive for so many years (he lived to be 110) that no-one questioned his authority. He wore the saffron robes of the Buddha, representing clarity, and ate only one meal a day, at noon. After his meal, he rolled himself up like a yellow silkworm and slept under a tree, if the weather was clement. In the evening, he drank a cup of warm milk with honey. He'd chosen a young student named Tim as his acolyte. This was considered a great honour for Tim, who stayed with him night and day, seeing to his every need.

Mr Bennett himself taught the action of digging, using a wooden articulated doll to demonstrate how to employ our own weight to conserve energy, when to lean, how to balance and attain rhythm. For a septuagenarian, he was a dab hand at digging. The centrepiece of Study was the Inner Octave of Man, the Enneagram, known as the Law of Seven. We learned how to use the Enneagram as a decision-making tool, where to bring in 'shocks' and when to begin a new octave. The entire thrust of this teaching was towards practicality aligned with spirituality. Nothing was mere theory; everything had to be experienced and the doing of the thing was analysed, discussed and meditated upon in retrospect.

Every Monday morning Bennett introduced a theme for the week, which we were asked to contemplate and to analyse how it affected our lives. Then, on Friday nights, the whole school met after dinner for the Theme Meeting. Anyone who wished could make observations about what had struck them about the particular theme during the course of the week. We were encouraged not to intellectualise or embellish our observations but to try to be as honest as possible, even at the cost of personal dignity or pride. We entertained subjects such as Likes and Dislikes, Material Objects, Sex, Sacrifice, Suffering, Ritual, Freedom and Intuition. Our meetings often lasted well past midnight and were vastly revealing, at times embarrassingly so. It was impossible to stand up and make an observation that was phony, as it was glaringly obvious to everyone in an instant.

To prevent the same people talking all the time, Mr B introduced a method of pulling names out of a hat so that you'd never know when it was going to be your turn. We were sometimes joined by visiting dervishes, professors, mathematicians or ex-students of Bennett's from London who found the whole exercise better than theatre in the West End – or so they said.

Huge upheavals had occurred in the garden. We had planted a kitchen garden the size of a football field to grow enough vegetables to feed the entire school, using bottles cut in half to protect the young seedlings until there was no more threat of frost. The restoration and reglazing of the old Victorian greenhouses was a task of magnitude, and raspberry canes had been lovingly put in place beside the kitchen garden.

There were weekends when every able body in the place was suborned to clear seven years of undergrowth from the flower gardens. A workforce of more than fifty people can be very effective, and when the clearing was finished a formal rose garden was laid out in the shape of an Enneagram and antique scented roses were planted to add authenticity. Lawns were re-established and there was great excitement when some rare botanical species were found growing wild next to the front drive.

It was decided that the school would invite the entire population of Sherborne village to spend a weekend as our guests so they could see first-hand what we were accomplishing and to allay their fears that we were a brigade of foreign freaks doing unmentionable things in the English countryside. We chose the weekend of Midsummer's Day, the 21st and 22nd of June 1972, for the festivities.

As students we had been divided into groups according to our 'Will Types', and Bennett delighted in changing the groups around just as we became familiar with each other's foibles. Each group was sent away to discuss and then decide what form our hospitality would take for the Midsummer event. Just as we were settling in to do this, Bennett changed all the groups around again so that we were thrown together with people to whom we'd never addressed a single word before. I became a member of the notorious Q group, the most argumentative, bloody-minded and ego-ridden mob in the school – the hard nuts of Sherborne. The idea was that each group would find their own spot somewhere, appoint two observers who took notes and were impartial (they were swapped over every two hours), and stay there until they could agree on their submission. The groups were only allowed to disperse and go to bed when they were certain of their choice.

Q group stayed put in a downstairs lecture room for two days. No-one left except to go to the loo. Food was brought in by our perplexed fellow students, who couldn't fathom what all the fuss was about. They'd decided upon *their* picnic lunches or donkey rides after an hour's gentle discussion but Q group was obstinate. We had a marathon battle on our hands. Half of us wanted to do an open-air production of *Midsummer Night's Dream* under the great larches, where there was room for hundreds of spectators, while the other half was determined that we should put on a fete with stalls to sell artefacts made by students.

It's hard to imagine how two such innocuous suggestions could arouse so much heated argument and obduracy. There were slinging matches and near fisticuffs as no-one would budge an inch. Mr B was delighted at the passion we displayed. He sat in on one of our vituperous exchanges and left exhorting both sides not to compromise. In the end, after an all-night session with impassioned pleas from both sides, we came to a sort of truce, having managed to concur that both the Shakespeare and the stalls were possible, but we would need the whole school to support our agenda.

I was to direct *Midsummer Night's Dream*, using as many students and children as I could muster. I decided to go all the way and not spare the postage. I had music composed and raised a large mound of moss-covered earth under the larch trees where Puck would cavort using Tarzan ropes to swing on. This was a massive operation, and we used the Enneagram as our guide while we subsumed nearly everyone in the school in the process.

Every morning at 4.30 a.m., before meditation, the production team and I would go out with wheelbarrows and shovels to bring earth in for the mound, which grew to enormous proportions. Those early-summer mornings when the dew made fairy tennis courts and early blackbirds sang as they gobbled up late worms were joyous occasions, even as we bent our backs and shovelled. I noticed something very strange had happened to the sun. As it rose I could look straight at it, and its surface pulsed with deep green contours that fluctuated into magenta. It was like tripping without drugs. I told Mr B and he laughed. 'Now your *real* energy's showing up,' he said, enveloping me in a huge hug. He seemed very pleased. 'You know,' he added enigmatically, 'the sun's the only man around.'

I cannot deny that I had been overwhelmed by Peter Brook's magnificent production of *Midsummer Night's Dream* at Stratford-on-Avon but, with our outdoor setting and a cast of at least fifty people, I had a chance to do something quite different and creative off my own bat – and I had eight whole weeks to do it in.

I found one of the most unlikely Pucks in the history of the countless productions of *Midsummer Night's Dream* that have been mounted since it first burst upon the Elizabethan stage circa 1598. A small wiry man with the face and agility of a Capuchin monkey, he was an American who professed to be of gypsy origin. He told me he was in esoteric training in Sherborne before he took up occult practices and higher maths – a heady combination. Immensely imaginative, he'd try anything, including swinging out of the trees from a great height, shrieking like a banshee and scampering through the audience.

My Bottom was a big Argentine whose English family had made a fortune out of cattle. They'd sent him back to the UK to attend boarding school when he was four years old. At the theme meeting on Sex, he'd distinguished himself by telling us all that he'd never had a satisfactory sexual encounter in his life, being then around twenty-six years old. Playing Bottom seemed to turn a key that opened his constricted personality. He was able to use the stentorian voice God had given him to rant, rave and act the fool. Because he was naturally a prude, this made his antics all the funnier.

I was used to directing the children as I had already done a Christmas play by Rudolf Steiner in which all the kids, plus a donkey lent to us for the occasion, performed in the great hall to resounding applause. Naturally, in *Midsummer Night's Dream*, they became the many fairies, pixies and elves flitting about. The musicians were positioned up the larch trees on pulleyed platforms which allowed them to descend and rise when required. The grand piano had been moved outside under an awning and the whole company danced Number 17 (the most famous of all the Gurdjieffian Movements) at both the beginning and end of the production.

By the last rehearsal, I'd lost my voice shouting and had reached a state of utter despair that we would ever coordinate the various elements that had been thrown together for this ebullient production. It was bedlam. We had worked with the intensity and focus of diligent ants whose very lives would be forfeit if we didn't get it right. It was like those early Hollywood movies when Mickey Rooney says to Judy Garland, 'Let's do a play!' and she says to him, 'Yeah! Where?' and he shouts, 'I know . . . in a BARN!' – except that, for us, it was 'on a MOUND!' and we'd built it. Just like in those films, the show had to go on, and when it did, no-one lost their balance and fell out of the trees or forgot their lines. Everything fell into place better than I could possibly have hoped. On the two occasions we performed the *Dream*, the audience loved it and cheered. A huge supper had been prepared by those not directly involved with the play, which was served to all alfresco after the show. Everyone was in such an elated state that spontaneous music broke out and everyone sang and danced their feet off for the rest of the torch-lit night.

But there was no rest for the production team. After the second performance, Bennett made us remove the entire mound of earth immediately. It turned into a scramble, a game with everybody wanting a go. Even Bennett himself dug a few wheelbarrows of loam while a herd of Friesian cattle watched baffled as we dumped a pyramid of earth in a far corner of their field. The play marked the end of the second third of the course and by now I was 'institutionalised'. She who had never been able to follow a rule in her life, for whom authority was anathema, the loner who loathed conformity had become a team player – well, almost.

Some of us had decided to test the veracity of the ideas we were learning, the most important being Bennett's projection of Future Communities. In the future, because of pollution, overcrowding and the deterioration of life in cities, groups of like-minded people, he said, would find places to initiate these communities. He contended that, if they understood what they were doing, they would be able to carry on fruitful lives in communication with the whole world, networking and doing business by computer. They would grow their own food, become self-sufficient, use solar energy and conserve the land they owned from pollutants and industrial farming.

What would hold these groups together was not just blood ties of the nuclear family but their ability to understand and accept each other, to meditate together, to practise energy-accumulating exercises and undertake imaginative new projects with input from everyone. He stressed the need for access to a constant supply of clean water, as he believed that water shortage and our ever-increasing dependency on oil were the two gravest problems facing future generations.

We searched the countryside within a twenty-mile radius of Sherborne for an affordable run-down farm to begin our experiment and found the perfect spot at Pinkney Parva, near Malmesbury, Wiltshire. Situated on ten acres of land, it was called Scot's Farm, but the locals had dubbed it Rat Castle.

The narrow road to Scot's Farm crossed a stream at the bottom of the hill before climbing in a curve to a courtyard, around which some stables and two tumbledown barns stood. A small honey-coloured Cotswold stone house was set back from the stables, one wing of which facing the stream was reputed to date back to the twelfth century. There was an array of rabbit-warren bedrooms, a cosy sitting room downstairs with a fireplace and the original stone floor. Along with the ten acres of land it cost twenty thousand pounds. Fourteen other students threw in their lot with me to try our experiment at Scot's Farm. I mortgaged my house at Coombe Springs to buy it, and long before we had finished the course at Sherborne we were planning and plotting how we should convert and rebuild the barns and mend the roofs.

Before the course came to an end I was allowed to go to London to take part in the tricentennial of Shakespeare's death at Southwark Cathedral, a gala evening arranged by Sam Wanamaker to raise funds for his proposed rebuilding of the Globe Theatre. The best actors and writers of the day performed songs, sonnets, poetry and speeches from the pulpit of the church. I was nervous and excited to be one of their number.

We were all invited to a splendid party after the performance.

Having been out of circulation for so many months, I found proximity to luminaries heady stuff. They were like open books. As I watched Prime Minister Edward Heath holding court, I remembered Mr B's exhortation: 'Look carefully into his eyes and see if he's a winner.' Heath's eyes roved around the room searching for a saviour but not even finding a life jacket. It wasn't because he'd drunk too much. I recognised a man bereft of hope. He was at that moment locked in a deadly battle with the Trade Unions but it was obvious that he wouldn't win it. It took the steely fist of Attila the Hen (Maggie Thatcher) to do that.

In the additional chapters of his autobiography, *Witness*, Bennett wrote the following about our course:

> In the final weeks of that inaugural course, I set all the students to teach one another what they had learned at Sherborne. I said that we can only truly possess what we share with others, and that *giving* is the necessary completion of *receiving*. I wanted them to go back and collect round them small groups to whom they would transmit the ideas and methods they had learned. So long as we remember, I told them, that we can do nothing and understand nothing with our *conditioned* nature . . . we shall be protected from the stupidity of thinking that we are better than those we teach.
>
> . . . As the course ended and I watched them go, I was astonished that so much had happened to so many. Some of those who looked least promising at the start had proved to be outstanding.

In my case, he was absolutely correct in his assertion that 'so much had happened'. I did not think in the same way. My centre of gravity had changed. I was putting into practice the ideas to which I had been exposed at Sherborne and adhesion to this was to shape the rest of my life.

While these momentous changes were happening in my life, Sean had found the woman who conformed to all his 'wife' criteria to perfection. Micheline Roquebrune, a French-Moroccan a few years older than Sean, had been married twice before – once to a very wealthy man who had settled enough money on her to last her for the rest of her life. She also had a ready-made family of three children and no connection to showbiz. Her son Stefan, by her second marriage, was the same age as Jason. But the cement of their relationship was a passion for golf that matched Sean's own. They met at a golf tournament in North Africa and have partnered each other ever since.

While Giovanna was at Millfield, hopefully availing herself of an education that would prepare her for whatever profession she wished to pursue, Jason had been having a very jolly time at Sherborne. Though I'm certain he learned many things that have stood him in good stead, scholastically he was ready for some old-fashioned three R's work – Reading, Riting & Rithmetic, as my old Gran used to say.

The day the course finished, I went straight from Sherborne to Pinewood Studios to commence a movie. Jason and I were to move into Scot's Farm three weeks later when I finished the film. In the meantime, Jason went to stay with his dad in Ireland where Sean was shooting *Zardoz*. My film, entitled *Hitler: The Last Ten Days*, starred Alec Guinness as Hitler while a group of eminent British actors (Simon Ward, Joss Ackland, John Bennett and Eric Porter) essayed the well-known and hated names of Bormann, Goebbels, Goering, Himmler et al. Barbara Jefford, my dressing-room partner of nearly two years in *Tiger at the Gates*, was playing Mrs Goebbels, so we had much to discuss comparing notes on the last fifteen years of our lives.

From the Meditation Room and soothing meadowlands of Gloucestershire, I was catapulted into a reproduction of the underground bunker where the elite Nazis spent the last ten days before the fall of Berlin. My role was as Hanna Reitsch, the most famous female test pilot of World War II, who trialled the first jet plane. I wore a Luftwaffe officer's uniform, clicking my heels and Sieg Heil-ing every time I entered or left Hitler's presence. It was like a mad dream.

Alec Guinness had one of those rare faces which, although bland when bare, can be transformed into anyone he wishes when the role requires it. It's not just the make-up; something seems to actually change in the very pores and texture of his skin. He had already demonstrated his incredible versatility playing eight eccentric victims of the d'Ascoyne clan – from effete aristocrat and dowager to drunken wastrel – in the 1949 classic *Kind Hearts and Coronets* with Dennis Price, and he surely couldn't have resisted the challenge of becoming Hitler when it was offered to him.

The story was adapted from a book by Gerhardt Boldt, for which he drew on the diaries of one of the secretaries present in the bunker to tell the sorry tale. Hitler, at his most cracked and compulsive, was evidently addicted to eating chocolate cake *mit schlag* (with lashings of cream), baked in the underground kitchen of the bunker. In those last days, he gathered a group of his top officers and intimates together for a chocolate-cake party at which he made them all swear an oath that they would commit suicide before they were captured. Some, of course, like Goebbels, actually did the deed, taking his wife and six children with him, but the wily Bormann escaped and was never found. Others, like Goering, were captured and stood trial at Nuremberg. My character, Hanna Reitsch, was alive and well and living in Germany at the time the film was made. She even sued the film company for misrepresentation of character.

Alec was quite phenomenal. So perfect was his impersonation and look that even Eva Braun might have mistaken the actor for her future husband. Alec asked me to come and sit in his caravan between takes and I still have a vivid picture of Hitler sitting comfortably in his armchair doing needlepoint. I had just seen *Lawrence of Arabia* and questioned him about his role as Prince Feisal, the Arab sheikh in that film, but he was not forthcoming, much preferring to exchange jam recipes.

Hitler: The Last Ten Days was withdrawn a week after its release because of complaints from the Jewish community. The producers agreed that Alec had portrayed Hitler too sympathetically.

As soon as I had shed my uniform, I hurried back to make the move into Scot's Farm with Jason. For two weeks we were alone together and, as there was no furniture, no stove and no electricity, we had a fine old time camping, cooking outside on an open fire, snuggling down in sleeping bags at night in the downstairs sitting room and thanking God that the weather held up. We had a competition as to who could tell the worst jokes.

I'd entirely forgotten that Jimmy Fraser had arranged for the writer and director of a new film called *The Wicker Man* to visit me on the first Saturday of our occupation of Scot's Farm. They arrived shortly after lunch in a chauffeur-driven Rolls-Royce, two gentlemen in overcoats – a Teddy Bear and a Tin Man. We had no drink in the house, so Jason was dispatched to the local shop down the hill and across the stream to buy anything he could. He returned with a bottle of damson wine costing forty-six pence.

I ushered the two men into the little downstairs sitting room and told them to make themselves comfortable. I could see them eyeing the two deckchairs, the old crating box, the pile of rubble from what had been the fireplace and a door torn off its hinges. We all sat down gingerly, me wearing a totally inappropriate purple spotted summer dress, while Jason served us very decorously with the filthy damson wine. The Teddy Bear was the playwright Anthony Shaffer, who wrote the blockbuster play *Sleuth*, and the Tin Man was his partner in an advertising company, Robin Hardy, who was to direct the film.

Tony was wearing an over-sized coat of the sort you see in thirties films. He was a well-covered man, in more ways than one, with chiselled features and drowsy blue eyes. I liked his voice. Tony and Robin began to discuss the film they intended to shoot in Scotland later on in the year and Tony explained that he had researched ancient pagan practices from pre-Christian times in *The Golden Bough,* the seminal study of mythology, magic and religion by Scottish anthropologist Sir James Frazer. He discovered records of human sacrifice in a ritual that consisted of the burning of a virgin each year, along with sheep, goats and pigs, in a giant effigy of a Wicker Man. The sacrifice was meant to ensure a fruitful spring.

The wonderful twist in the original script of *The Wicker Man,* as written by Tony Shaffer, is that the virgin is not the young girl whose disappearance the police officer is investigating. The virgin is the police officer himself, lured to the island to be the unwitting sacrifice victim. Edward Woodward had already been signed to play the police officer, Christopher Lee was to play Lord Summerisle and they wanted me to consider the part of Miss Rose, the fetching teacher and mistress of Lord Summerisle who schools her students in sex.

Tony told me afterwards that had I orchestrated or stage managed their visit to Scot's Farm, I could not have made them more determined to cast me in the role. He and Robin Hardy could talk of nothing on their way back to London but the eccentricity of this actress living in a ramshackle wreck with two deckchairs and a beautiful young son who served damson wine as though it was Louis Roederer Cristal.

In age-old esoteric tradition, the *murid* (teacher) sends his acolyte away when he becomes too dependent and begins to treat him as a saviour, his only support. Often, he passes his student on to another teacher so that he can acquire a different experience with another developed intellect. Unbeknownst to me, there were many students at Sherborne who fitted this category, some of whom had been sent by the man who was to become one of the most profound influences in my future life. His name was Bulent Rauf and he was a teacher of infinite subtlety and compassion. It was he who had sent the Argentinean who played

Bottom in *Midsummer Night's Dream* to Sherborne. When he saw the play, and the remarkable transformation of his former pupil from an anal retentive to an exuberant Bottom, he asked to meet me.

It was as his guest at a lunch of unrivalled degustation that I first became acquainted with Bulent. Like Bennett, he was an extremely tall man but he weighed some thirty kilos more. He had large, soulful brown eyes underlined with dark shadows, but his appearance was not at all sinister. On the contrary, his softly spoken voice was full of suppressed humour and his whole air was one of lightness. I was instantly captivated.

Bulent's life had been like a game of snakes and ladders from his birth in Cairo, in 1911, as the grandson of Ismael Pasha, Vice-Regent of Egypt, to being given twenty-four hours, in 1952, to collect his belongings and leave Egypt voluntarily or risk expulsion. As the husband of Princess Faiza, sister of King Farouk, he was persona non grata after Nasser deposed the king. His marriage to the princess came to an end very shortly thereafter and he arrived in England with barely the clothes he stood up in.

As Bulent read Turkish, Arabic and Persian, spoke three European languages and was a graduate of Cornell and Yale universities in archaeology, it's surprising that he didn't become an academic. Instead, he opened a restaurant in Kensington, London, where he prepared peerless gourmet delights of the Middle Eastern persuasion. His culinary creations still feature in the pages of *The Thousand Best Recipes in the World*.

A few years before our meeting, Bulent had remarried. Oddly enough, his second wife was a cousin of Elizabeth Bennett's, a great beauty by the name of Angela Culme-Seymour, who was also a watercolourist of some renown. However, this was just the outward show of Bulent's life. In reality, he was occupied with the teachings of the thirteenth-century Andalusian mystic Muhyiddin Ibn Arabi, known as the Sheikh al-Akhbar (the Great Teacher), whose works he was in the process of translating. Bulent taught through Ibn Arabi's *Fusus al-Hikam* (The Wisdom of the Prophets), all twenty-seven of them, from Adam to Mohammed.

Bulent's followers established a school called Beshara at Swyre Farm, not far from Sherborne, where Bennett would go every Thursday to lecture. These talks were later collected and published under the title *Intimations*. I was lucky enough to accompany Mr B on these trips, and listened with fascination to the impromptu words he spoke, so different from the way he lectured us at Sherborne. After one particularly enlightening talk, I was still in the room after the others had filed out. I saw Bulent kissing Bennett's hands as both a ritual acknowledgement of his status and gratitude for such a formidable talk. I couldn't imagine two Western professors kissing hands like that after a lecture.

After we had converted one of the barns at Scot's Farm into a fabulous Meditation Room, we gave a great inauguration party, inviting Bulent, Bennett, Bante Dharmawara, Anna Durco and Dick Holland – all our teachers from Sherborne – and, as the full moon rose, we did a resounding *zikhr* together. It is probably still reverberating through those metre-thick Cotswold stone walls today. Those of us living at Scot's Farm were still fully institutionalised. We rose to the morning bell, abluted and rushed to meditation, following the Sherborne timetable like robots, and worked at the conversion of barns and buildings with a perseverance that exhausts me if I think about it today.

Soon after I finished *Hitler: The Last Ten Days*, money from which augmented the barn conversion, BBC2 asked me whether they could shoot a documentary about what I had been doing for the past year of my life as part of a series called *One Pair of Eyes*. I never saw the finished film but, by all accounts, it was lovely to look at but rather whimsical. How could it have been anything else when the young BBC director had the idea of attaching long horns to our newly acquired ponies and running them up and down the orchards as unicorns in slow motion? I don't think he quite captured the practical side of our adventure. It's much easier for the Establishment to denigrate people who break away from conventional life by depicting them as woolly-headed eccentrics leading aimless lives of whimsy.

My next project was certainly eccentric but it didn't seem so to me. Even at our first meeting I had heard Mr B talk about the sect of Sufis called the Mevlevi, the Whirling Dervishes, and the image of a white skirt billowing out to make a spherical slow-spinning moon began to pervade my dreams. Bulent Rauf had explained to me that the white dress the dervish wears is a bridal gown symbolising his mystical union with God. The conical stone-coloured hat on his head represents his tombstone, his death to self-interest. He turns anti-clockwise in a moving meditation taking himself out of Time. His right hand is raised and open to receive *rahmat* (blessing) from above, which passes down through the transformer, his heart, and flows into the earth through his left hand, which is turned down to face the ground.

An idea was beginning to gestate in my head. I knew that in the central area of Turkey, in the great Anatolian plain where Konya lies, Catal Huyuk had been discovered by British archaeologist James Mellaart in the early 1960s. It is acknowledged to be the oldest city in the world, dating to as early as 8000 BCE. From the decorations on the walls it was clearly a matriarchal society, where Cybele, the mother and life-giver, was worshipped for thousands of years. My idea was to show how Cybele at Catal Huyuk and, after her, the Queens of the Hittites at Alaja Huyuk, then Diana of the Ephesians at Ephesus and, finally, the Virgin Mary at Maryameana, have turned the feminine force into the Whirling Dervish 'brides' of Konya, situated forty-eight kilometres from Catal Huyuk. I would call the movie *Turning*.

I sent a letter to Bulent outlining my idea for a documentary based on such a notion, expecting never to hear any more, but by return of post Bulent waxed lyrical about the possibilities of such a film to be shot in all the places in Turkey that I had mentioned. As an archaeologist, he would be pleased to lead the expedition and provide all the information he had accrued over a lifetime's study concerning these exceptional sites.

Bulent told me to meet him at the Turkish Embassy, where he had arranged an interview with the Ambassador to try to procure the help of the Turkish Government. It was almost too good to be true. The Ambassador agreed to pay all travel expenses for the crew, myself, Bulent and his wife, Angela, in return for three copies of the finished film and permission to show it at their embassies anywhere in the world for as long as they wished. We were only too happy to comply, but they had one deal-breaker: they insisted that every person who travelled to Turkey with our party should go to the embassy at least six weeks before our travel date and present their credentials so that they could check them out thoroughly before we left. These were the days soon after the film *Midnight Express*, an exposé of the Turkish prison system, hit the screens internationally and the Turks were ultra-touchy about their brutal image in the world.

Now all I had to do was get a crew, director and the rest of the money together. I put out all my feelers, signed on at the embassy and waited for the right person to come along and give us the money. But before any of this could be finalised, I was off to Scotland to shoot *The Wicker Man*.

In his foreword to *Inside The Wicker Man*, the book about what is now a cult film, Edward Woodward summed up the production as follows:

I'm sure that, like me, the others in the film have a wealth of strange, wonderful happy memories. I have never known a production like *The Wicker Man*. It was seven frantic weeks of sleepless nights, heavy socialising, fantastically hard work and a kind of wartime Blitz camaraderie. These days, movies are made with consideration for the sensitivity of the actors, the 'talent'. This was not true on *The Wicker Man*, which was shot in a frenzied rush, partly, I understand, for reasons connected with the inadequacy of the budget, partly because the weather exerted a certain malign influence on the proceedings. Whose idea was it to shoot a movie set at the height of spring on the west coast of Scotland during the onset of winter?

As far as the weather on the west coast of Scotland was concerned that year, I can vouch for the fact that we were amazingly lucky. For most of those seven crazy weeks, an Indian summer of warmth and serenity prevailed. Day followed day of perfect blue skies and windless golden glory. As for the 'heavy socialising' which Edward mentions . . . that happened mostly in the pub at Newton Stewart after the day's wrap. We all drank copious amounts of what we called the Big GM, Glenmorangie, a malt whisky of superior taste and quality, or else sloe gin, which was a speciality of the area. When the local doctor was conducting my insurance examination, I was surprised when, in ominous tones, he asked me if I drank.

'Well, sometimes,' I answered demurely.

'Then have a wee drappie of ma sloe gin,' he said, reaching under his desk. 'I make it maself. Soak the sloes for a year . . . works wonders for the constitution.'

There were deep and meaningful conversations in the pub after each day's wrap, fuelled by GM and fired by scintillating company – Edward, myself, Tony Shaffer, Ingrid Pitt, Britt Ekland, Christopher Lee, Paul Giovanni (who wrote the excellent score), Lindsay Kemp, who had taught David Bowie how to make up and be outrageous, and Seamus Flannery, who built and designed the mighty Wicker Man up on the cliff overlooking the sea at Burrowhead. Occasionally, we were joined by Tony's identical twin brother, Peter Shaffer, who was also the partner of Paul Giovanni. He wore a funny little skull cap and advised his brother on quotes from the Old Testament.

It was on one of these intense nights of struggle to make sense of our lives and what we were doing here that Tony Shaffer laid down a challenge that was hard for me to ignore, having just come from a year's study on this very subject. 'There isn't anyone in this world who can convince me that they know *why* Man inhabits this planet or that there's any sensible reason for him to do so,' he said, ordering another round for the lot of us. 'Nihilism rules, OK. There is no objective basis for Truth. All established authority is corrupt. End of statement.'

Edward and I said nothing. We were not about to cross verbal swords with Shaffer in his cups and at his most vitriolic.

'I thought one of you might like to debate me on the subject,' Tony continued. 'What about *you*?' he asked turning to me.

'No, no . . . but I might know someone who could.'

'Who?'

'A philosopher I know.'

'Where does he live? I'll go there.'

'Not tonight you won't,' said Edward. 'You're supposed to write that new scene by tomorrow.'

It was after this conversation that I noticed, every time I turned around on the set, Tony Shaffer was standing just behind me. I thought I must be imagining it, so I would change my position, only to find minutes later that Tony would be standing about a yard behind me, nonchalantly surveying the action, as though unaware of me. He invited me to go for a drive in his super-sensational, custom-built Citroën Maserati, which had doors that opened upwards. It was quite an unnerving experience as Tony had a nasty habit of revving up to 160 miles per hour on the motorway and then forgetting that there were cars ahead of us in the fast lane doing only a hundred.

I soon realised that Tony was one of the most amusing men I'd ever met, his trenchant sense of humour and razor-sharp wit cutting down the tedium of waiting around on the set. His answer to the black dog of melancholia that plagued him at intervals was the pleasure he took in real conversation, games, elaborate practical jokes and genuinely funny or ribald stories. He was grateful when I offered to teach the young girls involved in the film's fertility dance one of the Gurdjieffian Movements I had learned at Sherborne. 'The Little Tibetan' was performed by a dozen naked girls (actually, they wore body stockings) around a blazing fire set amid Stonehenge-like rock formations.

In *Inside The Wicker Man*, Robin Hardy wrote: 'Diane Cilento was very interested in the whole pagan, white witch thing, so she did the choreography for that scene. She suggested that she throw a little something into the fire to make it explode. She knew what she was doing, so we left her to it.'

In reality, I had discussed the idea with Tony the night before. He'd brought a book with illustrations to show me how the girls leap through the fire at the conclusion of the dance and explained what part the notion of parthenogenesis plays in it. The script included the following dialogue between Lord Summerisle (Christopher Lee) and Sergeant Howie (Edward Woodward):

Lord Summerisle: Parthenogenesis is literally – as Miss Rose would doubtless explain in her assiduous way – reproduction *without* sexual union.

Howie: What nonsense is this? You've got fake biology, fake religion! You should be bringing those children to Christ.

Lord Summerisle: Himself the son of a virgin, impregnated, I believe, by a ghost.

The words of the song that is sung throughout the parthenogenesis dance are:

> Take the flame inside you
> Burn and burn below
> Fire seed and fire feed
> And make the baby grow

It was on that very evening that Tony made his move, perhaps inspired by his own lyrics. 'I don't seem to be able to leave your room,' he said, as though paralysed.

'Why? What's wrong?'

'I don't think I can leave your room,' he repeated wryly, and this time it was quite clear what he meant.

'Ah,' I said, throwing a navel orange at him, 'you can eat this on your way home.' We laughed. He accepted the orange and defeat gracefully but he was a tenacious man. He could wait. The next day he had to go back to the States for a brief visit to see how his play *Sleuth* was doing on Broadway.

I liked Britt Ekland. As we were all staying in the not exactly five-star Kirroughtree Hotel in Newton Stewart, we were thrown together much of the time. It was like being back at boarding school, queuing up outside the bathroom and eating corned beef and bread and butter pudding at one big table. I have always admired a woman who can lock herself away in her room for a 24-hour self-maintenance job. Britt could do that and come out looking as though she had been in the hands of a Parisian beautician for a month.

Britt asked me to do a Tarot reading for her. Though Mr B had imposed a ban on Tarot at Sherborne, telling me it was baby stuff and I had to go beyond that, I looked at her cards. It was instantly clear that she was pregnant, that she would not live with the father of the child, a son, but that she would not be distanced from him either, and that she would move to a house overlooking the sea. In the pages of *Inside The Wicker Man*, Britt wrote that she was deeply shocked by the reading because the previous day she had discovered that she was pregnant by her then boyfriend, Lew Adler, but I seem to remember that she didn't find out for sure about her pregnancy until after I'd told her.

At the end of the shoot we decided to hold a pheasant and gravad lax party for the whole crew. Being Swedish, Britt would get her mum to send over a large batch of her homemade gravad lax, the Scandinavian version of smoked salmon. The fish, cured in salt and sugar, is pressed between bunches of dill, taking on the delicious flavour of that herb. It is truly scrumptious. I was to cook the pheasants and arrange for the hotel to provide all the trimmings. After all the overcooked roast lamb and spotted dick we'd been subjected to, it was to be a veritable feast.

When the gravad lax hadn't turned up by 8 p.m., and the guest of honour, Tony Shaffer, was also missing, we thought we'd have to call the whole thing off. But at 8.15 on the dot, as if by magic, they arrived together, Tony carrying the salmon and positively sparkling after his long drive from London in his outrageous Citroën Maserati. He swore he'd covered the distance between Heathrow and Newton Stewart in under six hours. We looked at each other. I was extraordinarily happy that he was there and I knew I wouldn't be throwing any more oranges at him that night.

Suddenly, I was back in the world where sensual love, betrayal, intrigue, jealousy and anxiety live. For nearly a year, I had been missing from what one old actress called 'the hurly-burly of the chaise longue'. I was opening a door that led somewhere quite different, to other emotions and another kind of struggle, but now the onslaught of passion stopped all that in its tracks, not forever, but just for the moment. There I was, reeling in love again.

Chapter Fourteen

We talked a lot, lying in bed in the lassitude after love-making. Tony quizzed me continuously about my time at Sherborne, intrigued by my descriptions of the exercises, theme meetings, fasts and silent meals, and he told me an elaborate wartime story about how he had volunteered while still a schoolboy at St Paul's to be parachuted into France as a boy spy.

The government was ever on the lookout for young idealists, and so Tony was inducted into the necessary combatant skills and undercover work at a special camp. His mangling of the French language changed his spy masters' plan for him, however, and he was sent instead to the coal mines in Wales to be an undercover 'Bevin Boy' (the politician Ernest Bevin had introduced the idea of sending conscripts to work in the mines for the duration of the war). Tony's task was to ferret out saboteurs and exterminate them. His identical twin, Peter, provided the perfect cover for him as they could alternate roles and be in two places at once.

Tony boasted that he had been very successful at his clandestine work and had seen off many traitors, but instead of the gasps of admiration that he had expected, I was filled with horror at the idea of him being a covert assassin. As soon as he saw my revulsion, he quickly changed his story and said the whole thing was a schoolboy fantasy ... but I was never sure. On his black-dog days, he always made reference to the unspeakable damage done to his psyche by such deeds from the past.

Tony was impatient to meet Mr B, so as soon as the filming of *The Wicker Man* was completed (and once he'd been amazed by the transformation of Scot's Farm from the dump it had been on his last visit) I drove him over to Sherborne.

We found Mr B rubbing his huge hands together, trying to keep warm in front of a wispy fire in his small sitting room. I went out to look at the dying vegetable gardens and the blooming greenhouses, the vestiges of our course. An hour or two later, Tony came looking for me. He had that look on his face that I came to know well. It was the abstracted face of a predator picking up the scent of prey, in tracking mode but not quite clear yet about what sort of animal is his quarry. There was a hint of fear and uncertainty aligned with a fierce determination to close in for the kill. He didn't say much except that Bennett was a remarkable man.

'Very quirky,' he added. 'Why do you think he talked mostly about General Wingate, the Chinooks and classical music? He fascinates me. He told me that I was to continue to work with you, undertake meditation, practise exercises. He thinks I'm your pupil.'

Tony caught me round the waist and squeezed me very hard. 'And he's right . . . I am.'

It was then that Tony began a peripatetic way of life that would become a pattern for the future: New York to check on *Sleuth* and various places in the UK to check on Diane and wife Carolyn and daughters, Claudia and Cressida. It was the stuff of a Wildean farce. And it wasn't long before another old plot piece for farce took place.

Tony's wife examined the contents of his beloved briefcase, a bulky affair in which he kept everything of value he owned. She found a letter from me in which, amongst other things, I had described one of the morning exercises. She confronted him with his affair. Tony must have come up with some very nifty explanations, sidestepping the real issue and depicting Mr B and my time at the school in glowing terms, because the outcome, bizarrely enough, was that Carolyn Shaffer enrolled herself and her children as students into the next course at Sherborne.

Meanwhile, I had found a backer for my documentary, *Turning*. It was arranged that we would leave for Istanbul in the first week in December, a contingent of four crew plus myself, Bulent Rauf, his wife Angela and her son as photographer. We'd shoot many of the ancient sites first, and then arrive in Konya in good time for the anniversary of the death of Jalaluddin Rumi (Mevlana) on 17 December, known as 'the wedding night' in recognition of his union with God. For one week only, beginning on that special day, the dervishes are allowed to perform the Sema, the ritual of turning, in an old basketball stadium in Konya. People flock to watch them in that week, but for the rest of the year the Sema is outlawed.

In 1924, Mustafa Kemal Atatürk, founder of the Republic of Turkey, national hero and humanist, introduced a series of radical reforms in order to drag his country kicking and screaming into the twentieth century. He abolished Arabic script and instituted a new Latin alphabet incorporating Turkish, decreed that Islam would no longer be the compulsory state religion, made primary education obligatory (most prominently for women), forbade the wearing of the fez and made a proclamation that, henceforth, only ugly women should wear the yashmak to cover their faces. Because Sufis (dervishes) were exempt from military service and paid no taxes, their ranks had engorged to such a degree that nearly everybody claimed to be *tassuuf* (on the Sufi path). Consequently, Atatürk outlawed the lot of them and closed the *tekke* (Sufi schools), in the knowledge that genuine Sufis would continue their work despite bans or banishments.

I had offered the young BBC director of *One Pair of Eyes* the job of directing our film, but as he had neglected to put his name down at the Turkish Embassy, he was forbidden to travel to Turkey. Bulent's reaction was to say to me, 'Of course, I always knew it would be *you* who directed it.'

We arrived at Yesilkoy airport in much different circumstances from when I was last there as Mrs James Bond joining her husband for the shooting of *From Russia with Love*. This time, I was the director of a government-sponsored documentary and had to pass through scrupulous examination. Our cameras were checked and we were rigorously questioned as to our locations and intentions before being allowed to leave, with explicit instructions not to film outside the strict guidelines.

It was bitterly cold but I never ever felt it. I think I was so fired up with the zeal of a first-time director that my temperature must have remained well over normal for the entire shoot. I wore a long false-fur coat with no sleeves, an extended muffler, high leather boots and a huge Russian hat. Our journeys were thrilling, as Bulent's insights into the archaeological sites we visited were remarkable. He had an intimate knowledge of the peoples, rituals and religion of each site, conveying such a feel of the reality of the past that time was eradicated and we could all imagine the place busy and inhabited by these ancient ancestors of ours.

Before we left London, Bulent introduced me to James Mellaart, the archaeologist who had uncovered the great mound in central Turkey that hid Catal Huyuk, the oldest known city in the world. To the astonished merriment of the locals, he had tramped around Turkey wearing a kilt, but, sadly, he was not allowed back into the country, having been accused of smuggling by the government after some of the priceless statuettes he'd found had turned up for sale in Switzerland.

Mellaart spent much time explaining to me the extraordinary 'Tetrad' lifestyle of the peoples who lived in Catal Huyuk some eight to ten thousand years ago. Over the centuries, families built huge apartment blocks with four-sided rooms on top of each other, the roofs of which became the thoroughfare and marketplace. Each side of the room was designated for a specific function: they slept on one side, ate on another, carried on their works on the third and buried their dead on the fourth side. All the walls were repainted with pure white mall every year and decorated with murals illustrating events in their lives.

Mellaart showed me slides of some of the murals that he had uncovered using dental tools, explaining that the colours were vivid when first discovered but quickly degraded to grey with exposure to the air. They showed men resplendent in leopard skins, leaping and dancing on the backs of giant bulls while netting animals. The women in the pictures were uniformly enormous and female skeletons recovered from the site revealed that they had borne an average of twelve children each. They stood at the centre of the action, solid and recognisable by their huge breasts, while the men cavorted around them like show-off schoolboys. These people worshipped Cybele, the mother goddess who is perpetually giving birth, and numerous statuettes of her were found at the site.

When we visited the Neolithic city of Catal Huyuk ourselves there was one small man guarding the whole place, still wearing his pyjamas under his uniform. He insisted that we take breakfast with him in his little hut, and he prepared tea with lumps of homemade bread and his own sour plum jam. I put him in the film, leading Bulent around the site. Bulent seemed to know everyone. We were invited into the kitchen of every restaurant we went to and were carried about Konya by a troupe of young dervish dancers who never seemed to sleep. Every night, after the Sema, they would take me off to listen to the sparkling music of the *neh* (flute), and the *zikhr* would go on until dawn. We were given fresh melon, mandarins and special Turkish delight with pistachios to eat but only water to drink. Sleep was a waste of time, but when it came, it was sweet and dreamless.

I got to know the dervish dance master, Ahmed Becan, very well, as I did the Sheikh, Suleiman Dede. There was also an 86-year-old dervish from Samsun, who could turn faster than all the rest; Jalaluddin, son of the Sheikh, who became a student of Bennett's at Sherborne; and Ergement and Bulent Ergene, brothers, who later came to stay at Scot's Farm and helped us put up our greenhouses. The dervishes made us welcome in their homes and I was witness to the sophistication and erudition of these men. Most of them spoke at least three languages and had passed from teacher to teacher to learn new skills with their hands.

Much to Bulent's fury and my chagrin, Hasan Shushud travelled all the way from Istanbul to see me, but some thoughtless person sent him away as I was out filming. We were shooting in the huge mosque where Jalaluddin Rumi is buried. Each tomb was surmounted by an enormous turban and a wealth of beauteous calligraphy inscribed on copper. While we were filming in the tomb, all the lights suddenly went out. We thought a fuse had blown but out of the shadows marched Madame Ayashler, Bulent's cousin. An Ottoman noblewoman and dervish who feared no-one, she was a truly formidable sight, waving her stick, wearing a hundred coloured scarves wrapped round her head and shouting at a group of men at the other end of the room, who cringed visibly. I couldn't understand anything she said but, evidently, the Minister of Culture, who was in the building on a visit, had ordered that all the electricity be cut off while the foreign filmmakers were present. Madame Ayashler was breathing fire, berating the minister in no uncertain terms and castigating the men mercilessly for their interference in our work. Within minutes the lights were restored.

We shot in markets in freezing Selcuk and Ankara, in classrooms where boy dervishes were learning German, in *chaihanas* where men played dominoes all day and in fields where women picked cotton and planted for the next year. I turned my camera on carpets, dervish hats, sheep being milked and people eating kebabs in the snow while their breath streamed out in ribbons around their heads. It was intoxicating, much more exciting than acting, and I revelled in being behind the camera. Filming the Sema in the old basketball court was pivotal to the entire film. I had two cameras to play with, so every day I chose new positions. One day we were at ground level, the next up in the ceiling. I managed to get huge close-ups, fish-eye lens shots and unusual top shots of great depth.

Once the filming in Konya was over, the party dispersed. Bulent, Angela and her son went straight back to Istanbul, while the crew and myself decided to drive back over the Ural Mountains. We were in pursuit of Halley's Comet, which was meant to be looming large and flashing its tail in the sky that year. Near midnight on the first night, as we climbed higher and higher, the weather turned sour, snow began to fall and the road became covered with black ice.

My second cameraman was driving cautiously as the road was treacherous, to say the least. We reached the summit with no mishap but it was on our descent that disaster struck. Right in the middle of the road ahead, hardly visible through the swirling snowflakes that battered the headlights, we made out a large old-fashioned farm truck laden with animals. The driver was standing in the road adjusting the ropes that held his cargo in place. We saw him from a far distance and applied the brakes but nothing happened. We just kept sliding down the mountain on the black ice, hooting for him to get out of the way. It was a slow-motion nightmare. He shot sideways and out of harm's way before we hit the truck. At first I thought it would be all right. The impact was not so great that anyone was badly injured. But the crates on the truck had all broken loose and, before long, the whole road was covered with goats, sheep and chickens, bleating and clucking their hearts out in the dead of night. The driver of the farm truck was yelling and cursing at us in Turkish but none of us could utter a word in reply.

Our immediate and overriding fear was that other cars would come over the summit and hurtle down to hit us. We hurried to get the precious film material and our belongings out of the boot, find a torch and dash back up the road to flag down any approaching traffic. Soon a large bus appeared and bore down on us. We waved the torch and shouted at the top of our lungs. There was the scream of hydraulic brakes as, in an awful replay of our slide, the bus slammed into our car with a sickening crunch, coming to a halt horribly near the edge of the cliff.

It was bedlam for about half an hour. Passengers piled out onto the road, tripping over scuttling goats and freaked-out chickens, and then two police cars arrived. We didn't know whether to be relieved or even more worried because out of the leading car stepped a lanky officer who looked rather like a rat-faced Gary Cooper. He took out his revolver, which was strapped loosely to his belt, and fired a few shots into the air to get everyone's attention.

We were pointed out as the culprits by the furious farmer, who shouted abuse at us. After much fist-shaking, we were bundled into the second police car and taken away to the police station to be questioned – but not before I had done a bit of fist-shaking of my own. I sat down defiantly in the middle of the road, insisting that our belongings and the undeveloped film come with us. I was petrified that all our wondrous work would be left to moulder on the side of this freezing Turkish roadway.

We arrived at an obscure little village where the pale light from a solitary café shone opposite the only other light in the main street, which issued from the cop shop. I was left in a bare room with all our baggage. I huddled in a corner next to the wood burner and tried to sleep. The two cameramen and the sound man had been taken off somewhere else and, though I listened hard, I could hear nothing but a lone dog baying at the moon and the eerie calls of night birds that could have been curlews.

The next morning, after a quick wash in freezing water, I was marched across the road to the café by a military guard and given an omelette to eat. Then I was marched back to my room and the rat-faced Gary Cooper type arrived to interrogate me, except that we had no common language. Somehow he made it known to me that my companions were in the cells and were being charged with dangerous driving. He mimed the farmer whose animals had been scattered across the mountain being very angry and bringing a case against them.

We stared at each other for some time while I endeavoured to put into practice things I had learned at Sherborne, like staying focused and

373

sensing my big toe. I took the opportunity to convey in sign language that I wanted to use the telephone. He agreed reluctantly and a phone was produced. With trembling fingers, I called Bulent's cousin, Madame Ayashler, in Istanbul. If anyone could get us out of this mess, it was the redoubtable Madame Ayashler. I prayed that she had returned to Istanbul.

Miraculously, the voice I heard on the other end of the line was none other than Bulent's. I could have fainted with relief but it was difficult to explain our predicament on a line that kept fading in and out. Eventually, he seemed to comprehend our precarious situation and asked to speak to the man in charge. I watched the face of the cowboy cop as it changed from suspicious to worried to official. He kept glancing at me during the conversation and clicking his teeth together. He put down the receiver and waited. Then he called a young boy and had glasses of tea brought in. This augured well. I had waited with Bulent at the government offices in Ankara for further permission to travel and I knew what glasses of tea meant – hang in there, it's only a matter of time and patience.

We hadn't finished our second glass of that stewed tea so favoured by the Turks when the telephone shrilled and the policeman answered it standing to attention. There was a great deal of verbiage and much nodding and frowning, and when the receiver was finally replaced, his attitude had changed completely. Some underlings brought an armchair into the room for me to sit in, after which a man appeared who spoke some words of French. He said he was a waiter who had lived in Paris for a short time. Through him, I learned that a car was being sent to collect us and take us back to Istanbul with our baggage and the precious film. The police officer saluted me as I left and, through my translator, I thanked him for his exemplary treatment. The boys had spent the night in a rat-infested cupboard in relative warmth but they were thankful to be leaving with nothing more than a few bruises and a good story to tell when they got back to London.

374

If Tony had been impressed by Mr B, he was felled by the charm of Bulent. Something about his courtliness and distinction made Tony squirm with pleasure. Knowing that Bulent had a weakness for smoked salmon, he would rush off to Harrods' Food Hall to buy a whole side and then top off his gift with two pounds of grapefruit peel dipped in bitter chocolate. While I was editing the film, we met often at Bulent's London residence, where he prepared mouth-watering Middle Eastern dishes, such as the Imam Fainted and Quail Loaf, while I recorded his voice-over for the film.

Bulent had invited me to his place in southern Turkey, which was in a village called Bitez, near the ancient town of Bodrum. Here, in a lovely house right on the edge of the Mediterranean Sea, Bulent and his pupils had undertaken the monumental task of translating the major works of the Great Teacher, Muhyiddin Ibn Arabi. I was thrilled to have been asked to participate – but first I had to complete the editing of *Turning*.

It took me a long time to pull the pieces of the film together. I worked in a studio in Soho with the editor Gene Ellis (aka the Genie), who was a sort of wizard in his own right. I was tireless, unable to sit down for a second. Hyperactive, I would stand behind the editor, jigging about, watching every frame, trying different things and probably sending him mad . . . but I had to get it right.

I took as my theme the following lines from *The Four Quartets* by T. S. Eliot:

At the still point of the turning world. Neither flesh nor fleshless;
Neither from nor towards; at the still point, there the dance is,
But neither arrest nor movement. And do not call it fixity,
Where past and future are gathered. Neither movement from
    nor towards,
Neither ascent nor decline. Except for the point, the still point,
There would be no dance, and there is only the dance.

I had asked Ergement, one of the young dervishes, to turn within a tiled square I had found in the floor of a nightclub in downtown Konya. I put the camera directly over his head and, after he had completed the ritual without which he could not turn, his huge skirt flared out into a sphere of whiteness as he unfolded into the perfect circle within the chequered black dance floor, his head being the 'still point'.

I spoke the words in the first half of the film, tracing the matriarchal society down to Maryameana, where the Virgin Mary is buried. Then I brought in the *neh* flute, with its mournful, yearning strains, and Bulent's voice took over to recite Rumi's poem, *The Song of the Reed*:

> Listen to the reed forlorn
> Crying since it was torn
> From its rushy bed
> A song of love and pain.
>
> The secret of my song, though near,
> None can see and none can hear.
> Oh, for a friend to know the sign
> And mingle all his tears with mine.
>
> 'Tis the flame of love that fired me,
> 'Tis the flame of love inspired me.
> Would you learn how lovers bleed?
> Then listen, listen to the reed.

The second half of the documentary explains what the dervishes are doing, how they look through the thumb and the forefinger as they whirl. They know who they are and they know where they are. They revolve in the place of the planets in our galaxy, the sheikh rising from his red sheepskin on the floor to take the part of the Sun. They are all engaged in a momentous collusion, a dramatic event which mirrors our galaxy and the universes – a collusion that brings about the transference of an energy that transfigures the world.

I finished the film with a magnificent montage sequence to illustrate the words of Rumi's poem *The Spirit of the World,* over which the original thirteenth-century music swelled majestically.

> I have circled a while with the nine fathers in each heaven.
> For years I have turned with the planets in their signs.
> I was invisible a while. I was hidden in him.
> I am the pangs of the jealous. I am the pain of the sick.
> I am both cloud and rain,
> I have rained on the meadows.
> Never did the dust of mortality settle on my skirt,
> > O Dervish.
> I am not of water, nor of fire.
> I am not of the forward wind.
> I have mocked at them all.
> Oh Sun, I am not Shamsi Tabrizi . . .
> I am Pure Light!
> If you see me . . . Take care!
> Don't tell anyone *what* you saw.

We finished editing, married in the sound track and music, graded the colour and finally printed copies. I walked down Wardour Street with two prints under my arm. It was a splendiferous day. Bulent and the Turkish Embassy loved it. The film was to be televised, having been bought by the Classics departments of both the BBC in Britain and the ABC in Australia. I had *finished* it and I knew beyond any shadow of a doubt that without my time at Sherborne I would never have had the tenacity to complete this complicated piece of work. Except for the births of my children, up until that moment, I had never felt such a tremendous sense of fulfilment and accomplishment in my life.

At Scot's Farm, the experiment of our 'future community' was progressing steadily but there had been shifts of population. Some of the Americans had gone home and Australians had arrived, notably my niece Adele, daughter of my sister Ruth, as well as my nephew Raphael, my brother Raff's son. Two important issues had become glaringly obvious. One was how to fund the conversions and glasshouses until we were selling produce; the other was that we desperately needed to delegate various areas of work. Meanwhile, we meditated together every morning. The energy was still high.

We'd met a family of farmers called Pegler from Foxham, near Christian Malford in Wiltshire, who had lived in the same ancient house (still called the New House) since 1730. Clearly, little had been changed since then.

Mr Pegler was West Country through and through. He had only one eye but was a connoisseur of dairy cows, especially Friesians. He owned three hundred of them and knew each one by name. He'd stand by the gate watching them all coming in to be milked. 'Now that one there is Foxham Viola 23,' he'd croon lovingly. 'She's the oldest cow in England, twenty-three years old and still going strong.' And on he would drone in his soft West Country accent, pointing out the special features of every cow like a litany. He sold us a gigantic black and white cow in calf called Buster (Foxham Viola 115). 'Now if that cow were a woman, she'd win a beauty contest,' he assured me, 'and very likely I'd marry 'er.'

He insisted we join the Friesian Society and register our future herd, which we did rather cornily as 'Moolooloo'. Buster's daughter Nicola, when she arrived, became Foxham Moolooloo 1 in Friesian Society terms. We had to milk these two marvels every day and were hard put to skim the cream, hand churn it and somehow use up the mountains of butter made daily. We put in a large strawberry patch that first year and sold punnets with our own cream in pub car parks at the weekends. The excess milk was used to feed the stray lambs that the farmer next door passed over to us to raise.

One of the outhouses was converted into a piggery and four large, bad-tempered sows – Regan, Goneril, Cordelia and Lassie – knocked down anyone foolhardy enough to enter their domain bearing food. The sows all had litters after an extended visit by George, an extremely greedy boar whose truly enormous testicles studded his rear like giant orange barnacles. He was even more aggressive than his consorts but his offspring were delightful little darlings, scampering about like an army of characters out of a Walt Disney cartoon.

The Lady Edith Foxwell (pronounced 'Fuxwell' by the locals), our neighbour from Sherston, used to bring her guests over to Scot's Farm to view its inhabitants, both animal and human, like a visit to an interesting zoo. She arrived in our courtyard with her entourage one Sunday just in time to witness Pippin, Jason's Jack Russell, having it away with one of the piglets. I saw her giving meaningful looks to her guests as if to say, 'You see? Even the animals here are at it like knives and forks with anything that moves.'

Edith herself was no slouch when it came to the sexual athlete stakes. She invited Tony and me over to her grand house in Sherston when we first arrived at Scot's Farm to drink champagne and meet her then lover, an Argentinean polo player some twenty years her junior. His belt was inscribed 'The Wild Bull of the Pampas' and, from then on, Tony and I always referred to him as TWBOTP. When Edith's daughters were at home, she would park him at Scot's Farm, where he would luxuriate on the lawn, getting a tan while flirting with anyone in his proximity, male or female.

Tony and I lived in the converted attic, which was reached by a short staircase coming up through the floor. I found a branch of a tree shaped like an arm that had an almost perfect hand on the end of it, which I carved into a handrail, index finger pointing up, holding the orb of the earth. It is still there. The windows came down to the floor through which a luxuriant pear tree was visible. In spring the tree hummed with bees, but in autumn, wasps came in their thousands to burrow in and eat the centres out of the rotting fruit before they succumbed to the cold.

There was a bathroom that overlooked the courtyard at the back. Tony brought his cat, Patrick, to live with us and he quickly discovered a way to get out of the bathroom window and over the roofs. He was a square marmalade moggy who had been the scourge of Tregunter Road but now his best trick was to catch shrews and bring them back to the bedroom half dead. He delighted in dropping them on the floor at eye level and playing the age-old dance of death with them in close proximity to one's head. It was not a pleasant sight to be greeted with first thing in the morning.

I *know* that Tony went away so often so that he could come back. He absolutely loved being met at the airport, where he would go through the same ritual every time. When the doors finally opened to disgorge incoming passengers, he would immediately see me waiting, but then play an elaborate game of pretending not to have spotted me. He was always very theatrically dressed for the occasion, sometimes wearing a wide-brimmed hat at a strange angle or carrying a stick. I had told him that I was a push-over for men who wore white suits with waistcoats, so he'd had several made by his tailor, Mr Holbrook. These he wore with black shirts and white ties, or vivid red shirts with lurid Jacques Fath ties. Then, quite suddenly, he would act as though he was seeing me for the first time and doff his hat, making ornate gestures. It was silly but lovely at the same time.

The meeting ritual was a prelude to lots of hugs, kisses, gossip, champagne and 'prezzies'. He would unpack his bags and bring out each marvellous offering with a flourish, saving the best until last. The presents themselves were carefully chosen and very expensive but never ordinary – always quirky and unexpected. I couldn't help revelling in the contrast with the dour Scot who had never been noted for his largesse.

I also got to know Tony's incendiary temper. Once, when he found out that I had introduced Michael, the director of *One Pair of Eyes*, to Mr B, he flew into an unbelievable rage for no reason that I could fathom and kicked a tree so hard that he dislocated his big toe. He was writing a play called *Murderer* at the time and had another one in the works, *The Case of the Oily Levantine*. On the backburner was a hilarious piece called *Widow's Weeds or For years I Couldn't Wear Black*. This last effort was the direct result of an adventure he and Robin Hardy had had when they were making a shampoo commercial about a widow who couldn't wear black to her husband's funeral because of her rampant dandruff fallout.

There is always something *diabolique* about Tony's plots. What makes them different from any other playwright's is that he dares to go much further than anyone in the thriller/detective genre. He called it 'the box within the box' syndrome. Once the audience thinks they have unravelled the mystery and guessed the outcome of the plot, there suddenly appears yet another twist to boggle their minds. When the dénouement finally happens, it's always unexpected and often shocking, as with *The Wicker Man*. He even called his private company Denouement Pty Ltd, and there have never been as many mispronunciations of one word, especially in Australia.

In one of the interludes when Tony was overseas, I got into our old farm truck and drove to Spain with Joe Minor, a fellow student from Sherborne who was then a resident at Scot's Farm. We were on a mission to bring back the furniture I had left at the *finca* in San Pedro before Sean sold it. Joe was a botanical scientist from New England, although

I fancy his interests had been diverted into substances of a more addictive persuasion before he arrived at Sherborne. He always wore a navy blue knitted beanie pulled well down over his ears so that only his cherubic little mouth was visible instead of his thinning blond crew cut.

Our journey through France and into Spain was uneventful, but soon after we arrived at the *finca* the Guardia Civil rolled up in force to advise us that we were under arrest for breaking and entering. As I had a key, this was demonstrably incorrect. Fortunately, Rafael and Anna (the gardener and housekeeper) trooped in and began to argue with the officers in charge, saying that all the furniture in the house was mine and that I should be able to leave with my belongings. The men knew Rafael and took his word without hesitation.

We loaded the truck with the antique carved furniture from Ronda and left before there could be any more commotion. All went well until we reached Lyons, where a motorcycle cop began to tail us. He pulled us over and told us to follow him to police headquarters, which we did. I began to think I was fated to spend half my life fending off foreign cops. We drove into a yard, where we were ordered to get out, but Joe would not budge. He stood waiting apprehensively near the truck, kicking at the earth, his hands pushed deep into his pockets. For a moment, I was worried that he might be carrying dope. The leather-clad cop regarded us with a sort of open contempt. It was as though he and Joe were chemically antipathetic the one to the other. At some point in his life, Joe must have had a very bad experience with cops.

We left Joe in the yard while I accompanied the policeman into an office. This French *gendarme* was so much smoother than his Turkish counterpart that it was laughable. He explained in concise terms that it was a grave offence to transport antiques out of France and asked to see my authorisation papers. I showed him my passport, which had been stamped at the Spanish border the day before, and assured him that the antiques did not originate in France but were heirlooms which I was taking back to England. He took my passport away, which was a bad sign, saying that the furniture would have to be unloaded and examined. It was clear that he thought we were carrying something other than furniture. I took out my camera and informed him that I must photograph every piece as soon as it was taken off the truck so we could make an insurance claim if anything was damaged.

It was a Saturday afternoon, I remember, because I could hear the commentary of a soccer match coming from the next room and excited voices barracking for the local Lyons team. I sat very still and sensed the back of my knees. This requires great attention. The policeman thought I was listening to the game and smiled.

'You like football?' he enquired.

'Oh, yes, I love it.'

'Okay,' he sighed and handed me back my passport. 'I'll let you go just this once. But if I catch you making any more trips through France with truckloads of fancy furniture, I will show no mercy.'

He actually got back on his motorbike and led us to the turnoff road out of Lyons. I tooted the horn in farewell, heaving a huge sigh of relief, but Joe sat scrunched over in his seat and remained silent all the way back to England.

The Spanish furniture fitted amazingly well upstairs in the second large barn and I managed to winkle the spiral staircase used in *Orpheus Descending* out of the Royal Court Theatre for a song. We converted one of the stables into a sauna bath and were making loads of Elderflower champagne for guests. It certainly beat 46-pence damson wine.

Bante Dharmawara came to live with us and conducted two ten-day Vipassana (Buddhist meditation) courses. We had to prepare everything to facilitate this. A doctor was on hand, as the stress of having no eye contact, no communication, not handling money and not looking in a mirror was too much for some people to bear. There were always dropouts and I knew that I would have found the course impossible had I undertaken it. It is a daunting test of will and stamina to meditate up to sixteen hours per day for ten consecutive days.

383

In his bright orange robes, Bante was a captivating and colourful creature. I can still hear Lady Edith's piercing upper-class voice exhorting her guests, 'Oh, *do* come and see this. It's priceless. There's a dear little gnome in yellow all curled up and asleep under an apple tree in the orchard!'

Scot's Farm was abuzz with activity. Even Tony went against his sworn philosophy that 'a country gentleman lifts nothing but his hat' and pitched in once in a while. He urged everyone to take part in erudite and witty conversations over dinner, as a year of silent meals inclined us towards merely fuelling the engine and leaving the table. He'd fly into tantrums, accusing wordless girls of being unforgivably boring. Tongue-lashings and diatribes were the staple for Tony, especially when the second bottle of wine kicked in. His bouts of fury made everyone laugh ultimately. No-one took him seriously and he was known – sometimes endearingly, sometimes exasperatedly – as Toenails.

We cooked on a large Aga stove, ground wheat by hand, taking turns at the hard yakka, and baked real bread every second day. It seems inconceivable, but by the end of 1974 we were nudging self-sufficiency, having set up beehives to cater for the sweet part of our diet. Every week or so we went over to Sherborne to reinforce our resolve and report to Mr B on our progress.

Tony had rented a little house at World's End in Chelsea as a pied-à-terre. I knew it to be a malevolent little hovel the moment I entered it. There are some houses which resonate forever with the evil deeds that have been performed in them and this was one of those. Jason, Giovanna and I were uneasy every time we had to stay in that house. Jason once told me that he'd seen an ugly man brush by him carrying a sack down the back stairs to the cellar. He was terrified by the encounter.

One evening in December, Tony and I returned from the theatre and supper at the Garrick Club in the West End and retired for the night to the upstairs bedroom, forgetting that we had earlier lit candles to create a romantic ambience in the room. Sometime in the early hours of the morning, from what was like a black pit fifty thousand feet under the earth, I heard a shrilling sound and tried to rouse myself. My body seemed to be paralysed and I couldn't breathe. I crawled across Tony to the telephone, fighting for oxygen. Someone on the other end was shouting, 'Mr B's dead!'

This one sentence impelled me out of bed and to the door. I wrenched it open and sucked some clean air into my lungs, coughing and heaving. 'HOLD ON! HOLD ON!' I screamed at the person on the other end of the line before dashing to the window and throwing it open. Freezing air rushed into the room and Tony moaned on the bed, so I knew he wasn't dead.

'Who is that?' I croaked into the phone.

'I'm calling from Scot's Farm. Is that you, Diane? You sound peculiar. We've been trying to get you all day to tell you that Mr B passed away this morning in his sitting room.'

I was so shocked that I was incapable of speech. 'I'll come back . . . later . . . today,' I managed to mumble, and put down the receiver.

I went to the bathroom and was horrified as I caught sight of my blackened face in the mirror. I dragged Tony out of bed. We were both choking on the toxic fumes we'd inhaled but we managed to pull ourselves together sufficiently to figure out that the candles had burnt down and set their plastic holders on fire. They, in turn, had fallen to the floor and set the carpet alight. The enclosed bedroom had filled with noxious smoke, and if not for that telephone call we would never have regained consciousness.

The untimely death of Mr B was a double blow. None of us had seriously envisaged a time when he would not be there. I still ponder the strange circumstances of his death.

On that morning, Dr Sharma was in his consulting rooms in London preparing to see a patient when, out of the corner of his eye, he caught sight of Mr B sitting on the high examination table with his feet off the ground. Sharma was stopped in his tracks, aware that something was amiss.

'You haven't, have you?' he asked.

'Yes, I have,' Mr B is purported to have said, smiling, and with that, he vanished.

Sharma immediately telephoned Sherborne and asked to speak to Bennett. Mrs B went to see if he had returned from his morning constitutional and found him sitting in his armchair, dead. His funeral was held at the church at Sherborne. There were hundreds of people there, all numbed by his sudden demise. It took ten men to lift his coffin, which seemed to occupy all the space in front of the altar. He was buried at Sparkford, the West Country village from which his family originated.

Our near-death experience left me with a lot of doubts about my relationship with Tony. I felt somehow that Mr B's passing had saved our lives but it was a warning. I was uneasy that I had virtually ignored the fact that Tony had a wife and two children, whom I saw often at Sherborne. I was 'ostriched' by the excitement and intensity of our love affair.

Then I received a desperate phone call from my mother, who told me that my dad was calling for me from his hospital bed. He had fallen off a verandah and lost his sense of balance. With this news, I felt I had been given my answer. Even though I adored Tony and found in him unique compatibilities, I felt that we should part. He was immersed in his new play *Murderer*, with Robert Stephens playing the lead in the West End. I knew he paid lip service to many of the Sherborne disciplines (like meditation) only because of me and I felt my life was far too directionalised towards things at which he secretly scoffed. I didn't know if I could live without him but I was determined to try.

The Queensland Theatre Company had offered me the part of Kate in Shakespeare's *Taming of the Shrew*. Normally, I would have politely declined, pleading my many responsibilities in England, but now it all seemed to fit. I would go back to Oz to see my dad, make a clean break with Tony by putting twelve thousand miles between us, and play a role which I had always coveted, in my own home town of Brisbane.

I agreed to do the *Shrew* for a modest fee if they paid round trips and accommodation. I would sign up for a limited season and bring my children out, after rehearsals, in time for the opening night. After writing a letter to Tony in which I explained my feelings and said good-bye forever, I flew off to Australia, lamenting the loss of my love but determined to make my homecoming mean something.

Dad was overjoyed that I had returned. He sat up in bed eating the apricots I'd brought him and insisted on recounting the whole saga of his fall.

'I was having a pee off the verandah, D, over on Bribie Island, not far from the marina. It was near to eight o'clock at night when some idiot, probably full of grog, took his boat out of the water and forgot to lower the aerial. It hit a power line and blacked out the whole area. Pitch dark, black as Newgate's knocker it was . . . lost my bearings . . . thought I was edging towards the door . . . ended up on the path ten feet below. Silly old duffer. I don't know how long I lay there but it was the weirdest sensation. There were no stars . . . only in my head. I couldn't tell which side was up. I don't recommend it.'

The first read through of the play was terrible. It was at once apparent that most of the cast assembled had never attempted to make sense out of Shakespeare's words in any of his plays. They mumbled or spoke like automatons with crossed wires. They didn't *want* to sound mentally deficient but fear intimidates and tongue-ties the most talented of actors. I looked across at Robin Ramsay, my wonderful and flamboyant Petruchio who had been brought up from Sydney to play opposite me, and he crossed his eyes at me meaningfully. We both knew that, to make the production work, we would have to do something radical – and very quickly.

With no discussion at all, we gave lessons from 8.30 until ten every morning for five whole weeks – voice production, parsing, diction, movements (Yat), making sense of the play and finding the skins in the piece, both banana and onion. With everyone warmed up and ready to go, rehearsals proper would start at 10 a.m. It wasn't long before we had an excellent and excited cast of young actors raring to go.

Allan Edwards, the director as well as manager of the Queensland Theatre Company, had arrived in Australia some years before after having done a stint at a repertory company in the seaside town of Clacton-on-Sea on the east coast of Britain. He was a brilliant marketing person and organiser but was only too happy to allow Robin and me to throw ourselves wholeheartedly into getting the best out of an untrained cast. Bille Brown was playing Tranio, one of Bianca's lovers. It was his first appearance on any professional stage, ushering in a prestigious and prolific career. A pumpkin-shaped Grumio, Petruchio's servant and the fool of the play, was played to perfection by the Brisbane actor Ken Kennett. There was so much talent in the cast that it was a joy to behold the blossoms beginning to open. Bill Phillips was a feather-footed Renaissance youth skimming the earth as Biondello; Bill Austen played my tetchy old dad; Peter Kowitz was a teeth-spitting tailor; and Greg Gesch was lord of the manor. Somehow, after a great many problems involving dress rehearsals and paying the theatre staff (but not the actors for staying on to get it right), we opened to ecstatic reviews.

We were doing the Christopher Sly version of the play, in which a troupe of wandering players re-enact the tale of *The Taming of the Shrew* for guests at a house party in the country. As the play begins with the arrival of the players at the manor, it was decided that each of us should learn some circus skills that mirrored his or her role. Being the Shrew, I aimed at fire-eating, an appropriate occupation for a combustible Kate.

I had been able to extinguish a lighted match in my mouth since I was ten, so I reckoned that I'd start with an advantage.

My teacher was a transvestite nurse from Toowoomba named Terri, who taught me by first taking a mouthful of water and spurting it out with no overlaps, never taking an inhalation. He explained that as it would not be water in my mouth but kerosene, with the added component of fire, I would burn my lungs out if I breathed in. Fun. I wasn't so sure about filling my mouth with kerosene at any time, let alone just before two and a half hours of Kate's ravings. But, as the I Ching says, 'perseverance furthers', and it wasn't long before I was attempting the real deal.

Handling such volatile materials makes you follow instructions to the letter. Under Terri's tutelage, I blew a magnificent burst of flame for the first time after a week or two of water practice. It gave me a truly fiery confidence, so I persevered some more and learned how to hold the kero in my mouth and blow at least five quick jets of fire into the air as I came on. This was my first entrance and I could hear the audience gasp, 'Is it really *her* doing that stuff?'

The one thing I loathed about the experience was the taste of kerosene in my mouth throughout the play, so I would gargle with Cherry-ade cough mixture at the interval. As any old actor will tell you, Cherryade cough mixture will cover a multitude of sins, kero included.

Lance Reynolds, who played the Prompter in *Shrew*, was also the originator of a band called the Silver Studs. He had organised the opening-night party on the second floor of the big hotel opposite Brisbane's SGIO Theatre. The band roared through a paper curtain on their huge silver choppers and belted out some heavy rock 'n' roll. Jason and Giovanna, who had watched our performance from stools in the wings of the theatre, were blown away. No-one wanted to go home. We knew we were a hit.

Everyone and his dog had to see *The Taming of the Shrew* and Allan Edwards did the obvious – he sold as many subscriptions as he could, not realising that there were not enough seats in the limited run to accommodate the new subscription holders. The outcome of this grave oversight was that the cast had to perform the play not only the regulation eight times a week (six nights plus two matinees) but were required to do it three times a day several days a week so that the management wouldn't go to gaol for fraud.

Believe me, it was no fun getting to the theatre at nine o'clock in the morning, knowing that three bouts of Kate lay ahead, and leaving the theatre half dead at around 11.30 p.m. Jason and Giovanna watched every performance from their position in the wings. Giovanna sometimes got herself up as a strolling player and made an entrance trying to juggle balls or tumbling. By the time they had to return to the UK for school, this exposure to the less glamorous side of the theatre had produced one daughter who swore she'd never go on the stage and one son who vowed he would.

It was still sweltering and I had to be extremely careful not to talk too much between performances as my voice was becoming very frayed. One boiling afternoon we were dashing down the front steps of the theatre to grab a quick bite between shows, still wearing our make-up, when a yellow cab drew up at the entrance almost in front of us. Out of it stepped an odd figure wearing a fully belted trench coat, his hat pulled down over his eyes, and carrying a battered suitcase. I only noted the garb because it was so unusual to clock a person dressed as Dick Tracy wandering about in Brisbane on a steamy Saturday afternoon. We raced past and down the street but were halted by a thunderous voice yelling, 'NOT SO FAST!'

The accent, timbre and choice of words were unmistakable. It could only be one person in the world and he was twelve thousand miles away. But, of course, he wasn't. He was standing there still holding his suitcase. What a momentous meeting it was. Tony offered no excuses whatsoever as to his presence outside the SGIO Theatre except to say that he couldn't stay where I wasn't. He took it for granted that

I felt exactly the same. I couldn't help laughing and laughing. No-one I have ever met could make me laugh like Tony. Just about anything in the world is forgivable when it ends in laughter, the great equaliser, the great emulsifier.

So Tony came to live with me at Spring Hill and immediately captured the hearts and minds of most of the young actors in our troupe. Bille Brown was particularly smitten. Here was a role model whose wit and theatricality fitted Bille's idea of playwright and *homme du monde*. The cast had changed but we were back to the intense midnight conversations about art, life and death that had started in Scotland during the shoot of *The Wicker Man*. Sumptuous after-theatre repasts were consumed by ravenous actors, Tony having scouted around Brisbane during the day to find out where the best smoked salmon and other exotic goodies were stocked. He was full of wonder at the price of genuine calf's liver (ten cents a kilo) and fresh oysters from Moreton Bay, which cost nothing in those days. I taught them all how to make real mayonnaise with egg yolks and virgin olive oil, and when they wanted to know the secret of what made it taste so special, I answered as my mother always did when asked the same question, 'I just spit in it, dear.'

By the end of the run, I was quite a wreck. I was back in 'burning-the-candle-at-both-ends' mode and suffering from an infected sore throat, bronchitis, flu and overexertion from wearing a waspie that squeezed my waist to eighteen inches. My brother David arrived at the flat armed with his medical bag and full of good intentions. He took out a syringe and looked at me expectantly.

'What's that for?' I enquired.

'I'm going to give you a quick penicillin shot. It will clear things up in a flash.'

'No, please, Dave, I'm allergic to penicillin.'

'Don't be silly, D. I know you and your excuses. It's only just a little prick – as the Bishop said to the Actress! Ha! Ha! Ha!'

In an instant, he'd jabbed me in the arm and was wiping the place with cotton wool. 'You see? That didn't hurt. You're worse than a child.'

Within the hour I was writhing on a bed of pain as huge red welts and wealds began to cover my body. They even blocked up my ears. David was confounded and kept repeating, 'But you should have told me. Why weren't you wearing a bracelet that *said* you were allergic?'

My brother Carl arrived next and administered adrenaline. He explained that what was happening to my body was like when the red telephone rings in the Oval Office of the White House. All systems are alerted and go into overdrive. I lay in bed for three days and Tony stayed closer than a skin graft. He sponged me with cool chamomile and was the perfect tender nurse. I had never seen him showing this passionate attention to anyone other than himself before and it welded me to him, more than any other thing he could have done. When I was well enough, we went over to my brother's place on Moreton Island and lay in the sun.

Far North Queensland (FNQ) has always exerted a strange power over me. Even the place names – the Daintree, Bat Reef, Mount Molloy, Cape Tribulation, Weary Bay. Perhaps I still had vague recollections of hearing my father cite these places in his tales of trips to the North.

Bill Austen, the actor who played my father in the *Shrew*, lived in FNQ but had come south to play Baptiste, lured by the idea of treading the boards once more and probably of spending a few months down in Brisbane. From January until May is the season known as 'the Wet', when a deluge can last for weeks. Insects appear in swarms, cane toads are in high sexual ferment and March flies can take a chunk out of your arm. It is not a favourite time of the year in paradise unless precautions have been taken.

Bill was also a master chef at a restaurant called the Nautilus in a broken-down little seaside village called Port Douglas. Port, as it is affectionately known locally, had been the mining supply town for the Palmer River gold rush. It had been bustling and boozy, with thirty or more pubs and rowdy houses, until 1917 when it was hit by two cyclones in one year, which flattened it. Captain Cook had originally called it Island Point because it projected into the sea like a pimple. Because of this it was said to attract cyclones, and Cairns became the central port in the area. Port Douglas became a backwater, its population dwindling to a couple of hundred eccentrics and a few prawn fishermen.

Maxie Bowden, gentleman spy and colonel in charge of the British zone of Germany after the war, actually owned the Nautilus restaurant and leased it to Bill on an annual basis. Max, a small, neat man with a matinee idol moustache, had eloped with Diana, his interpreter during the war. She was the niece of the Queen Mother. She made lovely jewellery from shells which Max, dapper in a military jacket and sarong, sold in the shop attached to the restaurant.

Arne Petersen, aka Peter the Dane, lived locally. He had made £100 million in the early sixties from the original hot-wax permanent-wave machines called Carmen Curlers. Single-handedly, he'd bought up most of the Daintree and planted acres of oil palms which he hoped to turn into margarine one day.

Then there was Bamboozelem, an 82-year-old magician who had once made lions disappear from the London stage and who now performed magic shows on Saturday nights in the bar at Port's Central Hotel.

An idea for a television documentary series had been buzzing around in my head for ages. The show, to be called *Individuals*, would seek out fascinating mavericks who had ended up at the end of the line in places like Port Douglas. They would tell their stories and have a chance to voice their most controversial views. I pitched the idea to producer Martin Williams, who agreed to supply a camera, sound, air fares and facilities to edit the film. It was a deal too good to pass up.

It was late June when Tony and I flew up to Cairns, that fragrant month when the temperature floats on twenty-six degrees Celsius. As anyone who has travelled it knows, the drive up to Port Douglas from Cairns is one of the most glorious and heart-lifting in the world. There is an ever-unfolding array of shapely hills covered with cycads and tree ferns, which give way to the purple-grey mountains of the Tablelands, cascading waterfalls and the deep green of a rainforest millions of years old. On the right is the sea, resplendent whatever the weather and dotted with islands – Double Island, Scout Hat, the Low Islands and Snapper in the distance. White sand, shaded by pandanus palms, she-oaks and ti-trees, dovetail into long rocky outcrops. It's better to be a passenger on your first trip up that road because you can't tear your eyes away from its magnificence. Bill hardly turned his head sideways as he drove us up the coast. He'd seen it all before, but my jaw was agape all the way. I could hardly wait to point my lens at this unspoiled piece of Australia that was like no other I had ever seen.

We settled into the Central Hotel on Macrossan Street – Tony, me, my niece Joey (one of my brother Carl's mirror twins) and the camera-man, a brawny bloke who could handle a camera like a piano accordion. Joey Cilento was to be the 'gofer' and write something about her experiences as practice for the career as a reporter she hoped to have.

I went to see Bamboozelem that night. He was a translucent little man with a transparent halo of white hair, and his speed and manual dexterity belied his eighty-two years. He ate razor blades, produced a live duck out of a burning dish and entangled grown men and women in steel hoops and then freed them with the flick of a finger. It was impressive stuff. We arranged that the next time he did his show, we would get Bill Austen and Arne Petersen to attend. As if by chance, he would pick the two out of the audience as his assistants so we could film them doing tricks, getting tied up in knots or whatever. Then, using freeze frame, we could segue into any moment of their lives that fitted.

Tony and I were a good team except that he wanted to stop filming for protracted lunches at the Nautilus every day, with what he called 'a glass of something remedial', and then maybe retire to bed for the afternoon. He didn't come when Arne and George Quaid Jr took me up the Daintree to a magic spot where the rainforest hangs out over the beach. This was long before tourists had discovered Cape Tribulation and we filmed its pristine splendour in a sort of frenzy as though, if we didn't get it in the can, it would disappear as soon as we turned away.

George Quaid Jr was in real estate but he had also been mayor of the Douglas Shire. He was sitting in his cupboard of an office in Mossman one day in 1972 when a wild white man wearing lederhosen walked through the door and demanded to buy up all the land from Cooktown to Mossman. It was Arne Petersen, who had landed his biplane on the beach near Cooktown and had walked the three hundred or so kilometres to Mossman through the Daintree. On the way he was overcome by the mystique and grandeur of the ancient rainforest, and now he wanted to own it.

George told me he thought Arne was either a crook trying to launder money or a delusional nutter, and he insisted on accompanying Arne to the bank to establish his credentials. It didn't take George long to realise that he'd hit the real thing. Speaking from his office in Mossman, he actually said on film, 'And so it was: for six days we *bought* and on the seventh day we *rested.*' His biblical turn of phrase befitted the exalted state this meeting afforded him because Arne made him a partner in the venture and offered him a third of the profits if he could survey and sell up the land. To this day, the repercussions of that deal still reverberate through the Daintree.

We shot Arne, who was a fitness freak and a Mason, jogging up and down mountains, swinging on ropes, visiting his cattle properties on the Tablelands and having meetings in the Adelaide Steamship Co. building, which he owned. He was a high-flier and a complete contrast to Bill Austen, whose life revolved around cooking epicurean delights, drinking brandy, smoking dope and acting. Bill had some wonderfully bitchy anecdotes to recount about when he was road manager for Marlene Dietrich's tours of Australia.

Bamboozelem produced a wealth of material from his early days with his disappearing lions in London. We filmed him in his sitting room surrounded by a glass menagerie, hundreds of miniature ornaments he had collected which seemed to me to be in deadly peril as his little dog frisked about the room, wagging his tail and leaping about.

We wrapped up the film with these three unlikely companions sitting around after the magic show, sharing a bottle of wine and exchanging their philosophies. Our time in FNQ came to an end but not before we had made firm friends with Max and Diana Bowden. We promised to return very soon.

Back in Brisbane, while I was editing *Individuals*, Tony was busy putting the final touches to a re-write of his new comedy/thriller *Widows Weeds* and working out an outrageous plot for *The Case of the Oily Levantine*, later called *Whodunnit*. We took an apartment in Auchenflower, quite near where my parents lived on the river. My father and Tony spent hours exchanging wicked stories, drinking and chuckling together. My mother, who was going deaf, couldn't pick up the nuances of their naughty stories, much to her chagrin. She kept asking me, 'What did they say, dear?' I would make up something innocuous to tell her and she would 'tsk, tsk' at their banality.

The more I looked at the pictures of the land we had shot in FNQ, the more I was convinced that HERE was the perfect place not just to experiment but actually to innovate a real 'future community'. Here there was clean water, pure air and pristine forests where no industrial waste contaminated the earth. Few people realise that FNQ was not colonised by white man until a hundred years later than the southern parts of Australia. Gold was not discovered in the Palmer River until 1872 and before that only the most intrepid of explorers had even visited the area. FNQ hadn't had as much time to be screwed up.

The rainforest Aborigines, the Yalanji people of the North, described by Captain Cook as 'far happier than we Europeans', had never inter-fered with the land. It remained in its sacred pristine state until white men came along with greedy eyes that saw only gold, red cedar, tin or copper. Those early pioneers were adept at ripping out of the earth any-thing they could turn into money. Once the gold ran out, they turned to cane and cattle. Already a third of the rainforest had been knocked down to make way for sugar cane.

I was determined to buy a big chunk of land and turn it into a rainforest sanctuary, a school or perhaps a prototype of Mr B's idea of a working future community. To earn some money I did a Neutrogena ad, which was strikingly successful, thanks to my recent high profile as Kate in *The Taming of the Shrew*. I drove back up north where Allison Pringle, a young Australian student who had been with me at Scot's Farm, was staying and looking for properties for me. She had found two possibilities – one in the Mowbray Valley and one in Whyanbeel, north of Mossman.

I was disappointed in the Mowbray Valley – it was too dry and the land was perched on the side of a cliff – but the moment I turned into the Whyanbeel Road and faced the imposing mountain, from which spurted two waterfalls and whose summit was capped by an outcrop of granite rock four hundred feet high, I knew I was in the right place. It wasn't just the physicality which clutched at me; it was as though I *knew* it, had visited it before when it and I had been different. The feel-ing was fleeting but no less real.

The actual property was a derelict farm with impacted soil, which had been settled as virgin land in the twenties when a timber trail was established to bring down the red cedar from the untouched rainfor-est that adorned the mountain. Later, an Italian family by the name of Sciacca tried their hand at growing cane there and built a little wooden house in 1956. They failed dismally, as the land was all hills, boulders and creeks. Eventually, they gave up and sold the farm to a man called Mulligan, an air-conditioning expert who wanted to diversify and fatten cattle. Like many pipe dreams, it never eventuated and the place had stood empty for seven years.

No-one seemed to have seriously considered buying it, even though it had everything I was looking for. Two creeks from the waterfalls on the mountain ran through the property and met at the bridge at the bottom of the hill. On that first viewing, I was taken to a special site in the rainforest that clinched the whole deal in my mind. There, where High Falls Creek ran down from the mountain, was a secret pool of such lucidity and beauty that I couldn't resist it. To have access to such a hidden wonderment (in my mind a sacred site) was all one could ask of life. I went to George Quaid Real Estate in Mossman and put a down payment on the property that very afternoon. The cost of 170 acres was forty-five thousand dollars. It was August 1975.

Back in Brisbane, Tony had finished *Widow's Weeds* and persuaded the Queensland Theatre Company to mount it amongst their next season's offerings. We left for London, in the knowledge that we would return.

All the time we were in Australia we were telephonically in touch with Scot's Farm where many improvements had been made in our absence. The oldest part of our conglomerate was a sturdy tower, where people reputedly huddled together on cold winter nights, using the heat that rose from the cows below to keep them warm. The roof had been remade and the cow pen transformed into a sunken dining room. A three-metre window was dropped in at one end of the room, giving us a view across the stream to the green sward where large Friesian cattle grazed peacefully. It was a bucolic poem made visual. The second barn upstairs had become a library filled with books and heated by a smart Scandinavian stove.

As we ate supper in the orchard in late August, with the full orange moon rising through the trees and the barn owls hooting, we congratulated ourselves on being witness to two of the most blissful but contrasting places on earth. It would be eighteen months before we returned to Australia and much water would have passed under the bridge in the meantime.

After consultation with Sean, Jason went off to Edgarley, the prep school of Millfield. It was handy to the big school, so I could drive down to Glastonbury on weekends and see both Giovanna and Jason at the same time. We had taken on a contingent of WWOOFers to help in the garden. Established in the early 1970s, the World Wide Organisation of Organic Food gathers young people from throughout the globe – backpackers, gap-year students, office workers who want to experience the land – who come and live on your farm, working five hours a day for food and keep. The only proviso is that the farm must be organic.

The problem for farmers is that you have to watch WWOOFers like hawks. On their first day at Scot's Farm, they came to me flushed with pleasure at their own worthiness and said, 'We've just pulled up all those thistles next to the back fence. There were ever such a lot of them.' I shrieked in horror. For two whole years, I had been nurturing those artichokes and, in one wonderful WWOOFer wallop, they were gone forever.

Tony's next big job was to adapt Agatha Christie's *Death on the Nile* for the screen. Having a high regard for the lady and the mystery genre, Tony was delighted when Christie and Sir Max Mallowan, her archaeologist husband, consented to dine at the Ivy with him and his twin brother, Peter, after seeing Tony's play *Sleuth*. When Miss Christie complimented Tony on the subtlety of his construction and the spontaneity of his surprises, he asked how she thought *Sleuth* compared to her play *The Mousetrap*, which has been running continuously in the West End since 1952. 'Oh,' she mused, downing the last of her dozen bivalves, '*The Mousetrap*? It's a silly little play.'

The twins couldn't resist. They added Miss Christie's own review of her play to those already on display outside *The Mousetrap* theatre: 'A silly little play.' – A. Christie. The management was so incensed that they insisted Michael White, the producer, move *Sleuth* to another theatre.

Lord Brabourne was producer of the movie *Death on the Nile* and the cast he assembled was illustrious, to say the least – Bette Davis, Maggie Smith, Mia Farrow, David Niven, Simon McCorkindale and, of course, Peter Ustinov as Hercule Poirot. Tony went off to Egypt terrified of drinking the water. He even cleaned his teeth in bottled water.

When we were in London, we often stayed at Victor Spinetti's house in Pimlico. We decided to formalise the arrangement and rented the upstairs part of Victor's house. One day, I went downstairs to find Victor lying in a tattered purple dressing gown on his sofa, picking at a cold sore on his face and bemoaning the fact that he had no work. I couldn't bear to see my lovely madcap Welsh Wop in such a woeful state. 'Get up!' he says I shouted. 'We missed the first Renaissance but we're not going to miss the second.'

So, off we went to Florence, Victor and I, on the spur of the moment to document The New Age Conference to be held in that fair city. Someone had seen *Turning* and thought it would be a good idea if the meeting of the world's most advanced alternative thinkers was recorded on film. They'd asked me to direct the film the very morning I spoke to Victor, but until I saw him lolling about, I wasn't sure that I would agree. Like all alternative events back then, there was no remuneration involved. I was expected to do the job for love and beg, borrow or steal enough money to present a finished piece of work at the end.

Amongst the members of the extraordinary group of intellects coming together in Florence were the architect, mathematician and inventor of the geodesic dome Buckminster Fuller, author Itzhak Bentov and the English eccentric Sir George Trevelyan. It seemed appropriate that the organisers should have chosen this special city, where Michelangelo and Galileo had lived and worked, as the forum to air their ideas about what the future held for us in the twenty-first century.

Victor and I landed in Rome and took the train to Florence. We had a bet on the way. I would pay him ten pounds every time we saw any bird other than a crow. I won. We found the river Arno filled with plastic bags and rotting rubbish. I couldn't believe that the inhabitants of Italy, where appreciation of beauty is fed to them with their mother's milk, could not see what they had done to their splendid country.

We stayed with the participants of the conference in a grand hotel overlooking the magnificent city and I was given a crew of three technicians who looked after us like doting Italian mammas. The Sound man even cooked pasta for us every evening knowing we had no money to eat out. As a Spinetti and a Cilento, we were considered to be family.

I tried to pick out the most cogent and radical of the theories presented by the participants while Victor conducted the interviews with great wit and deference. He fell madly in love with Itzhak Bentov, whose book *Stalking the Wild Pendulum* remains a classic to this day. Sadly, Bentov was killed not long afterwards in the 1979 Chicago air crash. I spent many nights talking to Buckminster Fuller. We had one of those instant *sympatico* relationships. The tetrahedron and its role in holding matter together was his credo. Though I loved him dearly, my mind just did not make the leaps needed to embrace his theories.

The thread that ran through everything at this conference was heightened consciousness. The hope was that the human race would somehow evolve to a new and higher level of awareness rather than sink in the opposite direction.

The film, which I called *The Human Race*, starts with a racing commentary but the runners are all concepts that man has formulated since the Big Bang – from Christianity through the Enlightenment, the Age of Reason, Existentialism, Communism, Nihilism, Nazism, Terrorism, Capitalism and all the other 'isms' man has ever come up with. It ends in chaos, with riders being dismounted and nobody knowing which horses are still in the race.

The commentary was written by Bille Brown, my fellow actor from the *Shrew* who had followed us over to the UK and was now staying at Scot's Farm. Victor Spinetti was the perfect linkman/interviewer, playing many different roles but predominantly the universal clown, with his huge Jolly Jack Tar laughing mouth and drooping lollipop eyes. In the film, he's first seen speaking from the pulpit in the Duomo, the famous cathedral of Firenze. He comes out of the great doors into the sunshine and a crowd gathers to find out who this whey-faced loon is.

When Joan Littlewood saw the film, she said of her old friend Buckminster Fuller, 'Poor old sausage. His mouth can't keep up with his mind.' It was true. What he said was marvellous but even I, hearing it hundreds of times in the editing room, could hardly make sense of it. Essentially, his message was that young people had to learn and then aspire to know more and more. He was so passionate that he concluded his galloping speech by staring straight into the lens, challenging anyone to refute him. I left that image of him glaring defiantly at us as his final word was snapped out.

As for Sir George Trevelyan, his clarion call rang out for all the world to hear. 'MAN IS THE MEASURE,' he intoned, speaking of architecture. 'There is no de-materialisation in our constructions. We are building edifices that stand like rocket guns pointing at the heavens.'

Possibly, it was Victor who learned more than anyone on this impromptu trip. He still refers to his life as BF and AF – Before Florence and After Florence. On our return to England, we had to pass through Rome again. It was around the time that Aldo Moro had been kidnapped, and we must have been searched twenty times. I dreaded another arrest. As our plane was cancelled, I found myself lumbered once again with all the undeveloped film, virtually hitchhiking my way back to the UK on an African airline, which was empty because no-one else dared travel on it.

After Tony returned from Egypt, we were able to take up Bulent Rauf's invitation to visit him in Bitez in southern Turkey.

Since Bennett's death, Bulent had taken over our small group at Scot's Farm as mentor and minder. We began to study his translations of the *Fusus al-Hikam*, a repository of Gnostic wisdom greater than any I have ever encountered.

We went to live in a mandarin orchard by the sea. It was spring and to wake up in a fragrant sun-flecked room next to the person you love with the scent of mandarin blossoms in your nostrils is one of the raptures of my life. I walked to our work session, which began at 9 a.m. sharp at Bulent's house. The strongest Turkish coffee I've ever tasted was served in little cups throughout the morning. There were students from all over the world, most of them from the United States and England, who were lively and eager to understand. There was rivalry between the four or five of us who took notes as Bulent translated straight from the page, consulting various commentators who had written treatises on the work in Turkish, Arabic and Persian. One's brain was forced to fire on all cylinders to comprehend the subtleties of the text and the many different inferences that lurked in the juxtaposition of the roots of Arabic words. Their implications were debated with passion and sometimes huge arguments.

At noon we finished, as Bulent said that the intensity of our attention evaporated after three hours. We went off for the rest of the day to jaunt about the countryside, swim, explore, watch camel-drivers washing their animals in the sea, quaff more Turkish coffee, eat luscious lunches and doze in the sun.

It was a splendid way to have a break because there was always a focal point of interest in doing the translations. Holidays can send you into a stupor of boredom unless there's something fascinating to contemplate, so in the evening we re-read our notes and tried to put them into cohesive sentences. The next morning, we compared what we had written and tried to settle on the definitive sentences of the translation. Further arguments ensued but these were mostly constructive and arbitrated by Bulent, who always had the last word.

The Turkish family who owned the house in the orchard where we lived asked us to their home for coffee nearly every day. Their hospitality was bountiful and consisted in the whole extended family of about thirty people sitting around the extremities of a reception room on lush Turkish carpets asking questions, telling family stories, listening avidly and serving an infinite variety of homemade delicacies – soused cumquats, pistachios, olives, dates, goat's cheese and, inevitably, Turkish delight.

We found a fisherman in Bodrum called Saleh Ozturk, who was willing to take us around the Ceramic Coast. He made delicious meals on board with the assistance of a lad of ten, who steered the boat while he was cooking. The sea was empty of other boats and we visited uninhabited islands still bearing traces of theatres, temples and docks. One was covered in small, squirming asps and Saleh told us that this island had been where Cleopatra took her holidays.

We sailed into ancient Knidos, on the west Anatolian coast, where Praxiteles sculpted four hundred years before Christ. There was nothing there except a closed archaeological site and a solitary restaurant on the water. It wasn't actually a restaurant but, if asked, the family who lived there would steam lobsters in seaweed for you. The lobsters were tethered alive on long strings that led into the sea and were pulled in when necessary. I have never tasted anything like that lobster in my life. We were slaves to gluttony and ate two each. When the time came to leave we were both tempted to just buy a little house and settle in. We lingered on but finally family ties prevailed.

Back at Scot's Farm, I could feel a foreign emotion tugging at me. I became fretful and couldn't sleep. I kept thinking that I had forgotten something terribly important that I had to do. Then, besides being irritable, I couldn't eat and spent my time trying to settle to any job that took my mind off whatever it was that was bothering me . . . which remained a mystery.

A word kept coming into my head. It was spelt W-A-S-I-F-A-S. I had no idea where it came from or what it meant. Perhaps it was something I had picked up during the translation. Maybe it was a malady. I wrote to Bulent and asked him what 'wasifas' meant, if anything at all. I told him of my malaise and how I couldn't feel comfortable doing anything at all until I discovered what was prickling me. I hoped he didn't think I was losing my mind.

He wrote back at once, asking me to come and see him as soon as possible. When I got there, he looked into my eyes searchingly. 'I recognise these symptoms. So who's been talking to you?' he asked.

'No-one,' I said truthfully.

'Do you not know what *wasifas* are?'

'I have no idea but they seem to have something to do with why I can find no rest.'

'There are different *wasifas*, particular to the order to which you belong. You are under the umbrella of Muhyiddin Ibn Arabi, whose works you have been engaged in helping to translate. Everyone comes to a place within themselves when it is imperative to go into retreat. You only come out when they are finished.'

'When what are finished?'

'The *wasifas*. It's very difficult. No-one has done them in England before that I know of. Can you spare some time out of your life?'

'Of course,' I said. 'If this is what has been making me feel as though I have lost my skin, I have no choice. I *must* do them.'

'We will help you. Everyone will do *zikhr* for you. You must have "a perfect servant" . . . someone who has already done them and knows what it is like. There are some short verses that you have to learn off by heart. I think it would be best if you do them at Swyre Farm.'

It was arranged that I go to Swyre Farm the next Saturday morning, where I spent the day quietly fasting and meditating to put myself into a collected state to begin the *wasifas* (repetitions). Tony took me down early and I can remember him looking at me as though he was delivering me to some sort of detention centre where I was to serve a sentence for an unknown but serious crime. I felt enormous relief that at last I could do something that would alleviate the gut-gnawing sensations of the past few weeks.

I met Abdullah, a member of the Rifai order of dervishes (the shouting dervishes), who had been sent to Bulent from Jedda. He was to be my 'perfect servant' and the only person with whom I would have any contact until I was finished. He would check up on me once a day to see how I was progressing and speak gently to me if I needed guidance. I was given a *tesbih*, a string of ninety-nine beads made from cedar wood, and a list of instructions of what I had to do.

Throughout the history of Sufism, each great teacher has passed down his special *wasifas* to those who come after him. It is as though he has made a recipe of his own special ingredients, words which are put together in a way that takes the proponent forward each day, led on a journey to what is necessary for him. On this extraordinary journey, the person who dares to travel uncovers what he needs to know about himself and his place in the universe. It is a private initiation and depends on the passion and the will of love.

In practical terms, you have to work very hard, never stopping until exhaustion overtakes the body. Your eyelids fall with fatigue and you just sleep where you are. Waking up means to continue the counting and the words, making sure that you are not skimping or leaving any out. Food is left outside your door but food is foreign to the person on this journey. It does not hold the answer to satisfaction.

The first day I thought it was going to be easy. I felt in control and got through the work without too much trouble. It was on the third day when I was doing the word for life ('*Haï*') that things beyond my control began to happen. With no warning, my eyes began to cascade with tears. I was weeping uncontrollably but still repeating the word for life. Then I saw my father in front of me. He was endeavouring to get out of bed but he could not and he was crying for me to help him, begging with outstretched arms. I didn't know what to do or what he wanted of me. He was covered with a horrible rash and in awful anguish. Somehow, without words, he was imploring me, entreating me to be his mother. In the end, I could do nothing but agree interiorly, and when he was sure that I had said yes inside, he fell backwards in the bed and disappeared.

I was exhausted, and lay on the floor with the reality of the encounter still filling the room and flying around my head. I was deeply shocked. Finally, I roused myself and had a shower before recommencing – but cautiously now, fearful that the power of the word would call forth other disturbing apparitions.

Each day, Abdullah would tap on my door to see where I was up to and how I was coping. Generally, he came late in the afternoon. I thought it best not to tell him about my father. It was on day five that I entered into another dimension. I was diligently working away, counting in rhythms using four or five and then three to break up the pattern, when, without warning, I was back at Sherborne on the morning I had been breakfast cook and Mr B had sent for us to come up to the Meditation Room.

I was perfectly aware that I was sitting on the floor at Swyre Farm doing my *wasifas*, but I was also outside the ballroom at Sherborne House, just letting myself in, having come up from the kitchen. I opened the heavy door and at first it seemed to be exactly as it had been on that morning, but when I looked more carefully I was amazed to see that not all the people present were the same.

I recognised Dick Holland, our history teacher, sitting on a small rattan stool on the other side of the room, but who was the woman dressed in a copper-green long dress that fell in cylindrical folds to the floor? She had an imperious face but great calm and wisdom. And there were many others that I did not recognise. I saw Bulent sitting there next to the imperious woman. I looked at his face and it became young again; his great coffee-coloured, remorseful eyes were luminous and the tumbling curls over his forehead nearly made me laugh. I saw Mrs Bennett, who was sitting near the piano, and she too became vibrantly young and beautiful.

I looked to the place where Mr B sat at the top of the room and there he was, just like on that other morning. He was talking but it was as though the sound had been turned down. There was something peculiarly false about him. As I watched, something flew out of him very fast, as though it was attached to a long piece of springy elastic, and disappeared past me. When I looked again, he had become a sepia drawing by da Vinci. I could see through him and he was beautiful, the essence of himself, pure and unadulterated. Whatever had been ersatz about him had been wrenched away and I noticed for the first time that the whole central area of the room was taken up with light-filled, kneeling beings facing away from me. I heard them murmuring, 'Yes, yes, he can come,' which was like the sighing of the breeze in the trees.

In the room at Swyre Farm, I continued repeating the particular word for as long as I could manage but it became too overpowering. I stopped and there was silence. I knew that I had been in two places at once and in two separate time slots. I had witnessed that time and space are illusions, that they do not exist in any other dimension outside this material one. The special morning that I had been reliving was the morning I had asked Bennett who it was that I had seen in my vision of the night before. He had said, 'You'll find out, you'll find out' – but I never had. With this revelation concerning time and space, I was sure that I would.

I think I went to sleep straightaway on the floor because, at daybreak, I was up. For the first time since entering the *wasifa* world, I looked out at the garden and the trees and, as it was very early, I decided to go for a walk.

It is important not to have human contact during the time of the *wasifas*, except with your perfect servant, who is careful not to interrupt or divert you from your journey. That morning it seemed that I was seeing everything around me as I had never seen it before, as though there was nothing that got in the way of our communing. I met an old farm horse down by a gate and was astounded at our encounter. It was like meeting an old friend. I returned to my room buoyant and full of exaggerated plans. I would learn sacred calligraphy; I would go to the source of the Blue Nile; I would visit the tomb of Muhyiddin Ibn Arabi in Damascus; I would keep hundreds of old horses and nurture them until they died. Of course, I did none of these things – except one.

For the remainder of the *wasifas*, on days seven and eight, I was forced to use a falsetto voice as my normal one had gone. In anticipation of Bulent's return, they were mowing the lawn outside my window and the noise was sending me crazy. On the last day, when I was nearing fulfilment, my *tesbih* broke, scattering the little cedar balls all over the carpet. It wasn't two minutes later that I heard the familiar tap on my door and there was Abdullah. I opened my mouth to tell him what had happened but he knew and was already picking up the beads and counting them to see if it was an auspicious number.

'You know, I am not far away and I heard you stop. I guessed what it was. It's not magic,' he assured me.

The day I finished, eight days after I had begun, Bulent arrived back from a short trip to Turkey and I was bursting with impatience to tell him everything. Of course, I had to wait in a ferment of emotional overload, going over my days again and again, trying to make sense of it all. When it was time for me to speak, a group of those near to Bulent, including Abdullah, met and I sat amongst them. It was what I imagine a military debriefing must be like. They asked me questions and I found it hard to repeat some passages without being overcome by feelings. I had to be objective and lucid. At the end, they embraced me and seemed extremely pleased, though no-one offered any explanations. It was for me to work it out. But having spoken, and been listened to, I felt as though I had been unburdened of baggage that had been weighing me down for years. I was as light as air and felt like prancing about and singing. Tony came to pick me up, expecting that I'd be exhausted but I was not. I was full of pleasure and ready for whatever life was about to present me.

CHAPTER FIFTEEN

*T*he land I'd bought in Australia kept haunting my dreams. A plan
for its use and development began to emerge from amongst the
morass of possibilities. I introduced the concept to Bulent of establish-
ing a school that would be a fusion of Bennett's ideas about future
communities and the methods to obtain greater spiritual awareness as
practised by Sufis. In fact, they were no different, except in the empha-
sis placed on study in Bulent's tradition and on meditational practices
and the Enneagram in Mr B's discipline. I thought that if I went on a
lecture tour showing the film *Turning* with the Florence documentary,
The Human Race, we could attract people who would be interested in
such ideas.

Bulent was surrounded by a group of dedicated people, some of
whom had been at Sherborne with me. They worked at Swyre Farm
but had also secured tenure of a glorious old wreck called Chisholme
House, which had been standing abandoned in about seventeen acres
of valleys and dales near Roberton in Scotland. The Chisholme group
had been beavering away on the building and outhouses for some years,
and by the end of the seventies there was a grand main house, now
habitable, with rooms for at least twenty people. There were also many ·
small cottages and a gatehouse for the regulars who lived there full
time. The whole place was, and still is, called Beshara.

It was decided that Hugh Tollemarsh, one of Bulent's closest students, would accompany me on a lecture tour of Australia and New Zealand, and that we would gather a group of people who would come early to FNQ for the first course to help prepare the place to open in April 1977. Bulent himself, who would be on a round-the-world trip at that time, would come and open the new school and stay for three weeks.

Tony and I mutually decided to call the place in FNQ 'Karnak'. The name was just right. Karnak is the spaceship that carries Beelzebub all over the universe in Gurdjieff's *All and Everything*. Tony also called the fatal paddle steamer in *Death on the Nile* the *Karnak* and we had recently read the history of ancient Thebes where Karnak, the Temple of Light, existed in its full potency some three thousand years ago. According to Herodotus, 250 different crafts were taught within those walls, including mirror gazing and dream interpretation, both respected professions of the time. The name kept presenting itself to us as though it had a will of its own.

My mum and dad came to our first lecture in Brisbane, after which my dad presented me with an old compass set he had used in his youth. He told me he had taken it on all his trips to New Guinea. My mother, although sceptical about the idea of what we were planning, was particularly attracted to the dark classic features of Hugh Tollemarsh, who was the epitome of everything she favoured in a man – serious, shy but commanding and, above all, good-looking. Had she been thirty years younger, she would have thrown herself at his feet. As it was, she followed us to Sydney and stayed at the same hotel, her old haunt, the Sebel Town House.

On the night of our lecture, she had the management prepare a supper of two dozen oysters each, followed by a cold collation of roast duck and salad, in a private dining room. She came in to see that all was perfect, recited a few of her favourite poems by Wordsworth to impress Tollemarsh, and left us to it, secretly hoping that after such an arousing repast we would fall into each other's arms and become engaged by the next morning. She was basically a romantic woman, for all her practicality, and had always disapproved of Tony, as she knew he was a married man. Of course, no such thing happened and we completed the tour. Tolle went back to England, having talked to many young people, some of whom would turn up at Chisholme over the years.

I brought Michael Pall over from Scot's Farm to be the designer of the verandahs we were going to build around the original house at Karnak. A blond Viennese boy with the face of a Renaissance angel, Michael had arrived at Scot's Farm one day on a huge black motorcycle, dressed entirely in black leather, with an Argentinean girl called Gloria on the back of the machine. They had just returned from an exploratory trip around India and were heartily sick of each other and ready to find something other than sex or guru-oriented enlightenment. Luckily for us, Gloria turned out to be an excellent coffee maker and Michael was a wizard carpenter.

I bought a long-wheelbase Land Cruiser that looked like a World War I ambulance and we began to load it from my mother's house on the river at Toowong. We knew we were starting from scratch in the rainforest, so just about everything imaginable went onto the back of that truck. We accepted any junk my mother was about to throw out. It went onto the truck and was battened down tight.

Bill Phillips, the young dancer/actor who played Biondello in *The Taming of the Shrew*, was coming with us. Since the play had finished, he had been in the UK doing a course at Sherborne with Giovanna. The last member of our expedition was my niece Miranda (Mandy), daughter of my brother Carl. She was a tall, gorgeous gazelle with reddish-brown hair and the wide eyes of a child. She was primed for adventure but was as even-tempered and smooth as I was volatile.

After spending three days on the road, we arrived at Cairns in the tropical north on a torrid and humid January evening, during what is called 'the build-up', prelude to the Wet. Basically, it is the season when the humidity builds up until it bursts and the Monsoonal Trough descends from New Guinea, bringing rains that sheet down so hard you can hardly see the hand in front of your face.

We debated whether or not to stay in Cairns for the night but finally decided that, as we were so near, we would press on. We reached Mossman by 9 p.m., where we were given directions to stay on the road to the Daintree and then keep turning left. By ten, we knew we were thoroughly lost and there were no lights showing from the few houses we passed. At last we stopped at a house where the faint glimmer of a TV screen was visible in one of the rooms. We banged on the door and a surly red-haired man answered. We asked him the way to Boulder Farm, as Karnak was formerly known locally. He screwed up his eyes and scrutinised me.

'You wouldn't be that fillum star who's supposed to have bought that dump, are you?'

'Yes, I think that might be me.'

'Aw, well,' he mused and then yelled, 'hey, kids! Come on, we're goin' to show the fillum star where she lives!'

Ken and his kids escorted us to the little house at Karnak, which was palely lit by a hoary moon when we pulled up. We had hurricane lamps in case we couldn't find the electricity but Ken leapt out of his 4WD in a flash, and was round the side of the house and had us switched on before we could blink. A thousand twittering bats swept out of the house and up into the sky the moment the lights came on. After thanking Ken, we sent him on his way with a few tinnies. We had arrived.

We put down a groundsheet on the floor of the main room and, exhausted, crashed out. The first thing we saw when we awoke the next morning was several rows of frogs' bottoms above our heads, all lined up on the glass louvres. They seemed to be bombarding us with frog poo as a counterattack for our invasion of their space.

It was hard to convince the bats too that this was not their house. For weeks, they kept coming back, hanging themselves up from every nook and cranny in the roof. This room, which we later painted blue, became (and still is) the Meditation Room.

The plans for our verandahs having been passed by the building inspector, a Mr Parsons, we spent the next three months labouring to get them built. We had to dig ninety-nine holes for posts and put in showers and loos so we didn't have to step outside and brave torrential rain. The post-holes filled with water and hundreds of noisy cane toads took up residence in them. They made a great racket, not realising their fate, which was to be built over. The little old house became three times its original size, the width of every verandah being four metres. We called it the Ritz.

The trick of working long hours in the tropics during 'the build-up' season is to have a handy creek running off a high mountain right there where you are sweating the days away. At regular intervals, you totter off to the creek, throw yourself in, wallow for some time and only emerge after your skin has cooled down to goose-bump temperature in the icy water. For twenty minutes thereafter, you are able to continue work in self-generated air-conditioning with the refreshing residue of water drying on your near-naked body. It's a special feeling.

We meditated together, ate hundreds of bananas (because we couldn't stop to cook) and fell to the floor every night as though we had been shot. There was a brief interlude when Michael Pall fell madly in love with Miranda and chased her around for a few days. Bill and I let them get on with it. When the madness had abated somewhat, it was back to the building trade. By the time the roof was going up, several of our future students had arrived and were rushing about trying to help, but mostly they got in the way.

I bought some double-decker bunk beds to put under the first bit of the verandah that had a roof and the house began to fill up with hungry mouths. The most pressing necessity was to buy a very large fridge. There was an old tractor with a slasher in the shed, which came with the property, so we were able to slash a wide swath through the guinea grass down to the creek for bathing. There was no time to do anything but struggle to finish the roof and the loos before the seventeen students, plus Bulent and his student Kamil Dupre, arrived. It was a marathon feat and undoubtedly the hardest I've ever worked physically in my entire life.

On the great day when the roof went on, we had a celebration. Max and Diana Bowden drove in from Port and Mr Ponzo, the cane farmer from down the road, brought his family. Just as we were toasting our magnificent structure, the skies opened and buckets of rain fell straight through a triangle of unfinished roof, in exactly the place where all the guests were standing. Everyone ducked for cover amid much mirth about our abilities as builders.

I have gauged over my time in the tropics that it takes at least a year to get over the initial fear of snakes, spiders and other creepy-crawlies that abound there. To become accustomed to the fact that it is *their* place too, and to cease feeling spooked every time you step off the verandah, is a sign that you are becoming a local.

I didn't know until later that a lot of money changed hands in bets in the local pubs concerning how long I would stay at Karnak. The Murdoch press had announced that I'd started a nudist colony in the Daintree and various documentary makers turned up to try to get a slant on what we were actually doing there. Because there was no pigeon-hole that the media could fit us into, and nothing sensational enough to generate the kind of copy that sells newspapers, they insinuated many things. It was widely believed that we were into the dope-growing business, or preparing to be, but it wasn't until our second year there that the police raided us. Rumours abounded and it wasn't long before we began to feel the backlash of being outsiders.

It started with the building inspector, Mr Parsons. He arrived one wet morning to inspect our verandahs and announced almost immediately that we would have to take them all down as soon as possible.

'Why?' I demanded.

'Because they are not two feet off the ground,' he informed me.

'Is that the *only* reason?' I asked.

415

'Yes. That's the law . . . two feet off the ground. Yours are only one and a half feet, maybe less. You'll have to take them all down by next week. I shall return then and expect to find all this dismantled.'

As soon as he left, we got to work with wheelbarrows and shovels, wearing sacks over our heads as we had to crawl under the house. With two teams working full time, we dug for days, taking turns: one person under the house to dig out the first layer of dirt, one to push the dirt back to the person waiting to shovel it into the wheelbarrow, and then the fourth member of the team to take it away to use as fill for our future front lawn. By the time Mr Parsons came back, we had dug out the whole house to be two feet off the ground. Triumphantly, we measured it for him to see. He was flabbergasted.

'How did you get these people to do that?'

'It's a question of us having somewhere to live, Mr Parsons,' I replied.

'Well,' he added outraged, 'you people can't live like this!'

'Why not?'

'You've got no privacy, that's why not! It's not right,' he announced, pointing to the road in the distance.

'But that road is miles away, Mr Parsons.'

'Yes, but people have got binoculars, you know!'

We left it at that and he stomped off angrily, to be known ever afterwards by the locals as Dug-out Parsons.

Bulent had asked me to select one of his students to come to be a supervisor at Karnak, someone who could hold the fort when I had to go back to the UK to work. I chose a young but exceedingly trustworthy man, Samadi Temple, whom I had been watching at Chisholme every time I went there. He was a slim boy with penetrating dark eyes and a quiet temperament that belied his youth. He also had an instinctive love of the land and no fears about facing hardships.

Bulent arrived from Tahiti in a sarong and broad straw hat like a character straight out of a Somerset Maugham short story. Because of

416

his bad hip, we carried him into the rainforest and up to the hidden lagoon where he swooned with pleasure at the sparkling waters, the blue Ulysses butterflies, the native orchids, the herringbone ferns up the trees and the shy white-tailed paradise kingfishers skimming the surface of the pool.

I took him to Mossman one morning in my second-hand Mini Moke with the fringe on top. Bulent weighed his side of the small vehicle down to the ground as he waved his hat to the Aboriginal children under the giant rain trees on the outskirts of Mossman.

'I know you! I know you!' they shouted as they ran beside the little car. 'You come from Adelaide . . . I seen you in Adelaide!'

'Never been there!' Bulent sang out.

'Yes, but we *know* you, Mister,' the voices called after us. 'We *knoooow yoooou!*'

When I took Bulent in to Port to sample Bill Austen's cooking at the Nautilus restaurant, Maxie Bowden came up to the table to have a drink and meet Bulent. With a shout of surprise, Bulent rose from his chair and enfolded the small Max in an embrace that obscured him completely.

'Max, is it you?' he cried.

'Good God! Good God! Bulent! Oh my God, I haven't seen you since . . . '44 . . . in Cairo. What are you doing here? How did you get here . . . and with this wicked girl?'

Maxie appeared shaken, beside himself, with tears in his eyes. He sat down and the two old friends went into a huddle, reminiscing for the rest of the evening. Bulent told me later that Max had been known throughout Cairo as a spy master who had contacts and networks all over the Middle East.

'I worked with him for a time,' Bulent said slowly. 'He was a very feared man there. This must be the perfect place for old spies to come and have their stings removed. Australia . . . it is hard to become impassioned about a cause in Australia. The idea would be subsumed and become inconsequential in this Never-Never land.'

I understood what he meant but that was for someone else to say, not for me. Australia, I knew, was the greatest challenge of my life.

The course was under way in earnest. Bill Phillips was a master at teaching Movements, Samadi had started study on the *Fusus al-Hikam*, and the students were occupied in every aspect of the Work, and planting trees and gardens. Meanwhile, I went back to Scot's Farm and Tony. For the next four years, Tony and I became the most consistent long-distance commuters in the world – covering the twelve thousand miles from Wiltshire to Whyanbeel and then back again so many times I hate to count.

It must be admitted that since the fateful day I picked up that book *In Search of the Miraculous* from the floor of the SAS hotel in Copenhagen, my life had changed radically. I had become less interested in playing an acting role unless it presented a major challenge. I was much more interested in the overview of the play or movie I was in – the other side of the camera, if you like. My stint at directing had whetted my appetite for having the whole vision, not just a partial view. I also had less interest in living a vicarious life, as actors often do. The actor's adventure lies in uncovering the part and using his own physical attributes to hone it into a creative exactitude – but he cannot afford to *live* it. When an actor becomes so identified with a role, he can often feel forced to act out the illusion in public so as not to disappoint his fans. Sometimes, the mask gets stuck so firmly that he cannot remember who he is underneath it. He cannot wrench it off, even in bed at night.

I was now intent on jettisoning all that was phony from my life, discovering the real thing and living it. I had tasted the poison, as the Sufis say. How could I accept anything less? The world was my oyster and it was up to me how I carved out the rest of my existence. I had freedom of choice, through my own volition, to expend my energy on furthering my acting career or making a pioneer experiment in the jungle of FNQ – whatever my intuition told me was right. I was determined to follow the inclinations of my secret heart, but money is always helpful.

I could not refuse the next part I was offered. It was in the 1978 British TV series *Tycoon*, and I was to play the lead, Diana Clark, the recent widow of the richest man in the world who'd inherited all his loot. It was a nice idea but a pity that the company producing the series was so skint they could hardly afford any production values at all. The richest woman in the world doesn't wear the same suit every day unless she's an eccentric.

What I remember most about *Tycoon* is that I had to spend a lot of time in Birmingham. I had worked for the director/producer, John Sichel, once before, in an episode of the *Thriller* series when I'd relished playing a 400-year-old witch in *Spell of Evil*. At the end of this tale of horror I was burnt up in a great fire, reverting to my ghastly witch persona to show my true age as I frizzled and fried. For this scene, four or five replicas of the 400-year-old me were made in case they didn't get it right on the first take. As there was one of these monstrosities left when the shoot was over, I asked if I might take it home with me, just to remind myself of what was in store for me in the future. I put it in the passenger seat of the car and drove off. When I was stopped for speeding on the M1, the police were horrified to see the witch sitting in the front seat, looking all of her four hundred years. They thought they might have a grisly murder on their hands. I kept her at the front door at Scot's Farm for years, where she was revered by many and dressed in new hats quite often.

After the wrap of every episode of *Tycoon*, I was driven home to Wiltshire by the delectable Christopher Gable, the dancer/actor who played my son. He always put on tapes of Maria Callas, from her early days, and I came to long for these drowsy journeys home with the honey sounds of that sublime voice soothing my soul. One night we arrived at Scot's Farm at about 1 a.m., to find that Tony had arranged an extraordinary dinner party with a salmon trout so big we had to leave the door of the Aga open to cook it. Once I'd got my second wind, we all raved on until dawn and then all went for a walk rather tipsily right around the property, greeting the cows and the sun, followed by Jason's Jack Russell, Pippin, who just loved to party.

Tony was embroiled with his plays *Widows Weeds* and *Whodunnit* both in the UK and Australia at this time. We were on the move continuously – a whirl of theatres, rehearsals, airports, slashing on the tractor, battening down for a cyclone, starry nights, study periods, Glastonbury to see my children, backstage at more theatres, opening nights, restaurants, champagne and more theatres . . . but not much definition.

I can recall that Margaret Thatcher entered our lives around this time. I met a man at one of Lady Edith Foxwell's Sunday lunches who came from Tetbury and had taught Mrs Thatcher to speak in that distinctive low-pitched drawl that became so imitated. He played us some hilarious tapes of her lessons and we all had a good laugh. It wasn't long before we didn't think that she was such a joke.

Bille Brown had written a play called *Tuffff*, which I directed at the Royal Court Upstairs. It's an endearing short play about three boys in Queensland and the angst of adolescent Australians in a battle of brain, brawn and the denial of emotions.

My nephew, Raphael, calling himself Raphael West, played the surfer. It received fabulous reviews and Raphael was besieged at the stage door every night by armies of gays. We got no offers of a transfer to the West End.

From directing *Tuffff*, I segued into playing the mother in Strindberg's *The Father* with Denholm Elliot at the Open Space Theatre. This was Charles Marowitz's swan song in his beloved theatre and the production received raves. Sean brought Jason to see it and they sat in the front row of the theatre-in-the-round space. It was disconcerting to be acting in a space where you could reach out and touch your son or your ex, so close is the contact with the audience. It didn't make it any easier that I was playing one of the ultimate bitches in theatrical history.

Joan Littlewood, whom I had known, revered and loved for years, came to see the production and made me an astounding offer after the show. Although I knew she had sworn never to work in the theatre again, I thought she was going to invite me to play a part in something she was contemplating directing. Instead, she asked me whether I'd like to direct the first production in the newly refurbished Theatre Royal Stratford East. This landmark British theatre was situated in the East End, where Joan had re-invigorated British theatre with such plays as *The Hostage, A Taste of Honey* and *Oh! What a Lovely War*.

In hindsight, I think Joan (who was a genius not only as a director but in stirring with a large spoon and then sitting back to enjoy the chaos she had created) chose me partly to infuriate Phillip Hedley, the new director of Stratford. She didn't think much of him and he had publicly called her 'a ragamuffin' and 'a nuisance'. Joan gave me some plays to read and suggested a melodrama by Dion Boucicault. I was thrilled, and selected *The Streets of London*. She also offered me her house in the East End to live in for the rehearsal period.

With only £3500 to mount the whole production, it was going to be a matter of tightrope walking and perseverance, with a large lump of luck. I found Hayden Griffin, my idea of the best set designer in the world, at the bar at the National Theatre, where he was having a pint with his mate, the ace lighting man Andy Phillips. With no further ado, I threw myself at their mercy and beseeched them to work on the show.

I flashed a challenge in front of their eyes – to make a fire onstage that would rival the spectacular scene created way back in the 1850s when Boucicault first produced the play in New York. Boucicault, an ingenious innovator, had devised a huge hand-operated roller which, when effectively lit and spun, cast the phosphorescent flames painted on it higher and higher. With some smoke and sound effects thrown in, it created the impression of a mighty conflagration, which always made the audience cheer. The production was so successful that Boucicault toured it all over the world for years, changing the title to correspond to each new place he went to so that it became *The Streets of London* in London, *The Streets of San Francisco* in San Francisco, and so on.

To save money, I thought that the scenes could be played bare stage against a series of Gustave Doré backdrops of Victoriana. Hayden and Andy succumbed to my entreaties and I was delighted to have such talent on hand. The whole look and feel of the show would have been impossible without their input. The actors who were attracted to the play were also perfect for their parts and a gang of the most talented thesps of them all – the East End kids – played the street urchins.

I'd decided I couldn't continue my affair with Tony. He demanded that I continuously match him in his drinking, smoking and carousing, which had increased big time. I had no intention of damaging my body, addling my brain and impeding my ability to meditate. I had begun to feel that we were embarked on a roller-coaster ride to mutual destruction unless there was time out to recover from the intensity of our relationship. I refused to see him at all while I was working on *The Streets of London*, so he laid siege to Joan's house, sometimes sitting in his car outside until dawn.

As the opening night of *The Streets of London* drew nearer, I hardly ever left the theatre. It's so different being a director. You have to hold a completely different set of priorities in your head, and after the curtain has gone up on that first night there's nothing you can do except walk up and down, gnawing your nails, hoping nothing disastrous will happen.

It was the audience that made *Streets* take off like a rocket. Very early on, they got the message and joined in to the max, hissing the villain, cheering the hero and loving every second of the dastardly plot in which members of a family become parted from each other in the big bad city and are ripped off unmercifully by a wicked landlord. The plot was very timely in its exposure of what happens when the threat of bankruptcy or war drives the price of gold sky-high overnight.

The first night was just amazing. When the great fire was reproduced by Hayden and Andy, the audience rose to their feet stamping and whistling. We had not foreseen that it could provoke such a reaction. We received a standing ovation and the cheering went on for what seemed like forever.

Tony came and was crying with delight. Victor Spinetti and Joan Littlewood were overwhelmed, saying it felt like old times. Jason was given his first toke of Mary Jane. He tells me that I passed out with exhaustion after a few glasses of champagne, and boasts that he drove me all the way back to Scot's Farm that night (being only fifteen at the time), but I cannot remember any of this because, as he says, I had passed out. Needless to say, next morning I found Tony in bed beside me.

I knew the play was a veritable hit when all the East End bad lads came and asked me whether there was anyone I'd like them to do over and *Punch* magazine published the plaudit 'The best thing to have happened in the theatre for a very long time!' It doesn't get any better than that on the streets of London.

It is my observation that if everything seems to be going wonderfully well, fate is about to do a volte-face and double-cross you. And so it was following our phenomenal success. After a packed run at Stratford East, *The Streets of London* was transferred to the West End – to Her Majesty's Theatre, no less. But how could Phillip Hedley (who had been made the Director of Stratford East) allow the new theatre's first success to transfer to the West End with another director in command? He could not and he did not. Just before the opening, I was sacked. Hayden and Andy were outraged . . . and so was I. I didn't attend the first night at Her Majesty's but I heard that, for the first time, the great fire roller apparatus broke down and nothing happened – no fire, no audience cheers. The most spectacular scene in the musical was a fizzer.

The experience left me questioning the validity of theatre and my place in it. I went to stay with Joan in Paris to lick my wounds. She lived in the servant's quarters upstairs in the house of Baron Philippe de Rothschild. This grandiose mansion overlooked the Paris morgue and we had long talks into the night, watching from the kitchen window while they brought in a steady stream of bodies.

Joan was cheerfully cynical and utterly down-to-earth – a valid iconoclast, a ruthless martinet in the theatre but, in the context of all that, sublimely romantic. Paradoxically, she was tough and level-headed, a good woman to know, as Baron Philippe was well aware. Within two minutes of meeting any attractive woman, Baron Philippe was wont to try to stick his tongue down her throat. He didn't have to make any of these token gestures with Joan. She lived at the Albany sometimes, his smart London pad, or at his chateau in the south of France. He kept her near him as a sort of stimulant and court jester. There was always something happening around Joan and she introduced him to the people he wanted to meet. I loved the way she passed out his Mouton Rothschild as though it was Spanish plonk.

She was a rover, Joan. Once she came to stay with me at Scot's Farm and brought a whole family of French gypsies with her who cooked continuously. We never got into the kitchen while they were there but they produced such lovely aromas and tastes of Provence that it wasn't too much of an imposition.

On the other side of the world, at Karnak, we were building a new house. It was called the Palace and cost all of five thousand dollars, plus a massive amount of labour. We located it at right angles to the Ritz, the main house, a hundred metres away from it in front of an enormous black bean tree, on the site of an old cattle loader which had been infested with snakes.

It all came about because they pulled down the Mowbray River Bridge. It was the habit of the Douglas Shire Council in those days to leave discarded timber on the side of the road for scavengers to pick up and take to their backyards, where it made a pleasant home for reptiles of all sorts until it mouldered away. The timber we collected from the Mowbray River Bridge was weathered like steel, and so it became the framework of the Palace. Michael Pall was again the designer. We hired a two-ton truck and went out every morning before dawn to collect slate from the Mowbray riverbed for the floor. A Yugoslavian called Boris showed us how to build an open fireplace of stone and we put solar panels on the roof to heat the water. It had a lot of rooms for students, as we were expecting quite a few for the commencement of our third course.

Not long before this course commenced, Maxie Bowden rang me in an agitated state, saying the bank was going to foreclose on him unless he found fifty thousand dollars and couldn't I persuade Tony to buy the Nautilus restaurant. I told him to speak to Tony himself. Tony was canny and played footsie with poor old Max for a while but before long he became the proud possessor of a run-down restaurant in Port Douglas, which he nicknamed the Naughty Lass.

All his life, Tony had craved to own two things: his very own vineyard and a smart restaurant where he could play mine host and drink as much as he liked without being thrown out. With great vigour, he set about turning the Nautilus into a smart restaurant. The vineyard would have to wait.

We decided to build a proper terrace using pink bricks, spiralling in the shape of a nautilus shell. This was shaded and surrounded guests as they dined, with an array of Alexander palms and coconuts creating a sort of green cathedral. Tony discovered a man who knew about bricks and design, so everybody from Karnak (all fifteen of us) came to learn how to create the Nautilus terrace – throwing and placing bricks with precision until we could have robbed any safe in the land, so sandpapered were our fingers.

Tony stocked the bar with a very special wine list selected by himself. We found a genius chef in the person of Jenny Watling, who loved making chocolate nautiluses, and Joh Bjelke-Petersen, Premier of Queensland, opened the dream place with fanfares of trumpets. Port Douglas was still a forgotten little backwater in the early 1980s, so it was quite a shock for the locals to have a jet-set fantasy food restaurant in their midst. After the first flush, they stayed away in droves. But it was impossible for even the most insensitive to ignore the uniqueness of its location, the splendour of our food, the rainforest and the Great Barrier Reef glittering in the distance. Slowly but surely, by word of mouth mostly, we became 'the only place to go'.

Tony's background in advertising stood him in good stead and every week we put an ad on the radio. He took great care in writing the material. Basically, the idea was simple: everyone in the world fancies having some dish that is their speciality, the dish they make whenever they want to show off their culinary skills, and our Sunday Brunches gave anyone in the district the chance to have a go. Tony kicked off the proceedings with Pommy Day, for which he ordered an abundance of beef on the bone from Toowoomba and cut huge slices for everybody, served with homemade horseradish and wicked potatoes (each packing about eight hundred calories), another of his specialities.

The rules were that we would buy all the ingredients to make the dish and would assist in any way to make the meal spectacular. Each protagonist would advertise on the radio with an ad, which Tony wrote specifically for them, and they could invite up to four guests to the brunch gratis.

Once the word was out, we had French Red Letter Day, Dago Day, Indian Summer, My Mother's Moussaka Day – and there were queues around the block every Sunday. I'm not sure whether the motives for coming to taste your worst enemy's or best friend's cooking were valid but everyone came. These lunches lasted well into the evening and we had to be very careful that Deadly Dave, the only policeman in Port, was not lurking in the heliconia bushes waiting to catch us serving drinks after hours.

It didn't take very long for the Nautilus to be voted Best Restaurant in Queensland, second to the Melbourne restaurant that won Best in Australia. It also didn't take long before there were some beady eyes swivelling in a northerly direction, noting the success.

Wily old Joh Bjelke-Petersen, who surrounded himself with a bunch of cronies, had been in power ever since anyone could remember. Joh introduced a state law at this time abolishing death duties, which brought about an immediate rush of settlers from the south into Queensland – people who quickly recognised the sense in passing on their hard-earned capital to their children and not to the Government.

There was such an exodus from other states that laws had to be revised to halt the flow to the North. Wave after wave of speculators swept in from Sydney and Melbourne, and to give the economy a bit of a shove, Joh offered land to any consortium prepared to build a five-star resort in FNQ. One company, Qintex, run by the young entrepreneur Christopher Skase, stepped in to claim eight hundred acres of absolute beachfront on Four Mile Beach in Port Douglas. Here, Skase built five acres of swimming pool dovetailing into the apartments, an eighteen-hole golf course and a resort that was a replica of roll-out Southern Californian glitz. He called it the Mirage. The rest of the land was allotted to million-dollar houses, which Skase offered to Elizabeth Taylor, George Hamilton and as many Hollywood stars as he could remember. It had taken less than ten years to turn the poor, forsaken, sandfly-ridden little backwater into the hottest real estate in Australia.

The success of the Nautilus had cemented Tony's presence in Australia. Now also a landholder, he began to take an active interest in local politics and the future of Port Douglas as a tourist destination. At Karnak our burgeoning population needed more housing, so when a man named Dick Francis told me he owned a former cane brothel on Syndicate Road and wanted to get it off his property, I jumped at the chance. He sold it to me for two hundred dollars if I agreed to remove it as soon as possible.

The logistics of transporting a whole house across the countryside and over some flimsy little bridges built in the 1880s are tricky to say the least. Though it wasn't far from Syndicate Road to Karnak, there were three bridges to negotiate and the planning had to be meticulously timed so that no neighbours would be inconvenienced. After much hassle with the council and contractors, the house was transported in the dead of night down to the chosen site, where it was raised eleven feet into the air and settled on stilts like a good Queenslander should be. We then built verandahs all the way around it, like the Ritz, but this time there was no digging out under the house required.

To differentiate it from the other houses, we called it the Chateau. To celebrate, Tony and I bought a big brass bed, which we placed in a small bedroom off the back verandah where we could watch the sun come up in the morning. The fact that the house wobbled slightly when you walked from one side of it to the other was rather disconcerting at first but was soon remedied by building parts in underneath. We again collected slate for the floor and put in a big bathroom with showers and loos, as well as several rooms for students and guests. Every house on the property was autonomous, with its own kitchen, but the cutlery and saucepans seemed to march around between houses of their own volition.

Tony went back to London several weeks before I did so that he could go to the fat farm and become 'trim, taut and terrific'. He didn't tell me of his plan to meet me at the airport looking very Giorgio Armani, wearing a new white suit with waistcoat, and then sweep me off to the Ritz, where he had booked a suite on the top floor overlooking Green Park.

I stopped at Perth on my journey out of Australia, only to be arrested for carrying a large sum of loose currency out of the country

428

(not in traveller's cheques). It was one of Mrs Thatcher's new edicts. I was taken off the plane but the police were very kind, putting me in the Hilton Hotel instead of the lockup. They even gave me a sightseeing tour of the hills behind the city. However, in London, Tony was in a lather because, although listed, I didn't arrive on the plane from Australia. Convinced I'd been kidnapped, he alerted the Qantas authorities, demanding an explanation. He was doubly infuriated when he heard I had been arrested, haranguing the airline officials and the Perth police in turn.

At last, I was released after buying traveller's cheques and there was Tony at the airport resplendent in white, doing his old trick of pretending not to see me until the last minute and parading his new finery topped off with a Panama hat. The luxury of satin sheets and breakfast in bed at the Ritz was the best antidote to the rigours of life in the jungle and being arrested by the police yet again.

What was becoming more apparent to me every day was that very soon a decision had to be made: I had to choose whether to put all my energy into Karnak and Australia or to withdraw from the Antipodes altogether and continue to expand Scot's Farm. I knew that to try to keep both of these places going at once was crazy. Both would end up failing.

At Sherborne, Mr Bennett had instilled in us the notion that it is imperative to watch for 'omens and portents'. Doors open and doors close in one's life constantly and it's stupid not to be watchful and intervene before a door slams shut in your face. What ultimately hardened my resolve to sell Scot's Farm and throw all my weight into Karnak was a series of 'accidents'.

The Turkish Government had been very pleased with the Whirling Dervish film *Turning*, showing it as after-dinner entertainment in their embassies around the world. Therefore, they were quite happy to sponsor me again to return to Turkey to shoot another film, a sequel to the first which I hoped to call *Learning*. The plan was to get a crew together and accompany Bulent and a group of his students through the length of Turkey, following the ancient Silk Route to the border, meeting Gnostics of different dervish orders, visiting the shrines of various saints and following the silk routes of the traders.

There is an old Sufi saying that says, 'Seek knowledge, even until China'. Like many of these obscure words of wisdom, it has a hidden meaning that bears explanation. The Silk Route ends in China, where the traveller/trader's destination lies. The word 'silk' has the same root in Arabic as the word '*salik*', meaning 'seeker of knowledge'. The seeker holds on to the golden thread, the teaching, and follows it as far as it will go, to his destination, China. All the way, he is acquiring knowledge. That is more or less the underlying meaning of the saying.

We arrived in Istanbul filled with aspirations of making an unforgettable film. Bulent was not so sure about being the linkman for the interviews, as he had just come through the experience of being the protagonist in a bestseller. One of his ex-students, Reshad Field, had written a book entitled *The Last Barrier* about his spiritual journey and dealings with Bulent, his teacher, whom he called Hamid.

Bulent said he didn't wish to be exposed any more but I brushed aside his qualms and set up the camera on the banks of the Bosphorus, looking up at the great hanging bridge that connects Europe and Asia. In the foreground, Bulent was talking to Ahmed Becan, the dance master of the Whirling Dervishes, who had entered a *tekke* (Sufi school) at the age of twelve. Bulent was questioning him about the teaching he had received before Atatürk had banned the schools. It was a great set-up.

The light was unnaturally bright, almost silver, coming out from behind a fleecy cloud, and then suddenly, with no warning, pelting rain came slashing down and drove us for cover. As we hurried to free the camera from its tripod, it was dropped on the slippery marble terrace and damaged beyond repair. To compound our woes, the next day there was a military coup and the government changed. People were running hither and thither and I saw a boy soldier dart through the railway station holding a Kalashnikov spitting bullets in one hand while dragging a shopping trolley with the other. A curfew was imposed and bands of soldiers marched through the streets with lanterns all night, on the lookout for anyone out after 9 p.m. I was itching to film the whole thing.

Of course, we tried to get another camera. We even had one sent out from London. I went to the airport and stood at the counter for three hours, begging to be allowed to take possession of it. I could have reached out and touched it but they were adamant: $200000 or no camera. I knew exactly how Tantalus felt. Now that there was a new set of officials in power, we had no leverage, no free transport and a film crew with long faces who had to be content with just going along for the ride. There is nothing more pathetic than a film crew without a camera.

All the way around Turkey, as we visited secret underground spa baths and caves where different sects of dervishes held their meetings, I was shooting the film in my head. When we arrived one night at the *tekke* of the Helveti dervishes in some obscure suburb of Istanbul, we were taken to a door which, when opened, led to the top of a staircase that looked down on a large room filled with students. In pride of place was a raised dais on which sat a very large man who we knew must be Muzaffer, the sheikh of the Helveti sect. He was wearing a voluminous striped kaftan, and as we looked down on him the entire lower half of his body began to shake and move about jerkily without his doing anything. We stood open-mouthed, wondering if this was some special Sufi practice for our benefit, but as he rose to greet us a small boy backed out from under the skirt of his robe. He had been massaging the man's massive legs. I shot that scene in slow motion in my head, inserting a long delay before we saw the emergence of the boy from between his legs.

By the end of the trip, I had shot an imagined masterpiece that

431

no-one would ever see except me. Yet, with all my frustration, I was immensely glad I had come. I couldn't help pondering whether Bulent had brought about the situation in some indirect way to give himself relief from awkward interviews and me a salutary lesson in patience and humility.

The final accident that swayed me in the direction of selling Scot's Farm and opting for Karnak happened to my son Jason. He telephoned me from school one day in great distress, telling me that he'd walked into the gym to discover a fellow student hanging by his belt. The boy was cut down while still alive and the sports master performed a crude but unsuccessful tracheotomy to try to save him. Jason was witness to the whole unfortunate incident.

I drove down to pick him up and bring him home. He was too upset to return to Millfield, so we decided that he should not go back there. Sean chose Gordonstoun, the Outward Bound School favoured by the Royal family, as the institution most suitable for his son. This meant that I couldn't drive up to visit him because Gordonstoun lies in the north of Scotland and it was a long and complicated journey.

Giovanna was now living in Oxford and studying carpentry. It was clear that both my children and all my original companions from Sherborne had moved into new spheres away from Scot's Farm. So, with much reluctance, I put it on the market. During the years of our tenure, we had converted three barns and several stables, sunk a dining room and renewed the roofs. The ten acres of land had two extensive greenhouses and was now productive, the soil having been reinvigorated and the outhouses repaired and made functional. Our experiment, by and large, had been successful. We sold the farm for five times as much as we had bought it for.

It did not harm the price that Prince Charles had moved into a place called Highgrove about two miles down the road. Tony and I had visited Highgrove when it was the home of President Roosevelt's son, FDR Jr. We found it a rather dark, dour house and my only memory of our visit is that booze flowed like water and the Roosevelts seemed inordinately interested in getting us into the tub with them.

And so the die was cast. On my return to Karnak at the end of the Wet, accompanied by two guests, I found that there was a plague of mosquitoes and that everything was amazingly overgrown. On the afternoon of the day I got back, Bari Brynl, the young man I had left in charge, was slashing the grass around the beehives when the tractor knocked one of them over and they all went down, in a domino effect. Bari was stung hundreds of times but managed to crawl to the creek, feeling his way along, having lost his glasses. We heard a sort of croaking and went outside to find him more dead than alive. His body had folded up like a deckchair while every orifice excreted whatever liquids were in it.

With the help of one of my guests, I managed to get him onto the back of the truck and drove at top speed to the hospital. I waited anxiously after they told me he was not responding to the massive doses of antihistamine they were pumping into him. After some very tense hours, he finally reacted positively and I left him in a stable condition and went home. In my absence, my guests had deserted the sinking ship. Karnak was denuded. They left a note to say that they had managed to catch a plane to Sydney. And so goodbye.

That moment is etched into my brain. I sat on the back steps of the Ritz, looking up at the mountain and wondering what the hell I had done. For half an hour, I entertained feelings of wonder at my own foolhardiness, then anger, bitterness and recriminations – but against whom? *I* had chosen to do what I was doing. *I* had burnt my boats and banished myself to a place as far away from civilisation as you can go. I had only myself to blame if I had taken on such a burden.

I looked at the sun setting behind the Devil's Thumb, the vast slab of grey and white granite on the top of the mountain the Aborigines call Manjal Jamalji. It is the place of Dimur, the Spirit of Fire, where he taught them how to use the fire sticks to make the spark, how to blow on the spark until it catches fire and flares up, how to feed the fire until it roars and how to wait until it burns down and becomes the place to cook food and curl up next to and sleep. I had made my choice and must live with it because it was where my intuition had led me. I was determined to follow the *tariqa*, the way, towards the getting of wisdom.

I heard the old tractor still chugging away near the beehives. No-one had dared go near it while the swarms of angry bees were still circling. I crept out to turn the engine off.

Silence . . . then the chorus of crickets, frogs, cane toads and scrub turkeys. Through the cacophony came the loathsome soprano whine of the mosquitoes. I lit the coils while the sky was darkening and the first brilliant stars were appearing. The flying foxes were taking off and the smell of grass was all around me. I breathed in. It was enough.

The reason for the plague of mosquitoes was stagnant water lying in a sort of hollow to the north of the Ritz, bordered on one side by enormous boulders. I think maybe Mr Sciacca, my predecessor, had once prepared the ground to plant rice by pushing the huge granite rocks back but, by now, the ground was just a swamp infested with mosquito larvae.

With the money from Scot's Farm, I hired a bulldozer and excavated the low-lying land to make a lake. The Water Board arrived to advise me at what point in the creek we could put in a pipe to gravity-feed the cavity with some of the purest water on the planet – water which rose in a spring on our mountain and tumbled 1220 metres before it reached the secret pool below and, from there, fed our lake. Therefore, mosquitoes *can* have a purpose. They can tell you where lakes should be. Nothing is for nothing.

Tony still had the flat at Victor Spinetti's, where he held court. While I was in Oz fighting the mozzies, he was in London and had gone into partnership with Lance Reynolds, the young Australian actor who'd played the Prompter in *The Taming of the Shrew*. Since then, Lance had become a very successful entrepreneur of pop bands like Air Supply. Together, they were taking Tony's new play *Whodunnit* (aka *The Case of the Oily Levantine*) on tour prior to its West End opening.

Our lives were crammed with projects and the feat was to keep juggling all the balls in the air, meeting to spend rapturous times together when we could. I was involved with a film called *The Last Tango with Rudolph Valentino*. Set in Sydney in 1975, it was about a woman still so obsessed with Valentino that she has a shrine in her house to keep her memory of him alive. Hilary Linstead was to produce it with Patrick Hockey, the painter, who was also the designer. I had written the script from a two-page short story and was set to direct the opus. I was particularly excited that Jeanne Moreau had expressed interest in playing the female lead.

The thunderclap sounded out of a clear blue sky. Tony was diagnosed with a tumour, a pituitary adenoma the size of a largish egg, right in the middle of his forehead. It was benign but increasing in volume daily. He sought the advice of his doctor, who referred him to a surgeon. Mr Andrews told him that if he didn't have it removed, he would surely go blind; however, if he *did* commit to the knife, he would lose his sense of smell as the olfactory nerve would have to be cut. He would also lose sight in one eye.

I begged Tony to seek other opinions, including alternative ones, but he was of a mindset common to those brought up in non-medical households who believe everything the allopathic doctor tells them as though he were an oracle. They have the same attitude to their bodies as they have to their cars – when something goes wrong, you take it to a specialist mechanic, park it in the garage and pay a lot of money, and when you come back to collect it some time later you drive it off with no worries. Everything is sorted. You can rev it up, do wheelies, drive it through dust storms or floods, and if it plays up again, back it goes to the mechanic, who'll tinker until it behaves itself again. Basically, you have nothing to do with the process of fixing it, or the process of healing in the case of the body. That's what you pay the quack for, and the more you pay him, the better the fix will be. To someone who comes from a medical background, this way of thinking seems like sheer madness.

Yet, as fate would have it, even before I could get to London to try and persuade him otherwise, Tony had committed himself to surgery, gone straight into hospital and had the operation performed. I don't think he had actually weighed up the consequences, especially of being without that most primal of senses, smell. The operation had cost him twenty-five thousand pounds, so how could it not work?

For six weeks, Tony remained in hospital, not even recognising his own mother. The surgeon was unable to reach some of the tumour, so it was only a partial removal. No-one quite knew what the outcome would be. He dropped from ninety-five to fifty-seven kilos during that time. I wasn't allowed to speak to him or visit, as I was not his wife or a relation, so I was left in a limbo of worry about his condition.

Then, through the post, I received a most amazing correspondence. It was in the form of one of those amateur actor's hopeful requests for an audition, addressed to Diane Cilento, Director of *The Last Tango with Rudolph Valentino*. There was a picture of Tony with a shaven head and a wicked-looking scar along his forehead which was signed 'Joe Bloggs: a recent snap'. With the photo was a request to audition for the part of Rudolph Valentino. His age, weight, height and past credits were included. He noted that he had played the dreaded dwarf Hugguth in a famous production of *Frankenstein* for Hammer Films (which was true) and that he'd always had a special affinity for Valentino because they were both born under the sign of Taurus.

I laughed and laughed, mostly with relief, because I knew that Tony was himself again.

As soon as he could travel, he came to Australia to recuperate. Terrified that the operation might have done some irreparable damage to faculties other than his sense of smell, he was incessantly getting me to test his memory with quotes from Shakespeare, historical dates or actors' names and what productions he'd seen them in. He missed not being able to swill a good wine around in the glass and inhale its aroma and, even though he always bought the most expensive perfumes for me whenever he travelled, he was truly devastated that he was denied what Mohammed called 'the best perfume in the world . . . the scent of one's beloved'.

I used to try to pass different smells on to him by osmosis, but I don't think it worked because he said that slowly but surely he was forgetting what it was like to have any sense of the air being permeated with odour at all. He renewed drinking and smoking with added fervour, as though making up for lost time. It was a compensation, like eating, and Tony never denied his appetites. The spin-off from Tony's operation that concerned me more than any other was the medication, without which he was lost. If he didn't have an injection of something called Synacthen every week, his energy level diminished so much that he had to go to bed. When the drug had been administered, it left him feeling sick for a short while and then hyperactive. It was supposed to jolt his pituitary and thyroid glands into action.

Soon after Tony's return to Oz, divorce proceedings were brought against him by Carolyn Shaffer. After a long legal wrangle, generous terms were agreed and he was a free man. Before long, my mother, vigilant of her daughter's reputation (which she should have known by then was nonexistent), put the hard word on Tony. I can picture the scene exactly as he described it. They had been out to lunch together and were walking through a shopping arcade in Brisbane. My mother, who had taken to using a stick by then, was stumping along when she suddenly came to a halt outside a jeweller's. 'When are you going to make an honest woman of my daughter?' she is purported to have demanded, waving her stick in Tony's face.

I can just imagine the myriad expressions that must have crossed Tony's face – surprise, as I had never expressed a desire to be married; consternation at the prospect of my mother wielding her stick in such a fashion; and delight at someone being so incredibly Edwardian. Tony told her that he had every intention of asking me to marry him, which he did. When he explained what my mum had said, I was surprised too, as my mother had never spoken to me about my relationship with Tony. I put it out of my head for the time being.

Tony and I travelled to Chisholme together that winter to see Bulent. We drove up to Scotland in a snowstorm after visiting Harrods to purchase Bulent's favourite Scottish smoked salmon and bitter chocolate-covered grapefruit peels. The weather closed down the moment we got there. It was so beautiful, and such a contrast from my humid, tropical haunt, that I sat for hours just looking out at the blanched wonderland where birds and squirrels fought to get to the feeding trays in the snow.

Since I had done the *wasifa* retreat at Swyre Farm, it had become a fixed part of the advanced course at Chisholme for all students, and Tony was determined to do it too. There were three candidates – Hugh Tollemarsh, Tony and an African-American architect named Bedi. On the morning they were to start the retreat, after their fast day, Bulent insisted that they eat a special breakfast with homemade cumquat marmalade and hot croissants. A long caravan of warm brown clouds in the shape of a camel train stretched out across the sky above the hill that stands to the north of Chisholme. We watched as the shapes slowly dispersed and then the three men retired to their rooms and began their own journeys.

Tony had a *tesbih* with five hundred beads, which he draped around his body as he counted. His room was next to mine so I could hear his voice droning on and on. When it would stop, I'd know he was either watching the creatures out of the window or had gone to sleep. Every night when I went to bed, he would have sneaked into my room and left a little *billet-doux* under my pillow.

Of course I knew that, for Tony, doing the *wasifas* was a sort of gift to please me. He never expected any manifestations or visions. When Tony sat in meditation, I knew that he just thought about things . . . never tried not to. He had neither the desire nor the ability to move away from a pragmatic approach, so he never knew what it was to let go. Although obsessed with the occult, mystery, murders, murderers and what lay beyond the known worlds, inside he was terrified to step into them.

By the end of the week, I could hear in his voice that Tony was getting very tired, so we called a halt. The snow was clearing and both of us had to dash off to different jobs. It was always such an effort to leave the world of sanity and the presence of Bulent at Chisholme and enter the fray again. I had been persuaded to do the opening of the new theatre at the Queensland Arts Complex in Brisbane, with 250 school-children, where I would perform in *The Three Legends of Kraaa*, written by Robyn Archer and designed by genius Nigel Triffid. Tony was off to London to discuss the second of Agatha Christie's Hercule Poirot films, *Evil under the Sun*.

The rehearsals and performances of this play are marked in my memory because my dad, who had been in poor health for some time at the Canossa Hospital, became gravely ill and died during the production. Canossa is a hospital run by Italian nuns and my father was their favourite, as he loved to speak Italian in his later years. He lay in bed with his eyes closed, saying he didn't want to look at the world any more. Tony and I used to visit to feed him lamb chops and mashed potato. He was very lucid sometimes and once gave us a cogent and fascinating dissertation on Flinders' imprisonment on Mauritius.

The young priest who conducted the funeral ceremony opened by saying that we were there to celebrate my dad's life. He wore a white flower-sprigged robe and all the nuns from Canossa sang an Italian hymn as a tribute. My father was not carried but wheeled into the chapel at the hospital in an open coffin. During the service, my mother approached his body and kissed him on the face with passion.

'Isn't he beautiful?' she cried, turning to face the whole congregation and slewing the coffin sideways in her agitation. Hands flew out to prevent it catapulting across the aisle but she saw nothing. Her features were illuminated like a child's and she seemed elated. It was a moment when you feel a great sob rising in your throat but it wasn't sad. I thought it was just as it should be but Tony was astounded. He couldn't believe my mother would have had the temerity to do such a spontaneous, uninhibited thing in public.

After my dad had been interred, I went back to the theatre to make up for the first night. I was playing three heroines lovingly created by Robyn Archer to demonstrate that women are not just pretty faces – an American-Indian woman who leads her tribe out of danger, a Japanese Bonsai tree woman who fights a giant, and a Scandinavian blacksmith woman who leaps off a castle. I put on my black wig and leather dress studded with beads to play the leader of the tribe of Native Americans in the first play.

The production, in the open air, took place where the theatre would later be built as part of the South Bank complex on the Brisbane River. The parents of the 250 children from various schools taking part in the plays made up the bulk of the audience but all the dignitaries were present as well. Excitement was building and the buzz of the first-night audience filled the air.

The play began well but thunderheads were building up ominously in the northern sky. I had to climb up a thirty-foot ladder towards the end of the play and stand like a figurehead scanning the horizons. I didn't look down when I got to the top, as the lights that hit me criss-crossed and were so strong that I became a bit dizzy. Swaying around at that height is not recommended. As soon as I felt the first splash of rain on my face, I knew that we were in for it. It wasn't light misty rain but the bucketing kind. A torrent of water descended almost immediately and I was transfixed, not daring to move. I looked down and saw that no-one was there. The crowd had run for cover while I was stuck up the ladder like the Christmas fairy with no tree.

I thought about my father going down under the ground and

didn't know whether I was crying or if it was just rain coursing down my cheeks. I stood out the storm, which lasted ten minutes . . . forever. When I finally descended very gingerly, my legs were shaking and the wet leather dress I was wearing, which weighed a ton, clung to my body like a huge dank hand. I felt as though the world had changed and I was on a different planet when my feet touched the sodden earth once more. When daughters lose their dads, a special link with reality has been severed. Your first protector/disciplinarian/myth-maker has disappeared from your life forever. You're no-one's little girl any more. It means being truly grown up and a feeling of loss hits you with great force.

Because of Joh Bjelke-Petersen lifting death duties in the state of Queensland, Tony moved all his monetary affairs to Australia and paid Australian taxes until 1996, when, for his own reasons, he stopped paying taxes altogether. We had leased the Nautilus restaurant to Mogens Bay Esbensen, a name chef who had lived in Thailand and learned his skills there. He created sumptuous dishes like warm duck salad and superior nasi goreng with herbs grown in our gardens. I was quite relieved not to have to open the menu as I sat on our handmade terrace, knowing that I had eaten every dish at least ten times.

Jason came to Australia for his sister Giovanna's wedding to Bill Phillips and stayed to shoot *The Boy Who Had Everything*, his first starring role. I played his mother in the picture but I wasn't enamoured of the role. Stephen Wallace was the director of this story of his life with his mum after her husband left her, which was traumatic and rather sad. Still, it was a giant leap for Jason, who had left Gordonstoun to play small parts in the Perth Repertory Company. When he appeared in a panto at the Rep as the Chong half of the Ching and Chong duo of Chinese laundrymen and declared that this was his chosen profession, I was quite surprised as he had always said he wanted to be a vet. I gave him three weeks of intensive Yat classes on the front verandah at Karnak before we embarked on *The Boy Who Had Everything* and found him to be responsive and intense, so I knew he *really* wanted to be an actor, not just a star.

The film was shot at Bondi Beach, where the breakers roll in and the surfing dreams of the nation were born. During the shoot, on Jason's twenty-first birthday, a very embarrassed young man delivered a gorillagram from the cast and crew. Jason acquitted himself well in the film, which won a Best Picture Award at the Moscow Film Festival. It was during this film that there was a call from London to ask whether a Mr R. Hood was available. Jason replied, 'Wrong number,' and hung up, only to get a call back from his agent, furious that he had not recognised her voice and her waggish way of telling him that he'd won the coveted role of Robin Hood. Jason was to be Robin of Sherwood in the 1984 TV series. With his long blond locks, he became a favourite with pre-pubescent girls. It had been bad enough being James Bond's wife . . . now I was Robin Hood's mother.

Tony and I were married under a flowering bauhinia tree in the garden at Karnak on 22 June 1985. After storms, wind and the remnants of the Wet season lingered on, the day of the wedding dawned bathed in golden light and with the promise of a perfect day. I sat in front of the theatrical mirror in the Chateau looking at my face. So many times had I made up these features for a performance and now, somehow, I felt renewed as though I had never seen myself before. Happiness pervaded my whole body.

'Did you realise it's the shortest day of the year in the Southern Hemisphere?' my brother asked.

'Ah, yes . . . but did *you* realise it's also the longest night?' was Tony's reply.

He wore one of his impeccably cut, stone-coloured suits while I had on a fabulous white bejewelled dress and wide-brimmed hat he had brought me from Los Angeles. The usual hiccoughs added to the stress of the final preparations. First, Tony's fly zipper broke just as he was going to take his place under the tree and then I got the heel of one of my stiletto shoes caught in a crack in the verandah. My brother Carl gave me away as my mother watched ecstatic from a wheelchair. After the ceremony, one of the guests collared Tony on the verandah.

'Did the film studios train those Ulysses butterflies to fly around your heads during the ceremony?' she enquired breathlessly. 'It was so clever and beautiful.'

'Of course,' replied Tony, egging her on. 'And did you notice that they were flying anti-clockwise?'

'It's so wonderful! You film people can do *anything* these days!' she enthused.

The wedding breakfast was held on the terrace at the Nautilus and later we flew to Lizard Island for our honeymoon. Known as Ungambikeela to the Aboriginal people of the Cape Flannery area, Lizard Island was the place of initiation for Aboriginal youths for thousands of years and was regarded as a sacred site for 'secret men's business', upon which no woman was meant to trespass.

In 1770, Captain Cook landed on the island and, clambering up the hill now known as Cook's Look, peered into his telescope over the Great Barrier Reef. He spied an opening between the deadly shoals where he could guide his ship the *Endeavour* out of danger and into open waters. Later, when Cooktown was established as the supply port for the Palmer River gold rush, a young girl called Mary, who played piano at French Charlie's Bar, was spotted by a bêche-de-mer (sea cucumber) fisherman named Robert Watson. He married her and swept her off to the little stone house he had built on Lizard Island. While he was away fishing and Mary was left with her new baby and two Chinese servants, Aboriginal men arrived, determined to rid the island of the female who had made her home in their forbidden territory. They speared and killed one of the Chinamen in the garden and Mrs Watson, her four-month-old baby, Ferrier, and the other Chinese servant, Ah Sam, fled to sea in the bêche-de-mer cooking vessel (now preserved in the Townsville Museum). They floated on the current for some days before running aground on a sand bank, one of a series of atolls called the Ribbons. Here, they died of thirst. Mrs Watson had kept a diary of the whole sorry affair and her death marked open season for the hunting down of Aboriginal tribesmen.

Ungambikeela is a superb example of a mainland island, lying like a curled lizard basking in the cerulean blue of the Pacific Ocean, almost a hundred kilometres off the north-east coast of Queensland. It has an ample lagoon on whose shores mounds of seashells ten metres deep (an ancient midden) are all that remains of the thousands of ceremonial feasts held over centuries for the initiates into Aboriginal manhood. In more recent times, Prince Charles, heir to the British throne, used the island as a retreat, far from prying telephoto lenses. The yacht club, where not only royals but marlin hunter Lee Marvin, goon Harry Secombe and other luminaries could be seen swilling Singapore slings in its bar, now caters to cognoscenti from all over the world. Giant goannas dot the lawns and the restaurant serves fresh seafood to die for.

We awoke on that first morning gloating in the knowledge that we had no telephones to answer, no students with horrible life problems to listen to, no schedule of classes, no rehearsals, no appointments – just days of delight, lying about reading, sleeping, love-making in the afternoons and being waited on hand and foot. It was a time to savour after so many years of slog. As we returned from a picnic lunch on the beach on our second day, we were hailed by a loud, cheery voice from a deck-chair on the front porch.

'Hello, you two! Thought I was bound to catch you sometime. How's the script going, Tony?'

'Oh God!' whispered Tony. 'It's Morris West. Let's hide.'

Morris West, author of many bestsellers, including *The Shoes of the Fisherman*, had commissioned Tony to write a film script based on his book *The World is Made of Glass*, about an incident in the clinical histories of Carl Gustav Jung when he treated a woman (unidentified) who was a sadist. Supposedly, Jung had been mightily attracted by this woman –

as a man, not as her analyst. Tony had been working on the project for months and Morris had been calling incessantly, asking to view the finished script. Foolishly, Tony had told Morris of our intended honeymoon destination. Now, here he was, occupying the main suite in the place and reiterating his demand to see the script of *The World is Made of Glass*.

There were few places in the resort to hide from Morris and his wife unless we stayed in our room all the time. They insisted on having dinner with us nearly every night, even though we protested, but Morris waylaid our arguments saying he had an important job that he wanted me to consider. He said he would pay me a great deal of money to go to Rome to do research for a new novel he was writing about some Papal scandal. He emphasised the fact that as I spoke Italian and could role play, I would be the perfect person for the job. I knew Morris was using this job to wind Tony up and refused his offer point-blank but Tony showed his anger the next day when we were out on a boat together.

We had sailed to a place called the Cod Hole, where we were snorkelling and feeding the mammoth spotted potato cod that were tame enough to eat out of our hands. One of them nipped Morris's thumb hard and drew blood. It's not sensible to hang around in these waters trailing fresh blood as predators converge from great distances to find and attack the source. Morris got out of the water in double-quick time and was being treated for his wound when Tony exclaimed tartly, 'Oh, what a pity! You won't be able to type out any more of your boring novels for at least a week.'

It was the beginning of an escalating tension between the two men, which resulted in a falling out of monumental proportions when Tony resigned from the job some weeks later at Morris's office high above Sydney Harbour. Morris was adamant that Tony should write a scene in which Jung masturbates clandestinely throughout a session with the woman. Tony refused, declaring forcefully not only that covert masturbation can't be made interesting for the camera but also that Morris was trying to turn a giant, in the person of Jung, into a pygmy. Morris was so incensed that they virtually came to blows. That was the end of their association. *The World is Made of Glass* never got off the ground, even though Morris employed another writer.

We came back to Karnak refreshed and took up residence in the Chateau, which was crowded with supervisors and children. Very soon, Tony had had enough, and was intent on building us a grand new house on the hill overlooking the lake. We decided mutually that I should gift him half of the fifty-five acres that the house would be built on and we drew up a contract with a lawyer in Cairns. Tony was surprisingly formal about our arrangement but it felt correct to be partners as land-owners as well as lovers.

We collaborated on the design of the house, which was the only house at Karnak not built entirely of wood. While the shell of the place was being constructed, we had two masons and their wives living with us. As I was cooking for everyone, I was delighted when the kitchen was finished. The Castle, as it was known, had a study/library where Tony wrote and a private verandah with a retractable roof. Here, he delighted in breakfasting in the morning sunlight while shouting abuse at a family of noisy kookaburras that scrounged tidbits and cackled continuously. There was a spacious mirrored bedroom, an Italian tiled bathroom and a wraparound verandah on the first floor. Tony boasted that it was the largest one-bedroom house in the Southern Hemisphere. He commissioned my brother David to design and make four stained-glass windows on the theme of the nine muses for his study and panels of local flora and fauna for the downstairs sitting room.

We took an apartment in Sydney overlooking the harbour bridge while I did the play *Agnes of God*. Tony was yoyo-ing back and forth to Hollywood discussing new scripts all the time. In rapid succession, he undertook *The Life of Bela Lugosi*, a dramatisation of the life of Charlie Chaplin and, after that, *The Glow*. Joe Levine asked Tony to adapt this timely tale of a sinister fitness epidemic amongst geriatrics in New

York's wealthiest families and the commission took us to the Big Apple for six months. Tony rented an apartment on the fifty-ninth floor of Trump Tower and I joined him there when *Agnes of God* was finished. Our windows went right down to the floor, through which we could watch the spectacular lightshows that transformed the Empire State Building and the Chrysler Building into light shows every night.

But there was another iron in Tony's fire. His play *Whodunnit* was on tour in Boston when we arrived. The company was locked into the usual turmoil that most pre-Broadway plays encounter before their openings. When we joined the production, Fred Gwynne, who played Herman in the hit American TV series *The Munsters*, had just taken over the leading role, necessitating a profound adjustment to his imposing six feet five inch frame within the cast, which eased the previously tense situation somewhat.

Gordon Chater, that superb comic master from Sydney, was hamming it up, shoving in lots of 'business' and stealing scenes as the butler while dear old Hermione Baddeley, at eighty years old, was snoozing peacefully on the sofa through most of her scenes. Gordon told a lovely story of how a profound silence descended throughout the theatre, interrupted only by some delicate snores, as Hermione was supposed to deliver a pivotal line. She awoke from her nap and thundered resentfully in a booming voice, 'Stop nudging me, Gordie, it's not my *turn!*'

Someone needed to pull the corset strings together. Tony made a wealth of suggestions and rewrote bits where actors felt uncomfortable. He had some slanging matches with the director, Michael Kahn, and we both went to the show many times to see that the actors were staying awake and not paraphrasing too many of his lines. When the show opened, it ran for nearly a year and although it wasn't *Sleuth*, it was a success not to be sneezed at.

When the horrors of *Whodunnit* and the splendours of Trump Tower were over, Tony and I went back to the wilds of FNQ to live in our very own nearly finished Castle. Over the next few years, Tony collected an assortment of curious and wonderful objects in his study – a vast carved silky oak manta ray as big as a grand piano, which we called 'Who Needs It', a large painting by Arthur Boyd of an Aboriginal boy standing in the water pointing up at the stars, a roll-top desk as large as my father's, and books – hundreds and hundreds of books, lining the shelves on every wall, right up to the ceiling.

Tony sat from morning until night, facing away from the Arthur Boyd in one of the special comfy armchairs we had brought out from Scot's Farm, writing in longhand in a notebook. He then typed out what he had written, making changes and improvements, on an old-fashioned portable typewriter that stood on his desk. The next stage was a clean copy of the script, begun by Lydia, his secretary, and finished, after many spelling corrections and cursing, by Mr T himself. He would rush to Copy Cats and choose a garish but apt colour for each new work and, with real glee, send the beautifully crafted piece off to London or Hollywood or wherever. No-one I know ever got so much pleasure out of finishing a work as Tony.

'It's all a load of shit, you know,' he would immediately say and then add pensively, 'Oh, I don't know. It could be rather good if they do it right.'

We had a Guy Fawkes Night party of Neroesque proportions to 'warm' the Castle when it was completed. Three pyrotechnists were hired to coordinate the fireworks display while Tony played Tchaikovsky's *1812 Overture* at 160 decibels, conducting the whole thing from the verandah. The guests never knew that the fire blazing up on the other side of the lake wasn't part of the spectacle because the reflection on the water was so perfect. Then, of course, came the exciting drama of us all rushing to extinguish the fire before it raged out of control. We ate 'muddies' on the verandah, washed down with Louis Roederer Cristal champagne. We had invited all the locals who weren't frightened to enter what they imagined must be a den of iniquity, as well as the jetsetters who always manage to appear when there's a party in the offing. It was a night to remember.

After the course that year, I received an unusual offer. Nasser Mirza, Professor of Middle Eastern studies at the University of Melbourne, wrote to ask me if I would like to participate in a private guided tour through Jordan and Syria with him. He was an Ismaili by birth and wished to visit his family near Homs in Syria. The trip coincided with one of Tony's London breaks, when he got his fix of West End theatre, saw his mother and daughters, showed off his tropical tan and came back to Australia via New York to catch up with his twin, Peter. It was perfect timing.

There was no time to think about the implications of such an adventure. I gathered together some of my past students, including Australian actress Rowena Wallace, and we were off to Amman, the capital of Jordan, within days. What I remember most about this city is walking around at night and sitting near a building site where there were lights, movement and men talking loudly. I knew the language they spoke wasn't Arabic. It turned out that thousands of Koreans were brought to Jordan every year to work day and night constructing new high-rises.

We went to the Dead Sea and, like good Australians, dived straight in. O Foolish Floundering Downunderers! It took a whole day to get over the pain of our stinging eyes. We climbed Mount Nebo and looked down at the dark green cultivation across the River Jordan, the Promised Land. It was from this very peak that Moses, who was not allowed to enter, viewed the Promised Land a short time before he died. Throughout the country, we met impassioned Palestinians who could talk, eat, breathe and hear nothing but the repetition of their unhappy displacement.

Professor Mirza was a guide with no equal. He took us to every place of interest and had an intimate knowledge of each. Some eighty kilometres south of the Dead Sea, we rode horses down the Wadi Araba, a corridor of winding sandstone sometimes only twenty metres wide, to that most mysterious 'rose red city half as old as time', Petra. At the end of the Wadi, the narrow corridor opened out to reveal the famous Treasury carved into the rock, where the Nabataean people stored their riches long before the birth of Christ.

Crossing the border into Syria, we spent two days at Crac de Chevalier, the largest Crusader castle in the world. Our visit there happened to coincide with that of some Russian astronauts who were being feted by the Syrian authorities, so they'd opened up places in the castle that had been off limits for years. The Knights Templar could ride right up onto the second and third level of the castle four abreast and the complex was designed in such a way that two more castles lay inside the outer one. No invader ever conquered Crac de Chevalier. It just fell apart, as there were only four ancient knights left to maintain the whole edifice.

I loved Palmyra. With its funeral pyres, pink palaces and slender columns rising from the desert floor, it is one of the most romantic places I have ever visited in all my travels. When someone died in Palmyra in those forgotten days, an image of the deceased was sculpted and they are so lifelike that even today we feel as though we know those people. I felt comfortable wearing Arab dress in Palmyra and was inspired by the story of Queen Zenobia, the Syrian Bodicea, who defied the Romans and fought valiantly to free her people. We were taken down under the ground at night to float through surreal caves in warm water filled with minerals, which is believed to enhance the skin and cure any ailments. We all slept until eleven the next day.

After Aleppo, where we lived in a rooftop apartment, we came at last to Damascus, the oldest continuously occupied city in the world. Our first stop was the gigantic Omayyad Mosque, where the head of John the Baptist, the coveted prize awarded by King Herod to Salome for her dancing, is preserved. Before they enter the mosque, all women have to don a peculiarly shaped garment made of black wool that covers not only the entire body but that has a hood so voluminous that it obscures the face as well. We looked like lumpen black bags of laundry dragging ourselves around the magnificent carpeted interior.

It wasn't on my journey *to* Damascus, like St Paul, that I had my epiphany; it was on my journey *out*. Nasser Mirza led us up the colossal mountain on our way out of town to a small mosque set in a busy suburban street. After again putting on the heavy black garment to hide our femaleness from the world, we walked down some interior stairs to a crypt where the local saint was buried. The moment I entered the cellar, with its tomb of green glass decorated with palm trees, I knew in whose presence I was. It had been sixteen years since that night at Sherborne when I saw the man in the garden prostrate on the ground, his back towards me, making his obeisance. I had never ceased thinking about him and who he might be. Mr Bennett had said I would find out one day and he was correct. It was Muhyiddin Ibn Arabi.

I sat down on the floor in the burial chamber and that same overwhelming feeling of wellbeing I'd had so many years before crept over me. I have no recollection of the passing of time until being aware that my companions were tugging at my sleeves, telling me that we had to leave. I had been there more than two hours.

Before we left Syria, I went back to the tomb of Muhyiddin Ibn Arabi, this time by myself, but the old mullahs wouldn't let me in. They said they were doing *zikhr*, which was true. I could hear their voices in unison chanting the names of God, *Ya Wahid al-Ahad* (the One and Only), as I sat on the steps outside, with tears spurting from my eyes. One of the mullahs came out and threw a handful of boiled sweeties over me as I sat there. When I didn't pick them up, he went back into the chamber looking bewildered and rather disturbed. I was still there when they finished the *zikhr* and filed out. Two of them lifted me under my arms and quite gently carried me up to street level and put me in a cab. I was still wearing the hideous black garment and was shoeless.

I have no explanation for my behaviour, nor can I say what the connection is between myself and the virtually unmarked tomb of a saint on a hill in Damascus. However, I do know that my encounter at Sherborne with the Sheikh al-Akhbar (the Great Teacher, as Ibn Arabi is also known) was not an aberration and has been singularly the most motivational happening of my life.

As soon as I got back to Karnak, my mother telephoned to say that I must come down to Brisbane to say goodbye to her as she was going to die, and that she wanted me to perform a great favour for her before she went.

She was sitting up in bed with one of those tubes through her nose when I arrived. She seemed very composed as she explained that she wanted me to record Thomas Gray's *Elegy Written in a Country Churchyard* for her. When my mother couldn't sleep at night she liked to repeat poems to herself, but if she couldn't remember all the verses she was in torment until morning, trying to get hold of the words and worrying that she was getting senile dementia. I went to the ABC and recorded all the poems she loved to professional standard.

My mother had also insisted that my sister Margaret come up from Melbourne, and with my brother Carl we sat on her bed and jollied her up, making her laugh. She was rather matter-of-fact about her impending demise. A day or so later she called us to her bedside again and told us that she had provided a sum of money for each of her six children. She gave me strict instructions that I was to do something important and meaningful with my inheritance, not just buy a European car. 'Well,' she concluded, 'you can all go home again now because I feel much better and have decided not to die yet. Thank you for coming.'

So off we went – Carl to his home and six lovely children in Redland Bay, Margaret to Melbourne and her easel, and Tony and I to London. Tony had arranged a very special trip for us, something everybody dreams of doing once in their lifetime – taking the *Orient Express* across Europe and Russia in a luxury compartment, watching the countries flash by while you eat, sleep and have a lovely time with your best love.

We broke the journey in Vienna, where Jason was filming *The Train*, the story of Lenin's triumphal return to Russia after years of exile in Switzerland. When our train pulled in to the station, Jason was waiting for us, looking incredibly handsome, but he seemed very stilted and nervous when we hugged and didn't tell his usual fistful of dreadful jokes. As soon as we were alone, he turned to me and, with great tenderness, told me that my mother had died and that I must go back to Australia as soon as possible.

I had a difficult job obtaining flight connections and asked my family to delay the funeral for a day or two until I got there. True to her word, my mother had been meticulous in the dispersal of her life's collection of 'things', each having been marked with the name of the person it was to go to. She had remembered all of her twenty-six grandchildren with money as well as a memento of herself and my dad. She had even written out the hymns she wanted sung at the church service.

There were so many people at the funeral that they spilled onto the pavement and into the street. Members of Parliament, the Premier of Queensland, Joh Bjelke-Petersen, and his wife, Flo, families of rich and poor alike, bag ladies, her colleagues from the *Courier Mail*, university alumni, nurses, patients and many of those she had brought into the world all came to see her off.

After she had been laid to rest beside my dad, we all went back to her house on the river at Toowong and drank to her life and death. Gathered in a circle, everyone told their favourite anecdote about her. I wish I could remember all those mad stories. We laughed and laughed, wiping our eyes, but there was always the nagging feeling that she was the glue that held the family together and, without her, we would drift apart. I was very happy to be in the midst of my family listening to such funny loving tales about someone who had lived her life filled to the brim with works of generosity for other people.

I have never doubted that my mum was a truly remarkable woman but I know that until the day she died she never thought of me as anything other than a naughty little girl who got away with it. She was so proud and surprised when I did anything that she considered worthwhile that it was worth anything to evoke that surprise from her. I read a beautiful poem by Muhyiddin Ibn Arabi at the church:

> Dearly beloved!
> Let us go towards Union
> And if we find the road
> That leads to separation,
> We will destroy separation.
> Let us go hand in hand.
> Let us enter the presence of Truth.
> Let it be our judge
> And imprint its seal upon our union
> Forever.

Chapter Sixteen

No matter what age you arrive at, it is always a shock to discover you are an orphan. After my mother's death, her presence haunted me and I wondered what she wanted me to do with the sixty thousand dollars that was burning a hole in my pocket.

I threw myself into the course that year with renewed vigour. Karnak had grown in status and complexity over time so that the course now included Gurdjieff Movements (taught by my daughter, Giovanna), meditational practices, cooking, baking bread, personal creative projects, Yat acting and movement classes, and the comparative study of religions and philosophers.

In order to gain practical knowledge of how to use Hazard in life, we began every course by embarking on an adventure together. One year it was exploring the Quinkin caves near Laura to discover new Aboriginal art on their walls. Another year, we climbed the rugged 1220-metre mountain at Karnak that's topped by the giant granite outcrop known as the Devil's Thumb. The way up the mountain is through our property, so we didn't have to travel anywhere, just up. Two of the new students, a young couple with a five-month-old baby which was being looked after back at Karnak, had left the group to follow the sound of a waterfall and had got lost.

It seemed unthinkable that a lactating mother would willingly leave her five-month-old baby, so at the crack of dawn next morning

I set off up the mountain again with three other students. We coo-eed and shouted ourselves hoarse all day and returned very worried and dispirited by evening to find that the missing couple had turned up just after breakfast, fed the baby, devoured half a dozen eggs and retired to bed to sleep off their fatigue. That night my legs felt as though they had been pummelled with sticks. I had been up and down the mountain twice in two days.

On the 1987 course we went to a wild, uninhabited beach called Weary Bay. A mob of Aborigines passed us on their way out, chattering about a monster crocodile they had been frightened by, but we ignored their warnings and built our camp between the lake and the sea.

The idea was that we only took staples such as rice, tomatoes and garlic, and foraged for the rest of our food – fishing and netting together or scouring the sands for pipis and other edible shellfish. There is almost nothing in this world more pleasant than snuggling up around a gum-scented fire on a beach in the tropics with a billion stars blazing overhead, digesting a tasty meal of hand-collected pipis and rice.

At around two in the morning, as the fire died down to embers, the dogs suddenly went berserk. There was something lumbering around in the bushes on the lake side of our camp. We were all awake in a flash and on our feet, throwing wood on the fire and yelling like banshees to scare off whatever had sent the dogs into such a frenzy. We could feel it there, watching us from the darkness.

No-one slept for the rest of the night; the dogs were wild-eyed and scared, and we had to hold them down. Early next morning we took the Aborigines' advice and got out of there. Later, our friend the Flying Doctor told us that he had seen the biggest croc he'd ever sighted from the air as he flew over Weary Bay that morning. He reckoned it measured nine metres – 29.5 feet long.

In the last three months of the ten-month course at Karnak, students devoted much of their time to projects of their own choice. Using their creative imagination they undertook something they had always wanted to do but had never got round to – whether it was sculpting, making an oven, composing music, painting, writing or carving. One girl designed and made a sundial out of different coloured stone which still stands in the garden today.

For study, I combined the works of J. G. Bennett, which encompass a number of subjects – the Enneagram, Sex, Hazard, Future Communities and the Dramatic Universe – with the writings of the thirteenth-century mystic Muhyiddin Ibn Arabi, as translated by Bulent Rauf in Bitez. They complemented each other perfectly, even though they were written more than five hundred years apart.

The students that year were a particularly interesting group, being of various nationalities, ages and socio-economic backgrounds. Included amongst them was Seb (Sebastien), a blazing redhead who is my sister Margaret's son. Tony took part in most of the classes, although he had no interest in meditation or movements. He presented a series of lectures about the construction of both films and plays and was working with Jeremy Johnson, a brilliant young Australian playwright, on a series for American TV. Bille Brown came up from Brisbane to lecture on Giordano Bruno's School of the Night, a secret society of free thinkers with which Christopher Marlowe and Shakespeare were reputedly associated. Also, the Perth psychoanalyst Irene Rix Weaver, head of the Jungian Society in Australia, spent many months at Karnak as a guest teacher.

We decided to give a public performance and invited actors up from a Townsville theatrical group called Tropic Line, run by Jean-Pierre Voos, to do a play called *The Chocolate Frog* by Australian playwright Jim Neill. It was set in a prison cell, so we built one on the verandah of the Ritz. We invited locals to come, and when they arrived we had everything set up to shock the life out of them. People dressed as police officers escorted them through the back of the house and they were required to fill out a form in order to enter. The policemen patrolled the audience, preventing them from smoking or talking too loudly, so that most of the spectators believed that they were watching real criminals, inmates of a prison who'd been allowed out to demonstrate what it was like in their cell. It was clearly an overwhelming experience for the audience, as most of them had never been to a genuine theatrical performance in their lives. It was wonderful, too, for the actors to see what a powerful impact theatre can have when there is no suspension of disbelief.

The germ of an idea began to form in my head, which I put to Tony. Why not use my mum's money to build a permanent stage where we could demonstrate the Gurdjieff Movements and put on performances, like *The Chocolate Frog*, and readings of interesting works, including his new plays? He thought it was a brilliant concept, but where would we put it?

There was a five-acre paddock, where we kept our milking goats, which backed onto the lake. Here, with all the students in tow, we walked up and down trying to find the perfect spot. The communal project that year was the construction of a set of terraces with a slate staircase leading down to the lake from the Castle. We chose a section of lakeside opposite the terraces for the stage, just where the famous fire had burnt on Guy Fawkes Night. From his study, Tony would be able to look across the lake and see what was happening backstage. In front of the stage, a large hill of earth would be piled up and long wooden benches would accommodate the audience. It would be rough but practical.

When a project is the offshoot of an unpredictable impulse, someone always seems to turn up without whom the whole crazy idea would crumble into a pipe dream. A young architect, Barry Lake, arrived out of the blue and was only too pleased to take on the challenge of tackling 'a different, modern kind of stage in the middle of nowhere'. To integrate it with the rest of the architecture at Karnak, he used poles and designed it with nine sides in the shape of a spaceship or teardrop. The roof had a trajectory pointing up to the skies and the stage itself was double the width of any standard theatre, nearly thirty metres across, because obviously there were no size constraints. The proscenium arch was made in a classic Greek design and, at the back of the stage, we inserted wide copper panels so sound would resonate.

It was not difficult to get the plan passed by council, so we went ahead and built the stage. The result was even better than we could have hoped. It was quite thrilling to discover that the acoustics were amazing, utilising the large V-shaped back to the stage, the copper panels and the lake behind.

We began by inviting our friends to witness performances of movements and all sorts of impromptu singing sessions. Musicians with guitars, flutes and violins seemed to turn up from nowhere and stay for hours, attracted by the great sound they were producing on that stage. We bought a classic old upright piano from a piano tuner who was getting divorced and didn't want his wife to get her hands on his beloved instrument.

Australian playwright David Williamson came to holiday at Karnak with his wife, Kristen. I had met Kristen at a conference in Mount Abu in Rajasthan, where she was reporting on an extraordinary meeting about meditation for a national newspaper. At that time I didn't know that we were both married to famous playwrights. By chance, we roomed together and spent the first evening giggling at the strange decorations on our walls. There was a baby Krishna who lit up and winked his eyes when you moved around him and a life-size photo of Prajapita Brahma, founder of the Brahma Kumaris World Spiritual Organisation, who stared at us through the door of the bathroom, which inevitably had no water in its taps. Kristen and I became firm friends on that trip and she promised to bring David to visit when we got back to Australia.

They stayed in our old suite at the Chateau and loved it, although they were somewhat mystified by the assortment of students and by what we did all day. We walked on the hard, wide sands through the maze of snarled driftwood trees at Wonga Beach, drank some vintage reds, and Tony and David argued all night. It was a joyous time. They encouraged us to build a proper auditorium with seats and to open a bar/restaurant for hungry and thirsty travellers. They thought the time was ripe to do something about the cultural wasteland that was Port Douglas and Mossman.

It was hard to believe what had happened to Port Douglas since we'd been there in 1975 to shoot the documentary about a crumbling, forgotten backwater by the sea in FNQ. Now the tourists were pouring in, as Port had become a 'destination' for the rich and famous from June until December. Christopher Skase, whose Quintex Group had been responsible for building the Mirage, was innovative in many ways. He had all Arnie Petersen's spiky oil palms dug up at vast expense and brought from the Daintree to line the road from the turnoff to Port, some four kilometres. It changed the entire aspect of the place and gave it a sort of Mediterranean look. Skase and his wife, Pixie, sailed around in a magnificent yacht furnished with Louis XIV antiques and hosted parties at a shopping complex where Louis Vuitton, YSL and Ermenegildo Zegna jostled for space under its galvanised-iron roof. Hundreds of boats, junks and schooners lay at anchor in a brand-new marina where, every day at 9.30 a.m., busloads of tourists were bustled onto Quicksilver hydrofoils for their day of fun on the Great Barrier Reef. Each week, the price of real estate increased exponentially, and with it the rates.

However, there was one glaring deficiency: visitors and locals had nothing to do at night. Of course, there were restaurants, our own Nautilus included, but, after that, cane-toad racing doesn't do it for most people. After much discussion, Tony and I decided that we could open the theatre to the public for six months of the year, mounting plays that would tour nationally after being staged at Karnak. We would model ourselves loosely on Glyndebourne, the famous private theatre built in 1934, outside London on the way to Brighton. Like Glyndebourne, we planned to host opera, professional entertainers, local talent and school functions. It was an exciting prospect and we approached the Douglas Shire Council with our plans.

As soon as we submitted our application to construct an amphitheatre, bar and restaurant, the proverbial shit hit the fan and didn't stop flying for well over two years. There were petitions signed by Whyanbeel Valley residents who were concerned that we would be corrupting the morals of minors by introducing alcohol and drugs into the community. It was a well-known fact, they said, that persons connected with the theatre were all homosexuals and paedophiles. It mattered not that the society in our northern parts was notorious for incest, child abuse and wife beating. In reality, I believe that the Whyanbeel Valley was already well established in dope-dealing circles for the quantities of superior cannabis grown in its rich alluvial soil. Those who profited from this lucrative horticulture were determined that there would be no intrusions.

So many barriers were put in our way that it was obvious there was a collective effort to thwart the whole venture. We had become the unsuspecting targets of a concerted assault, and had we been less passionate people, we would have given up after the first unpleasant salvos were fired. We had no idea why there was so much antagonism towards the building of such an exciting venue in their midst. Looking back, one can laugh and say how crazy it all was, but at the time it was simply devastating and had some lasting evil effects.

Probably the most unscrupulous and vile act of sabotage was the one perpetrated against Tony. Arriving home from his usual swim on Four Mile Beach, he told me that a funny thing had happened to him that afternoon. He had just come out of the water and returned to his Toyota when a police car had pulled up beside him and two police officers had got out. With smirks on their faces, they told him to get into their patrol car, as they wanted to talk to him. He complied, sitting in the back seat between them. There had been a complaint about Tony exposing himself on the beach, they told him. Someone had seen him jogging with his swimming shorts around his ankles. Tony was astounded, but managed to laugh, 'How could I possibly be jogging if my shorts were around my ankles?'

The police officers were not amused. There were witnesses, they advised him in an unpleasant, menacing manner.

'Who?' asked Tony.

'Never you mind,' they sneered.

Finally, the officers let him out of the car with a warning and he came home utterly flummoxed. The next thing we knew, the local rag, the *Mossman Gazette*, printed a front-page story about Tony being arrested for indecent exposure. Inevitably, it was picked up by news agencies all over the world but the story was particularly beaten up in all the London papers. Just as inevitably, to Tony's horror, his old mum read the story.

Of all the men I have ever met in my life, Tony Shaffer was the least likely ever to be a flasher. A natural reserve about displaying his body was one of his characteristics. He loved dressing up in flamboyant, expensive finery, which gave him dash, but, without doubt, he would have been mortified beyond measure to expose any part of his anatomy that might allow his physical inadequacies to be remarked upon. Most men of his age group have the same organic shame about their bodies.

Tony's mother rang him, just as mine had done when that spurious story had appeared in the newspapers inferring that both Sean and Paul Newman were my lovers. She demanded to know what he was doing, and though he told her a thousand times that the story was a blatant fabrication, her only response, like my mum's, was to enquire, 'Why then was it *printed in the paper?*' They both belonged to a generation who took the printed word as gospel.

There were no witnesses, of course, and the matter never came to court, but the damage had been done. Needless to say, the retraction was buried in the most obscure pages of the paper. The biographical scripts about Charlie Chaplin and Bela Lugosi that Tony had lavished so much love and attention upon were relegated to the backburner by the Hollywood Studios, as was *The Glow*. His play *This Savage Parade*, though produced at the King's Head in Islington with a good cast, did not transfer to the West End. Tony's despair was manifested by a marked escalation in his drinking habits. I could feel the build-up of frustration in him and, worse still, the spin-off of the life-support medication and steroids he had been on for over five years was kicking in. He was diagnosed as diabetic, and his mood swings were daily ordeals.

Despite all this, we persevered with the theatre, trying to get building permission. The next objection put forward by council was that our neighbours would be disturbed by the noise. As the nearest house was through a wood, over a river and at least half a kilometre away from the stage, I pointed out how unlikely this was. The councillors, all of whom were cane farmers, looked bewildered when I described the funnel effect of the V-shaped back wall of the theatre, the copper inlays and the superior acoustics.

'What's *ack . . . koo . . . sticks?*' one of them asked, shaking his head at the others as though I was talking about nuclear physics.

I put together a short film to demonstrate what the finished complex would look like, and to explain how the presence of such an eco-tourist destination in the rainforest could prove to be a boon to the area. Joh Bjelke-Petersen had been ousted from government, in the wake of the Fitzgerald Inquiry into Corruption, and Queensland had a spanking new premier in the person of Wayne Goss, a young and approachable lawyer. I showed the film to Goss, who immediately offered a dollar-for-dollar deal and sent a letter of recommendation to the Douglas Shire Council encouraging them to give us any assistance necessary in the project, which was to be named Karnak Playhouse.

The letter served only to get us in deeper mire with the council. Far from complying with this missive from the premier of the state, they were determined to show their disdain for the new young Labor premier, for a Pommy who wrote plays and for a female person with a reputation. A large dead pig was dragged into our driveway and left to rot there. It was the tall poppy syndrome in spades.

One of the councillors, Don Watson, wrote an article, which wasn't printed in the *Mossman Gazette* but in the *Cairns Post*, in which he said I was the object of a 'witch-hunt'. The building inspector changed our plans for the auditorium radically every time we submitted them and made it impossible for us to put a cover over the theatre unless we reconstructed. Next, we were denied a liquor licence. The only way to get around this punitive measure was to purchase a Special Event Licence every time we held a performance.

At around this time, two new people entered our lives at Karnak. A woman named Diane Morgan arrived unheralded from the United States, although she was already known to Tony as the ex-CIA investigator who had ferreted into the accounts of Peter Shaffer Pty Ltd (his brother's company, which handled *Sleuth*) and discovered a discrepancy of eighteen thousand dollars. Having retrieved the money, she was now dangling another fat carrot in front of Tony – the promise of a six-figure pay-off from monies she claimed were still owing to him.

Mrs Morgan came with her partner in crime (literally), the ox-like Ian, whom she passed off as her lover. However, our students, who had overheard the pair talking, quickly informed me that this was merely pretence. Mrs Morgan was the arch-prototype of the female I had avoided all my life. Long-bodied and horsy-faced, with prominent teeth, hennaed red hair and a rasping Midwestern American accent that defied contradiction, she was exceedingly bossy. I disliked and distrusted her on sight.

I put them in the Chateau and watched with alarm as they took crates of champagne up to Tony's study each day. Their manner was incredibly obsequious and unsubtle. Every comment Tony made, however innocuous, would be greeted as though it was an oracle and they leapt upon any slight joke he made, laughing uproariously for minutes on end.

The most depressing thing about their dreadful pantomime was that Tony loved it. Somehow, within days, Mrs Morgan had persuaded Tony to sell the Nautilus restaurant, although I intervened when he was about to accept a price that was $200 000 less than its worth. In the end it was sold for a million dollars and Mrs Morgan was in and out of Cairns seeing Tony's lawyer and (as I suspected rightly) doing her nefarious deals. I made no secret of my disapproval of Mrs Morgan and informed Tony that I was going into the bush to stay in the jungle house until she left.

At last, the two of them decamped from the Chateau and went off to stay at the most expensive place in Port Douglas, the Mirage. Mrs Morgan then persuaded Tony to give her the Sidney Nolan painting he had on his wall, saying that she would sell it for him in the States and make a great deal of money. She also convinced Tania Heben, a painter who had been living at Karnak, to let her take a great number of her paintings as well, promising she would launch Tania's career with a lavish party in Hollywood. Personally, I cannot imagine how this blatantly obvious criminal took in either Tony or Tania – but so it proved.

Once she had possession of the Nautilus money, the Sidney Nolan, Tania's pictures, and whatever else she could get her hands on, Mrs Morgan flew off to the USA and disappeared. Tony sued her in absentia for fraud in connection with the Nolan and won the case but the woman, the money and the paintings had gone forever. A year or two later, her bogus lover, Ian, got in touch with Tony, sending him a snapshot of the interior of a warehouse purported to be in Hawaii. It was crammed with objects that the magpie Morgan had filched from her victims, prominent amongst which were Tania's pictures and the Nolan. Ian offered himself as a go-between to make some deal but Tony suspected another 'sting' so he didn't reply. I agreed with his decision.

Meanwhile, our snail-like progress towards building the auditorium, restaurant, bar and foyer/front of house went on. A man from Melbourne, Barrie Semmens, and his wife, Maureen Hafner, replaced the previous rip-off occupants of the Chateau. Barrie had one of those minds that could comprehend and apply trigonometry. He designed and built a primitive tower and, using leverage based on unfathomable trigonometric calculations, was able to raise the huge poles into place, thus saving us close to fifty thousand dollars for the hire of an industrial crane. Maureen looked after the office and coordinated the elements that were coming together at last. Hopefully, it would culminate in two opening nights of magnificent entertainment and enchantment.

On 8 August 1992, the little cane train bound for Karnak Playhouse's inaugural night left Mossman crowded with excited guests. They were served complimentary champagne as the train chugged through the cane fields, many of which had been lit, over creeks and through backyards until it arrived at its destination. By the skin of our teeth, amidst men hammering and last-minute splashes of paint being applied, we managed to be ready to greet them with all the glitter and gaiety of a grand first night.

Only hours before, I had stood overlooking the stage with the new building inspector while the set of Tony's play, *Murderer*, was being assembled.

'Is that a working oven you've got in that kitchen on the stage?' he'd asked.

'Yes. The leading man has to take a piece of smoking roast beef out of it in the first scene.'

'Then you'll have to get building permission for the kitchen to be there, you know. Six weeks it takes to go through.'

'But it's only a set! It comes apart in five minutes.'

'You still have to have permission.'

As director of the play, I made the decision to go ahead anyway. It was too late for building inspectors. This was about live theatre, not a bunch of bureaucrats.

Tony hit the exact note when he wrote in the programme:

What is it that makes live theatre so different from films and TV? Basically, it is just that – it is live – not shadows. It can respond to its audience at the actual time of playing, and can allow the audience to respond and change itself – to transform, to leave the building in a state completely different from the way it entered it – enlivened, enlightened, even edified.

And how does one achieve all this? By involving the risk of accident by being alive. And it is this very 'liveness' that can create a sense of an Event or a Celebration or an attack on Reality . . . it makes no difference which.

My son, Jason, looking impeccable in tails, was the MC for that first night. It turned out to be a scintillating mix of talent and, with the nearness of the stars in the sky, the moon rising over the trees and the sounds of the jungle, it was a magical experience none of us will ever forget. The Premier of Queensland, Wayne Goss, formally opened the theatre after Robyn Archer had yodelled, Dance North had danced like demons in a ballet called *Women's War Too* and the Brisbane Festival Quartet had played works by Mozart and the Australian composer Peter Sculthorpe.

I'd managed to procure a thirty-metre blood-red curtain for *Murderer*, Tony's classic play about a man who has decided to take 'the sinful way to salvation', which was our second night's offering. The sinful way to salvation was a theme that had exercised Tony's mind all his life and he questioned various intellectuals, mystics and masters of philosophy about it continuously. In my production of *Murderer*, as the house lights dim, the audience sees a gruesome murder taking place, distorted in shadow play behind the crimson curtain and orchestrated by the crashing, discordant chords of the opening of the first movement of Brahms' Piano Concerto No. 1 in D Minor, Op. 15. As the music fades, the murderer's voice is heard:

'To become a murderer . . . that, in the last few years, has crystallised into my single, constant, unappeasable passion. Not a casual killer in a barroom brawl, or a senseless slayer in a squalid domestic squabble . . . but a great *classic* murderer – a man who understands the true nature of the act of murder, who actually knows that once a man has killed deliberately, his inhibitions are destroyed because he has fully looked on mortality . . . and his soul is freed! My ambition is to join that alien clan of which no member knows the other and set my face against the world. And my aim is to ensure that, if I cannot be famous, at least my crime will make me infamous for all time.'

The proposition of the play is thus established within the first thirty seconds, but from then on, nothing is what it appears. Tony lovingly embraces the thriller/mystery/black comedy genre while at the same time satirising it, always staying one step ahead of the audience. He goads them into thinking they've discovered the outcomes and then rips the carpet from under their feet with another shifting plot change.

Tony and I sat with Wayne Goss and his wife, Roisin. I could feel Tony squirm with delight when Wayne turned to him and announced in his authoritative lawyer's voice, 'Yes . . . Ah, yes . . . I can see where you're going now, Tony. I've got it all sorted out.' He then proceeded to explain his solution to the plot (mistaken, of course) but wicked Tony just smiled and said, 'Well done, Wayne. Thank God we have a man of superior intellect in politics at last.'

During the play, there was one glorious moment when the murderer, played by John Stanton, had stripped off to his briefs and was busy rushing from the kitchen downstairs, where he was eating a huge roast beef sandwich, to the bathroom upstairs, where he was dismembering his victim in the bathtub. Every time he mounted the steps, the whole audience hooted with laughter. John was baffled. He surreptitiously checked his underwear, and was relieved that it wasn't the cause of such hilarity, but howls of laughter continued to dog his departure from the kitchen every time. Flying down the stairs faster than usual on his fifth descent, John caught our naughty pussycat having a gnaw on the roast on the kitchen table, which she had been craftily leaping on each time he went up the stairs. Inevitably, several people asked me in the interval how I had trained a cat to perform so remarkably.

Like every director, I sat frozen with terror that something ghastly would happen, but, apart from the cat's antics, nothing did and the entire audience rose at the curtain to give *Murderer* a rousing reception. Though it had been an incredible effort to mount such a play, it was the best gift that I could ever have given Tony.

The run of the play was not a week old when we heard it. It was the noise of claxons, hooters and trumpets of the kind made by football crowds. The actors on the stage could hardly hear each other, let alone convey anything to the spectators. Delini Wijeyesekera, a former student at Karnak who was originally from Sri Lanka and who now looked after the bar at the theatre, came with me to investigate. The noise was so loud that we thought there must be a group of people just beside the stage, but there was no-one there. I followed the source of the cacophony, which led right down to the creek. I crossed the water, taking off my shoes and leaving them on a rock, and walked through the trees and up a slope to where I could see lights in the distance. All the while, the sounds grew even more deafening. Halfway up the long slope a tableau came into view . . . a tableau so extraordinary it took my breath away.

On the lighted patio of the house ahead of me, I saw a giant amplifier. There were figures prancing around in front of it with trumpets, horns and hooters. They were being egged on by a larger figure and there was someone else in the background. All of them were laughing. They were oblivious to anything other than making as much noise as possible and they seemed to be tireless in their efforts. I shouted out but my voice was but a whisper in the din they were creating.

When I drew nearer, I saw that there was a boy of about thirteen, a girl of eight or nine and an older man with grey hair who seemed to be in charge of the proceedings. The only way I could think of attracting their attention was to throw a stone past them onto the back wall. The boy noticed straightaway, and shouted, 'There's someone there!'

The older man immediately whistled and shrieked for his dogs, to set them on me. I stopped dead in my tracks, frightened of being savaged by the pig dogs, but they just ran past me and away to the river. The man and the boy started searching the bush with torches, so I came forward and was caught in the headlights of a truck being driven by another man, who I recognised as the boy's father. He was the person who had written a raft of letters to the local paper opposing the theatre.

The boy held a baseball bat over my head, asking his father if he should hit me. A surreal conversation followed.

'Why are you doing this?' I asked.

'We're going to get you, you know,' the father threatened.

'What did we ever do to you?'

'We're going to get you for trespassing.'

'She threw a stone at me, Dad!' shouted the boy.

'And we'll get you for the attempted assault of minors, as well,' the man yelled.

'Do what you will but stop this disgusting noise,' I said and left them, walking back the way I had come, picking up my shoes on the way. I was extremely shaken and found it hard to explain to Tony what had happened. It just seemed so mad.

The story was blown out of all proportion by the newspapers and I appeared as a vicious lunatic who had thrown stones at toddlers. Of course, when the case finally came to court, the judge, hearing the true story of the amplifier and the threats, threw out the case. When asked whether I wanted to sue them, I declined, knowing that it would only drag the affair on and on and incite more threats and bad blood in the district.

We were beset by problems from every side. In particular, there had been a major and insupportable blowout of costs. With the expenses of our brilliant opening and actors' salaries, having brought them from Melbourne to do only two or three performances a week instead of eight, we were $900 000 over budget. We thought of touring the play, as we just did not have the numbers to fill the theatre every night, but that would have meant another outlay of funds that was beyond our means. We had to consolidate, rethink the whole enterprise and try to pay off the debts in dribs and drabs. We came so near to bankruptcy that we consulted accountancy experts for guidance on the most effective way to go about handling such an eventuality. However, with the enormous generosity of those around us – like Jason, who gave us the residue from his educational package, Tony's brother, and many others – we managed to weather the storm. We had to take out a bank loan, which took what seemed like an eternity to pay off, but by 1994 we were back in business and taking on a mammoth production of *Midsummer Night's Dream*.

Before that, we played host to twelve students from the ATYP (Australian Theatre for Young People), Nicole Kidman's old school. They stayed for two weeks of master classes given by the top teachers in the land, including the late Australian playwright Nick Enright, David Williamson and John 'Cha Cha' O'Connell, choreographer for the film *Strictly Ballroom*. Tony undertook classes in play construction and I gave lessons in subtext and motivation. It was a heady mix.

David and Kristen Williamson's son Rory was one of the students, and a lively lot they were. They shot their own extremely obscure film in the Palace, where they were staying, and showed it to us on their last night. We invited the public to see what a couple of weeks of intense theatrical work could produce in a group of teenagers and with Delini's assistance I cooked enormous amounts of food. This was our initiation into what was to become the way we kept the theatre ticking over.

Unforeseeable good fortune came our way in the persons of David Helfgott and his wife, Gillian, who arrived one morning at the theatre. It was one of those days when time seems suspended and an hour stretches out into eternity. Gillian and I sat upstairs looking over the lake at the waterlilies and empty theatre, drinking chilled wine and talking, while the butcherbirds clarioned and David played and played

471

on my old upright piano. After finishing one piece, he would look over at us with the face of an expectant child and Gillian would call out, 'Oh, David, play "Clair de Lune",' or 'Play that lovely Mazurka you adore,' or 'Oh, David, just keep playing!' He would respond at once with the alacrity and pleasure of a willing child, so that Gillian could continue our conversation. 'The piano's the best minder in the world,' she told me.

It was decided that they would come back and stay at the Chateau for a short holiday while David put on a special concert at Karnak. When I tried to discuss money for such an event, Gillian demurred. 'No, David wants to do this one for free as you were such a good friend of Rix Weaver and we have to give something back, you know. We've been so fortunate.'

The other generous genius to enter the annals of Karnak Playhouse as a saviour was Jane Rutter, the flautist. Jane came to Karnak in the early 1980s as a member of Posh (a radical chamber music group), long before the Playhouse had ever been thought of. She was very young and had just returned from Paris, where she'd studied with flute masters Alain Marion and Jean-Pierre Rampal. From them she learned not merely music but a philosophy of life – romanticism, freedom of spirit, the mystique of the *artiste* dedicating herself to love affairs and excesses, a mélange of Bohemian ideas gleaned from Colette and Jean-Paul Sartre with a dash of Edith Piaf and a drop of Sancerre thrown in.

We all went up to the secret waterhole where the creek flows off the mountain and opens out into a glorious fringed pool, where platypuses snuffle through the residue at the bottom of the lake and the air is crackling with negative ions from the freezing water that falls four thousand feet. Jane shucked off her clothes in a flash, draped herself along an overhanging branch and played on her silver flute. It wasn't exhibitionism, as no-one had ever worn bathing suits at this magical place. There would have been something sacrilegious about putting bits of latex or any other sort of impediment between your skin and this healing water from the mountaintop.

I can still hear the pure sounds of *Syrinx* by Debussy across the limpid water as she played. We are all framed forever in that moment and space – the luckiest people in the world, lost in the crystal sounds of flute and water, with the filtered sun flickering through the over-hanging trees. Jane always plays that same Debussy piece when she comes to Karnak, relating the story of the pursuit of Syrinx, the river nymph, by the satyr, Pan. That day, she *was* the nymph, a mythologi-cal being who had found her habitat. *Syrinx* has become her Karnak signature piece.

When Jane became a solo artist, a star able to carry an evening's entertainment, she came back to Karnak and did a sell-out concert, but that wasn't enough for Ms Rutter. She was avid to act and determined to compose music. Why not cast this ethereal being with a flute as Titania, Queen of the Fairies, and have her compose the music as well?

It was an ambitious project we undertook – but nothing ventured, nothing won. Having built such a theatre we had to use it. For this pro-duction, we called upon a cross-section of schools – Trinity Anglican in Cairns, Trinity Bay School, Mossman High and Miallo Primary schools. The James Cook University teachers, including Jean-Pierre Voos, were also roped in and given bits of Shakespeare's *Midsummer Night's Dream* to rehearse. The principals – Jane as Titania, David Jenkins as Oberon, Brendon O'Connor as Puck and Sarah Walker as the First Fairy – stayed and rehearsed at Karnak. I chose a shy Aboriginal boy called Patrick from the Mossman Gorge Community to be the Changeling Child and with him came the Mount Molloy Dancers and the Bamanga Bubu Ngadimunku Aborigines from the Kuku Yalanji Community. The cast numbered seventy-nine and counting.

In the last week, the teachers brought the participants to Karnak and they camped in the grounds. I had to use a loudhailer and became hoarse with shouting but, somehow, it all came together. Like the old saying goes, 'It's bound to be right on the night', and it was. From the moment Jane's Balinese wedding music rang out and the fire-blowers (including myself) shot flames into the air from their mouths, it took off. With all the parents barracking, we had a sell-out.

We took the play to Townsville, to the Botanical Gardens. When I asked for an estimate of the number of people likely to turn up, they told me two hundred. On the day of the performance, the actors found it difficult to get to the performance area, so great a crush was there. Two thousand came.

The success of *Midsummer Night's Dream* emboldened us to seek new schemes to keep the excitement going. We knew that we couldn't afford to transport actors from the capital cities and pay union rates of fifteen hundred dollars a week for two performances, plus per diems. The cost was prohibitive. We had to devise some way of making the theatre work, week in and week out, with a bread-and-butter show and then mount our own productions when we had accrued enough money.

In London I had been overwhelmed by experiments with laser light, so I put out feelers to find how we could harness this fascinating new technology for our purpose. Fortuitously, Telstra was launching a new logo at the Cairns Civic Centre to celebrate their corporate branding, using the first 3-D colour laser brought to the North. They had employed a company called Technofear, run by two young Sydneysiders (cousins), one of whom was a laser freak like me. His name was Dean Holland and it was he who digitised the images, joining up the dots three-dimensionally by hand. Tony called him, explaining that we were thinking of acquiring a laser, and asked if he could help. He could.

On our next visit to Sydney we visited Dean's studio in Cronulla, where we sat in a small darkened room filled with prop smoke (known as fog juice – user-friendly and odourless) and watched as he produced miniature figures made of brilliant light in an endless variety of hues. They ran, jumped and turned cartwheels in the air. To me, it was true magic and I found it impossible to look away. Afterwards, we went to lunch together and shook hands on a deal: Dean would sell us a colour laser, come up to Karnak for three months and stay at the Ritz with his

474

lady, Tracey, and their three daughters while digitising the images for our laser drama. An air-conditioned room would be built into the V of the back wall of the theatre to house the sensitive laser equipment and computer at a constant temperature of twenty degrees.

The laser show was called *Creation* and the script we wrote together was designed to please all ages. Employing every device – smoke, lasers and sound – to maximise the effect, it begins with the 'Big Bang'.

[*Complete blackout*]

Tony's deep, reverberating voice as God swells from the blackness: DARKNESS! There are a few scattered sounds as pulsating, concave shapes pass through the smoke that pervades the auditorium.

Voice: The state of not knowing where you ARE! [*Suddenly*]
                   FEAR . . . !

[*Subliminally, a death's head and skull hit the smoke*]

Voice: Your eyes begin to pick up shapes . . . [*More weird shapes
                   whiz by with crackling sounds*] And you realise . . . there
                   is no such thing as darkness . . . There is only that
                   place . . . where there is no *light*. So . . .

[*There is lightning, and strange firecracker sounds are heard from far away*]

Voice thunders: LET . . . THERE . . . BE . . . LIGHT!'

[*The voice swells to a monumental crescendo and reverberates as the laser flashes white lightning and rips the sky asunder with a protracted display of* LIGHT]

It is overwhelming. Through the elements of laser imaging, voice, sound effects and music, the narrative carries the audience from the beginnings of life on this planet, through the greening of Gondwana-land and the era of the dinosaurs, to the advent of Man in the person of an Aboriginal boy. He stands, one foot upon his knee, leaning on his spear in a halo of laser light. He is made of flesh and bone.

The history of this particular area of the earth's surface unfolds, from Aboriginal legends through to the coming of Captain James

Cook, who spent six weeks careening his boat here. We found a passage in his log about the Australian Aborigines, which Tony read out in Cook's North Country accent: 'They may appear to some to be the most wretched people on earth, but in reality they are *far happier* than we Europeans. They live in a tranquillity which is not disturbed by the inequality of condition; the earth and sea of their own accord furnish them with all things necessary for life . . .'

The elders of the Kuku Yalanji Community, our indigenous rainforest people who have inhabited the Mossman Gorge and surrounding lands for forty thousand years, gave us permission to use their legends about the coming of Fire and the conquering of Urambu, the Flesh Eater, by Goobidi, their Protector. We recorded their stories with five young Aboriginal girls at Select Sound Studios in Cairns, where British expatriate Nigel Pegrum, former percussionist for the Small Faces, the Pretenders, Steeleye Span and Uriah Heep, was another link in our enterprise.

Luckily for us, Nigel had married a Queensland girl, Carmel Webb, whom he'd met on Dunk Island, and had relocated to Cairns, where he'd set up his state-of-the art sound studio. He is a perfectionist and *Creation* would have been impossible without his assistance. Tony and I stayed in Cairns for a week, working night and day with Nigel to complete the CD-ROM so that Dean could choreograph his images to the audio. Tony, Dean, Nigel, Mark Marshal (Dean's cousin) and I all lent our voices to the CD as sailors on the *Endeavour* and I was recruited to do bird calls and any other weird ambient sounds. Donald Hall and Jane Rutter composed other sections of the original music, and when all the strands had been pulled together we brought the children from the Gorge Community into the mix to mime the stories in an interface with the laser 3-D images. It remains a unique example of multimedia magnificence.

My niece Adele came to work in the office and arranged bank accounts for each of the children we employed. I picked them up on

Wednesdays and Saturdays in a bus that Tony had bought for me as a birthday present, after Delini and I had prepared a symphony of salads, curries and roast chicken with lemon and tarragon for the guests, using our own rare fruit.

Creation garnered a rave review in Queensland's *Courier-Mail*, which described it as the most innovative happening in theatre for ten years, and the *Bulletin* described Karnak Playhouse as a national treasure. We had no money to do publicity but word of mouth was beginning to spread and it began to make a difference. Slowly but surely, we paid off our debts.

A pattern began to emerge that had been foreseen many years before by Bulent Rauf. Back in 1977 when he had come to give us his special blessing and inaugurate Karnak, I had asked him why it was that I was constrained to take myself to the ends of the earth and undertake something that was seemingly impossible. I told him I didn't think I could do it, that I wasn't strong enough or committed enough to stick it out. He thought for a long time before he answered. At last, he spoke:

'You know, there are some things which you already know that will give you your answer. There is a saying, "A back was never made too weak to support the burden it had to carry." That is one thing you do *not* know yet. Another saying says, "We shall try them until we know." This is also for the future. But what you *do* know is that your instinct led you here and everything that has happened to you in your lifetime has brought you to this moment when you are to define yourself by the impulse that set this adventure in place. There is only the necessary and the impossible. It happened, so it was necessary; any hypothetical is impossible after the event. Remember, you can drown in "if".

'You have a distinct destiny, like everybody. That is why we asked to be here, in this place, in the beginning. You were actually born in this strange, geographically detached land of the Never-Never, Down Under, beyond the burnt stump – all the names conjured up in people's imaginations to describe remoteness. But this attribute may prove to be its greatest blessing. Who knows? Just as it is an integral feature in your destiny, so *you* are in *its* chaptering out of time. The greatest stumbling block for mankind is despair. It is considered a sin, but man has also been gifted with its antidote, if you like to call it that – a sense of the absurd, humour. Man can always – in fact, *must* – laugh at himself and the monstrous absurdity of being born, knowing only one thing for certain, and that is that he must die. He has a limited amount of time to find out what he is doing here and who he actually is. It is the choice of each individual to undertake these questions. If not now, when? You will always suffer from other people's envy. But that is also a challenge, so do not feel sorry for yourself. Stay close to what you have learned because it will be there that you will find all the succour you need to carry you through the times when you feel your back will break.'

It was at this time in my history that my back was showing distinct signs of breaking. I went to sit in the Meditation Room every day, sometimes feeling that I could not get up again . . . or that I did not want to get up. It was a temporary collapse of will, but every time I was about to throw in the towel, put Karnak on the market and run away, something would happen to change the mood, our fortune, the future.

During the six-month season the theatre was open for business, my stint of mowing the grounds, maintaining the theatre, putting on plays, skimping and saving, never taking a salary and holding everything together with chewing gum would leave me on the verge of despair. It was different for Tony. He didn't have the same fervour in these matters. His great contribution was that he would always have some holiday planned – Bali, Mexico, Cuba, La Jolla, Morocco or Santa Fe. He was adept at fixing the perfect reconcilers, pointing out new horizons, smells and sights, and so I stumbled on, impervious to the strife and struggles.

We embarked on a series of plays, modest two-handers with low overheads – *Deceptions* with Rowena Wallace and Peter Moore, and a new American thriller set in New York called *Galatea's Hands*, both of which we toured to Port Moresby in New Guinea. The two young actors in *Galatea's Hands* were products of southern schools of acting and both were extremely talented. When Sarah Walker played the First Fairy in *Midsummer Night's Dream* she established an abiding link with the Aboriginal children, helping to rehearse them and bring them up to performance level. They adored her. She had the knack of amusing them while at the same time making them pay attention. I have never met such observant children in my life. Tony once gave me a quandong seed on a chain. When I wore it, all of the children shouted out from at least fifty metres away: 'Quandong! Quandong seed!'

I was at first a bit worried about Sarah's co-star, Julian Leather. The play called for the actor to dig deep down into the emotional depths of a young man who has killed both his parents. An obsessional psycho, he lures an unsuspecting young model from his sculpting class to pose for him. Our rehearsals are always times of discovery, but Julian was a revelation. With each performance, he expanded to fit the role. Watching an actor in full flight, in control of the material but still trying things out, is a surprisingly valuable experience.

Both Sarah and Julian had to appear nude in the context of the play, which is set in a sculpting studio. It wasn't gratuitous nudity, but when we went to New Guinea the management refused to let them strip.

'But there are women everywhere here with bare breasts wearing virtually nothing,' I argued.

'Yes, but they're black.'

They were adamant. If no clothes, then no show, so I went out and bought one of those hideous bodysuits which are supposed to hide the naughty bits and preserve modesty. In fact, no more obscene garment exists that I know of. Sarah got into it and looked ridiculous. I made a great show at the dress rehearsal of demonstrating the use of the suit and then told Sarah to take it off for the performance. No-one said anything, and at the party after the show I remarked to the manager how successful the suit had been. He agreed.

Within a year or two, both these brilliant young actors were dead. It still seems an implausible sentence to have just written – that Sarah and Julian both left the stage, never to return.

First, Sarah wrenched herself away from Karnak after many misgivings to try her fortune in her native Melbourne. Some months later, she went to a wedding, drank some champagne, did a scene from *Absolutely Fabulous* and ingested a tab of Ecstasy. She went home to bed, but when her boyfriend came to collect her the next day, he could not revive her. The police wouldn't release her body to her parents for quite some time, as they were conducting so many tests but, finally, her ashes were brought back to Karnak.

It would have been incorrect to allow Sarah's passing to go unremarked. All of us were devastated, including the Aboriginal children. Her parents, brothers, boyfriend, grandparents – in fact, the whole Walker clan – arrived bearing Sarah's ashes, and we prepared the ceremony taught to us by Grandfather Morning Owl (James A. Barnett, a Native American pipe-carrier from Sedona, Arizona, who had been visiting Karnak to do Sweat Lodges for some years). All the mourners met in the theatre upstairs, where we were each allocated a partner and given paper and pens to write a letter to Sarah. In our letters, we were to ask Sarah any questions that remained unanswered in our minds, tell her what we specifically loved about her and conclude by saying goodbye. Once the letters were completed, we all walked hand in hand through the bush to the hidden waterhole in the rainforest where we had swum together so often.

We had built a huge fire in the clearing, and it was here that we read out the letters, not our own but those written by our partners. All of them were moving and different. Then, each person came forward to say goodbye, throwing their letter into the fire. The smoke rose above the trees, where the sulphur-crested cockatoos screeched out their warnings of our presence to each other. We then moved down to the water's edge, where Sarah's brother gave a eulogy and gently released her ashes into the clear water where her remains merged into the ever-flowing stream that empties itself ultimately into the sea. I never visit the spot without thinking about her.

With Julian, it was different, I think. I only heard about his death some weeks after it had happened. No-one seemed to have a clear picture of how it had come about. I was told that Julian was in the habit of sitting out on the window ledge of his apartment in the evening, smoking a joint, looking out over the vast metropolis and ruminating. His father told me that perhaps he was thinking about his beloved sister who had died. One evening, he either lost his balance or slid into oblivion intentionally. As I understand it, his death occurred when there was no-one there, no-one to say goodbye to and no-one to tell us how it happened. Potentially, I believe he was a great actor, but no-one will ever know that now.

My son Jason had been in Russia with Michael Caine shooting a film called *Bullet from Beijing*. His co-star in the flick was a very desirable young lady who had appeared in *Ferris Bueller's Day Off* and *Legend*. Her name was Mia Sarapocciello but she was known professionally as Mia Sara. Jason had always been rather guarded in his attitude towards girlfriends – not secretive, just not what my mother would have called 'forthcoming'. I suspect Michael Caine played matchmaker with Jason and Mia Sara. He whispered to Jason that Mia was secretly mad about him and to Mia that Jason was lost in love but too shy to make the first move. This method of attraction through a third party works every time, having been used in the plots of numerous plays, including Shakespeare's.

The outcome of all this romantic persiflage was that Jason went to live with Mia in Hollywood. When Tony and I visited them on our way back to Oz, Jason was busy sanding her floors and renovating – a sure sign of the nesting instinct – so we were not particularly surprised to hear that they had driven to Las Vegas one day and tied the knot without informing their respective parents.

The next time I saw Jason was when he brought his already pregnant wife to stay at Karnak early in 1996. I housed them in the Chateau, in the suite reserved for the stars. It had a theatrical mirror with light bulbs of various colours and its own loo – luxury. The first morning I went to have breakfast on their verandah, I found Mia swiping at the little black native bees that often hover around jams and honey.

'These flies are really bad,' she winced. 'Have you got some spray?'

'They're not flies. They're small black native bees. They don't sting. They make black honey. They don't hurt anybody.'

'No . . . no,' she said. 'They're flies.'

'I promise you, they're bees!'

'I know they're flies and there are ants with green abdomens walking all over the handrails,' she said in disgust.

'Yes, green ants . . . they live here too. They make a great drink. The Aborigines drink it. It's cool, like lemonade.'

I knew I was not convincing her. In the tropics, you either learn to live with insects or you leave. That day, Mia went shopping with Jason and spent a small fortune on sprays.

'Jason and I are *clean* people,' she said firmly, and I could tell she hated everything about Karnak.

A welcoming concert had been arranged in which many performers were appearing – Jane Rutter flauting, Nigel Pegrum performing with his band and a bevy of schools doing bits of their plays. It was meant to be a joyous occasion called 'The Jason and Mia Show', and Jason was hosting it, but as soon as Jane started playing, the chainsaws started up from over the river. This was the rednecks' new way of disrupting performances. Jason was outraged but Mia never said a word. She wasn't surprised.

I had envisaged that maybe Jason and Mia would take over the theatre one day and spend some time in the rainforest, but it was quickly apparent that Karnak would be the least likely plan for their future. Jason had bought a cottage in Scotland in a place called Lillies-leaf-under-Melrose, where sheep and cows graze in tranquil verdant meadows, where no small black native bees or green ants or rednecks dwell, where nothing disturbs the bucolic peace of the seasons and all is under man's control. It was understandable that he would prefer a safe environment where no threat of hurricane or other hazards disturb sleep.

My daughter Giovanna had also left for foreign parts and now lived in Santa Fe, New Mexico, where she was pursuing an academic career at Antioch University, completing a Masters Degree in Environment and Community as well as teaching the Gurdjieff Movements. Her marriage to Bill Phillips had fallen apart and she was soon to meet the great love of her life, Randal Swedberg. Tony and I rented a house in the centre of Santa Fe to be near G and my nephew, Seb, who had married there and was studying jewellery making. We motored around, visiting Taos, Ghost Ranch, Albiquiu, where the artist Georgia O' Keeffe painted, and the cliff dwellings of the Anasazi Indians. We sampled tamales and green chilli sauce and enjoyed the desert.

I am immensely proud of both my children, as they are people whom, even if I were not related to them, I would love to know. The fact that neither of them wants to live in Far North Queensland is of no consequence. Everyone finds a place that chimes with their special needs and I have never made them feel guilty about their preference for somewhere else. We are thrilled to see each other when we meet, and they put up with my eccentricities and are protective and loyal towards me. I think that's about all you can expect from your children.

By 1997, when we added a gold rush segment to *Creation*, Tony's health had begun to deteriorate. I noticed it especially when we went back to the recording studios with Nigel and Tony's voice had lost that vibrant quality which had made it so distinctive. A less constitutionally strong body would have buckled under the duress Tony placed upon it. He smoked incessantly, sometimes two cigarettes at once when he forgot that he had one lit already. The medication he was taking turned his stomach into a factory for bile, and if he didn't sit down to eat by 7.30 p.m. he lost any appetite for food, and was interested only in drinking well into the night until he was legless.

I was working the spotlight on the night of the new laser show, when the gold rush was added, which made it impossible for me to be with Tony during the performance. It was his habit to stand at the long red cedar bar at the back of the stalls during the show and drink, sometimes making very loud comments. His presence was not often intrusive but Delini, who worked the bar, would try to curb the supply of champagne at times. If Tony noticed, he could become verbally offensive. On this particular night he was not to be denied and could be heard shouting at Delini to open another bottle. By the end of the show, Tony wasn't too stable on his feet.

When people are excited by the performance they have just witnessed in a theatre, they can be reluctant to go home. They linger and buy a few more drinks, waiting for the performers to appear. Sometimes they sit down with us and eat another dinner, attracted by the proximity to live actors, so we often don't get out of the theatre until the wee small hours.

It was very late when I finally helped Tony into the car and drove up the hill to our Castle. I pulled into the garage, adjacent to the stone stairs that led down to the road and the lake, and had just reached the back of the car as Tony heaved himself out of the passenger seat. He staggered to his feet and turned to go down the hill rather than towards the house. I watched, horrified, as he tottered towards the stairs, his pace gaining momentum as though he were sprinting, until he raced forward at an angle of forty-five degrees down the seventeen wide steps. He landed on his head with a sickening crunch.

I shouted out to Dean Holland, who was still in the theatre across the lake, and we both rushed to where Tony lay moaning on the road. We got him into the car and Dean drove us to Mossman Cottage Hospital while I held Tony in the back seat. A young intern was summoned, but upon examining Tony he found no serious damage. I couldn't understand how Tony, having fallen on his already damaged head, had not been further injured. Tony himself was sure he was dying, so they kept him in overnight – or what was left of it. I wanted to stay but was not allowed, as they told me he was being placed in a public ward.

The next morning, X-rays were done and he was released. By that evening, Tony was back in the bar. He seemed impervious to his accident but complained that he was finding it difficult to raise his right elbow, the arm that lifts the glass to the lips, so he made much of having to use his other hand to lift his arm while drinking. As the diagnosis based on the X-rays was inconclusive, I found a guy named Emad who was adept at massage and repairing torn ligaments in athletes. He put Tony through some rigorous exercises but the problem with his arm persisted, becoming a constant source of worry and frustration.

Tony and I were invited by a Canadian film company to go on a journey of two days and a night on the *Queenslander*, a luxury train which chugged its way from the south-east of the state all the way north to Cairns. It was the perfect change of pace we both needed. We took the opportunity to talk about Tony's new play, away from the telephone and the demands of working in a live theatre. Even the camera crew didn't intervene in our discussions.

I had been thrilled when Tony had told me that he had a new play in mind. He had a pool of plots stored in his head and every so often he would drag one to the surface to become the subject of his intense scrutiny, sometimes writing a rough outline as a guide. The stories he was interested in had one common feature: they all centred on murder. This particular plot was quite simple but also diabolical. An old woman, who is completely paralysed except for the ability to blink her

485

eyes, overhears her daughter-in-law planning the murder of her son with her lover. How can she avert his death? And if she cannot, how can she bring the murderers to justice?

Tony wanted to call the play *The Thing in the Wheelchair*. He thought my idea was a winner – that the daughter-in-law is an amateur actress who is playing Lady Macbeth when the murder plot is hatched. Her lover and co-conspirator is a bowser attendant at the local filling station, who she has got into the theatre to play the Second Murderer. The play was to be set in the sixties with the subtitle *The Lady Macbeth of the Suburbs*.

By the time we got off the train, Tony was greatly excited and eager to get to work, but first he wanted to go to London to see about his arm problem, visit his old mother who was ailing and spend Christmas with his daughters. I was to stay on, finish the season and join him in the New Year while the theatre was under wraps for the Wet. The next thing I heard, after some worrying calls about certain sadistic masseurs, was that Tony had had another hugely intrusive operation on his back and was unable to move at all. His daughter Claudia telephoned to warn me that Tony was completely incapacitated and relying on a 24-hour nursing care service.

It was January and freezing in London when I arrived. I had left Australia as the humidity soared to a hundred and a tropical cyclone was imminent. Tony, a small croissant shape under the covers in his bed, was drugged, pale and disinterested in the world. When I roused him to give him a kiss, he reeked of that undergrowth smell of the unwashed. A red-haired girl from Perth, Western Australia, was sitting upstairs in the large airy studio flicking through a magazine. This was his day-time nurse, Margaret. I asked her when Tony had last had a bath. She said she was terrified of his sudden ranting furies and had not managed to wash him properly in the week she had been at the studio.

My initial job was to try to bathe him. He couldn't get into the bath, so Margaret and I stood him between us in the shower and I scrubbed him thoroughly. He made a big fuss, but I knew he felt much better afterwards. When this difficult task was accomplished, I walked down the Fulham Road in search of some warm clothes. The chill factor in the London wind allied itself with the dirt lifting in small whorls from the pavement. Perhaps it was because I had been travelling for thirty-two hours but the people I passed looked disgruntled and sour. I felt like a stranger in a strange land until I entered the supermarket, where everything was exactly the same as everywhere else – the same brand names, the same marketing, the same rubbish that we wander around with in the same trolleys.

In the weeks that followed, Margaret and I pushed Tony all over London in a wheelchair, which is hard work until you learn the trick of managing the pavements and finding the ramps. We wheeled him over to his mother's place in Chelsea one evening, squeezing him into the twee little elevator and up to his mum's apartment overlooking the River Thames. His mother, coiffed as always by her old Irish retainer, Martha, shrieked when she saw the emaciated man in the wheelchair.

'Oh, heavens! Oh, good Lord! Tony, is it you? You look older than I do!'

I thought it was incredibly cruel of her but Tony just grinned and quaffed his champagne. His mother did not offer Margaret or me any.

'Don't worry,' Martha whispered in my ear. 'She's just forgotten who you are. She doesn't remember anyone any more.' I did not believe it for a second.

Tony was agitating to get back to the Australian warmth, far from the wintry days and bitter nights. Before the operation, he had been given some exercises to practise underwater but the local swimming pool was far too crowded. The trip to the Antipodes was too arduous for someone in his condition to undertake in one hop, so I began to think about how we could break up the journey and somehow stimulate his interest in something – anything. He was dejected, certain that he would never walk again, and work on his new play was out of the question.

For a long time, we had been talking about going to Sri Lanka. We had even been booked to stay with Delini's parents in Colombo some years before, but they cried off at the last minute and asked us not to come because of the civil war. People were being blown up in the cities with alarming regularity. Since then, so much had happened in that country. Delini's father was murdered in the street and her mother had a stroke and died. It was time for Delini to return to her native land and lay her ghosts to rest.

Before we left the UK, we visited Jason, Mia and Dashiell, their new baby boy, in their cottage in Scotland. It was a nightmare in the wee housie with the narrow staircase that Jason and I had to negotiate, carrying Tony up and down. The two dependents, Dashiell and Tony, got on like a house on fire. As Jason said, 'It takes one to know one.' They exchanged secret knowing smiles while demanding instant and constant attention from all three of us. We loved them both to distraction but together they upped the stress factor by 300 per cent.

I returned to London exhausted but ready to plan our journey home like a military operation. Delini and Robert Kemp, a friend of many years who was also a brilliant set designer, would fly from Australia to Sri Lanka and await our arrival from London later the same day. We would then lift Tony and his wheelchair into a specially hired car and drive to Anoma Beattie's house, where we would occupy a small cottage at ground level. It would take Tony a day or so to recover from the trip, by which time our transport for the rest of the trip would be waiting at the door.

The Sri Lankans had put their heads together and worked out a list of awesome adventures in rapturous settings to stimulate Tony's senses. Anoma Beattie (née Wajarawardene) lives in a lovely house in the centre of Colombo with a walled garden and shaded verandahs. A gifted painter, she was until recently married to the son of the Admiral of the Fleet, Lord Beattie. Everything went swimmingly until we reached the small cottage in her garden, where Tony collapsed. We put him to bed in the tiny bedroom that opened out into the garden.

When a doctor was called, we didn't expect that ten people would turn up. They crowded into Tony's room like a scene straight out of a Marx Brothers film. One was taking Tony's temperature, another his blood pressure and yet another his pulse, while several nurses, dressed in full regalia, were jostling each other as they sterilised needles. Two of the doctors chattered at the top of their lungs, one of them questioning me about Tony's medication and the other giving a running commentary on Tony's condition, as he lay comatose. Once the injection had been administered, they swarmed out like a plague of noisy locusts moving on to fresh pastures.

Our time in Sri Lanka was spent in what was perhaps the most comprehensive traversing of any island I have ever done. We went everywhere, but before we left Colombo there was the unique religious festival of Perahera to whet Tony's appetite for things to come. We watched as elephants plodded through the streets on their way to the park, where some were painted a magnificent shocking pink in preparation for the massive annual event that went on for hours, commencing with a procession of saffron-clad monks holding fans shaped like bodhi leaves.

This was followed by an astounding pageant of people, some swinging enormous flaming braziers on chains, which were replenished with kerosene along the route. There were devils, dwarves, dancers wearing droll masks to look like European tourists, dogs, monkeys and dragons. The highlight was a train of elephants, one of which carried a replica of the ornate gold casket that holds the Sacred Tooth Relic, housed in the Temple of the Tooth in Kandy. This venerated molar of the Buddha is believed to have been brought to Sri Lanka in the third century, hidden in the tresses of a princess. We had very good seats in the front so that Tony, although unable to stand, could see everything. He watched disinterestedly as the parade passed by.

After the Perahera, we went south to Galle to stay in Sinbad, a spectacular resort which, alas, was all but washed away in the tsunami caused by the Sumatra–Andaman earthquake on 26 December 2004. It was a blessing that Robert Kemp was so physically strong because he was able to carry Tony into swimming pools and lift him out again. At last, I saw a glint of the old Tony as he began his underwater exercise regime. The sun shone down on the lushness of that gorgeous island, which was not called Serendipity for nothing, and Tony was happy that he shared the pool with only a few intrepid Germans who were not fazed by fearsome stories of terrorists.

From Sinbad, we motored down to visit a most elegant and triumphantly personal creation, the garden estate of the late Bevis Bawa, which was called 'Brief'. Laurence Olivier had stayed as a guest when he was married to Vivien Leigh, during the making of *Elephant Walk*, and most visiting thespians tried to wangle an invitation over the years that Bevis held court. There were no guests at all when we arrived. A smiling, fawn-faced man showed us some sinister black flowers shaped like bats, which Delini was determined to plant at Karnak, and he ushered us through the deceptively simple, cement-floored house filled with marvellous works of art, including many sculptures of male nudes done by Bevis himself. Every wall opened to the omnipresent garden. We left feeling inspired to create a comparable garden at Karnak.

After a drive of ten hours we reached our next destination, the shabby old colonial rest house at Anuradhapura where the young Queen Elizabeth had stayed and which had remained in a time warp since then. Sri Lanka has many of these relics of colonial rule when British tea plantations covered the highlands and nostalgic Brits replicated their passion for the seedy guesthouse for genteel travellers. I could see that Tony felt immediately at home in the atmosphere of Britain in the thirties. The rest house could have been the perfect setting for one of the Agatha Christie murder mysteries which were so dear to his heart.

Unfortunately, very early on in our travels, Tony discovered a new drink – arrack (a strong liquor distilled from fermented palm sap, rice or molasses) and ginger beer. Throughout the rest of the trip, he drank copious quantities of this seemingly innocuous libation, which actually packs a punch like a mule. He had acquired a long straw to suck it through, as he was unable to lift his glass, and invented a curious way of smoking by lowering his head to his left hand. We could not stop him smoking several packets of Benson & Hedges a day.

The combination spelt trouble, especially at night, when Tony could become tetchy and find the slightest problem infuriating. For the first fifteen minutes, after the initial shot of his arrack, he was the most amusing and loquacious wit in the Western world, but as soon as the alcohol kicked in he would shout at staff and become abusive. When I lost his precious straw, he became apoplectic and berated me for hours until I got him another one.

While Tony's mood swings and tantrums had been occurring for some time, he was now becoming exasperated by his inability to walk or climb to the various sites we visited. We took it in turns to wait with him while the others climbed Sigiriya mountain or visited the rock temples at the ancient city of Polonnaruwa. He came into his own when we arrived at Kandy, however. It happened that all the elevators had broken down in the hotel where we were staying and we knew Tony would never make it up the imposing forked staircase leading up to the rooms. I spoke to the manager and explained that Tony had just had an operation. The man gazed at me with large compassionate eyes brimming with tears as he described his father's recent demise after a surgical intervention and, within minutes, ten beefy men arrived bearing a golden sedan chair fit for an emperor. Tony was transported up the stairs in style, glowing with pleasure and scoffing at us poor mortals who had to trudge up behind him.

But the place that leaves the greatest impression on my mind, and where Tony was at his happiest in Sri Lanka, was a tea plantation high in the mountains. Ann and Rohan Gomis, childhood friends of Delini's, welcomed us on our first night with the entire garden lit by a trail of lamps. We followed them towards a magical scene arranged by

Nande, the overseer, who had shot a wild boar on the property and was barbecuing some of the marinated meat on a fire in front of the barn. The sky was filled with stars and the crisp mountain air spiked our appetites. We drank and laughed together, embraced as family.

Six weeks later, we returned to Colombo. I felt as though I had run several marathons, rather than having been on a holiday, but we agreed that Tony's flagging interest in life had been somewhat restored. One of the last visits we made in Sri Lanka was to a temple called Issipathanaramaya, built by Delini's great-grandfather. The white *dagoba*, or stupa, rose like an immense meringue into the cerulean sky. The dome, containing relics of the Buddha, symbolised the path to divinity. Doves cooed and bowed to each other and we all sat under the giant bodhi tree in the grounds of the temple. Time had taken a backward step and there was peace. The bodhi is the tree under which Buddha sat and said, 'I shall not get up until I *know*.' Every bodhi planted at a Buddhist temple is a descendant of that very tree, and we now have two burgeoning bodhi saplings at Karnak, grown from seeds we collected at Issipathanaramaya.

Our journey was broken again in Singapore but, at last, we arrived home, surrounded once again by all the familiar things. Our dog Max (half dingo and half Great Dane) greeted us with a great show of affection and would have knocked Tony off his feet if he hadn't been restrained. I realised that life at Karnak would be very different with Tony unable to undertake even the simplest operation. I was determined to do everything I could to bring him back to health, and began to talk about the play again.

'What a bummer,' said Tony ruefully. 'I thought we'd call it *The Thing in the Wheelchair* but . . . now I *am* one!'

For a long time, a marine biologist called Karl had been one of the favoured 'sons' Tony would take up to his study for endless hours of stories, music, philosophy and drinking. Karl had lost one of his eyes when he was a boy, and he wore black eye-patches of differing shapes, sometimes sharks, sometimes schooners. They gave him a raffish, seafaring look. I thought Karl would make the perfect companion/helper for Tony and we agreed that he should come to stay at Karnak and take Tony to the Mossman Swimming Pool for his underwater routine every day. It was unspoken that he should also be his drinking buddy and, as such, try to lessen Tony's dependence on the sauce.

A specialist came from Cairns to advise on the best procedure in caring for an incapacitated person. She told me where to put all the stainless-steel supports – next to the loo, in the shower – anywhere the patient needs to hang on to something so they don't fall down. She arranged for us to get a stipend of thirty dollars, the sum given by the government to carers every two weeks. Thus, the recuperation of Anthony Shaffer began.

Karl lasted two days. When he came to me to say goodbye, all he would say was, 'He's a hard man.' After that, it was up to me. Every single day, we would go to the Olympic swimming pool in Mossman in the morning, never venturing near the big fifty-metre one but to the children's learning pool which had a roof and was no more than a metre and a half deep. And every day we went through the routine, maybe three times, depending on how strong Tony felt, and every day he got stronger. The theatre was still closed for the Wet but I was in preparation for the new season. Tony was astonished that I had managed to put by enough money from the previous season to pay for maintenance and the upgrading of the theatre in the off-season.

One of our ex-students, Michael Verban, had agreed to build the theatre's dressing rooms, showers and toilet, in return for board and lodging for himself and his son, Jamie, who had been born at Karnak in the Palace. Karnak was now humming with activity, and some of it spilled over into Tony's recovery plan. I was very well aware of what a terribly difficult place Karnak was to be ill in – just the physical distance between houses and the unevenness of the earth were challenges.

I was thrilled when Tony began to use his walker and then graduated to two walking sticks. The first time he attempted to complete the whole distance from the Castle to the theatre was a triumph. We began to talk seriously about *The Thing in the Wheelchair* again, but not ruefully this time. Tony revised his rough draft of the script and sent it to his agent, Kenneth Ewing, in London. Kenneth replied almost bluntly that he thought the play was too cruel and lacked subtlety.

We discussed the matter at length and then he had a long conversation with his twin, Peter, in New York. As usual, they came up with a new twist to the plot with amazing synchronicity. At the same moment, they both thought of Gilbert and Sullivan. Why not make the husband and his mother G & S fanatics? As in *Amadeus*, Peter Shaffer's work about Mozart, the music was out of copyright and able to be used throughout the play. It had a ready-made audience who had listened to and loved the catchy tunes since forever.

I wrote a front story for the play, incorporating the accident that paralysed the old mum, and bought recordings of every G & S operetta that had ever been performed. Tony listened to them over and over again to choose the most appropriate pieces to 'suit the action to the word'. He was really excited by the project and his health improved in leaps and bounds. A new successful play on his horizon was better for him than any medication in the world.

Once Tony had graduated to walking with only one stick on level ground, I felt it was time for him to see someone about his teeth, which had been troubling him greatly. He wanted to consult the dentist he knew in London and I thought it was a good idea for him to go.

Before he left for the UK, Tony took a driving test but was so wayward that the examiner refused to let him drive the car home afterwards. The police impounded my little Mazda and Tony had to wait for me to pick him up. He was greatly incensed and cursed the sergeant roundly. Nevertheless, he took my car later without telling anyone and drove to Cairns to do some business. I was on tenterhooks until he returned, wondering how I'd got myself into the uncomfortable and uncharacteristic position of being Tony's nanny and nurse instead of his wife.

The new season at Karnak Playhouse opened in June, and from then on we were able to serve up a rich fruitcake of entertainment. David Helfgott returned to perform his arch favourite modern classic, *Rhapsody in Blue* by Gershwin, and Frank Productions brought Oscar Wilde's *Salome* to the stage. An enormous blood-red moon illuminated the set of *Salome*, casting a baleful light over the proceedings. The effect was superb when the real full moon rose in the sky opposite the red one and they both lit up a production of such precision and wit that I knew it could only have been achieved with Jacqui Carroll's big bamboo stick banging away during hour after hour of rehearsals. She never actually hit any of the actors.

Jacqui Carroll and John Nobbs, founders of Frank Productions, have worked like demons to make their company the formidable, Suzuki-trained, disciplined outfit it is. I love to watch their progress every year as they grow in esteem and style. The whole company stays at Karnak for several weeks when they perform and, that year, John built us a pontoon for the lake out of old fog juice bottles and fence palings. It still sits on the lake in full view of the audience.

For our Christmas show at the end of that year, I used it to transport a singing drag queen known as Miss Pencil Vania across the lake while she belted out a song about not being 'a fucking drag queen'. She made a magnificent entrance onto the stage, carried from the bank by four massive oiled-up body builders. It was now seven years since Karnak had opened and I was beginning to feel that we had cracked it, as audiences packed in for our performances and we were not actually losing money every year.

I dashed off to Santa Fe, New Mexico, to attend the wedding of my daughter to Randal Swedberg, after which they both came back to

Australia to make their home in Marrickville, Sydney. Everyone had said that they were a disastrous match, both being opinionated and having gargantuan intellects, but in all my years of marriage-watching I have never seen a couple who were so compatible. It was a joy to be with them.

Later, they came to Karnak and did some cooking demonstrations, accompanied by the brilliant Lindsay Pollok, who whittled and bored flutes out of large carrots and played them to everyone's merriment. We called the show *The Art of Food*. I introduced the Jiddagirri Dancers, an Aboriginal group from Ravenshoe, into the *Creation* laser show and a very talented Bama woman, Dee Murphy, brought her own personal saga from the Jute Theatre to the stage at Karnak, which she called *Bedtime Stories with Auntie Dee*.

Yet, all the time I was thinking about our play, *The Thing in the Wheelchair*. I knew beyond any doubt that it was paramount to find a Stella, the Lady Macbeth of the suburbs. Without someone ultra-special in the lead role, it wouldn't work. I gave the play to Christine Johnson, who had sent audiences into a frenzy with her indescribable mix of bird calls and singing people's hair, but she'd just had a knee reconstruction and was taking a protracted convalescence away from acting.

Jane Rutter had asked me whether she could do an innovative, improvisational performance with dancer Kathryn Dunn, a show she called *Flute Spirit*. Jane was very excited by the combination of body movement and flute, as well as the prospect of working with Kathryn. Jane and her son, Bertie, then seven, came up to Karnak with Kathryn and her three-year-old daughter, Ava. The children swam in the lake and played on the pontoon while their mums worked on the stage only a few metres away. I watched their rehearsals with fascination.

Kathryn's dance background was an eclectic one. After training in Australia, she won a scholarship to the Royal Ballet in London, moved back to Oz to join Graeme Murphy's Sydney Dance Company as a freelance artist and then worked with Chunky Move before touring with the Bangarra Aboriginal Dance Theatre as the only white member. Her striking physical appearance was enhanced by her lofty stature and she moved with a litheness and ease that I had never witnessed before. This was the result of a yoga workout she undertook every day, which was so gruelling that I was exhausted just watching her. Her overall presence was quite breathtaking and everyone who saw the performance of *Flute Spirit* could talk of nothing afterwards but Kate, swearing that they had been inspired to begin movement classes instantly. When I heard her reading a fairy story to Ava, I listened intently. This was not the high-pitched adenoidal voice generally associated with dancers but a well-modulated one without pretensions, a voice that came from the right place. I could do something with that voice.

I gave Kate the script of *The Thing in the Wheelchair* and talked to her about playing the role of Stella. She read the play and thought about my proposition but was very unsure of undertaking a role that entailed her speaking Shakespeare and displaying such raw emotions. Kate said she would only do it if she came back to Karnak for at least a month before the commencement of rehearsals to work one-on-one with me, taking acting lessons with particular attention to her voice. I agreed immediately and assured her that I would guide her through the difficult shoals of playing such a part, and that if it wasn't going to work out I would tell her so after a week of intense rehearsal.

That night, during our evening telephone call, I told Tony that I thought I'd found our Stella and that we could go ahead with our plans to mount the production. He'd been having a bad time with his teeth, and they could not be saved, but he told me he'd arranged a wonderful trip for the two of us to Morocco when the season was over and the theatre would be dark.

We decided to ask Robert Kemp, who had been with us in Sri Lanka, to design the set, so before heading off to Morocco I went to stay with him at his home in Byron Bay. I had to talk him through the script and sort out how we could manage a two-storey set with a working inclinator (or chairlift), a practical bathroom, two bedrooms, a balcony and room for a car to drive onto the stage. It was a big ask. As the play was set in the Swinging Sixties, it was natural that we should involve Nigel Pegrum. We also had to record all the G & S songs and some live duets sung by mother and son.

When I arrived in London in January 2000 en route to Morocco, Tony was very worried about his mother, who had been ailing. We went to see her before we left but she was lying in bed, unconscious without her false teeth in, so I knew she was oblivious. She would never have received her beloved son in such a state.

We left London for Morocco, and I was intoxicated by its smells and colours. The richness of everything – textiles, pottery and natural cosmetics – was phenomenal, and we went to buy carpets from the Tuareg, the blue people who inhabit Paul Bowles' book, *The Sheltering Sky*. If Sri Lanka's rest houses were vestiges of British colonialism in a remote outpost of the Empire, so the Gazelle d'Or, our five-star hotel in Taroudant, was the French equivalent in far-flung Morocco. It was built by wealthy French settlers and was now the sanctuary of celebrities like John Mortimer, who exposed their bodies to the warmth of the North African sun nearly all winter long.

We were having lunch by the hotel pool under pepperina trees when Tony was called to the telephone. I could see by his body language that something was amiss. He limped slowly back to the table, looking up at the sky but seeing nothing, eyes glazed, shoulders slumped.

'She's gone,' was all he said. 'Ma's dead. I should never have come.'

CHAPTER SEVENTEEN

e had to wait in the dusty airport at Taroudant for hours. When one is travelling on a pre-sold package, tourist operators loathe changing your schedule, even if death has intervened. We missed our connection in Paris and had to stay there overnight. I could see Tony's health deteriorating by the minute, and by the time we reached London he was a wreck. There was a recurrence of the anal haemorrhaging he suffered periodically and the doctor was called.

I realise now that this was a manifestation of the diverticulitis, the inflammation of a pouch in the colon, which had plagued him for a long time. It seemed he wouldn't be able to attend his mother's funeral after all. However, after much medication, he was fit enough to make the journey with his brothers, Peter and Brian. They stood together at their mother's graveside on that bleak January day in North London while her remains were committed to the cold earth next to her husband's.

I knew that Tony was devastated and tried to comfort him as best I could. As Tony was the eldest son, the Shiva, the Jewish wake, was held at his studio in Kensington and I rushed off to Selfridges to procure all the traditional kosher foods required. At least sixty people crowded into the spacious room to witness an impressive service. A cantor sang ancient Hebrew incantations, a lone candle burned and the three brothers sat on small stools wearing yarmulkes on their heads while everyone filed past wishing them good health.

I flew back to Australia to prepare for our production of *The Thing in the Wheelchair* while Tony stayed in London to oversee yet another touring production of *Sleuth*, which he called 'my old warhorse'. He was bringing his younger daughter, Cressida, out to Karnak later in the year, but in the meantime there was much to be done.

The Thing in the Wheelchair was budgeted for $100 000. The cost included the making of a video tape by a young filmmaker named Sean Byrne, as we needed to have a complete record of the performance that we could view after the event. It was no mean feat to find the correct actress to play the eponymous 'thing in the wheelchair' – an old woman who can convey everything only through the blinking of her eyes, who can remain utterly still while being picked up, brutally scrubbed in a tub and shaken about like a rag doll. Buzz Whiting, an actress from the Rondo Theatre in Cairns, was recommended to me. Not only could she sing, she fulfilled the role perfectly in every respect. I'd had nightmares about the difficulty of the part and Tony and I had even discussed the possibility of using a doll rather than a live actor. However, Buzz was a director's dream. She sailed through the play, bringing such quality and sympathy to the role that she quickly became the darling of the entire cast.

Rory Williamson, son of David and Kristen Williamson, was a natural for the role of the lover/co-murderer. He was no stranger to Karnak, having been on the Australian Theatre for Young People course. Extremely tall and good looking, he made a perfect foil for Kathryn Dunn. Emma Jackson, a vibrant young actress from Sydney, came up to play the feisty girl next door while Russell Wicks and Howard Turner, both from Cairns, completed my brilliant cast.

True to her word, Kate Dunn arrived long before rehearsals began and we embarked upon an intense period of preparation. She is one of the most intelligent and gifted artists I have ever worked with, and I was amazed at how quickly she trapped ideas and made them her own. It was thrilling to watch her blossoming in the role.

Tony had come home for Christmas with Cressida, just in time for the birth of eight puppies, offspring of Max and our other dog Molly. Tony and I were both excited by the prospect of mounting a new play and the Castle was filled with people, music and dirty little puppies. We built an enclosure off the front verandah for them before they ripped everything to pieces and, with Cressida, we would sit out on the deck in the late afternoon sun watching their incessant fighting and feeding as we sipped cool unwooded chardonnay.

When rehearsals proper started, the gears changed and I had no time to do anything but think about the work in hand. There were re-writes and re-jigging, scenes were cut and actors lost lines they loved, which is always the way with a new play. Everyone got to have their say and the cast knitted together into a tight group within days. I encouraged Kate to use her body as much as she felt was necessary and the result was that all the other actors were freed up too, especially Rory Williamson. She taught him how to whirl her around so that their love scenes were positively acrobatic.

I was blessed to find a terrific stage manager in Terri Gonzales from Sydney. She was a rock, a professional of awesome competence, and I would have been lost without her. It was she who kept track of all the changes and rewrites so that slowly but surely the play began to emerge. There were some blistering rows, as there always are in rehearsals when actors have not learned their lines, nerves fray, tempers flare and none of it seems to make sense. We were working in the forecourt area upstairs in the theatre, and had laid out overlapping guidelines on the floor to represent both levels of the stage. This nearly sent Tony out of his mind, as he couldn't tell which level we were working on. He would try to leap up and stop the actors in full flight when he thought they were in the wrong position and became abusive to Terri Gonzales when she called for quiet.

Every evening, I would review the emails that had arrived during the day and deal with whatever was necessary. In nearly every batch there would be attachments to open and print out for Tony from the Shaffer Studio. I never actually read them, as they were endless corrections of his forthcoming memoirs, *So What Did You Expect?* When I asked Tony who was sending them, he told me that an American editor from Peters, Fraser & Dunlop, his agent, was staying in his studio. I had no inkling that there was anything odd about the correspondence but I thought it strange that Tony kept changing his story of this female person who inhabited his apartment in London. One time he told me that she was going to teach Cressida sculpting and another that she was a stalker who was in love with him. However, as my mind was fully occupied with directing the play, I had no time to think about Tony's London foibles.

When opening night came, I was a bundle of frazzled nerves held together by sheer determination that the play would carry the audience along with its energy and black humour. I wasn't worried about the actors – they were all fabulous – but I was concerned about the core of nastiness buried in the text. I didn't know whether the audience would sit through what amounted to the blatant mistreatment of a defence-less old woman. I should not have been perturbed. They lapped it up and the reviews were raves. I was so proud of all of us but Kathryn Dunn was singled out in every review and that pleased me even more. Ken Coterill, a respected reviewer for the national theatre magazine, wrote:

At the centre of this cyclone of a thriller is the superb Kathryn Dunn as a Lady Macbeth figure, whose body alternated from the highly sexual to that of a vulture. Nowhere in the play was Dunn more alluring than in the murder scene where, stripped to her underwear, she donned a gas mask and cackled as the gas disposed of her husband.

The thing in the wheelchair, observing all the plotting, is Buzz Whiting, Dunn's incapacitated mother-in-law, who can only communicate by blinking her eyes. There are shades of Zola's Therese Raquin here as Buzz frustratingly attempts to tell the world how her son really died. Terrific acting from Buzz . . .

Get in now to say you've seen it during its world premiere because this one is a stunner and will be headed for the West End or I'll eat my hat.

Another reviewer from the *Cairns Post* wrote:

Cilento approached the text with a bright and energetic comic style. Flashes of the director can be seen in most of the performances. This is a welcome attribute. Kathryn Dunn as the suburban Lady Macbeth, Stella, commanded most of the attention and deserved it. Her physical ability to portray wit was exceptional. Dunn never swayed from her goal, with motivations and diversions all as sharp as the fresh air provided by this magnificent outdoor venue.

Patti Humphreys, a reviewer from the Gold Coast, went overboard and said she thought that *Thing* was even better than Tony's *Sleuth*.

We were elated to find that all the hard grind had paid off. The film crew finished their re-shoots of bits they had missed, and after six scintillating performances, with the applause still ringing in our ears, we struck the set, hung up the costumes and went off to our respective homes, well pleased with ourselves. It was the beginning of June 2001.

David Williamson had come to several performances (which wasn't surprising as his son Rory had a leading part) and had written glowingly about the play to everyone he knew in the business, including his agent, Tony Williams. It was decided that I would travel down to Sydney to meet Tony, who would facilitate a national tour, take the tape to London to show to West End producers and arrange for a production there. I arrived in Sydney full of plans and confident that we were a shoo-in. It is a fatal combination.

It was horribly obvious that Tony Williams was dying. His face had a yellow-grey tinge and he was filled with a desperate energy that told the story. He was well aware that he had cancer and had only a few months to live. He was hanging on to what he knew best – brokering deals for writers and producers to work together for the betterment of both, with 10 per cent of the gross for him. He introduced me to two young entrepreneurs, assuring me that they were the future tycoons of theatre's resurgence. Very quickly, I learned that young producers are not interested in straight plays with casts of eight actors, chairlifts and large sets that cost a bomb to move. They are interested in one-man shows with no sets, revivals of well-known musicals and marquee names that you don't have to get out and sell. We fitted into none of these categories. They loved the tape but passed on the adventure.

I was disheartened but not defeated when I flew off to stay with Tony at the studio in London. I found that he'd had somewhat the same experience with producers there, and he was also having huge rows with the company publishing his memoirs. It seemed he had bagged a well-known celebrity and his publishers knew the man would sue them the day after the book appeared. They refused to leave the offensive material in the book and Tony refused to take it out. It was a stand-off.

Jason's marriage to Mia had just fallen apart, and he had asked me to come to Scotland to stay with him and Dashiell while they had a period of adjustment. Summer in Scotland with my son and delightful grandson was the best therapy in the world after my intense period of work, so I did not say no. But when Tony asked me whether he could come with me, I did say no. I knew from nearly thirty years of close association with my husband that in a situation where those present would be my son, my grandson and him, he would compete for, if not demand, my complete attention. He was miffed.

Had I known the outcome of this slight I would not have driven off so happily with Jason and Dashiell up the M1 through the glorious Lake District to Carlyle and Jedburgh. I revelled in the freshness of early summer. We laid out and planted a massive garden, painted the front of the house and pottered about the countryside, visiting ancient Floors Castle and numerous adventure playgrounds. Only fifteen minutes away, through Jedburgh and Roberton, was Chisholme House, which was still taking students and offering courses. I drove over early one morning and walked up to the top of the hill to where Bulent Rauf, my teacher, is buried. So much had happened since we had all climbed this hill before the morning Tony and Hugh Tollemarsh began their retreat. I did not feel sad but was overcome by a sense of wonderment at how the unfolding of time carries us along inexorably towards a culmination. I had begun to understand what Sufis call being lost in the love affair, and had intimations of what would be a 'culmination' in my own life.

We drove back to London to Jason's flat in Camden Town to find his friend Graham staying there. As space was limited, Jason suggested that I go back to Tony's studio a day early. My flight back to Australia was only a day or two later, so Jason and Dash drove me to Tony's apartment in Fulham Road. We rang the doorbell and knocked but there was no answer. I looked through the keyhole and saw Tony standing at the bottom of the stairs as pale as a sheet. When he finally opened the door, he looked as though he was going to faint.

Jason carried my bags to the small bedroom but there was an open suitcase already on the bed. The room was littered with bits of female apparel and the bathroom was filled with cosmetics. Tony's face told us all there was to know. 'Why didn't you come back when you said?' he mumbled. 'You weren't supposed to come until tomorrow.' It was like a scene from one of his own plays, or a French farce, but at that moment

I didn't think it was at all funny. I was furious. I left with Jason and that evening we had a long discussion about what I should do. Here we were, Tony and I, having just inaugurated a new and exciting work together, ready to commence selling it worldwide, and Tony was doing another Mrs Morgan on me.

Jason told me that I should see a lawyer before I left, just to clarify what my position was, whether a trial separation was necessary and where I stood as to the co-authorship of the play. We looked up lawyers in the Camden Hill area and I telephoned one of the firms but they could not see me until the following week. The second number I called was a lawyer by the name of David du Pre. The address in Albany Road was within walking distance from Jason's flat, so I called and made an appointment for the next morning at 11 a.m. My plane was departing at seven that evening.

David du Pre's chambers were up a narrow staircase, at the top of which I was ushered into a tiny office by a woman called Gaye Osborne, who sat me down and gave me some tea. She was a pleasantly rounded woman with apple cheeks and candid eyes and I trusted her immediately. I tried to explain the ridiculously complicated scenario to her. Although I saw her eyes flicker once or twice, she was not fazed by the theatrical and geographic challenge of my story. I felt relief that I had told someone impartial what was happening in our lives. I wanted to wait, to step back from the situation, before I did something irrevocable. Gaye agreed and we parted.

I had hardly set foot in the street before I realised I had left my coat behind so I retraced my steps and was halfway up the stairs when I heard much chortling and excited chatter above my head. David du Pre, Gaye and one of the secretaries looked over the banisters at me and they all stopped laughing at once.

'I left my coat,' I said by way of explanation. 'Is there a problem?'

Gaye spoke first. 'It's just that we are all astounded by the coincidence. You see, when David had the office over in South Kensington in the early eighties, he acted for Carolyn Shaffer in her divorce from Anthony.'

On my return to Karnak, I was instantly swept up in mowing and pruning, continuing the battle to hold the jungle back that takes place whenever I am away for any length of time. It was the season for chainsaws, whipper snippers and waiting for mountainous piles of debris to dry so that we could burn them off.

The next I heard from Tony was when he rang to say that he was in hospital in Ireland. Several yards of his intestines had been removed from his lower abdomen after near-fatal complications from an attack of diverticulitis and peritonitis. He told me how he had swelled up like a pregnant woman and complained that it was his doctor's fault, as he hadn't been informed that he had to watch his diet. He couldn't wait to get out of hospital, he said, because they wouldn't let him smoke. They had fitted him with a colostomy bag but he was to have another operation at a later date to have more intestine and the offensive bag removed. When he asked if I'd had any luck arranging the tour of Australia with the play, I told him I hadn't. He said he missed me. I asked if his American woman friend was with him, to which he replied 'No, she's wandered off.'

'Where to?' I asked.

'Over a cliff,' he answered.

Then, the events of September 11, 2001, occurred and changed the state of play forever. The most remote thing from anyone's mind was taking a 1960s black comedy/thriller on tour around Australia. When Tony was allowed out of hospital, he recommenced telephoning me nearly every day, full of conspiracy theories and fearful of his impending operation. It was scheduled for 5 December. I remember because that was my father's birthday. Tony insisted that he did not want to spend winter in the bitter cold of the Northern Hemisphere and asked whether it would be possible for him to come home to convalesce. I said yes, and he seemed content, but as I was busy sweeping the verandah at the Chateau one day, a telephone call came through from London. It was Tony's brother, Brian. He said he was sorry to tell me that Tony had died that morning, 6 November.

It drizzled at Tony's funeral. I could not help feeling as though I had got mixed up in a location shoot for one of those British spy series – the ones that always begin with a funeral and then, in flashback, reveal a trail of skulduggery and mayhem. It was an unhappy affair and when it was over I was given a lift to Camden Town to see my solicitor, Gaye Osborne. It was only the second time I had met her and circumstances had now changed radically. As Peter Shaffer was Tony's executor and I was chief beneficiary, Gaye planned to approach Peter's solicitors to sort out any problems of death duties and back taxes. Little did we know that four years later, nothing would have been concluded and Tony's heirs would be left in the lurch without a penny.

Later, I had to go back to London to testify at a hearing in the High Court to establish where Tony was legally domiciled at the time of his death. A woman who claimed to be Tony's mistress, but who had only known him since late 1998, contended that he was domiciled in England rather than Queensland, Australia.

Gaye procured the services of barrister Martin O'Dwyer, who was concise, authoritative and elegant. Although it was considered unlikely that we would win, I knew as soon as the opposition appeared that we were in with a fighting chance. The woman in question had already lost a similar case in Italy and her objective was clear from the start. She took the stand to give us a performance of tears and protestations, but when asked by Mr O'Dwyer what she would have done had Tony returned to Karnak after his operation, the mask slipped. In a voice that would have struck terror into the heart of any man, she proclaimed, 'I would've MADE him take care of me!'

In the event, we won the case. Even so, there was no movement in what I have come to call 'the Wide Sargasso Sea', a body of water notable for its stagnant wasteland of rotting seaweed. Granted, Tony's affairs were in disorder and the tyranny of distance between Oz and the UK makes things difficult, but four years is just too long to have to wait for a resolution. Shakespeare's idea on the subject is short and sharp: 'Let's kill all the lawyers'.

Gaye Osborne, being the exception to the rule, has been my inform-ant and lifeline from twelve thousand miles away in each new twist of the plot. I realised long ago that to stress about the situation was stupid and not at all productive. After we staged our 'Tribute to Tony', which Jason and I hosted, I got on with the business of attempting to keep the theatre open and not be compelled to sell Karnak to live. I have put together a company called KEEP (Karnak Exceptional Events & Promo-tions) designed to do just that – keep Karnak intact.

Soon after I returned from the funeral that Christmas, Giovanna and her husband Randal shouted me to a holiday. Sensitively, they chose the Sunshine Coast, north of Brisbane, knowing that I had been brought up there. They rented an apartment near the sea so I was able revisit all my old childhood haunts, now radically changed but still pre-cious to my heart. I went back to swim on the beach at Mooloolaba and walked to the end of the Spit where our old house had stood. There now is a yacht club and real estate worth billions.

My son-in-law, Randal, was always a kindred spirit and I was infi-nitely grateful to him for his kindness to me. The miracle was that, after so many peaks and troughs, Giovanna had at last found her soul mate. Then, in October 2003, Randal died from a lymphoma of the lung brought about, so his doctors told us, by exposure to radioactive material. He was raised in Española, only several miles downwind of Los Alamos, New Mexico, where the atom bomb tests were conducted.

Randal's funeral was a complete contrast to Tony's. Brilliant sun-shine lit the grove of gum trees as he was lowered into the parched

Australian soil. Kookaburras cackled and the congregation of his friends pressed forward to bless him on his way. It was a tragedy for G. As we drove down to Melbourne to spend Christmas that year with my sister Margaret and her husband, Geoffrey Maslen, I could not bear to look around at her face and see it suddenly suffuse with blood, the prelude to an uncontrollable outburst of tears.

Randal and Giovanna had been members of a community of Sufis under the guidance of Dr Mohsen Labban, an Egyptian professor of economics, who came to make his home in Sydney after working for the United Nations for many years. Giovanna has since married Randal's best friend, Ian MacGregor, who is studying horticulture at Sydney University. My son, Jason Connery, has become not only an actor but also a director who is now so sought after that trips to Australia are on the backburner. However, I shall hopefully visit him on the set of one of his grand movies as 'The mother of the Director'.

The strange thing about my life today is that the tempo has not slackened. The passing years are supposed to bring you nearer to a time when you work less and take it easy, but the opposite has been true for me. The older I get, the harder I have to work. I do not resent this. When I look around me at the beauty of Karnak, the word 'work' does not seem to apply; it is more a question of guardianship and an ongoing expansion of creativity. I never cease to be surprised that it is all *here* – the lake with ducks, the gardens, the theatre, the houses, the rare fruit trees, the carambola, lychee and mango orchards, bananas and passionfruit vines. I must accept the fact that without a fortuitous and truly awesome amount of help, none of this would have been possible.

I cannot disregard my Sherborne vision of the man in the garden and my subsequent discovery of the identity of my mentor, Ibn Arabi, the great teacher. I opened a book by Michel Chodkiewicz about him very recently and came upon this passage, which opened the door to the mystery just a little more.

> Ibn Arabi is not only an archivist and interpreter par excellence of sacred knowledge. Through his invisible presence, beyond death itself, he maintains and transmits a spiritual impulse or *baraka* which, when the circumstances require it, comes to quicken individuals and groups, to re-establish the ways of sainthood, and to restore what can be restored of true Islamic order.

> Hence the importance of his spiritual teaching, whose course, like an underground river, may suddenly surface for a while into the light of day, and leave the imprint of Ibn Arabi on one of the branches of an existing group of people somewhere in the world. Hence too, the importance of his physical appearance in the visions of Sufis down through the ages and to our own time. From Sadruddin Konevi [ancestor of Hasan Shushud Konevi, the Turkish teacher of J. G. Bennett, for whom I translated at Sherborne] to the sage Abd el Kadir, a long succession of people, known and unknown, have been guided, aided and instructed by a teacher whom the grave did not divide from those who were still alive.

It seems but a breath away since I walked along the beach at Mooloo-laba as a little girl with the full moon stretching out a path across the water straight to me. What has happened in between is like a dream. Everything is different but nothing has changed. I am still that child, ready for the next impression to present itself. But I am also old now. Like tempered steel, or better a loaf of grainy bread, I have been through the fire and been 'cooked'. May God make me 'tasty'.

EPILOGUE

MECCA, JULY 2005

*T*his is the most monumental, momentous place I have ever visited in my life. It did not arrive at this distinction for nothing. The living hopes of millions of men and women are focused here in the vibrational pull towards the rose-scented black damask cloth that covers the Kaaba, where the black stone, said to be the beating heart of mankind, is enshrined.

For twenty-four hours a day, seven days a week, whatever their colour, race, age, sex or shape, the stream of souls contained in bodies moves and encircles the Kaaba anti-clockwise. They carry their children on their shoulders, lead ancient parents, wheel the crippled, chant pleas for mercy or shouts of praise, tears streaming down their faces that shine with the fulfilment of a lifetime's desire.

In spite of the constant deterrent of the WIBs (Women in Black, aka the Black Bags), who patrol like an army of crows with their male counterparts, the *Wahabites*, pushing pilgrims along, reprimanding them for anything they deem a misdemeanour, the masses still arrive. There are literally a million pilgrims a day, buoyed up by thousands of years of tradition, love and the promise of redemption.

The great ones were here ... *are* here ... on this very spot ... from the beginning. The patriarch Abraham, his son Ishmael and, after them, Muhammad – they set up this place. They built it and blessed it with the enormity of their *baraka* and it remains the magnet of hearts to this day, timeless and just as intense as when the black stone was reset in place by Amin, the Trusted One (Muhammad's name at that time).

It is said that the stone was once a pure white meteorite that fell to earth and that it turned black over the ages by taking on the sins of mankind. It was already black by the time Amin devised the diplomacy of sharing the task of replacing it. He allowed a member of each of the four bickering tribes to hold a corner of the cloth while it was reset. It is still in that place today, revealed at a corner of the Kaaba, and the millions passing it seven times on each circumambulation try to get nearer and nearer so they can touch or kiss it. This is the culmination of the journey.

Physically, the Kaaba is situated at the centre of a vast mosque, open to the sky. Three hundred metres on every side of it is laid with blazing white marble. All day and night, amid the mosaic of people who circle, a bevy of Bengali cleaners in blue scamper. They quickly cordon off a strip of marble with a coloured cord and then five or six of them run, pushing a surging wave of soapy water ahead of them. They are followed by others with six-foot-long mops who swipe up the residue and the glittering white marble dries in seconds in the 45-degree heat. It is done with such precision and finesse that it is hardly noticed by the throng that moves inexorably onwards.

No-one notices the jostling either. It is all part of the experience of joining with a million others in the celebration of the spiritual arrival home. To undertake this journey called Umra (the visit) is not for the faint-hearted. I had been invited by a group of Sufis living in Sydney. The idea of a visit to Mecca, the forbidden city, seemed unthinkable – the heat, the knowledge that a woman cannot enter or leave Saudi Arabia without a *mahgrem* (a close male relative) being fully responsible for her, the fact that I had never worn a *hijab* in my life. All of these things made the journey seem impossible. And then I had a dream.

In my dream I saw my heart being engraved with the Arabic symbol for Allah over and over with pokerwork. I could see the decorative calligraphy burnt all over my heart. The next morning I caught sight in the mirror of a dark brown mark the size of a ten-cent coin on my chest, right over my heart. It had not been there before.

I remembered that, way back when I was at Sherborne, Mr Bennett had told us that everyone has a home in one of the religions, even if he rejects it outwardly, and he asked each of us to answer, without thinking, where we thought we belonged. He himself was a Christian, he said, but I answered unhesitatingly . . . Islam.

Then later, I visited Bawa Muhaiyaddeen, the Tamil sage who lived in Philadelphia, and he answered my question when he said, 'You are a Christian because you believe in Jesus and you are a Jew because you believe in all the prophets including Moses. You are a Muslim because you believe in Muhammad as a prophet and you are a Sufi because you believe in the universal teaching of God's love. You are really none of those, but you are all of those because you believe in God . . . And once you believe in God, there is no religion. Once you divide yourself off with religions, you are separated from your fellow man.'

I knew I had to come to Mecca.

Using the scaffolding of Muhyiddin Ibn Arabi's verse, my greatest desire is that:

My heart has become capable of any form.
It is a pasture for gazelles, a convent for Catholic nuns,
The tables of the Torah, and the Book of the Koran.
It is a theatre in the jungle, a red rock,
A kitchen where the dragon and the dove
Sit down and sup together.
I follow the religion of love,
Wherever the wings of love take me
That is my flare path and my way.

INDEX

516

Text credits

The author and publisher would like to thank the following copyright holders for permission to reproduce their work.

Zuleika Dobson by Max Beerbohm, published by Random House (Modern Library), 1998
The Politics of Experience by R. D. Laing, published by Penguin Books, 1967
Extract from 'The Town of Two Knights: Sir Harry Oakes', Sangerville Public Library website
Witness by J. G. Bennett, published by Bennett Books, 1962
Inside the Wicker Man by Allan Brown, published by Sidgwick & Jackson Ltd, 2000
Dialogue from *The Wicker Man* by Anthony Shaffer, reproduced with permission from Canal Plus
Dialogue from *Murderer* by Anthony Shaffer © Peter Shaffer Limited
Programme notes by Anthony Shaffer, reproduced with permission from Peter Shaffer Limited
Review of *The Thing in the Wheelchair* in the *Cairns Post*, excerpts courtesy of the *Cairns Post*
An Ocean Without Short: Ibn Arabi, the Book and the Law by Michel Chodkiewicz, published by State University of New York Press, 1993

Photograph credits

BLACK & WHITE SECTION:
Page 3   Popperfoto/Australian Picture Library
Page 6   Top: John Oxley Library, State Library of Queensland; Middle: © Australian Picture Library; Bottom: © Australian Picture Library /John Chillingworth
Page 7   Bottom right: Getty Images
Page 8   Top left: Newspix/News Ltd; Bottom right: Newspix/News Ltd
Page 10   Top: © Australian Picture Library
Page 12   Top: Getty Images; Bottom right: A. Purcell/Courtesy of *The Age*
Page 13   F. Burke/Courtesy of *The Age*
Page 15   © Corbis/Australian Picture Library

COLOUR SECTION:
Page 10   Top: Newspix/Brian Cassey; Bottom: Newspix/News Ltd
Page 13   Mike Lawn/Rex Features/Austral International
Page 14   Top: AFP/Getty Images
Page 16   Mike Lawn/Rex Features/Austral International

All other photographs from the author's personal collection.

Every effort has been made to contact copyright holders of material reproduced in this book. The author and publisher would appreciate hearing from any copyright holders not acknowledged here.